Council Tax Handbook

Martin Ward

10th edition updated by Alan Murdie

Child Poverty Action Group

CPAG promotes action for the prevention and relief of poverty among children and families with children. To achieve this, CPAG aims to raise awareness of the causes, extent, nature and impact of poverty, and strategies for its eradication and prevention; bring about positive policy changes for families with children in poverty; and enable those eligible for income maintenance to have access to their full entitlement. If you are not already supporting us, please consider making a donation, or ask for details of our membership schemes, training courses and publications.

Published by Child Poverty Action Group
94 White Lion Street, London N1 9PF
Tel: 020 7837 7979
staff@cpag.org.uk
www.cpag.org.uk

A CIP record for this book is available from the British Library

ISBN: 978 1 906076 79 5

Child Poverty Action Group is a charity registered in England and Wales (registration number 294841) and in Scotland (registration number SC039339), and is a company limited by guarantee, registered in England (registration number 1993854). VAT number: 690 808117

Cover design by Devious Designs

Typeset by David Lewis XML Associates Ltd
Printed and bound in the UK by CPI Group (UK) Ltd, Croydon CR0 4YY

The author

Alan Murdie (LLB) barrister, is a lawyer and consultant, specialising in local taxation and welfare law. He has edited this book since 1998. He was co-founder of the Poll Tax Legal Group in 1990 and is co-author of *Enforcement of Local Taxation*, published by the Legal Action Group. He writes and lectures extensively on local government finance issues and has been involved in many legal test cases.

Acknowledgements

Many people have provided valuable information and suggestions with respect to the ninth edition of this book and a number deserve a special mention.

I would like to express my gratitude to Martin Ward who originally wrote the first two editions of the *Council Tax Handbook*, upon which this new edition is broadly based.

Thanks are due to David Paterson, Paul Moorhouse and Michael Spencer for checking the relevant law. I am also particularly grateful to Robert Telfer for his knowledge of, and contribution on, the law in Scotland.

I would also like to thank Nicola Johnston, Kathleen Armstrong, Clare Gardner and Katherine Dawson for editing, proofreading and indexing the book.

Thanks are also due to staff and volunteers at Nucleus Legal Advice in Earl's Court, London, members of the Institute of Money Advisers, Karen Buck MP, Baroness Molly Meacher of Spitalfieds, Jan Luba QC, the Reverend Paul Nicolson, Joanna Kennedy and Henu Cummins of the Zacchaeus 2000 Trust, Peter Tutton, Debt Policy Officer of the Citizens Advice Bureau, members of the Enforcement Law Working Group, members of the Benefits Legal Group, Val Stevenson of The Pavement, David Magor, John Roberts and Gary Watson of the Institute of Revenues Rating and Valuation, Janan Akkad, and Councillor Ben Grower of Bournemouth, all of whom have provided information and insights on different aspects of the tax and appeals system, and its impact on vulnerable people since the last edition. The library staff of the Honourable Society of Lincoln's Inn again gave invaluable help with obtaining key references.

Alan Murdie

The law covered in this book was correct on 1 January 2014 and includes regulations laid up to this date.

Contents

Abbreviations

AA	attendance allowance	HMRC	HM Revenue and Customs
CA	carer's allowance	IB	incapacity benefit
CTB	council tax benefit	IS	income support
CTC	child tax credit	JSA	jobseeker's allowance
CTR	council tax reduction	MP	Member of Parliament
CTRRP	Council Tax Reduction Review Panel	NI	national insurance
DCLG	Department for Communities and Local Government	PC	pension credit
		PIP	personal independence payment
DHP	discretionary housing payment		
DLA	disability living allowance	SDA	severe disablement allowance
DWP	Department for Work and Pensions	UC	universal credit
ESA	employment and support allowance	VOA	Valuation Office Agency
EU	European Union	VTE	Valuation Tribunal for England
HB	housing benefit	VTW	Valuation Tribunal for Wales
HMCS	HM Courts Service	WTC	working tax credit

Introduction

This is the 10th edition of this *Handbook* to appear since council tax came into operation in 1993 and its aim remains to be to provide a practical source of reference and advice to taxpayers, advisers and professionals in local government and those involved with the administration of justice. Once again it is hoped that it will prove of practical use to the many thousands of people currently experiencing difficulties with the council tax, those engaged in providing help and advice to the public and to all those charged with interpreting and applying the relevant law in an administrative or judicial capacity.

Regrettably, the on-going need for a book such as this was tragically demonstrated by the narrative verdict delivered in June 2013 at an inquest into the suicide of Peter Williams, an inventor of considerable talent, who had taken his life after being bankrupted for council tax. Although the Dunstable Coroner did not attribute blame to local authority concerned, he nonetheless stated that the inflation of his council tax debt from £1,350 to £70,000 'may strike the man in the street as remarkable'.[1]

Sadly, Peter Williams is unlikely to be the last such case and indeed is representative of a growing number of middle-class people caught up in a council tax enforcement process that can easily spiral out of control, just as it already has with an enormous number of poorer people dependent on benefits and low paid work who find themselves in court, as highlighted in the introduction of the previous edition of this *Handbook*.

This edition details the biggest change in the history of the council tax since 1993, following the enactment of the Local Government Finance Act 2012. The Act has not attempted any simplification or rationalisation of the system but has removed some of its fundamental features, including a number of the previous nationally available discounts and full support for those who needed most help with paying. These particular features were considered essential to the principle of fairness for all taxpayers when the tax was established under John Major in 1993, as well as to its smooth operation and viability as an effective revenue raising system. The year 2012 thus represents 'Year Zero' for the council tax, when some of its core principles were jettisoned, along with any case for it being simple to understand and administer. Perhaps most significantly, the principle of protection for those on benefits and low-incomes has been removed entirely, with the exception of protection for low-income pensioners. Effectively, following the abolition of the national system of council tax benefit from 1 April 2013, the

Act has re-introduced an anaemic version of the poll tax or community charge in many areas.

Under the Local Government Finance Act 2012 responsibility for council tax support is delegated to hundreds of different local authorities across England, and similarly in Wales and Scotland according to the schemes decided by the Welsh and Scottish governments.

This has been presented as part of a 'localism agenda', but as enacted constitutes wider abandonment of responsibility by national government for the conduct of local taxation affairs.

With no consistent nationwide system now in existence, in England alone there are 326 separate local schemes in operation for the 326 different billing authorities. The complexities of this system, and the effect on taxpayers, have been wholly underestimated by the government. For instance, in April 2013 the government predicted 14,000 appeals to be heard by the Valuation Tribunal for England over local support decisions. In fact, up to 1 November 2013 there had been only 60. This might be misinterpreted as indicating a system of support that is working with unparalleled efficiency. In fact, it represents a system where no one actually understands what is going on. How else could the government have made an error of over 99 per cent in its estimates? In any event, the tribunal procedures are far too complex for all but a relatively small number of taxpayers to be able to access without specialist advice and help. Unfortunately, it remains the case that despite the best efforts of this *Guide* and its author, many competent advisers remain unaware of the full role of the tribunal system. Current cuts in legal aid and advice funding have further reduced the pool of specialist knowledge available to help taxpayers.

Undoubtedly, the policy of cutting loose local authorities to steer their own course is certainly an adventurous one, legally and constitutionally. Schedule 1A of the Local Government Finance Act 1992 (inserted by Schedule 4 of the 2012 Act) permits authorities to draw up local council tax reduction schemes each year. As legislation goes, it is all rather vague but the implications and liabilities are huge. The Coalition Government has engineered the biggest shake-up in local taxation in two decades and walked away, leaving authorities to create brand new support systems, with little guidance as how the task is to be accomplished. Local authorities now bear rule-making powers and functions normally entrusted to the Secretary of State.

Previously the province of DWP lawyers, parliamentary draftsmen and indeed Parliament itself, such demands would prove rather challenging. Certainly, such an outcome was never envisaged at the time the council tax was created in 1992 and few professionals in local government could ever have imagined what would be thrust upon them. No one can envy their position.

Consequently, local authorities – or a small number of officials employed by them – have the unique task of creating localised systems of support for the most complicated local tax system ever levied in the UK.

That the levying and enforcement of local taxation has become a difficult and complex business will be obvious from even the most casual inspection of the relevant statutes, rules and regulations and comparison even with earlier editions of this *Handbook*.

It would be wrong to attribute blame for all the problems that are now emerging to the impact of the 2012 Act. Many problems have been building up for a decade. Following the Local Government Act 2003, the council tax was subject to very little reform or amendment by way of primary legislation until 2011, and certainly none which made any meaningful impact on the position of those least able to pay. Unfortunately, the plan to revalue dwellings in England by 1 April 2007 was abandoned in October 2005, meaning that council tax valuations remain based upon a set of theoretical values which are now nearly a quarter of a century old. Instead, an ever increasing number of regulations were issued by the Department for Communities and Local Government, making the administration of council tax ever more complex in theory and in practice.

Within this labyrinthine system, the position of many of those dependent on benefits is an increasingly difficult one, combined with the effects of the full raft of welfare reforms which have been introduced since 2010 by the Coalition Government, including:
- the benefit cap;
- housing benefit cuts in both the private and public rented sector, including size restrictions (the 'bedroom tax');
- the abolition of the social fund and replacement with localised welfare assistance (in Scotland, with a national Scottish Welfare Fund);
- the replacement of disability living allowance with personal independence payment;
- a three year freeze on child benefit; and partial means-testing for higher earners;
- an extension of the jobseeker's allowance sanctions regime.

Taking just the latter measure, the operation of this sanctioning, including cuts in benefit of up to three years, it remains to be explained how a claimant, who has been means-tested to get the benefit and who suffers a complete stoppage of money, can then be expected to pay her/his council tax. If a person has no income, s/he can scarcely be expected to meet, for instance, 15 or 20 per cent of her/his local council tax bill. Even more remarkable is the assumption by some local authorities that the percentage of council tax to be paid by anyone who is unemployed should be increased once a person has been out of work for more than a year. No case has yet been made as to how such a punitive approach to the unemployed will result in anything other than an increase in irrecoverable debts and bankruptcies. If taxing the unemployed unaffordable sums is considered to be a sound scheme for raising local taxes, the thought processes of policy makers responsible can only be described as an example of what anthropologists term 'magical thinking'.

However, such ironies, contradictions and irrationalities aside, there is a wider general concern as to how many vulnerable debtors are being treated by the administration and enforcement processes for council tax, not least that many are being served with demands for payment which are in error or unlawful.

The danger of corner-cutting in local tax proceedings was identified over a generation ago by the higher courts[2] and unfortunately it has become all too common in the council tax system, even among those local authorities which strive to follow the rules. Perhaps inevitably, the council tax has become open to abuse, by administrators and outsourced companies who can use their position to obtain and extort sums which have no basis in law. Unfortunately, there is evidence that too many examples of this cannot be attributed to merely negligent or even innocent errors on the part of either humans or computers. The complexity of the system, the looseness of effective controls and scrutiny, and the vulnerability of many of taxpayers all result in a system of taxation which is wide open to abuse at official level, both by public and private sector employees who have been empowered to administer and collect the tax or apportion benefits and support. Although wrongful and excessive charging has long been acknowledged as a danger with enforcement by bailiffs (eg, £230 charged in Slough for seizing a doormat), it is disturbing to realise that fraud and misfeasance against taxpayers may also be deliberately perpetrated in other areas of council tax administration by those in official positions of responsibility.

Details given in this *Handbook* reflect concerns that exists over the question of local authority costs being added to the issue of summonses, and the failure in many cases of magistrates' courts to record liability orders in the correct form, if at all, a concern identified by the Court of Appeal as long ago as 2005.[3]

Hitherto, examples of financial abuses committed against taxpayers at an official level, having been only picked up sporadically in Parliament, in occasional Ombudsman reports and in individual cases by advisers and taxpayers and in local newspapers. Indeed, it appears that there is still prevalent a widespread culture of disbelief and denial that this could take place in the collection of local taxes, a myopia comparable to that which originally existing on the expenses of Members of Parliament or the newspaper telephone-hacking scandals which have embroiled a number of national newspapers. However, a conference held by the Scottish Institute of Revenues Rating and Valuation in December 2013 was informed that fraudulent threats to the public purse are far wider than generally recognised. This, together with extensive feedback obtained since the last edition of this *Handbook*, demonstrates that such dangers are real and cogent.

However, it must be said that although the system is failing millions of taxpayers, the possibilities for evasion of the council tax are now greater than at any time in the past 22 years, certainly for mobile members of the population or those who are simply disdainful of official processes or decide to declare a 'non-payment campaign' in the spirit of that which brought down the poll tax between 1990 and 1992. Many unemployed taxpayers have suffered benefit cutbacks which mean that they lack the financial resources to pay, as pointed out above. Ironically, the practice of sanctioning jobseeker's allowance means that it is a measure imposed by the DWP that is triggering an unofficial non-payment campaign in areas of high unemployment.

Substantial root and branch reform will undoubtedly be forced upon the council tax as the contradictions and defects accumulate and become more apparent to politicians, the courts and the public. In the meantime, it is hoped that this *Handbook* will provide help, advice and support to those having to deal with council tax problems in practice.

Alan Murdie

Notes

1 www.bbc.co.uk/news/uk-england-beds-bucks-herts-22820105
2 *R v Liverpool Justices ex parte Greaves* [1979] 77 LGR 440
3 *R(on the application of Mathialagan) v Southwark London Borough Council and another* [2004] EWCA Civ 1689 Court of Appeal.

Chapter 1

Overview

This chapter covers:
1. Introduction (below)
2. Administration (p2)
3. Chapter summary (p3)
4. Legal background and references (p8)

---

1. Introduction

This *Handbook* describes the council tax as it operates throughout England, Wales and Scotland. It should be of value to taxpayers, advisers and administrators.

Council tax is best understood as a cross between a land tax and a personal tax. It was originally introduced in 1993 by the Local Government Finance Act 1992 after the failure of the short-lived system of community charge or 'poll tax' which operated in England and Wales between 1990 and 1993. The scheme of the original 1992 Act has now been substantially altered by the Localism Act 2011 and Local Government Finance Act 2012. Council tax is levied on domestic dwellings, but the number of people and the type of people who are living in a dwelling affect the amount of tax to be paid and who should pay it. Increasingly, more emphasis is placed on the personal element of the tax than the property element. This *Handbook* provides a guide to the relevant rules.

There are a number of differences in the way the scheme operates in England, Wales and Scotland. In some chapters, these variations are indicated as they arise; in others, there are separate sections on the different arrangements.

Following changes under the Local Government Finance Act 2012 there are many local variations as to the support which is available for those on low incomes.

One of the fundamental principles upon which council tax was originally conceived was that the poorest in the community would be protected by council tax benefit (CTB) covering up to 100 per cent of their council tax liability. Between 1993 and March 2013, central government funded the CTB system for those on welfare benefits or low incomes.

As part of the 2010 spending review, the government announced that it would reduce spending on CTB by 10 per cent and localise it from 2013/14.[1]

From 1 April 2013, CTB has been abolished and replaced by locally determined council tax reduction schemes. Local schemes have created new administrative functions within the council tax system with councils being given powers equivalent to those which existed under specified social security legislation relating to council tax. Local authorities have increased financial autonomy and responsibility for support for pensioners, those on low incomes and on benefits. From April 2013, the amount of support available in each area to a local taxpayer is decided by each individual local authority. As a result, the amount of support that a low-income taxpayer is entitled to receive can vary widely, so that the position of one low-income taxpayer in one part of England and Wales is no longer the same, or broadly equal to, that in another part of the UK. The position is more consistent in Scotland.

Domestic rates are still payable in Northern Ireland. This *Handbook*, therefore, does not apply to Northern Ireland.

2. Administration

In England and Wales, district councils, metropolitan districts and London boroughs, unitary authorities, the Common Council of the City of London and the Council of the Isles of Scilly are responsible for setting the council tax, as well as billing and collection in their area. They are known as 'billing authorities'.[2] In 2009, the number of district councils in some regions was reduced, and further amalgamations are taking place over the next few years. Currently, in England, 326 councils collect council tax: 201 district councils, 33 London boroughs, 36 metropolitan district councils and 56 unitary authorities.

In Scotland, new single-tier, all-purpose councils were introduced in April 1996, replacing district, island and regional councils. Both billing and levying is performed by these local authorities. Scottish local authorities remain legally obliged to collect Scottish Water charges (for household water and waste water). These charges are included in the annual council tax bill.

Although local authorities set and levy the council tax in their area, the actual day-to-day administration and collection of council tax in a number of areas may be carried out by a private company acting on behalf of the local authority. These companies operate under contracts with the local authority and may also be responsible for administering benefits and enforcing non-payment of tax, acting in the name of the council. In July 2013, the functions which an independent contractor can undertake in England were extended to include notifying applicants about reductions, ascertaining liability and the collection of penalties.[3]

3. **Chapter summary**

The following provides an overview of the scheme and summarises the related chapters in the *Handbook*, which describe particular aspects of the scheme in greater detail.

Chargeable dwellings (Chapter 2)

The council tax is a tax on a domestic property known as a 'dwelling'. Not all properties count as dwellings. A property that is not a dwelling is usually subject to non-domestic rates. In England and Wales, the listing officer at the local Valuation Office Agency office and, in Scotland, the assessor, decides whether or not a property is a dwelling. An appeal may be made against a decision that a property is, or is not, a dwelling.

Valuation (Chapter 3)

In England and Scotland, dwellings are allocated to one of eight valuation bands by the local listing officer or assessor on a list which first came into operation on 1 April 1993. In England, newly built dwellings are also placed in a band which reflects their hypothetical value at 1 April 1991. In Wales, dwellings are allocated to one of nine bands on a list effective from 1 April 2005 based on their hypothetical value on 1 April 2003. Information about the dwelling and its valuation band appears on valuation lists maintained by the listing officer at the local valuation office, or the assessor in Scotland. The public has the right to inspect and obtain copies of the valuation list. A proposal may be made to change, and an appeal can be made against, a dwelling's valuation band.

The amount of tax (Chapter 4)

The amount of council tax payable varies between and, in certain instances, within local authorities. Before the start of each financial year (April to March), each local authority must set an amount of council tax that enables it to meet its budgeted expenditure and the budgeted expenditure of certain related bodies. For example, in England and Wales, the county council raises money via the district council's council tax. The power of the Secretary of State to cap amounts set by local authorities has been removed but the Secretary of State retains important powers to fix and determine how local authorities calculate the amount of tax. In 2011 the government introduced a right for taxpayers to call for local referendums where a rise in council tax is 2 per cent or more in any financial year compared with the previous year. This is frozen for the year 2014/15.

The council tax payable on each dwelling depends, in the first instance, on the valuation band to which it has been allocated. Different valuation bands apply in England, Wales and Scotland. These reflect the different range of property prices in the three countries. There are a number of ways in which the council tax payable on a particular property may be reduced, and these are examined in the following chapters.

Local authorities have a discretionary power to reduce council tax bills. They can do so in individual cases (eg, to prevent financial hardship) and in groups of cases – eg, if several properties have been affected by flooding.

Exempt dwellings (Chapter 5)

Certain categories of dwelling are exempt from the tax. New exempt categories have been added and the definition of others amended since the tax was first introduced with more local flexibility in the period and amount of the exemption granted. The exemption may be either indefinite or for a fixed period. No council tax or Scottish Water charges are payable while the dwelling is exempt. An appeal may be made if a local authority refuses to grant an exemption. There is no time limit for obtaining exemptions.

Liability (Chapter 6)

Council tax is usually payable by someone aged 18 or over who is solely or mainly resident in the dwelling. If there is more than one such person, the liable person is the one with the greatest legal interest in the dwelling. Normally, it is the owner or the tenant who must pay council tax. However, in some circumstances, a non-resident owner may be liable instead of a resident – eg, a dwelling which is in multi-occupation where residents do not form part of the same household.

If the liable person is married or in a civil partnership, or living with someone as though they were married or in a civil partnership, the partner is normally jointly liable for the council tax even if s/he has no legal interest in the dwelling. Also, if two or more people, other than partners, have the same legal interest in the dwelling, they may all be jointly liable for the council tax. Special rules apply if a liable person or partner is 'severely mentally impaired' or a full-time student.

The local authority has the right to obtain information from a variety of sources to identify liable individuals. An appeal may be made against any decision by the local authority on liability.

Disability reduction (Chapter 7)

The amount of council tax payable on a dwelling can be reduced if the dwelling has certain features to meet the particular needs of someone (either an adult or a child) with a disability. The fact that a dwelling is occupied by a person with a disability is not sufficient in itself; what is necessary is that there is an additional room, or a room which is adapted, to meet the needs of a disabled resident of the dwelling. Annual applications must be made for these reductions and they may be backdated up to six years. An appeal may be made if the local authority refuses to award a disability reduction.

Discounts (Chapter 8)

A council tax bill is based on the assumption that there are two or more residents aged 18 or over in the dwelling. If there are more than two, the bill does not increase, but it may be reduced by:

- a variable percentage if the dwelling is no one's sole or main residence; *or*
- 25 per cent if it is only one person's sole or main residence; *or*
- 25 per cent if all but one person fail to be a 'disregarded person'.

In deciding how many people are solely or mainly resident in the dwelling, certain categories of people are disregarded – effectively, the dwelling is treated as if these people were not actually living in it. The local authority must consider whether a discount applies in any particular case.

From April 2013, local authorities have greater powers to alter the amount of discount awarded on certain dwellings. The Local Government Finance Act 2012 gives local authorities greater discretion over the amount of council tax that they collect on long-term empty dwellings. These decisions are made by the authorities themselves. In addition, individual local authorities may also grant special discretionary discounts in certain situations.

Appeals may be made against the local authority's decision not to apply a discount.

Council tax reduction schemes (Chapter 9)

Until March 2013, local authorities paid council tax benefit (CTB) to people on low incomes to help them pay their council tax liability. Councils could claim most of this money back from the Department for Work and Pensions, which compensated them directly for any loss of council tax income.

This system was substantially changed by the Welfare Reform Act 2012 and the Local Government Finance Act 2012. Councils now receive grant funding from the government equal to 90 per cent of the value of the CTB previously paid to them. This national system, which operated uniformly throughout England, Scotland and Wales, is now replaced by local council tax reduction (CTR) schemes, with each council setting its own individual level of support for its own area.

By 31 January 2013 each local authority was required to draw up its own individual CTR scheme to assist council taxpayers in its area as it sees fit, within a broad framework prescribed the Secretary of State for Communities and Local Government. These provisions continue to apply for 2014, with some amendments in Wales.

A default scheme applies if a billing authority's area failed to make a scheme on or before 31 January each year. Eligibility for a reduction scheme is based on a means test. Pensioners on low incomes receive most protection under all schemes.

In addition to the reductions under its scheme, the local authority retains a discretion to reduce an amount payable in council tax. This can be exercised either in individual cases or for certain classes of persons.

As a consequence of the introduction of local reduction schemes, many people previously protected from having to be pay council tax on account of low income are expected to pay.

Bills and payments (Chapter 10)

Council tax is not payable until a demand notice (bill) has been issued and served (including by electronic means) on the taxpayer. Liability for council tax arises on a daily basis, but bills are raised on the assumption that the circumstances on which they are based will remain the same throughout the year. The council taxpayer is required to report changes in circumstances which affect the bill to the local authority.

You have a right to pay council tax in instalments. There are usually 10 each year. However, from April 2013, taxpayers have a new right to choose to pay their council tax bills in 12 monthly payments, rather than a maximum of 10.

If a first demand notice is issued part way through the year, the number of instalments is reduced. Local authorities may also offer council tenants up to 52 instalments so that they can pay their council tax with their rent payments. Local authorities also have the power to enter into special payment arrangements with individual taxpayers, to offer discounts for lump-sum payments and adopt non-cash payment methods. These schemes have to be agreed in writing beforehand.

Enforcement (Chapter 11)

The local authority may use a variety of measures to ensure that a liable person pays the tax and any related costs and penalties. These methods range from issuing reminders to taking legal action. If someone fails to pay council tax, a local authority may apply to a magistrates' court for a liability order (or, in Scotland, to the sheriff court for a summary warrant).

A liability order (or summary warrant) enables the local authority to:
- make deductions from the debtor's earnings;
- seize and sell the debtor's goods;
- obtain a charging order against the debtor's home;
- request that deductions are made from certain welfare benefits;
- use bankruptcy proceedings to make the taxpayer bankrupt;
- if the taxpayer is a councillor, obtain deductions from her/his councillor's allowances.

Legal costs are added when the local authority applies for a liability order or a summary warrant. Further costs may be added with particular enforcement methods.

Enforcement action by way of bankruptcy can be challenged through the County Court or on appeal to the High Court.

In addition, English and Welsh local authorities may apply to the magistrates' court for a warrant committing the debtor to prison, but only in certain limited circumstances. Imprisonment can only be used as a last resort where it is established that the debtor has the means to pay but has failed to do so.

Both the magistrates' court and the sheriff court have the power to remit the debt (in whole or in part) if the debtor is unable to pay, but in England and Wales this only arises on an application to commit a debtor to prison.

There are various ways of appealing against a liability order or against improper enforcement action, including to the magistrates' court, the County Court or the High Court.

Appeals (Chapter 12)

Many decisions concerning council tax can be appealed. Appeals can be made against:
- valuation;
- the amount of reduction under a local CTR scheme;
- liability;
- completion notices;
- calculation of the amount of tax;
- penalties.

Complaints to the Ombudsman and civil action for redress for maladministration (Chapter 13)

In some cases, local authorities or the private companies working for them make mistakes in the administration of council tax, which cannot be rectified by appealing.

Such errors may fall within the remit of the Ombudsman. The Ombudsman seeks to obtain redress for people who have experienced injustice as a result of maladministration. The Ombudsman may conduct an independent investigation with a view to obtaining a remedy. Complaints may be resolved by a local settlement or proceed to a full investigation. If a complaint is upheld, the Ombudsman may recommend compensation for the person bringing the complaint.

If the Ombudsman is unable to provide a remedy, or as an alternative to using the Ombudsman, there may also be the possibility of a claim against the local authority or individual officers for wrong-doing under civil law.

4. **Legal background and references**

The legal framework for the council tax is contained in the Local Government Finance Act 1992, as amended by the Local Government Act 2003, the Localism Act 2011 and the Local Government Finance Act 2012. The Act includes sections and Schedules that apply throughout England, Wales and Scotland, as well as sections and Schedules that apply exclusively to one or other of the two jurisdictions. The functions of the Secretary of State were transferred to the Scottish Ministers by s53 of the Scotland Act 1998.

The Acts enable the Secretary of State, the Welsh government or the Scottish government to formulate legislation (statutory instruments) in the form of regulations which contain and amend the details of the scheme. In practice, it is these regulations that govern the operation of the council tax. Different sets of statutory instruments apply to England and Wales and to Scotland. Additionally, certain statutory instruments only apply to England or to Wales or Scotland. Most of the regulations have been amended since they were first made and others substituted. The original text of many of these regulations is available at www.legislation.co.uk but subsequent amendments are not always included.

Following the Local Government Finance Act 2012 local authorities are now responsible for setting the level of reductions which apply in their area for people on low-incomes. Each local authority is required to draw up a council tax reduction (CTR) scheme which applies from the start of each financial year. With the exceptions of pensioners and certain prescribed categories of support set out in regulations made by the Secretary of State, each local authority is left to devise the support scheme and level of support for its own area as it sees fit for persons of working age. Consequently, there is no national set scheme of support for persons of working age and there is widespread variation between different councils. Reference needs to be made to the appropriate local CTR scheme published by an individual authority. However, these rules have legal effect and are binding on the authority, and appeal rights are to the valuation tribunal remain consistent and standardised throughout England and Wales, with separate provisions applying in Scotland.

Relevant caselaw is also identified in the appropriate paragraphs of this *Handbook*.

Electronic communication

Under powers derived from the Electronic Communications Act 2000, local authorities in England, Wales and Scotland may serve certain notices and information required for council tax by electronic means. These provisions require the agreement of the taxpayer to be effective. Information and notices may also be served electronically on local authorities by taxpayers, although to be effective in law the communication must be recorded on a local authority computer. Electronic communication can also be used to alter lists and for appeals.

Freedom of information

The Freedom of Information Act 2000 (and in Scotland, The Freedom of Information (Scotland) Act 2002) enables anyone to seek and obtain information held by state bodies, subject to certain exceptions. The Act may be used to discover information about aspects of the council tax, both national and local, in addition to information which is already available to the public (such as the valuation list). If a request to supply information is unreasonably refused, an appeal can be made to the Information Commissioner. Not all information is available – eg, personal records.

Personal data held on computer can also be obtained under the Data Protection Act 1998. The person who is the subject of the data can obtained copies of the information by way of a subject access request. The cost of this is up to £10 and can be more for paper-based health records (see http://ico.org.uk).

Practice notes and implementation letters

In addition to the legislation, the Department for Communities and Local Government (in England), the Welsh Government and the local authority associations have together produced, and periodically revised, a series of 'practice notes'. These advise on the interpretation of the legislation and on administrative arrangements, and highlight a number of good practice points. There is no Scottish equivalent. The Department for Communities and Local Government also produces council tax 'implementation letters'. These advise local authorities about the latest changes in legislation or decisions of the courts. Points from the implementation letters are periodically included in revisions of the practice notes. While the legislation is binding on local authorities, neither the practice notes nor the implementation letters have the force of law and local authorities are not bound by them. Particularly useful comments from the practice notes are included in this *Handbook*. The Valuation Tribunal also issues a newsletter (*Valuation in Practice*), which may be consulted online, and a selection of guidance notes.

The president of the Valuation Tribunal for England has issued a series of *Practice Statements* which apply to the conduct of hearings and the procedures to be adopted with appeals. Details of these are published on the Valuation Tribunal website. Guidance has also been issued by the Valuation Tribunal for Wales.

Notes in the *Handbook*

References to the law are given in notes at the end of each chapter. The notes usually begin with the letters E, W or S or a combination of these, indicating references to English, Welsh and/or Scottish law. The abbreviations used in the notes can be found in Appendix 4.

Legal and other references

Local authorities publish details of their local reduction schemes for council tax which should be available online.

Statutes and regulations governing council tax are available online but are not updated. Butterworth's loose-leaf work, *Ryde on Rating and the Council Tax*, reproduces all the relevant English and Welsh legislation and the practice notes. Large public reference libraries should have this two-volume work.

CPAG's Housing Benefit and Council Tax Reduction Legislation consolidates the legislation on council tax reduction schemes in England, Wales and Scotland.

Shelter and the Chartered Institute of Housing annually produce a *Guide to Housing Benefit and Council Tax Rebates*.

Rating and Valuation Reporter covers changes to council tax and reports decisions of the courts in valuation and local taxation matters. Other unreported decisions may be available on LEXIS, a database of court decisions and law reports; some judgments are also available at www.judiciary.gov.uk.

The most detailed guide to enforcement in England and Wales remains the Legal Action Group's *The Enforcement of Local Taxation: an advisors' guide to non-payment of council tax and poll tax* (2000).

Detailed information on proceedings in the civil and criminal courts, which may involve council tax matters, can be found in specialist works of law and procedure, published annually. Note that the rules of civil procedure which apply in the County Court and High Court do not have an equivalent in council tax proceedings in magistrates' courts. Details of appropriate procedures in the magistrates' court can be found in the annual *Stone's Justices' Manual*.

Policy changes and council tax research can be found on the Department for Communities and Local Government website at www.communities.gov.uk.

Information on valuation matters and appeals can be found at the Valuation Office Agency website at www.voa.gov.uk and the Valuation Tribunal website at www.valuationtribunal.gov.uk. The Valuation Tribunal website is regularly updated with summaries given in recent valuation tribunal decisions.

Individual local authority websites may also provide useful information on the payment and collection of council tax in local areas. It seems likely that the provision of information in this area will increase in the next few years, and some local authorities are developing schemes to share information with advice agencies, such as Citizens Advice Bureaux, at a local level.

Reports of Ombudsman decisions in England are at www.lgo.org.uk.

Future changes

This *Handbook* is up to date as the law stood on 1 January 2014 and the benefit rates referred to in Chapter 9 are those that apply from 1 April 2013 and 1 April 2014. Rates for future years will be on www.gov.uk.

The system of council tax reduction schemes operated by local authorities must be reviewed by the Secretary of State by April 2016.

Notes

1. **Introduction**
   1   HM Treasury Spending Review 2010,
       Cm 7942, 2010 p50, para2.42

2. **Administration**
   2   **EW** s1 LGFA 1992
   3   The Council Tax Reduction Schemes
       (Detection of Fraud and Enforcement)
       (England) Regulations 2013 No.501

Chapter 2

Chargeable dwellings

This chapter covers:
1. Chargeable dwellings (below)
2. Dwellings in England and Wales (below)
3. Dwellings in Scotland (p18)
4. New and altered properties (p20)

1. Chargeable dwellings

Council tax is payable on any dwelling which is not exempt (see Chapter 5). Properties on which the tax must be paid are referred to as 'chargeable dwellings'.[1] The definition of a 'dwelling' is therefore a fundamental one for council tax purposes.

In most cases, whether or not a property constitutes a dwelling is not in question. Houses, flats, bungalows, cottages and maisonettes used for domestic purposes all normally count as dwellings. However, sometimes it may not be clear whether or not a property constitutes a dwelling. This might occur, for example, if one property consists of a number of dwellings or if a number of properties constitute one dwelling. Whether or not a specific property constitutes a dwelling is one of the grounds for making a proposal to alter the valuation list (see Chapter 3) and could be the subject of an appeal (see Chapter 12).

The definition of a dwelling which applies in England and Wales differs from that which applies in Scotland. In the majority of cases, however, the effect is the same.

2. Dwellings in England and Wales

What counts as a dwelling

The legal definition of a dwelling for council tax purposes in England and Wales is not straightforward. The Local Government Finance Act 1992 defines a 'dwelling' as any property which:[2]

- would have been a 'hereditament' (ie, a rateable unit – see below) for the purposes of s115(1) of the General Rate Act 1967 if that Act had remained in force (see p13); *and*
- is not shown, or required to be shown, on a local or a central non-domestic rating list (see p16); *and*
- is not exempt from local non-domestic rating; *or*
- is a 'composite hereditament' (see p17).

What is not a dwelling

The Act specifically excludes certain properties from being dwellings, unless they constitute part of a larger property which is itself a dwelling. These are:[3]
- a yard, garden, outhouse or other land or building belonging to, or enjoyed with, property used wholly for the purposes of living accommodation; *or*
- a private garage which either has a floor area of not more than 25 square metres or is used wholly or mainly to accommodate a private motor vehicle; *or*
- private storage premises used wholly or mainly to store domestic articles.

These exclusions mean, for example, that a garage used to keep a private car that is not part of a larger property does not constitute a dwelling and should not be included in the valuation of any other dwelling.

In England, property is a dwelling if it is used for the microgeneration of electricity or heat by alternative energy sources such as biomass, biofuel, wind, water unless it forms part of a larger property which is itself a dwelling.[4]

Hereditaments

The General Rate Act 1967 charged general rates on domestic and non-domestic property. Section 115(1) of that Act defined a **'hereditament'** as a 'property which is or may become liable to a rate, being a unit of such property which is, or would fall to be, shown as a separate rate item in the valuation list'. The exact identity of the hereditament has been the subject of numerous legal cases. In the leading case on the issue, Denning LJ said:[5]

'Where two or more properties are within the same curtilage or contiguous to one another, and are in the same occupation, they are as a general rule to be treated for rating purposes as if they formed part of a single hereditament. There are exceptional cases, however, where for some special reason they may be treated as two or more hereditaments. That may happen for instance, because they were valued at different times, or because they were at one time in different occupations, or because one part is used for an entirely different purpose. Where the two properties are in the same occupation but are not within the same curtilage nor contiguous to one another each of them must as a general rule be treated as a separate hereditament for rating purposes: and this is the case even though they are used by the occupier for the purposes of his one whole business.'

In the same case, Parker LJ said that the following should be considered when determining what is a hereditament:
- whether two or more parts of the premises are capable of being separately let;
- whether the premises form a single geographical unit;
- whether, though forming a single geographical unit, the premises' structure and layout consist of two or more separate parts;
- whether the occupier uses the whole of the premises for one purpose or whether s/he uses different parts for different purposes.

Dwellings in a state of disrepair

In some cases, a property may be in such a state of disrepair that it cannot be classed as a dwelling at all. It could be so derelict that even with a reasonable amount of repairs, no one could be expected to live in it. Such a property ceases to be a hereditament and may be removed from the valuation list altogether.

When deciding whether a dwelling should be removed, a key test is whether a reasonable amount of repair work would make it habitable. If the answer is 'no', the dwelling can be taken off the list entirely. Past valuation tribunal decisions on this question show that the state of dereliction must be severe and it must be uneconomical to undertake repairs. A tribunal may establish that if it were unreasonable to undertake repairs and no reasonable owner would attempt them, the dwelling should be removed from the list.

Note: the actual intentions of the landlord or owner are not relevant. The tribunal looks at the actions of a hypothetical reasonable owner. Thus, an owner or landlord who is willing to spend more than what a reasonable person would to repair a property may still have the dwelling removed from the list for the period it is uninhabitable. For example, in one case, a valuation tribunal held that a dwelling with dangerous electrical wiring and lacking a gable wall should not appear in a valuation list while undergoing rebuilding.[6] The building was uninhabitable during rebuilding and failed to meet the definitions of a rateable hereditament. If a dwelling can be repaired, it should remain on the valuation list and may be entitled to an empty dwelling exemption for 12 months while the repairs are carried out. For more information on exemptions, see Chapter 5.

Self-contained accommodation and 'granny flats'

If a dwelling is considered to be a single dwelling under the definition of a hereditament (see p13), but consists of more than one 'self-contained unit' of living accommodation, the local authority will treat each self-contained unit of accommodation as a separate dwelling.[7]

A '**self-contained unit**' is a building, or part of a building, which has been constructed or adapted for use as separate living accommodation. Local authority listing officers are advised to look for living and sleeping accommodation and at least minimal separate cooking and washing facilities before they decide that the property constitutes 'self-contained' living accommodation. For example, a property that contains more than one self-contained unit (eg, a large house that has been adapted to provide a separate 'granny' annex) should be treated as two or more dwellings. The annex may then be an exempt dwelling if unoccupied (see Chapter 5). Key factors that will be taken into account include whether a self-contained unit or annex has all the features necessary for independent living.

If a living unit does not have independent outside access, it does not necessarily mean it is part of a single dwelling.[8]

The view of the occupier (eg, if s/he says that the accommodation is used as a games room rather than living accommodation) will not prevent a listing officer from deciding that a separate dwelling exists.

Identifying a 'self-contained unit' is a two-stage process. The listing officer must first determine that a hereditament exists and to what extent, and only then go on to consider whether the hereditament contains any self-contained units.[9]

If you are an 'interested person' (see p33), you can make a proposal to the listing officer not to show your home as a separate unit of accommodation on the valuation list. The process of making a proposal is described in Chapter 3.

Buildings in multiple occupation

The listing officer has the discretion to treat a property which would otherwise be considered to be two or more separate dwellings as a single dwelling if it:[10]

- consists of a single self-contained unit, or such a unit together with or containing premises constructed or adapted for non-domestic purposes; *and*
- is occupied as more than one unit of separate living accommodation.

This could apply, for example, to a property occupied by more than one household, but where the residents share facilities such as kitchens or bathrooms – eg, a group of bedsits, a hostel or a care home. The listing officer must exercise her/his discretion reasonably and should take into account all the circumstances of the case, including the extent to which the parts of the property that are separately occupied have been structurally altered.

The listing officer's decision that a property with a number of different households is, or should be treated as, only one dwelling rather than several may have an impact not only on the single dwelling's valuation band but also on liability and entitlement to discounts or benefits. In one case concerning general rates, it was held that at least four factors should be considered by a valuation officer when exercising her/his discretion.[11] These are:

- the degree to which facilities, such as kitchens and bathrooms, are shared;
- the degree of internal adaptations, such as entrance doors;
- the degree of identifiably of separate parts;
- the degree of transience in the occupiers' residence.

The higher courts have confirmed that the above principles continue to apply with the test that is sometimes referred to as the 'bricks and mortar test', by looking at the reality of what has actually been constructed rather than at the intentions of the owner (see Chapter 6).[12] However, if two flats are converted to a single property, a new dwelling is created for council tax purposes.[13]

Houses in multiple occupation have to be registered with the local authority (see Chapter 6).

Converted sheds and garages

In areas with high rents and a shortage of accommodation, some people have transformed sheds and garages into places to stay for migrant workers. These may pose problems for local authorities in the future. Converted sheds and garages may be excluded from the category of 'dwelling' or may be part of the owner's dwelling. Even if they are treated as dwellings in their own right, in most cases it is likely that the owner will be held liable for the council tax (see Chapter 6).

Property on the non-domestic rating list

Property is **'domestic'** if it is used wholly for the purpose of living accommodation. If it is not in use, it is still considered to be domestic property if its next use will be domestic. Most non-domestic property, such as business or industrial property, is shown on either the local or central non-domestic rating list. Such properties are not dwellings for council tax purposes, but are subject to non-domestic rates.

Caravans and houseboats

A pitch for a caravan and a mooring for a houseboat are hereditaments (see p13) and are, therefore, capable of being considered dwellings for council tax purposes if they are occupied by a caravan or houseboat (including a boat which is no longer navigable[14]) which is someone's sole or main residence (see p77). If not in use, even if the pitch or mooring is empty, it is still considered a dwelling if it appears that its next use will be domestic, but it may be an exempt dwelling (see Chapter 5). Boats and caravans may themselves be classed as hereditaments and treated as domestic dwellings. For a boat or a caravan to constitute a hereditament, the key question is the degree of permanence in its position.

If a boat is moored at one spot or a caravan parked on the same pitch for a substantial period, its value may also be included in the valuation of pitch or mooring for banding purposes. Where a dwelling boat or caravan occupies a mooring or pitch for 12 months or more, the value of the boat or caravan should be included in the band value, even if it moves away for brief periods, of say, two to four weeks, provided it then returns to its original mooring or pitch.[15] The question to be asked is whether the occupation can be characterised as that of a 'settler' or 'wayfarer'. If the latter, then only the mooring or pitch should valued.[16]

Holiday caravans and other caravans used for non-domestic purposes are subject to non-domestic rates. However, if you keep a caravan at home for use on holidays, you are not liable to pay non-domestic rates or council tax on it.

Timeshare property

Timeshare accommodation does not count as domestic property and is subject to non-domestic rates.

Composite hereditaments

A property is a **'composite hereditament'** if only part of it is used solely for the purpose of living accommodation. For example, some rooms in a property may be used only for business purposes and others used only for domestic purposes. Council tax is payable on the domestic portion and non-domestic rates are payable on the business portion. It is possible to appeal against a decision that a property is a composite hereditament, or against a decision on the proportion of a property that is used for domestic or non-domestic purposes. The key question is whether the character of a dwelling house has been lost.[17] For example, a dwelling in which a room or garage is predominantly used for business purposes may be classed as a composite hereditament. However, the fact that someone works from home does not necessarily create a composite hereditament. In *Tully v Jorgensen (VO)*,[18] the appellant worked from home because her disability meant she was unable to travel to work on a daily basis. The room she used had not been structurally adapted for business use and contained normal domestic furniture. Outside of office hours, the room reverted to normal family use. No one visited for business purposes and if meetings were required, they took place elsewhere. Consequently, the room was part of the ordinary domestic accommodation of the household.

When valuing a composite property, a listing officer is expected initially to value the property as a whole, and then apportion the relevant amount between domestic and non-domestic parts.[19]

When assessing the domestic portion of a composite hereditament, the listing officer must take into account the amount of the property that could reasonably be attributed to domestic use. The Court of Appeal has ruled that, provided the listing officer does so, s/he can value the domestic portion by any method s/he chooses.[20]

Dwellings in different locations

The location of a dwelling is a major determining factor in how much council tax is payable. Different local authorities may have different levels of council tax for dwellings in the same valuation band (see Chapter 4). Additionally, where there are parish or community councils, different parts of the same local authority may have different levels of council tax for dwellings in the same valuation band.

If a dwelling (including a dwelling that is part of a larger single property) falls within the area of two or more local authorities, or two or more parts of an authority's area, it should be treated as being in the area in which the greatest part of the dwelling is situated.[21]

3. **Dwellings in Scotland**

In Scotland, a '**dwelling**' means any lands and 'heritages' - ie, rights that exist with the land, such as farming and fishing rights:
- which consist of one or more dwelling houses with any garden, yard, garage, outhouse or pertinent other area belonging to and occupied with the dwelling house(s); *and*
- which would, but for the fact that it is a dwelling, be entered separately in the valuation roll.[22]

The valuation roll is now limited to recording the details of non-domestic and part-residential properties. Details of domestic dwellings are now contained in the valuation lists.

A Scottish dwelling includes:
- the residential part of part-residential property (see p19); *and*
- part of any premises that was apportioned on 1 April 1989 as a dwelling house.

It includes caravans, but only if they are someone's sole or main residence.

What counts as a dwelling

Certain types of property are explicitly included or excluded from the Scottish definition of a dwelling. The following properties are specifically included in the definition of a dwelling if, but for the fact that they were dwellings, they would be entered separately on the valuation roll:
- a garage, carport or car parking space wholly or mainly used, or last used, for private motor vehicles;[23]
- certain private storage premises used, or last used, wholly or mainly to store domestic articles (including cycles and other similar vehicles);[24]
- bed and breakfast accommodation operated on a commercial basis by a person living there for letting to not more than six people a night;
- student halls of residence which include shared facilities;
- accommodation owned by the Ministry of Defence which is, or is likely to be, the sole or main residence of at least one member of the armed forces;
- school boarding accommodation;
- any part of a communal residential establishment with shared facilities for residents, including those parts of a hostel or care home (as defined for the

purpose of a discount – see p118) which are used wholly or mainly as the sole or main residence of a person employed there. **Note:** the other parts of this type of accommodation in which the residents live are not dwellings, but are subject to non-domestic rates.

Note: some of the above dwellings are exempt from council tax (see Chapter 5).[25]

What is not a dwelling

Certain properties are specifically excluded from the Scottish definition of a dwelling, but may be subject to non-domestic rates. These are:
- certain huts, sheds and bothies which are no one's sole or main residence;
- certain self-catering holiday accommodation which is no one's sole or main residence;
- women's refuges (except any part which is the sole or main residence of an employee of the voluntary organisation managing the refuge);[26]
- timeshare accommodation.[27]

If a dwelling is served by a combined heat and power station, the pipes, risers and other plant connected with the power station are not treated as part of the dwelling (and so are ignored for valuation purposes) except insofar as they fall within the solum (upper soil), garden, yard or garage of the dwelling.[28]

However, all pipes and risers for the transport of water between a power station and a block of flats (or tenement) are treated as part of all the dwellings in the tenement insofar as these pipes and risers are located in or on land pertaining to the tenement. If the power station benefits only the tenement, it (and all the associated plant) counts as part of each dwelling. They are allocated equally between the dwellings they serve.

Part-residential property

Certain properties with a mixed domestic and non-domestic use, such as private nursing homes and hospitals (see p18 and p118), are divided into their relevant parts. The non-domestic element is entered on the valuation roll and the domestic element is entered on the valuation list and is treated as a dwelling for council tax purposes.

Premises that are used for commercial or sporting purposes (known as '**part-residential subjects**') are treated differently. The property is shown on the valuation roll, but an apportionment note on the roll indicates the net annual value and the rateable value based on the residential and non-residential use of the property.[29] The residential part counts as a dwelling for council tax purposes. **Note:** those parts of a women's refuge, hostel or care home (see p118) used as accommodation for residents rather than employees are specifically excluded from the definition of part-residential subject.[30]

4. **New and altered properties**

A new dwelling may be created either by a new building or by the structural alteration of an existing property. A new dwelling is considered to come into existence for council tax purposes from the day a completion notice is served, or from the completion date contained on the notice, if later.[31] In the latter case, this is if a dwelling is not completed, but the local authority believes it is substantially completed and it can be completed within three months from the date the notice is served.

A new or altered dwelling does not require a completion notice once someone starts to live there.

If a new or altered dwelling is unoccupied, it may be exempt from council tax for a period (see Chapter 5). If a new dwelling is created by the structural alteration to a building, the former dwelling(s) is considered to have ceased to exist on the completion date.

Completion notices

The local authority (in England and Wales) or assessor (in Scotland) may serve a completion notice on the owner of a building which has been completed or which can reasonably be expected to be completed within three months.[32] This notice proposes a completion day for the building.

The proposed completion day becomes the actual completion day unless the owner appeals. Before the outcome of the appeal, the proposed completion day is treated as the actual completion day.

Appealing against a completion notice

Any disagreement over the date on a completion notice can be raised in the first instance with the local authority (in England and Wales) or the assessor (in Scotland), but appeals must be made within particularly short time periods (see Chapter 12).

In England and Wales, appeals should be made directly to the Valuation Tribunal for England or the Valuation Tribunal for Wales within 28 days of the notice being sent (see p235).[33] The president of the tribunal may, however, allow an out-of-time appeal if you have failed to meet this time limit for reasons beyond your control.[34]

In Scotland, an appeal must be lodged with a valuation appeal committee within 21 days of receiving the completion notice.[35] This is done by writing to the assessor, stating the grounds of the appeal and enclosing a copy of the completion notice.

Notes

1. Chargeable dwellings
1 **EW** s4(1) and (2) LGFA 1992
   S s72(6) LGFA 1992

2. Dwellings in England and Wales
2 s3(1) LGFA 1992
3 s3(4) LGFA 1992 and in England as amended by the Non-Domestic Rating and Council Tax (Definition of Domestic Property and Dwelling) (England) Order 2013 No.468
4 The Non-Domestic Rating and Council Tax (Definition of Domestic Property and Dwelling) (England) Order 2013 No.468
5 *Gilbert (Valuation Officer) v Hickinbottom & Sons Ltd* [1956] 2 All ER 101 (CA)
6 *Z Munter Farms Ltd v Pettitt* [2006] RVR 332
7 CT(CD)O
8 *Vaziri v Listing Officer* [2006] RVR 329
9 *Rawsthorne (Listing Officer) v Parr* [2009] EWHC 2002 (Admin)
10 CT(CD)O, as amended by The Council Tax (Chargeable Dwellings, Exempt Dwellings and Disregards) (Amendment) (England) Order 2003 No.3121
11 *James v Williams* [1973] RA 305
12 *R v London South Eastern Valuation Tribunal and Neale ex parte Moore* [2001] RVR 94; *Baker (LO) v Gomperts* [2006] All ER D 1 July; *Listing Officer v Callear* [2012] EWHC 3697
13 *R v East Sussex Valuation Tribunal ex parte Silverstone* [1996] RVR 203
14 *Nicholls v Wimbledon Valuation Officer* [1995] RVR 171
15 para 6.2 Council Tax Manual Practice Note 7 – Application to Council Tax to Caravan Pitches and Moorings, VOA
16 *Reeves (LO) v Northrop (LO)* [2013] EWCA 362
17 *Guthrie v Highland Region and Western Isles Assessor* [1995] RA 292
18 *Tully v Jorgensen (VO)* [2003] RA 233
19 *Listing Officer v Monmouth School* [2009] EWHC 2720 (Admin)

20 Reg 7 CT(SVD) Regs; *Atkinson and Others v Lord* [1997] RA 413
21 CT(SVD) Regs; see also Practice Note No.10

3. Dwellings in Scotland
22 s72 LGFA 1992
23 CT(Dw)(S) Regs
24 CT(Dw)(S) Regs
25 CT(DPRS)(S) Regs
26 CT(D)(S) Regs
27 CT(Dw)(S) Regs
28 CT(Dw)(S) Regs 2010
29 s72(8) and Sch 5 LGFA 1992
30 CT(D)(S) Regs

4. New and altered properties
31 **EW** s17 LGFA 1992; Sch 4A LGFA 1988
   S s83(1) and Sch 6 LGFA 1992
32 **EW** s17 LGFA 1992; Sch 4A LGFA 1988
   S s83(1) and Sch 6 LGFA 1992
33 **E** Reg 21(5) VTE(CTRA)(P)Regs
   W Reg 29(4) VTW Regs
34 **E** Reg 21(6) VTE(CTRA)(P) Regs
   W Reg 29(5) VTW Regs
35 **S** Sch 6 LGFA 1992

Chapter 3

Valuation

This chapter covers:
1. Who is responsible for valuations (below)
2. The listing officer's and assessor's powers (p24)
3. How dwellings are valued (p25)
4. Compiling and maintaining valuation lists (p29)
5. Inspecting the valuation list (p30)
6. Altering a valuation list (p31)

1. Who is responsible for valuations

England and Wales

In England and Wales, the valuation of dwellings for council tax purposes is carried out by the Valuation Office Agency (VOA), which is part of HM Revenue and Customs (HMRC). There is a listing officer at the VOA for each local authority. The listing officer has various duties in relation to compiling and maintaining the valuation list, and is independent of the local authority.[1] The term **'listing officer'** in this *Handbook* refers to any listing officer and any other officer appointed by HMRC's commissioners to carry out their functions.[2]

Details of your local Valuation Office and listing officer can be found at www.voa.gov.uk or by telephoning 0300 0501 501 (England) or 0300 050 5505 (Wales).

Scotland

In Scotland, the assessor and any deputy assessor for each local authority decides which valuation band should apply to each dwelling in the area.[3] The assessor is a professional valuer who must comply with any directions on valuations given by HMRC commissioners.[4] The assessor is appointed and employed by the council.[5] Details of assessors can be found at www.saa.gov.uk.

Appointees

The commissioners (in England and Wales) and the assessor (in Scotland) have the power to appoint other people, such as private surveyors, to carry out valuations.[6] The commissioners and the assessor are able to supply these appointees with relevant information obtained under their various powers – eg, any survey report obtained for rating purposes.[7] If the person assisting with the valuation discloses that information for reasons other than valuation purposes under the provisions of the Freedom of Information Act 2000, data protection purposes or in legal proceedings, s/he may be imprisoned for up to two years and/ or fined.[8]

Complaints

If you are unhappy with a valuation decision, see p28 and Chapter 12.

To complain about the poor performance and maladministration (as opposed to the actual decision) of any local listing officer, write initially to the office concerned. Examples of maladministration include failure to reach the quality of service expected, delays in dealing with enquiries and letters and providing inaccurate or misleading information or bad service from a member of staff.

If the response to your complaint is unsatisfactory, in England and Wales a complaint can be made to the relevant regional director of the VOA.

In England, if you are not satisfied with the regional director's response you can put your case to the Adjudicator. The role of the Adjudicator is to review the handling of complaints brought against the Insolvency Service, HMRC and the VOA, and can recommend action to put matters right. The VOA will accept the Adjudicator's recommendations, unless there are exceptional circumstances. You can refer a complaint to the Adjudicator's Office in writing or by telephone (see Appendix 1).

If you are unhappy with the Adjudicator's recommendations, you can complain to the Ombudsman. Since the VOA is a central government agency, the complaint is to the Parliamentary and Health Service Ombudsman, not the Local Government Ombudsman/Public Services Ombudsman, whose role is described in Chapter 13. Contact your MP if you are pursuing a complaint with the Parliamentary Ombudsman.

In Scotland, a complaint may be made to the Valuation Joint Board using the complaints form. If you are still dissatisfied at the end of the procedure you can complain to the Scottish Public Services Ombudsman (SPSO).

The SPSO is the final stage for complaints about most public bodies that provide public services in Scotland. The SPSO will only consider a complaint after you have completed the assessor's complaints procedure. **Note:** complaints must be made to the SPSO within 12 months of when you became aware of the matter subject to complaint.

Contact the SPSO for advice and to request a complaint form on Freephone 0800 377 7330.

2. **The listing officer's and assessor's powers**

The listing officer and assessor have powers to:
- enter dwellings; *and*
- obtain information from a past or present owner, occupier, the local authority and certain other people.

Powers of entry

A listing officer and any assistant with written authorisation from the listing officer (in Scotland, the local assessor or deputy assessor) may enter, survey and value a dwelling.[9] At least three clear days' written notice must be given. The three-day period excludes weekends and public holidays. Normally, the official concerned should try to arrange a suitable time for access and give you at least seven days' notice.

Listing officers will carry identity cards and ask your permission to take photographs.[10]

Someone who intentionally delays or obstructs the official may be liable, on summary conviction, to a fine not exceeding level 2 on the standard scale.[11]

The owner's and occupier's duty to provide information

The listing officer or assessor may require the present or past owner or occupier of a dwelling to supply information to assist her/him to carry out the valuation.[12] If the information is in the owner's or occupier's possession or control, it should be supplied within 21 days of a written notice being served. Failure to comply with this requirement, without reasonable excuse, may result in a fine of up to level 2 on the standard scale.[13]

A current or past owner or occupier could be liable to be imprisoned for up to three months and/or for a fine up to £1,000 if s/he makes a false statement.[14]

The local authority's duty to provide information

The listing officer or assessor may require the local authority to supply information about a property to assist her/him to carry out the valuation. In addition, if any information comes to the notice of a local authority, which it considers would assist the listing officer or assessor in her/his duties, it should provide that information.[15] In practice, the local authority will identify new dwellings and refer existing ones that have been altered.

Right to use other sources of information

Certain other individuals and organisations, such as the former community charge registration officer and, in Scotland, the district council, must also supply information if the listing officer or assessor requests it.[16] A listing officer or assessor may also take into account any other information available from other sources.

3. **How dwellings are valued**

In **England and Scotland**, each dwelling is valued on the basis of what it might reasonably have been expected to realise on the open market, subject to certain valuation assumptions, if sold on 1 April 1991 by a willing seller.[17]

When valuing a property, the question asked is: 'What was this dwelling worth on 1 April 1991, assuming there was a buyer available and the valuation assumptions applied?' (see p26).

The use of 1 April 1991 for all valuations has meant that adjustments for changes in prices over time have not had to be made. However, with changes in property prices since 1991, the construction of many new dwellings and the alteration of others, an assumed valuation date of 1 April 1991 has become harder to justify or maintain. As a result, the Local Government Act 2003 introduced a new 10-year cycle of revaluations, but the process has so far only been completed for Wales (see below).

Plans for a general revaluation in England by 1 April 2007 were abandoned in March 2006 when the Council Tax (New Valuation Lists for England) Act 2006 was passed. This removed the requirement for a revaluation to be undertaken every 10 years and future revaluation dates will be set by regulations. At present, the government has no plans to undertake a revaluation in England and council tax valuations will continue to be made based on a theoretical sale price on 1 April 1991.

This may pose a problem in valuation appeals, as obtaining reliable data on the price of properties in 1991 becomes more difficult as time passes.

In **Wales**, a revaluation of dwellings was completed on 1 April 2005, using the relevant date of 1 April 2003. The closing date for most appeals by taxpayers in Wales against the new valuation was 31 December 2005, with only limited rights of appeal thereafter (see Chapter 12).

Under the Localism Act 2011, Welsh Ministers have been given the power to determine the date of the next revaluation in Wales rather than be bound by the timetable laid down by the Local Government Finance Act 1992 which would require a revaluation on 1 April 2015. Any order for a revaluation decided by Welsh Ministers must be approved by the Welsh Assembly. Until the date chosen (or until 1 April 2015 if none is decided), the question to be asked is: 'What was this dwelling worth on 1 April 2003, assuming there was a buyer available and the valuation assumptions applied?'[18]

Theoretical and actual value

The valuation for council tax purposes represents a *theoretical* value of what the property was worth on the relevant date (see p25), not its actual value. Thus, a dwelling which, in reality, may have been in a bad state of repair will be treated as though it had been in a reasonable state of repair, as this is one of the valuation assumptions applied to all dwellings regardless of the circumstances. Similarly, fixtures inside a dwelling are ignored. For example, it makes no difference whether there is a modern kitchen range installed or no modern kitchen fittings at all. A council tax valuation must be made applying all the theoretical assumptions, regardless of what the actual situation was or might be today. The consequences of this are that the *actual price* that a property achieved when put on the market in 1991, or since, will not be its value for council tax purposes unless the two figures happen to coincide. An actual sale price would simply count as evidence towards what a property was worth for the purposes of a council tax banding valuation, applying the valuation assumptions.

A dwelling built since 1991 has to be valued by imagining it as if it had existed in 1991 and then applying the valuation assumptions to it to determine what it was worth. From this theoretical valuation, the dwelling is then allocated within a valuation band.

Banding details of domestic properties can be found at www.voa.gov.uk. **Note:** the government is also proposing to allow the Valuation Office Agency (VOA) to share information it holds on the sale prices of dwellings before 2000, which is currently confidential unless used in a valuation appeal (see Chapter 12).

The valuation assumptions

To make all valuations on a common basis, properties are not only assessed on the basis of their market value on 1 April 1991 in England and Scotland (1 April 2003 in Wales), but are also subject to certain valuation assumptions. The factors that affect the market value of a property include the number of rooms, its age, the construction materials used, the presence of a garden and the nature of the neighbouring environment. Many factors can affect value, and once these have been taken into consideration, the following statutory valuation assumptions are then applied.

Valuation assumptions
– The sale was with vacant possession.
– In England and Wales, a house was sold freehold and a flat (ie, part of a building divided horizontally to provide living units) was sold on a lease for 99 years at a nominal rent.
– In England and Wales, the dwelling was sold free from any rent charge (ie, rare rental payments on freehold land usually associated with covenants) or other duty or obligation.

- In Scotland, the dwelling was sold free from any 'heritable security' – ie, any mortgage is paid off.
- The size, layout and character of the dwelling, and the physical state of its locality, were the same as on the day the valuation was made.
- The dwelling was in reasonable repair.
- If there were common parts (eg, a hallway shared with another dwelling), these were in a reasonable state of repair considering the age and character of the dwelling and its locality, and the purchaser would be liable to contribute to the cost of keeping them in such a state.
- Fixtures designed for a person with a physical disability (see below), which increase the value of the dwelling, were ignored.
- The dwelling's use was permanently restricted to use as a private dwelling.
- The dwelling had no development value other than that attributable to any development for which no planning permission is required.

Note: the above assumptions are applied, whether or not they exist in fact.[19]

Reasonable repair

The dwelling is presumed to be in a reasonable state of repair, regardless of whether it is or not.

However, a distinction may be drawn between a dwelling which is in need of repair and a dwelling which is in such a poor state that it no longer should be classified as a dwelling or hereditament, and no longer be on the valuation list.

In *Wilson v Jo Coll (Listing Officer)*,[20] the High Court accepted that there may come a point at which a property is so derelict as to be incapable of repair. A valuer or tribunal must avoid confusing the concept of the existence, or continued existence, of a hereditament on the one hand, from the separate question of the proper valuation of a hereditament on the other. If a dwelling is in such a state of disrepair that it cannot be classed as a hereditament, it should be removed from the valuation list. Listing officers are expected to ask the question: 'Having regard to the character of the property and a reasonable amount of repair works being undertaken, could the premises be occupied as a dwelling?'[21]

If the answer to this question is no, the dwelling should be removed from the valuation list. If it is yes, it should be valued using the assumption that it is in a reasonable state of repair.

Fixtures for a person with a disability

'**Fixtures**' are items in a dwelling which are permanently attached to it, such as a sink, lavatory or lift. The value of fixtures should be ignored in the valuation if they:[22]

- are designed to make the dwelling suitable for use by a person with a physical disability; *and*
- add to the dwelling's value.

In other words, the dwelling is valued on the basis that those fixtures are not present. There is no requirement for someone with a disability to live in the dwelling. Such fixtures may have been taken into account during the valuation process. If this is the case, the listing officer or assessor should be advised of this possible oversight.

However, the presence of fittings and adaptations may be relevant to obtaining a reduction in valuation (see p32). There is also a separate disability reduction scheme for people with disabilities. This is described in Chapter 7.

Dwellings with mixed domestic and business use

In England and Wales, properties which include both a domestic and non-domestic component (known as 'composite hereditaments' – see p17) are valued on the proportion of the market value which might reasonably be attributed to the domestic use of the property. The valuation is based on the same rules and assumptions outlined above, except that the assumption that the property is permanently restricted for use as a private dwelling is ignored.

Scottish farmhouses, crofts and fish farms

In Scotland, dwellings such as farmhouses or cottages and croft houses connected with agriculture or fish farms are valued on the assumption that their availability is restricted to being used in that way. This lowers the value of the property and may lead to its being placed in a lower valuation band. When valuing a dwelling for council tax, the effect of a planning condition restricting occupation to a person mainly employed on a farm must not be ignored.[23]

Proposals and appeals on valuations

The use of valuation assumptions (see p26) means that a dwelling's valuation band may not reflect its actual sale price in 1991 (2003 in Wales). Consequently, the actual selling price of a dwelling would not necessarily be useful evidence to support a proposal to alter its value on the valuation list (see p31) or at a valuation tribunal or a valuation appeal committee hearing, unless the actual sale price happened to match the council tax valuation using the statutory valuation assumptions.

The valuation assumptions are applied whatever the condition of the dwelling (but see below if energy efficiency measures have been added). Thus, a valuation for council tax purposes may differ from a valuation for any other purpose. The assumptions are applied in every case regardless of the actual circumstances on the relevant day (ie, 1 April 1991 for England and Scotland, and 1 April 2003 for Wales) and used by valuation tribunals and valuation appeal committees and the High Court and Court of Session when considering appeals against banding decisions.

To be successful, a proposal to alter a dwelling's banding or an appeal must apply the assumptions described on p26.

Energy efficiency measures

The addition of energy efficiency or renewable energy measures, such as ground source heat pumps, insulation or solar panels, affect the value of a dwelling for council tax purposes. If the property is sold and the measures have increased the value of the dwelling into the next council tax band level, it is possible to change the dwelling's valuation. However, in practice, only substantial improvements would be likely to move a property up a band on its sale, and energy efficiency measures in isolation are unlikely to do so.[24]

4. Compiling and maintaining valuation lists

The listing officer or assessor is responsible for compiling and maintaining each local authority's valuation list.[25]

Compiling the list

In **England and Scotland**, the valuation list in operation was compiled on 1 April 1993 and came into force on that day. In **Wales**, the current list came into force on 1 April 2005. Before its compilation, the listing officer or assessor should have taken such steps as were reasonably practicable in the time available to ensure that the list was accurate.[26] Any new lists must, as far as is reasonably practicable, be accurate on the date on which they are compiled, and so the listing officer or assessor must revalue properties before the publication of each list. As soon as is reasonably practicable after its compilation, a copy should be sent to the local authority. The local authority should deposit this at its principal office.[27] You can access the valuation list (see p30), but the local authority does not have to advertise its availability.

Maintaining the list

The listing officer or assessor must maintain the list for as long as is necessary for the purposes of the council tax.[28] The listing officer or assessor notifies the local authority on a regular basis of any alterations to the compiled list to take account of new dwellings, demolitions, successful appeals and other changes. For the purpose of determining which valuation band (see p43) is applicable to a dwelling for any day, the state of affairs at the end of the day is assumed to have existed throughout that day.[29] This reflects the fact that council tax is a daily tax, payable for each day a dwelling falls into a particular valuation band.

5. **Inspecting the valuation list**

Everyone has the right to inspect the valuation list. Access to this information must be provided free of charge and at a reasonable time and place.[30]

You can check the council tax banding of an individual property and inspect the valuation list in England and Wales online by providing the address, postcode and billing authority area on the Valuation Office Agency website at www.voa.gov.uk. Valuation lists for Scottish local authorities are at www.saa.gov.uk.

You can make copies or transcripts of the list, or parts of the list. Alternatively, you can request that the local authority, listing officer or assessor supplies a copy, but a reasonable charge may be made for this service. If you are intentionally obstructed from exercising your rights in relation to the valuation list, the person responsible for the obstruction may be liable, on summary conviction, to a fine not exceeding level 2 on the standard scale.[31]

What the valuation list shows

A valuation list must show the items identified below.[32] The list does not contain any personal information. The omission from a list of any matter which should be included does not make it invalid.[33]

The contents of a valuation list
– Each dwelling in the local authority's area.
– Each dwelling's valuation band.
– A reference number for each dwelling.
– A marker indicating properties with mixed domestic and non-domestic use (England and Wales only).
– The effective date on which there has been an alteration.
– An indicator showing that an alteration has been made following an order of a valuation tribunal or a valuation appeal committee or the High Court or Court of Session.
– Notes indicating that a dwelling is a private garage or domestic storage premises (Scotland only).

There is no statutory requirement for how the contents of the valuation list should be laid out. Listing officers and assessors typically order their lists alphabetically, by postal towns, then by streets within each town. Within each street, numbered addresses are shown first, then named-only addresses in alphabetical order. Addresses which cannot be allocated to any street are shown at the end of the list of addresses in each postal town under the heading 'within billing authority area'. Addresses that are not allocated to a postal town appear at the end of the list.[34]

6. **Altering a valuation list**

A current valuation list can be altered by the listing officer or assessor following:

- the receipt of a proposal from an interested party or the local authority; *or*
- a successful appeal to the Valuation Tribunal for England (VTE), Valuation Tribunal for Wales (VTW), valuation appeal committee in Scotland, or to the High Court or Court of Session.

A dwelling's valuation band may be altered if:[35]

- the listing officer or assessor is satisfied that the valuation band is incorrect – eg, because of a clerical error;
- the listing officer or assessor is satisfied that the dwelling would have been allocated to a different valuation band had the valuation been carried out correctly;
- there has been a 'material increase' (see below) in the value of the dwelling since it was placed on the list and all, or part, of it has been sold or let on a lease for a term of seven years or more;
- there has been a 'material reduction' (see p32) in the value of the dwelling;
- part of the property has started to be used, or is no longer used, for business purposes, or the balance between business and domestic use has changed;
- there has been a successful appeal against the valuation band shown on the list.

The Valuation Office Agency (VOA) should normally tell you within two months if it has decided to alter the list.

A 'material increase' in the dwelling's value

A **'material increase'** in the value of a dwelling means any increase which is caused (in whole or in part) by any building, engineering or other operation carried out in relation to the dwelling.[36]

This would apply to building or other works which either increase the size of the property or add to its market value. However, the material increase only has an impact on the dwelling's valuation once the dwelling (or any part of it) has been sold. In England and Wales, this also applies if the dwelling is let on a lease for seven years or more.

In **England**, the increase takes effect on the council tax banding from the day the alteration is entered on the list.[37] In **Scotland and Wales**, it takes effect from the date the sale or lease was completed.[38]

Even if a dwelling has not been sold or let on a lease of seven years or more, if a revaluation takes place in England in the future (see p25), all material increases will be taken into account in setting the banding for the dwelling concerned.

A 'material reduction' in the dwelling's value

A **'material reduction'** in the value of a dwelling should lead to an immediate revaluation. This, if sufficiently significant, will also lead to an immediate re-banding of the dwelling. This only applies, however, if the material reduction is caused (in whole or in part) by:[39]

- the demolition (but not partial demolition during other building or engineering work) of any part of the dwelling; *or*
- any change in the physical state of the dwelling's locality; *or*
- any adaptation of the dwelling to make it suitable for a person with a physical disability.

Changes in the physical state of a locality give the greatest scope for proposals to change a dwelling's valuation band – ie, so-called 'blighting'. Such changes include, for example, a change in the character of the immediate environment brought about because of a road-widening scheme, the deterioration of surrounding property or a change in the use of nearby business premises.

The reduction in value should post-date the entry of the dwelling on the valuation list. In one case it was pointed out:[40]

> '[in]… some cases the reduction may follow very swiftly upon the change, in other cases it may not do so. It may take time after the change is known about before the impact of it is realised and it begins to affect the prices which people are prepared to pay for the affected dwellings.'

In **England and Wales**, an alteration to the list reflecting a reduction in value takes effect from the day on which the circumstances that caused the reduction arose. However, if that day cannot be reasonably established, the alteration takes effect from the day the proposal (see p33) was served on the listing officer or, in any other case, from the date it was entered on the list.[41]

In **Scotland**, a material reduction takes effect from the date the value fell sufficiently to affect the property's banding or the start of the financial year in which the proposal is made, whichever is later.[42]

How dwellings are revalued

When one of the conditions for the potential alteration of a dwelling's valuation band exists, there should be a revaluation. This should be made on the basis of the rules and assumptions on p26.

In **England**, this means that the dwelling's value, taking into account its current state, is still based on what it would have sold for on the open market by a willing vendor on 1 April 1991.[43] If the change in value is only small, it might not be sufficient to move a dwelling from one valuation band to another.

In **Scotland and Wales**, a material increase is assessed on the date the sale or transaction took place. In the case of a material increase in the value of the dwelling, the date of alteration takes effect from the date of the transaction, even if the increase is not identified for several years. The effective date of the alteration should be the day on which the first sale of the dwelling subsequent to the material increase is completed. If the change in value is only established some while after the first date of sale, the liable person may be faced with a backdated bill.[44]

If a dwelling ceases to be a composite hereditament, if there is a reduction in the domestic use of a dwelling or if a new dwelling comes into existence, the relevant date is the date of the alteration to the property. If a number of changes have taken place, the change in the valuation list is taken from the date of the last change.[45]

Obtaining an alteration

If a list is inaccurate, a **'proposal'** may be made to the listing officer or assessor for an alteration to the list. In many instances, there are time limits for this (see below). Making a proposal is also the first stage in the appeal process (see Chapter 12).

Who can make a proposal

Any 'interested person' can make a proposal to alter the list. An **'interested person'** on any particular day is:[46]
- the owner of the dwelling;
- anyone who is liable (either solely or jointly) to pay the tax on the dwelling;
- in the case of an exempt dwelling (see Chapter 5) or a dwelling on which the council tax has been set at nil, the person who would otherwise be liable to pay the tax.

Thus, a person who is in receipt of a council tax reduction under a local authority's reduction scheme (see Chapter 9) is entitled to make a proposal to change the banding of the property.

Local authorities in England can also make proposals to the listing officer.[47]

Time limits

A proposal may be made at any time if:
- a property should be excluded from or included on the valuation list;[48]
- there has been a material increase (see p31) in the value of the dwelling and a relevant transaction;
- there has been a material reduction (see p32) in the value of a dwelling;
- part of a property starts to be used or is no longer used for business purposes, or the balance between business and domestic use has changed.[49]

In the following circumstances, however, there is a time limit in which to make a proposal.

- **Proposals concerning a valuation band on the original list.** Except in limited circumstances, the time limit to make a proposal has now expired.
- **Banding proposals made by a new resident/owner or concerning a new property.** A proposal can be made within a six-month period if:
  - someone first becomes liable for the council tax on a particular dwelling; *or*
  - the dwelling (eg, a new home) is first shown on the valuation list after 1 April 1993 (1 April 2005 in Wales).[50]

  Such a proposal cannot be made, however, if:
  - it is based on the same facts that have already been considered and determined by the VTE, the VTW or valuation appeal committee in Scotland, or by the High Court or Court of Session; *or*
  - the new taxpayer is a company which is a subsidiary of the preceding taxpayer; *or*
  - the preceding taxpayer is a company which is a subsidiary of the new taxpayer; *or*
  - the change of taxpayer has occurred solely because a new partnership has been formed and one of the partners was a partner in the previous partnership.[51]
- **Appeal decisions concerning a comparable dwelling.** A proposal may be made within six months of an appeal decision on another comparable dwelling if this gives reasonable grounds for arguing that the valuation band of the dwelling in question should be changed.[52]
- **Proposals concerning an alteration to the list.** If the listing officer or assessor has altered the list in respect of a dwelling, a proposal can be made within six months from when the notice of the alteration was served.[53]

Making a proposal

You must make the proposal by writing to the listing officer at the local office of the VOA (the address should be on the council tax bill) or the local assessor.[54] Standard forms and explanatory notes are available from these offices to assist with the proposal. The completed form, or alternatively, a letter should contain all relevant information including:[55]

- your name and address;
- the capacity in which the proposal is being made – ie, whether you are the liable person or the owner of the dwelling;
- the dwelling to which it relates;
- the date;
- the way in which you propose the list should be altered;
- the reasons for believing the list to be inaccurate, the relevant facts, any evidence supporting those facts and any relevant dates, such as the date you

first became the liable person or the date when a material reduction in the dwelling occurred.

Evidence

A wide range of evidence can be used. You can use sales evidence for up to two years either side of 1 April 1991 for your property or similar properties in your locality. Evidence that similarly sized properties to yours are in a lower band may be used. There must be no more than a 10 per cent difference in size comparison between these properties and yours. Evidence of significantly larger properties within the locality in a lower band may also be accepted. No more than five comparable properties should be supplied – if you supply more than five comparable properties only the first five are considered as part of the case.

Normally a proposal can only deal with one dwelling. In England, however, a proposal can be made for more than one dwelling if:[56]
- you make the proposal in the same capacity (eg, as the owner) and each of the dwellings is within the same building (or 'curtilage') as the other(s); *or*
- it arises because a property is shown as a dwelling when it should not be or should be shown as a number of dwellings.

The proposal should be addressed to the listing officer or assessor for the relevant area and delivered or posted to the appropriate address. Keep a copy and obtain some proof of postage or, if delivered by hand, a receipt.

If you are acting on behalf of another council taxpayer to challenge a council tax band, the VOA expects you to:
- provide a form of authority to act on the taxpayer's behalf which must be signed and dated by her/him not more than six months before it is supplied;
- check whether you are entitled to make a valid proposal on the proper form, either on the internet or supplied by the local valuation office;
- provide relevant evidence to raise doubt over the accuracy of the band (see above);
- supply a completed property details questionnaire.

Response of the listing office

In **England and Wales**, the listing officer should write within 28 days acknowledging receipt of the proposal, unless the proposal is considered to be invalid (see p36). In **Scotland**, the assessor should write acknowledging receipt of the proposal within 14 days. The acknowledgement letter should include details of the procedures that will be followed.[57]

Joint proposals in Scotland

In Scotland, other interested people (see p33) may write to the assessor indicating that they wish to support the proposal.[58] Provided the proposal has not been withdrawn or referred to the local valuation appeal committee, the original proposal should then be treated as a joint proposal.

Invalid proposals

Different procedures apply to invalid proposals in England, Wales and Scotland. If the listing officer or assessor fails to identify an invalid proposal at this stage, the point can still be raised at an appeal hearing.[59]

England

In England, if the listing officer considers that the proposal is invalid, you will be sent an 'invalidity notice'. This should be done within four weeks of her/his receiving the proposal. This notice gives:[60]
- the reasons why the proposal is considered invalid; *and*
- you a right to make a further proposal in relation to the same dwelling (see below) or to appeal against the invalidity notice to the VTE (see p38).

The listing officer may withdraw an invalidity notice at any time by informing you in writing.

Unless an invalidity notice has been withdrawn, you can:
- make a further proposal, but only once and only if the original proposal was made within the appropriate time limit. If you make a further proposal, the earlier proposal which resulted in the invalidity notice is treated as withdrawn; *or*
- appeal to the VTE. You must send the tribunal a copy of the invalidity notice, together with a written statement. This should include the address of the dwelling and the reasons why the proposal is considered invalid. Action on the original proposal is suspended until either the listing officer withdraws the invalidity notice, or the VTE or High Court reaches a decision on the validity of the proposal. If the listing officer withdraws an invalidity notice after an appeal has been started, s/he must inform the tribunal. See Chapter 12 for more details on tribunal hearings.

Scotland

In Scotland, a distinction is drawn between proposals that are considered invalid because:[61]
- you are not an appropriate person to make a proposal or because it is out of time; *and*
- you did not include the required information.

In both instances, the assessor must write to you within six weeks of receiving the proposal giving reasons for the decision and describe your right to appeal to the assessor within four weeks. If no such appeal is made, the matter will end. If you did not include the required information, the letter must give reasons for the decision and should also identify the information that needs to be supplied. You may either:

- supply the information within four weeks; *or*
- appeal in writing to the assessor within four weeks.

If the information is not supplied or an appeal is not made within the four-week period, the assessor treats the proposal as invalidly made and that is the end of the matter.

If an appeal is made in either case but the assessor still considers the appeal invalid, s/he should inform the secretary of the local valuation appeal committee in writing, within four weeks, that an appeal has been made. Details of the proposal and the assessor's reasons for considering the proposal invalid should also be given.[62]

Wales

In Wales, if the listing officer believes that a proposal has not been validly made, s/he may serve an invalidity notice on you. This must be done within four weeks. The notice must explain the reasons for her/his decision and that you can either make a further proposal or appeal to a valuation tribunal. If you make a fresh proposal, the original is treated as withdrawn. The fresh proposal must be made within four weeks of the invalidity notice being served.

What happens after a valid proposal has been made: England and Wales

Within six weeks of receiving a valid proposal, the listing officer should send a copy to anyone else who appears to be liable for council tax on the dwelling. Copies should also be sent to the local authority if it has informed the listing officer in writing that it wishes to receive a copy of a class(es) of proposal, and your proposal falls within such a class. Each copy should be accompanied by a statement of the procedures to be followed.[63]

Following the receipt of a valid proposal:

- the listing officer may agree to the proposal (see below);
- all interested parties may agree to a different alteration to the list (see below);
- an appeal may be made to the VTE/VTW(see p38);
- the proposal may be withdrawn (see p38).

The listing officer agrees to the proposal

If the listing officer agrees to the proposal, you and the liable person (if different) should be notified that the valuation list will be altered accordingly. The valuation list should be altered within six weeks of the date of the letter.[64]

Agreeing to a different alteration

Before an appeal, it is possible for the listing officer to agree an alteration to the list that is different from that proposed, but with which you agree. This requires the agreement of all interested parties. If such an agreement is reached, the listing officer should alter the valuation list within six weeks of the date of the agreement. The original proposal is treated as having been withdrawn.[65]

Appealing to the Valuation Tribunal for England or the Valuation Tribunal for Wales

If the listing officer has made a decision and served a notice on the proposer, the taxpayer and any other competent person, an appeal can be made to the VTE/VTW (see p235).

An appeal must be made within three months. If an appeal has not been made within this time, the President of the tribunal can authorise the appeal if the delay has arisen because of circumstances beyond your control.

The appeal is started by serving the tribunal with a copy of the decision notice, together with the following information if this is not contained in the decision notice:

- the address of the dwelling;
- the reasons for the appeal;
- the name and address of:
  - the appellant;
  - the proposer (if different from the appellant);
  - the listing officer;
  - any other person who appears to be a taxpayer;
- any other interested person.

Where, after an appeal has been made to the VTE under regulation 13 of the Council Tax (Alteration of Lists and Appeals) Regulations (disagreement as to proposed alteration), the listing officer alters the list in accordance with the proposal to which the appeal relates, the listing officer must notify the VTE and the appeal is treated as withdrawn on the date on which the notice is served on the VTE.[66]

Appeals are described in Chapter 12.

Note: you cannot make a second appeal on the same facts if one has already been determined against you.[67]

Withdrawing the proposal

You may withdraw the proposal at any time before an appeal by writing to the tribunal, or orally at the hearing. If a proposal is withdrawn at the hearing, it will not take effect unless the panel consents. Each party must be notified in writing of a withdrawal, and the date on which the proposal is withdrawn should be confirmed. Each party has the opportunity to begin a new appeal about the decision by serving a written notice. This must state that the new appellant wishes to proceed with an appeal and the reason for it.

In the past, it was not unknown for the valuation office or for local authority staff to attempt to encourage people to withdraw their proposals and appeals.

Such 'persuasion' included claims that a tribunal had previously rejected a similar appeal, so an appellant had no prospect of success. Remember that a tribunal decision on any point is persuasive, but not binding, on subsequent tribunals (see Chapter 12). If you are subject to improper pressure over an appeal by an official either in the valuation office or from, or acting on behalf of, the local authority, you should make a formal complaint (see p271).

What happens after a valid proposal has been made: Scotland

In Scotland, once a valid proposal has been received:
- the assessor may agree to the proposal (see below);
- an appeal may be made to a local valuation appeal committee (see below);
- the proposal may be withdrawn (see p40).

The assessor agrees to the proposal

If the assessor thinks the proposal is well founded, you (and any joint proposer) should be advised of this in writing. The list should be altered within six weeks of the date of the letter.[68]

Appealing to a local valuation appeal committee

If the assessor thinks that the proposal is not well founded and it is not withdrawn, s/he should refer the disagreement to the local valuation appeal committee. This should be done within six months of the day the assessor received the proposal.[69]

If the assessor has previously issued an invalidity notice on the grounds that:
- you are not an appropriate person to make the proposal or because the proposal is out of time, the six-month period starts from the day the assessor withdrew the notice or you won the appeal against the notice;
- the proposal does not include the required information, the six-month period starts from the day that all the relevant information was supplied or the day you won the appeal against the notice.[70]

A proposal may be adopted by another interested person (see p33) if the original proposer seeks to withdraw it. In such cases, the six-month period starts from the date the person informed the assessor of her/his wish to adopt the proposal.[71]

The appeal is initiated by the assessor writing to the secretary of the valuation committee, advising of the appeal. The following information should be included:[72]
- proposed alteration of the list;
- date on which the proposal was received;
- name and address of the proposer;
- grounds on which the proposal was made.

Appeals are described in Chapter 12.

Withdrawing the proposal

The proposal may be withdrawn at any time by writing to the assessor.[73] If none of the proposers are currently liable for the tax on the dwelling, the assessor must write to at least one currently liable person telling her/him about the proposed withdrawal. An interested person (see p33) has six weeks from the date of the letter to advise the assessor that s/he wishes to adopt the proposal. From that date, it is then treated as having been made by that person.

Notification of an alteration

Within six weeks of altering the list, the listing officer or assessor should write to the local authority stating the effect of the alteration. The local authority should alter its copy of the valuation list as soon as is reasonably practicable.[74]

England and Wales

In England and Wales, the listing officer should also write to the person who is currently liable for the tax on the dwelling within six weeks of altering the list, advising her/him of the effect of the alteration and the process by which a proposal and appeal may be made.[75] This obligation to notify does not, however, apply if the alteration was made solely to correct a clerical error, or to reflect:

- a decision of the listing officer that a proposal is well founded; *or*
- an agreed alternative alteration; *or*
- a change in the address of the dwelling concerned; *or*
- a change in the area of the billing authority; *or*
- the decision of the VTE/VTW or the High Court in relation to the dwelling concerned.

The listing officer should take such steps as are reasonably practicable to ensure that the letter to the liable person is sent no later than the letter to the local authority.[76]

Backdating in Wales

Following revaluation in Wales in 2005, it was discovered that a small number of dwellings had been wrongly placed in a valuation band not only in in terms of their assumed value at 1 April 2003 but also on the previous valuation list dating back to 1993, resulting in their having been placed in the wrong band for more than 10 years. In such cases, the VOA was backdating the amendment to 1 April 1993 and local authorities were obliged to refund any overpayment of council tax. However, following an amendment to regulations, backdating is only possible for six years from the date the entry is altered.[77]

Scotland

In Scotland, the assessor must notify a liable person within six weeks of the alteration being made. Where the alteration involves the addition of the dwelling to the list, the owner must also be notified within six weeks of the alteration.

Additionally, the assessor must notify a liable person within six weeks of the alteration being made if:

- an alteration has been agreed, but the proposer is not a liable person at the time of the alteration; *or*
- an appeal decision has led to the alteration of the list but none of the parties to the appeal is a liable person on the date of the alteration.[78]

The above notification should include a statement about the process by which a proposal may be made. The assessor should take such steps as are reasonably practicable to ensure that the above letters are sent no later than the letter to the local authority.[79]

Notes

1. Who is responsible for valuations
1 **EW** s20 LGFA 1992
2 **EW** s26 LGFA 1992
3 **S** s84(1) LGFA 1992
4 **S** s86(5) LGFA 1992
5 **S** s86(10) LGFA 1992
6 **EW** s21 LGFA 1992
   S s86(7) LGFA 1992
7 **EW** s21 LGFA 1992
   S s86(8) LGFA 1992
8 **EW** s21 LGFA 1992
   S s86(9) LGFA 1992

2. The listing officer's and assessor's powers
9 **EW** s26 LGFA 1992
   S s89 LGFA 1992
10 VOA Service Standards
11 **EW** s26 LGFA 1992
   S s89 LGFA 1992
12 **EW** s27 LGFA 1992
   S s90 LGFA 1992
13 **EW** s27 LGFA 1992
   S s90 LGFA 1992
14 **EW** s27 LGFA 1992
   S s90 LGFA 1992; The Criminal Justice Act 1991 (Commencement No.3) Order 1992 No.333

15 **EW** s27(6) LGFA 1992
   S s90 LGFA 1992
16 **EW** s27 LGFA 1992
   S s90 LGFA 1992

3. How dwellings are valued
17 **E** s21 LGFA 1992 and CT(SVD) Regs
   W s21 LGFA 1992 and CT(SVD) Regs, as amended by CT(SVD)(W)(A) Regs
   S s86(2) LGFA 1992 and CT(VD)(S) Regs
18 s22B(3) LGFA 1992 amended by s80 LA 2011
19 *R v East Sussex Valuation Tribunal ex parte Silverstone* [1996] RVR 203
20 *Wilson v Jo Coll (Listing Officer)* [2011] EWHC 2824 (Admin)
21 Council Tax Manual Practice Note 4 – Disrepair, Building Works, Temporary Disabilities and Flooding, VOA
22 **E** s21 LGFA 1992 and CT(SVD) Regs
   W s21 LGFA 1992 and CT(SVD) Regs, as amended by CT(SVD)(W)(A) Regs
   S s86(2) LGFA 1992 and CT(VD)(S) Regs
23 **S** Reg 3 CT(VD)(S) Regs; *The Appeal of Grampian Valuation Joint Board* [2003] RA 167 Sc
24 Parliamentary Answer by John Healy, Minister for Local Government, 13 December 2007

4. Compiling and maintaining valuation lists

25 **EW** ss22 and 22B LGFA 1992
   S s84 LGFA 1992
26 **EW** ss22 and 22B LGFA 1992
   W CT(SVD)(W)(A) Regs
   S s84 LGFA 1992
27 **EW** ss22 and 22B LGFA 1992
   S s85 LGFA 1992
28 **EW** s22 LGFA 1992
   S s84 LGFA 1992
29 **EW** s2(2)(b) LGFA 1992
   S s71(2)(b) LGFA 1992

5. Inspecting the valuation list

30 **EW** s28 LGFA 1992
   S s91 LGFA 1992
31 **EW** s28 LGFA 1992
   S s91 LGFA 1992
32 **EW** s23 LGFA 1992 and CT(CVL) Regs
   S s84 LGFA 1992 and CT(CVL) Regs
33 **EW** s23 LGFA 1992
   S s84 LGFA 1992
34 Council Tax Guidance Manual 3.4.1

6. Altering a valuation list

35 **E** CT(ALA)(E) Regs; VTE(CTRA)(P) Regs
   W CT(ALA) Regs
   S CT(ALA)(S) Regs
36 **E** s24 LGFA 1992
   S s87 LGFA 1992
37 **E** Reg 9 CT(ALA)(E) Regs
38 **W** Reg 14(2) CT(ALA) Regs as amended
   by CT(ALA)(A)(W) Regs
   S Reg 19 CT(ALA)(S) Regs
39 **E** s24 LGFA 1992
   S s87 LGFA 1992
40 *Tilly v Listing Officer for Tower Hamlets*
   [2001] RVR 250
41 **E** Reg 9 CT(ALA)(E) Regs
   W Reg 14(5)(a) and (b) CT(ALA) Regs as
   amended by CT(ALA)(A)(W) Regs
42 Reg 19 (5) CT(ALA)(S) Regs
43 **E** CT(SVD) Regs
   W CT(SVD)(W)(A) Regs
   S CT(VD)(S) Regs
44 *Lothian Valuation Joint Board v Campbell*
   and Campbell [2011] CSIH 47
45 **E** Reg 6 CT(SVD) Regs, as amended by
   CT(VALA)(E) Regs
   S CT(VD)(S) Regs, as amended by
   CT(VD)(S)(A) Regs
46 **E** Reg 2 CT(ALA)(E) Regs
   S Reg 3 CT(ALA)(S) Regs
47 **E** Reg 4 CT(ALA)(E) Regs
48 **E** Reg 4 CT(ALA)(E) Regs
   S Reg 5 CT(ALA)(S) Regs

49 **E** Reg 4 CT(ALA)(E) Regs
   S Reg 5 CT(ALA)(S) Regs
50 **E** Reg 4 CT(ALA)(E) Regs
   S Reg 5 CT(ALA)(S) Regs
51 **E** Reg 4(5) CT(ALA)(E) Regs
   S Reg 5 CT(ALA)(S) Regs
52 **E** Reg 4 CT(ALA)(E) Regs
   S Reg 5 CT(ALA)(S) Regs
53 **E** Reg 4(2) CT(ALA)(E) Regs
   S Reg 5 CT(ALA)(S) Regs
54 **E** Reg 5 CT(ALA)(E) Regs
   S Reg 6 CT(ALA)(S) Regs
55 **E** Reg 5 CT(ALA)(E) Regs
   S Reg 6 CT(ALA)(S) Regs
56 **E** Reg 5 CT(ALA)(E) Regs
57 **S** Reg 7 CT(ALA)(S) Regs
58 **S** Reg 12 CT(ALA)(S) Regs
59 **E** CT(ALA)(E) Regs
   W CT(ALA) Regs
   S CT(ALA)(S) Regs
60 **E** Reg 7 CT(ALA)(E) Regs
61 **S** Regs 8 and 9 CT(ALA)(S) Regs
62 **S** Reg 10 CT(ALA)(S) Regs
63 **E** Reg 8 CT(ALA)(E) Regs
64 **E** Reg 9(3) CT(ALA)(E) Regs
65 **E** Reg 9(4) CT(ALA)(E) Regs
66 Reg 19(7) VTE(CTRA)(P) Regs as
   amended by reg 2 VTENDRCT(E) Regs
67 *Hakeem v VTS and London Borough of*
   Enfield [2010] EWHC 152 (Admin)
68 **S** Reg 14 CT(ALA)(S) Regs
69 **S** Reg 15 CT(ALA)(S) Regs
70 **S** Reg 15 CT(ALA)(S) Regs
71 **S** Reg 15 CT(ALA)(S) Regs
72 **S** Reg 15 CT(ALA)(S) Regs
73 **S** Reg 11 CT(ALA)(S) Regs
74 **E** Reg 12(1) CT(ALA)(E) Regs
   S Reg 16 CT(ALA)(S) Regs
75 **E** Reg 12 CT(ALA)(E) Regs
76 **E** Reg 12(4) CT(ALA)(E) Regs
77 **W** Reg 14 CT(ALA)Regs as amended by
   reg 2 CT(ALA)(A)(W) Regs
78 **S** Reg 16 CT(ALA)(S) Regs
79 **S** Reg 16 CT(ALA)(S) Regs

Chapter 4

The amount of tax

This chapter covers:
1. The valuation bands (below)
2. Reducing the amount of tax payable (p46)
3. Discretionary reduction (p48)

1. The valuation bands

Each year, local authorities must set a council tax to help pay for their expenditure and that of related bodies. They must publish the amounts of their council tax in at least one local newspaper within 21 days of setting them and calculations must be made before 11 March each year preceding the start of the council tax financial year on 1 April. Failure to do so, however, does not invalidate the amounts set.[1] The set amount of council tax and Scottish Water charges for each dwelling depend on the valuation band to which it is allocated. Different valuation bands apply in England,[2] Scotland[3] and Wales.[4]

England and Scotland

The original bands from the 1993 valuation list continue to apply in England and Scotland until the next general revaluation date.

Valuation bands in England

Valuation band	Range of values
A	Up to £40,000
B	£40,001 to £52,000
C	£52,001 to £68,000
D	£68,001 to £88,000
E	£88,001 to £120,000
F	£120,001 to £160,000
G	£160,001 to £320,000
H	£320,001 and over

Valuation bands in Scotland

Valuation band	Range of values
A	Up to £27,000
B	£27,001 to £35,000
C	£35,001 to £45,000
D	£45,001 to £58,000
E	£58,001 to £80,000
F	£80,001 to £106,000
G	£106,001 to £212,000
H	£212,001 and over

Wales

Before 1 April 2005, the valuation bands for Wales were as listed in the table below. These values apply to any calculation of council tax for a dwelling in Wales before 1 April 2005. This may arise if there is a question of backdating an exemption (see Chapter 5) or discount (see Chapter 8).

Valuation bands in Wales before 1 April 2005

Valuation band	Range of values
A	Up to £30,000
B	£30,001 to £39,000
C	£39,001 to £51,000
D	£51,001 to £66,000
E	£66,001 to £90,000
F	£90,001 to £120,000
G	£120,001 to £240,000
H	£240,001 and over

From 1 April 2005, dwellings in Wales fall into one of the following bands, based on a theoretical valuation date of 1 April 2003.[5] These bands apply to all domestic dwellings from 1 April 2005. A transitional relief scheme to reduce bills for people who were affected by certain banding changes operated for three years until 31 March 2008.

Valuation bands in Wales from 1 April 2005

Valuation band	Range of values
A	Up to £36,000
B	£36,001 to £52,000
C	£52,001 to £73,000
D	£73,001 to £100,000
E	£100,001 to £135,000

F	£135,001 to £191,000
G	£191,001 to £286,000
H	£286,001 to £400,000
I	£400,001 and over

How the amount of tax payable varies between bands

The council tax payable in any local authority depends on the valuation band in which the dwelling has been placed. The lower the value of the band, the lower the bill will be. The amount of tax payable on dwellings in the same area varies between valuation bands in England and Scotland in the following proportions:[6]

6(A):7(B):8(C):9(D):11(E):13(F):15(G):18(H)

This means, for example, that the tax payable on a Band H dwelling is three times more than that payable on a Band A dwelling and double that of a Band D dwelling. The local authority has no discretion to vary bands or the relative proportion of tax paid within each band.

In 2013/14 in England, the average council tax payable on a home in Band D in London is £1,302. In shire counties the average figure for band D properties is £1,510.[7] In Scotland, the average council tax payable on a home in Band D is £1,149.[8]

In Wales from 1 April 2005, the amount of tax payable on dwellings in the same area varies between valuation bands in the following proportions:[9]

6(A):7(B):8(C):9(D):11(E):13(F):15(G):18(H):21(I)

This means that those in the top Band I in Wales will pay three-and-a-half times more than those in the lowest Band A.

In 2013/14 in Wales, the average council tax payable on a home in Band D was £1,226.[10]

Daily liability

Liability to pay the tax arises on a daily basis. The situation at the end of the day is assumed to have existed throughout the day.[11] The amount payable for the day is the annual amount set by the local authority for that year for dwellings in the relevant valuation band, divided by the number of days in the financial year (365 or 366).

2. **Reducing the amount of tax payable**

Individual dwellings

The amount payable in respect of a specific dwelling may be reduced by:
- an alteration to the dwelling's valuation band (see Chapter 3);
- a fixed period or indefinite exemption (see Chapter 5);
- a disability reduction (see Chapter 7);
- a discount (see Chapter 8);
- council tax reduction under the local support scheme (see Chapter 9);
- adopting certain payment arrangements, which may offer a discount (see Chapter 10);
- a discretionary reduction (see p48).

Tax capping and referendums

Under the Local Government Finance Act 1992, the Secretary of State could originally limit the amount of council tax set by individual local authorities (known as 'capping'). The government could use this power to instruct councils to set a lower budget if it considered their budget requirement and council tax to have exceeded what it considered a reasonable amount. When this power was exercised, the result was that lower bills might be issued to residents. The Localism Act 2011 removed this power and instead introduced that any local authority (including police and fire authorities) wanting to raise its council tax above a set threshold must call a referendum of all registered electors in its area.[12]

The threshold is proposed by the Secretary of State and approved by the House of Commons. For 2013 it was set at 2 per cent. As a consequence some councils have increased the amount of council tax by 1.99 per cent for 2013/14 so as to avoid the possibility of a referendum.

The Act also enables the Assembly to make provision for Wales corresponding to the council tax referendum provision as applies for England.[13]

With a few exceptions, each local authority calculates its level of council tax according to the schemes laid down by the Local Government Finance Act 1992 as amended by the Localism Act 2011. The exceptions are the Greater London Authority, which calculates two basic amounts of council tax,[14] because the special expense of the Mayor's Office for Policing and Crime relates to only part of the Greater London Authority's area.[15] For London, for the financial year beginning on 1 April 2014 the Mayor is required to prepare and present a draft consolidated budget to the Assembly on, or before, 10 February 2014.[16]

The Secretary of State issues principles that define what should be considered excessive council tax. One or more principles may be set.[17] The set of principles must include a comparison between the relevant basic amount of council tax for the year under consideration, and the preceding year. The principles which the Secretary of State uses for a financial year must be set out in a report laid before the House of Commons by a set date. Where the report is not laid, or not approved by resolution of the House of Commons, no principles can take effect and no authority's relevant basic amount of council tax can be determined as excessive for the year.[18]

Local authorities, major precepting authorities, fire authorities and police and crime commissioners are required to determine whether the amount of council tax they plan to raise is excessive.[19] An authority proposing an excessive increase is also required to make substitute calculations, based on a non-excessive council tax level.[20]

If a local authority does not make the substitute calculation within a set time period, it will have no power to transfer any amount from its council tax collection fund to its general fund, effectively freezing the council tax collected. This restriction continues to apply until the authority makes the required substitute calculations; where a precepting authority fails to make the required substitute calculations the billing authority is not able to pay anything to the precepting authority until the calculation is made.[21]

Provision for a council tax referendum

If an amount set by a local authority in England is deemed excessive it can be challenged by a local referendum giving electors the right to vote on the increase. If a referendum takes place and the majority of voters veto the increase, the substitute figure of council tax applies. A billing authority must make arrangements to hold a referendum where the billing authority itself has set an excessive increase in council tax, conducted under a statutory scheme laid down in regulations.[22]

The referendum can be held at any time of the authority's choosing subject to this being no later than 22 May 2014 or a date specified by the Secretary of State by order.[23] The wording of the question for the referendum and the form of the ballot paper are prescribed by the Secretary of State in regulations.[24]

Failure to hold a referendum

If a local authority fails to hold a referendum on time (see above), the local authority's substitute calculations will have effect, or that of a precepting authority where one is involved. The billing authority must inform the Secretary of State of the result of the referendum. Where the result of the referendum is that an authority's excessive increase in council tax is rejected the authority's substitute calculations have effect for the financial year.[25]

These provisions first applied in the 2012/13 financial year but no authorities held a referendum in either 2012/13 or 2013/14. For the 2013/14 financial year, the principles stated that billing authorities could not raise their council tax by more than 2 per cent without holding a referendum. An exception was made for billing authorities which are in the lowest quartile of council tax in their category (ie, local authority, fire authority, or police and crime commissioner), which were only required to hold a referendum if they planned an increase over 2 per cent *and* over £5.

As a way to avoid a referendum, it is now also possible for a local authority of its own volition to substitute a new council tax requirement for a financial year after it has previously made a decision. This power may only be exercised where the substitute amount calculated would not exceed the previous amount set.[26]

Where it appears that an authority is unable to discharge its functions effectively or to meet its financial obligations unless it sets an increase in council tax which exceeds the principles, the Secretary of State has a power to direct that the referendum provisions do not apply.[27]

The Secretary of State may give a direction that the referendum provisions do not apply where it appears that, unless the authority's council tax calculations of an excessive amount are permitted:

- the authority will be unable to discharge its functions in an effective manner; *or*
- the authority will be unable to meet its financial obligations.[28]

Challenges to a referendum

A referendum may be challenged on a limited number of grounds in an election court or by way of judicial review – eg, as the result was not in accordance with the number of votes cast or a corrupt practice has occurred.[29]

3. **Discretionary reduction**

England and Wales

A local authority in England and Wales can reduce the amount of council tax payable on any dwelling or any class of dwelling by any amount it sees fit under section 13A of the Local Government Finance Act 1992, as inserted by the Local Government Act 2003. Under the rates system, local authorities had the power to reduce the amount payable in a case of poverty, but with council tax the power extended beyond this.

From 1 April 2004, local authorities had a discretionary power to reduce council tax bills. Local authorities can reduce sums payable in individual cases (eg, to prevent financial hardship) and in groups of cases – eg, if several properties have been affected by flooding. A reduction might be applied, for instance, if someone could not get her/his council tax benefit backdated, or if an application for benefit was made within the correct time limit, but was never processed.

However, such reductions are little used as many taxpayers do not know about the power and some local authorities appeared unaware of its existence or lacked procedures whereby an application could be considered.

Following the introduction of localised council tax reduction (CTR) schemes (see Chapter 9), the power to grant a discretionary reduction has been repealed and re-enacted as section 13A(1)(c).

The power may be exercised as the billing authority for the area in which the dwelling is situated thinks fit. It can include a reduction granted in addition to a CTR award, and could cover periods not otherwise covered by a CTR scheme.

A local authority has the discretion to reduce the amount of council tax to nil.[30]

A reduction can be made in respect of sums of council tax that have accrued in previous financial years, including arrears.

The power under subsection (1)(c) may be exercised in relation to particular cases or by determining a class of case in which liability is to be reduced to an extent provided by the determination.[31]

The classes of people might include victims of flooding or persons in receipt of particular benefits or in respect of personal circumstances – eg, pregnancy.

Meaning of hardship

There is specific provision for reductions for persons considered to be in financial need.[32] The local authority should exercise its discretion with this in mind in an appropriate case.[33]

This can cover persons the authority considers to be in financial need on an individual basis, or classes of persons whom the authority decides are in general need, such as certain groups of employees.[34]

The term 'financial need' is not defined but it should be given a wide interpretation, in accordance with existing caselaw.

It has been held by the courts that 'To need is not the same as want. "Need" is a lack of what is essential for the ordinary business of living.'[35] Financial need may be distinguished from such terms as 'hardship' and 'poverty'. Poverty has been considered as usually involving 'extreme financial stringency such that the applicant has some difficulty in meeting the conventional necessities of life.'[36] Accordingly, the term 'financial need' can cover persons not in a state described as poverty but who nonetheless may be or who are experiencing difficulty in meeting ordinary bills and household expenses in the course of the financial year unless support is given. The term 'financial need' is a lower threshold or test than poverty or hardship and may also include persons who are, or who will be, in debt unless support is given. Note that a person is not required to be without any money or assets, with certain amounts and types of savings being allowed.

It would appear that a local authority needs to consider all the circumstances of an individual person or the circumstances of a particular class – eg, persons entitled to means-tested benefits. A local authority is required to base its decisions on evidence.

Duty to act reasonably

A local authority must act reasonably when exercising discretion by considering all relevant factors, disregarding irrelevant ones and not acting perversely.[37] Explaining the scope of the power to reduce a council tax bill in Parliament in 2003, Lord Rooker stated: 'The billing authority would, of course, have to act reasonably and would have to justify to [their] auditors what [they] had done.'[38]

There has not yet been any caselaw on how the discretion should be exercised specifically with a CTR under section 13(1)(c) or its predecessor, but the matter has been considered by the Local Government Ombudsman.[39] In December 2004, Redcar and Cleveland Borough Council decided that all empty homes in its area should pay the maximum 90 per cent council tax. Mr and Mrs Weaver (pseudonyms) bought a bungalow in the local authority district and renovated it, but then faced hostility from people in the area and decided not to move in. When they received a bill, Mrs Weaver wrote to explain their circumstances. The Council refused the reduction, stating that it had set the maximum discount and that the scheme 'does not allow for any individual discretion'.

The Ombudsman ruled that the blanket policy adopted by the Council was wrong in law, and that the local authority had no basis for claiming it had no discretion on whether to grant a discount or not in individual cases. Parliament had given it a discretion and the Ombudsman said that a local authority should consider cases on an individual basis. The failure to do so amounted to maladministration, and the Ombudsman directed the authority to give proper consideration to Mrs Weaver's request and invite her to state her reasons for seeking the reduction. Having considered her reasons, the Council was directed to give its reasons for either accepting or rejecting the application, as well as establishing proper arrangements for considering such cases in future.

Applying for a discretionary reduction

You should apply for a discretionary reduction in writing and provide supporting evidence. An application for a discretionary reduction can be made at any time.

The application for a reduction should be made to the chief executive of the local authority. A local councillor may be able to assist in making the application.

When making an application, it is advisable to include a full income and expenditure breakdown, together with that of any other household members. Many local authorities will request this if the application is being made on grounds of poverty or hardship.

The local authority may request evidence in support of the application and expect you to show that you have done everything reasonable to resolve the problem leading to difficulties with paying.

The authority is also likely to consider relevant factors such as whether you have received all relevant reliefs and reductions and whether council error has contributed to the situation.

A record should be kept of any application, as it may be useful evidence to rebut possible allegations of 'wilful refusal and culpable neglect' if the local authority seeks to pursue enforcement action in the event of non-payment. See Chapter 11 for more information.

Appealing a discretionary reduction decision

In England and Wales, you can appeal against a refusal of a discretionary reduction by an authority and where the authority has acted unreasonably or made an error of law.[40] These are the equivalent of grounds which would apply in a judicial review to the High Court. The appeal goes to the Valuation Tribunal for England or the Valuation Tribunal for Wales. For information on appealing decisions on discretionary reductions, see Chapter 12. In theory, a local authority's refusal to consider an application might be challenged within three months by judicial review in the High Court, but if the valuation tribunal is used as the route of appeal first, the time limit for any subsequent High Court appeal is 28 days.

Scotland

From 1 April 2005, Scottish local authorities can apply a discretionary reduction to empty dwellings and dwellings that are second homes owned by the same person and are in the same local authority area.[41] This may alter the amount of the usual discount given to an empty property (see Chapter 8). The minimum reduction is 10 per cent and the maximum reduction is 50 per cent. If you are required to live away from your usual home as a condition of your employment, the reduction is 50 per cent.

A dwelling is job-related if you or your spouse or civil partner are required under a contract to live there – eg, a manager of a public house who is required to live within or near the premises, domestic staff, and service personnel who need special security arrangements which require them to live in other dwellings.

A dwelling is also job-related if you or your spouse or civil partner are a minister of religion and you live there in order to perform your ministerial duties.

Notes

1. The valuation bands

1 **EW** s31A(11) LGFA 1992
   S s96 LGFA 1992
2 **E** s5(2) LGFA 1992
3 **S** s74(2) LGFA 1992
4 **W** s5(3) LGFA 1992
5 **W** s5(3) LGFA 1992
6 **E** s5 LGFA 1992
7 *Council tax levels set by local authorities in England: 2013 to 2014*, DCLG, 22 August 2013
8 *Band D Council Tax 1996-97 to 2013-14*, Scotland Government statistics
9 **W** s5 LGFA 1992
10 Welsh National Statistics from the Welsh Government were released on 21 March 2013
11 **EW** s2 LGFA 1992
   S s71 LGFA 1992

2. Reducing the amount of tax payable

12 Schs 5 and 6 LA 2011; paras 4-28 Council Tax (Conduct of Referendums) (Council Tax Increases) (England) (Amendment) Regulations 2013 No.409
13 Sch 6 and para 187 Explanatory Notes LA 2011
14 ss88(2) and 89(3) Greater London Authority Act 1999
15 The Local Government (Structural Changes) (Finance) Regulations 2008 No.3022
16 Sch 6 Greater London Act 1999 as amended by Greater London Authority (Consolidated Council Tax Requirement Procedure) Regulations 2013 No.3178
17 s52ZC LGFA 1992
18 s52ZD LGFA 1992
19 s52ZB LGFA 1992 inserted by Sch 5 LA 2011
20 s52ZF LGFA 1992
21 52ZW LGFA 1992
22 Local Authorities (Conduct of Referendums) (Council Tax Increases) (England) Regulations 2012 No.2012
23 s52ZG LGFA 1992; Local Authority (Referendums Relating to Council Tax Increases) (Date of Referendum) (England) Order 2013 No.2862

24 Local Authorities (Conduct of Referendums) (Council Tax Increases) (England) (Amendment) Regulations 2013 No.409
25 s52ZH LGFA 1992
26 ss49A and 49B LGFA 1992 as inserted by s78 LA 2011); s52ZP LGFA 1992
27 ss52ZR to 52ZW LGFA 1992
28 s52ZR LGFA 1992
29 Reg 20 Local Authorities (Conduct of Referendums) (Council Tax Increases) (England) (Amendment) Regulations 2013 No.409
30 s13A(6) LGFA 1991
31 s13A(7) LGFA 1991
32 s13(1)(c) LFFA 1992
33 s13A LGFA 1992 inserted by s10 LGFA 2012
34 s13A(2) LGFA1992
35 *R v Gloucestershire County Council and another ex parte Barry* [1997] 2 All ER 1 HL
36 *Windsor Securities Ltd v Liverpool City Council* [1978] LGR 502, Court of Appeal, per Cumings-Bruce LJ
37 *Associated Provincial Picture Houses v Wednesbury Corporation* [1948] 1 KB 223
38 *Hansard*, Grand Committee, 16 June 2003, col 217
39 Complaint against Redcar and Cleveland Borough Council (05/C/03367)
40 Council Tax Reduction Appeals Practice Statement VTE/PS/A11: 22 May 2013, paras 25-30
41 The Council Tax (Discounts for Unoccupied Dwellings) (Scotland) Regulations 2005 No.51

Chapter 5

· ·

Exempt dwellings

This chapter covers:
1. Exempt dwellings in England and Wales (below)
2. Exempt dwellings in Scotland (p64)
3. How exempt dwellings are identified (p69)
4. Notification of exemption (p70)
5. Penalties (p71)
6. Appeals (p72)

As originally designed in 1992, the council tax and, in Scotland, Scottish Water charges were only payable for chargeable dwellings and certain classes of dwelling were treated as exempt from council tax on a national basis, regardless of where they were situated.[1] No council tax is payable on a dwelling on any day when it falls into an exempt category. The local authority must take steps each year to establish which dwellings in its area are exempt. When determining whether a dwelling is exempt, the state of affairs at the end of the day is assumed to have existed throughout that day.[2]

However, following consultation in autumn 2012, the government reduced the number of dwellings entitled to a complete exemption on a national level throughout all of England and Wales (but not Scotland). Instead, it increased the powers to award discounts to dwellings as a particular local authority determines (see Chapter 8).

The government intends that extra revenue raised by authorities under these changes will be used to reduce council tax levels and increases.[3]

1. Exempt dwellings in England and Wales

From 1 April 2013, the types of dwellings which are treated as exempt from council tax on a national basis is reduced. Two classes of dwelling in England – Classes A and C – which relate to empty homes are no longer classed as automatically exempt on a national basis but may be on a local basis if an individual council decides otherwise.[4]

Class A covered, for a 12-month period, empty homes requiring or undergoing major repair work, or undergoing structural alteration, or having undergone either if less than six months had elapsed since the works were substantially completed.

Class C covered homes that were empty for a six-month period or less – eg, following completion. Empty properties and second homes in England falling into these two categories are no longer treated as receiving an automatic exemption and are liable for 100 per cent of the council tax.

Now any reduction on these two classes of property is awarded as a discount only if your local authority decides that a discount should be given (see Chapter 8).

Exemptions may still be claimed for previous years in some cases and you should check whether your local authority makes provision for certain classes of dwelling (see Chapter 9).

From 1 April 2013, the classes of dwellings that are entitled to an exemption under council tax are those set out in the Council Tax (Exempt Dwellings) Order 1992 as amended by the Council Tax (Exempt Dwellings)(Amendment) (England) Order 2012.[5]

These changes do not apply in Wales where these categories remain as exempt dwellings after 1 April 2013.

'Exempt dwellings' applies to different types of dwelling which are vacant.

The term **'vacant'** refers to a dwelling which is both:[6]

- unoccupied; *and*
- substantially unfurnished.

The legislation contains no definition of 'substantially unfurnished'. In practice, many local authorities regard a dwelling as **'substantially unfurnished'** if there are insufficient furnishings to enable someone to live in the dwelling. However, the quantity of furniture present in the dwelling, in relation to its size, should be the determining factor, ignoring anything other than 'furniture' – ie, appliances, fitted wardrobes, TV and carpets. Thus, a studio flat with a table, two chairs, a sofa and a bed (plus a cooker, washer/drier and TV) would be substantially furnished, but the same goods would not make a four-bedroom house substantially furnished.

The legislation defines an **'unoccupied dwelling'** as one in which no one lives and an **'occupied dwelling'** as one in which at least one person lives.[7] There is, however, a significant distinction between occupying a home and being solely or mainly resident in it (see p77). While the same person may occupy two or more dwellings at any one time, s/he can only be mainly resident in one of them. The local authority must consider each case on the particular facts.

From 1 April 2013, an unoccupied dwelling is exempt from council tax if:[8]

- it belongs to a charity and was last used for that charity's purposes (see p56);
- it was previously the sole or main residence of someone in prison (see p57);
- someone has died in it (see p57);

- it is a property in which occupation is prohibited by law (see p58);
- it is being kept for occupation by a minister of religion (see p58);
- it was previously the sole or main residence of someone in a hospital, care home or certain hostels (see p58);
- it was previously the sole or main residence of someone who is receiving care in a place other than a hospital or a home (see p59);
- it is owned by and was previously the sole or main residence of someone who is resident elsewhere providing personal care (see p59);
- it was previously the sole or main residence of a student who is resident elsewhere or a person who will become a student within six weeks of vacating the dwelling (see p60);
- it is in the possession of a mortgage lender (see p60);
- it is an annexe and may not be let separately (see p61).

In addition, a local authority may make a class of dwelling exempt by way of a discount that reduces the amount of council tax payable on a dwelling to zero (see Chapter 8).

Long-term empty properties

From 1 April 2013, other empty properties do not receive any discount or exemption and are subject to 100 per cent of the council tax charge. This includes any short periods where the property is empty and where it is undergoing structural repair or alteration work or is unoccupied and unfurnished such as newly built properties. Where such properties have been empty for two years or more they are classified as 'long term empty properties' and liable for a 50 per cent premium, as allowed by the Local Government Finance Act 2012 whereby a council taxpayer may be liable for up to 150 per cent of the council tax charge.[9] For further details see Chapter 8. Exemptions may still be claimed for previous years in some cases and local reduction schemes may also make provision for certain classes of dwelling.

Before 1 April 2013, a dwelling in England and Wales was exempt for a maximum of 12 months if it:[10]
- was vacant (ie, unoccupied and substantially unfurnished) or was undergoing major repair works to make it habitable; *or*
- was undergoing structural alteration which has not been substantially completed; *or*
- had undergone major repair work to render it habitable, but has remained continuously vacant since completion for less than six months; *or*
- had undergone structural alteration, but has remained continuously vacant for less than six months since the alteration was completed.

The vacant dwelling remained exempt for as long as it required the major repair work or for as long as the work or alteration takes, subject to the 12-month limit.

The words 'habitable' and 'major repair work' were not defined in the legislation, apart from the fact that it includes structural repairs. However, in *Summers v Salford Corporation*, Lord Atkin stated: 'If the state of repair of a house is such that by ordinary user damage may be caused to the occupier, either in respect of personal injury to life or limb or danger to health, then the house is not in all respects reasonably fit for human habitation.'[11] For Class A to have applied, the property had to be vacant and required, or was undergoing, major repair work 'to render it habitable', which is not the same as to render it habitable for letting purposes, or to render it marketable in the case of a tenanted property.[12]

In a Scottish case, the word 'habitable' must have been intended to refer not only to the physical attributes of the buildings but to their being 'habitable' in all senses of the word, including the sense of being legally habitable.[13]

The phrase 'substantially completed' is also not defined.

In deciding whether a dwelling has been vacant, any period of not more than six weeks when it was not vacant is disregarded.[14]

Vacant dwelling recently repaired or altered

Before 1 April 2013, a vacant dwelling remained exempt from council tax for an additional period of up to six months from the day on which the repair work or structural alteration was substantially completed. In deciding whether a dwelling has been vacant, any one period of not more than six weeks during which it was not vacant is disregarded.

Classes of exempt dwellings in England and Wales

Unoccupied dwelling owned by a charitable body

An unoccupied dwelling owned by a body established solely for charitable purposes is exempt for up to six months from the last day it was occupied. For this exemption to apply, the charity must be the freeholder or hold the most inferior (ie, shortest) leasehold interest for a term of six months or more. The dwelling may be furnished or unfurnished. The exemption only applies, however, if the dwelling was last occupied in connection with furthering the objectives of the charity. When deciding the day on which the dwelling was last occupied, any period of occupation of not more than six weeks is disregarded.[15]

This disregard is a device to avoid abuse of the exemption. Without the disregard, the owner could ensure that the building is occupied for a few days near the end of the six-month period and thus trigger the exemption again for a further six months. This exemption can be repeated each time the dwelling is unoccupied following a period of occupation of six weeks or more, provided the above conditions are met.

Almshouses and refuges are typical examples of properties that would be exempt.

Vacant dwelling

A vacant dwelling (one that is unoccupied and substantially unfurnished, or an unoccupied caravan or houseboat) is exempt for up to six months.[16] This exemption applies both to new and previously occupied dwellings. Any one period of not more than six weeks during which the dwelling is occupied is disregarded when deciding if the dwelling has been vacant.

Dwelling unoccupied because the former resident is in prison

An unoccupied dwelling is exempt indefinitely if the former resident is in prison or certain other forms of detention and the dwelling was previously her/his sole or main residence (see p77).[17] For the purpose of this exemption, a person is considered detained if s/he would be regarded as such for the purpose of a council tax discount. See Chapter 8 for more information.[18] The definition includes people detained under immigration or mental health powers, but not those in prison for non-payment of council tax.

This exemption includes not only former residents who were owners (ie, the freeholder or the leaseholder with the shortest lease of six months or more) but also a former tenant or licensee, whether or not s/he is the person who is liable to pay council tax on the property.[19]

The dwelling is also exempt if the owner or tenant was previously the sole or main resident and, since the end of her/his imprisonment, has been in a hospital, care home, hostel or other accommodation where care is provided, or if s/he has been providing personal care to someone else.

Example
On leaving prison, Geoff moves in with his elderly mother to look after her. Geoff's former home remains exempt.

Unoccupied dwelling in which someone has died

A dwelling is exempt if it has been unoccupied since the former resident's death and the only person liable for the tax on the dwelling would be the deceased's personal representative, and no grant of probate or letters of administration have been made.[20] The exemption ends six months after a grant of probate or letters of administration have been made.

Before 1 April 1994, for this exemption to apply, it was enough that the dwelling was unoccupied and that the only person who would otherwise be liable was the personal representative of the deceased owner; it was not necessary for it to have been unoccupied since the death of the owner. From 1 April 1994, unoccupied dwellings are also exempt if the deceased was a tenant or licensee, and an executor or administrator is now liable for the rent. The exemption applies for each day for which the executor or administrator is liable for rent and lasts up to six months after the grant of probate or letters of administration. This is designed to discourage landlords, who would become liable for the council tax following a tenant's death, from pressing for the property to be cleared immediately in order to benefit from the six-month exemption for vacant dwellings or, alternatively, from seeking to pass on to the deceased's relatives or estate the council tax payable on the dwelling which is now unoccupied, but not vacant.

In all cases, any one short occupation of less than six weeks following the death is disregarded. Thus, the exemption is not ended if, for instance, a relative stays at the dwelling briefly in order to arrange the deceased's affairs.

The Valuation Tribunal for England has upheld a decision by Epsom and Ewell Borough Council that members of a trust to whom a council taxpayer had transferred her bungalow to protect it from family business liabilities were not entitled to claim the exemption following her death. Although the bungalow was treated as part of the deceased's estate for inheritance tax purposes, it belonged to the trustees.[21]

In addition, this exemption does not apply if the deceased left the dwelling to a beneficiary in her/his will. In this case, the beneficiary becomes the taxpayer at the date of death, as s/he is deemed to become the owner for council tax purposes on that date. This situation may arise at the death of a spouse or partner who was living apart, or if a relative who was living in the dwelling succeeds to the tenancy. However, there may be an argument for an exemption if the executor is given any discretion over the dwelling that might affect whether the beneficiary can occupy it.

Dwelling in which occupation is prohibited by law

In England, a dwelling is exempt indefinitely if its occupation is prohibited by law, including a condition imposed by planning control under the Town and Country Planning Act 1990.[22] It is also exempt if it is being kept unoccupied because legal action is underway to prohibit its occupation or to acquire it under a compulsory purchase order. However, a dwelling on which a local authority has served a repair notice does not qualify for an exemption, even if the occupant has to move out temporarily.[23] If the dwelling is actually occupied (eg, by squatters), the dwelling is not exempt from the charge. The squatters will normally be liable to pay the tax. See Chapter 6 for more information on liability.

Unoccupied dwelling held for a minister of religion

An unoccupied dwelling, such as a vicarage, is exempt indefinitely if it is held to be available for occupation by a minister of any religious denomination and from where s/he will perform the duties of her/his office.[24]

Dwelling unoccupied because the former resident is in hospital or a care home

An unoccupied dwelling is exempt indefinitely if it was previously the sole or main residence (see p77) of an owner, tenant or licensee:[25]

- who would be disregarded for the purpose of a council tax discount because s/he is a patient in hospital, or is in a care home or certain hostels; *and*
- who, since s/he last occupied the dwelling, has either been in that type of accommodation, in detention, or receiving or providing care elsewhere.[26] The care must be required for one of the reasons listed below.

During temporary stays in hospital, people remain liable for council tax at their normal address. However, if your main residence is a hospital, your previous home is exempt from council tax, provided it is unoccupied.[27]

Dwelling unoccupied because the former resident is receiving care elsewhere

An unoccupied dwelling is exempt indefinitely if it was the sole or main residence (see p77) of an owner, tenant or licensee who now has her/his sole or main residence elsewhere and where s/he is receiving personal care (but not a hospital, care home or certain hostels).[28] The personal care must be required because of her/his:

- old age; *or*
- disablement; *or*
- illness; *or*
- past or present alcohol or drug dependence; *or*
- past or present mental illness or disorder.

To qualify, the former resident must have been resident in such accommodation, or in prison or detention centre, or in a hospital, care home or hostel since the dwelling last ceased to be her/his residence.

This exemption applies if the former resident was an owner and, in England, if s/he was a tenant or licensee, irrespective of whether s/he was liable for council tax on the dwelling. In Wales, this exemption extends to former tenants only if the person has been absent for the whole period since the dwelling last ceased to be her/his residence.

Dwelling unoccupied because the former resident is providing care elsewhere

An unoccupied dwelling is exempt indefinitely if it was previously the sole or main residence (see p77) of an owner, tenant or licensee who is now solely or mainly resident elsewhere because s/he is providing personal care to someone.[29]

This exemption applies to former residents who were owners, as well as tenants or licensees, irrespective of whether they were liable for council tax on the dwelling.

The carer does not have to be disregarded for the purpose of a council tax discount. However, the person being cared for must require the care because of her/his:

- old age; *or*
- disablement; *or*
- illness; *or*
- past or present alcohol or drug dependence; *or*
- past or present mental illness or disorder.

The carer must have been absent from her/his own dwelling since it was last occupied because s/he has been providing such care.

Dwelling left unoccupied by a student owner

An unoccupied dwelling is exempt indefinitely if it was last occupied as the sole or main residence (see p77) of its owner who is now a student and s/he:[30]
- has been a student since s/he last occupied the dwelling; *or*
- has become a student within six weeks of leaving the dwelling.

'Student' has the same meaning as for council tax discount purposes (see p108). If there are joint owners of the unoccupied property, all of them must be students and at least one of them must have been solely or mainly resident there on the last day it was occupied, and the last one must have become a student within six weeks of the day it was last occupied as a sole or main residence.

Example

Josie is a single student studying in London. She left her former home in Plymouth and came to London three weeks before her course was due to start. Josie owns a flat in Plymouth, which remains unoccupied apart from when she returns for short periods during college vacations.

The flat in Plymouth is exempt because it is unoccupied and Josie became a student within six weeks of having been solely resident there. It remains exempt when Josie returns in the vacations because, during these times, although it is occupied, the sole resident is a student. If Josie decided to let the flat in Plymouth to a tenant it would cease to be exempt because it would no longer be unoccupied. However, it would continue to be exempt if the new tenant were also a student.

Unoccupied dwelling in the possession of a mortgage lender

An unoccupied dwelling is exempt indefinitely if a mortgagee (ie, a bank, building society or finance company) is in possession under the mortgage.[31] This would arise, for example, if the lender has repossessed the property because of the borrower's failure to keep up her/his mortgage payments.

Unoccupied dwelling held by a trustee in bankruptcy

An unoccupied dwelling is exempt indefinitely if the liable owner is a trustee in bankruptcy under the Insolvency Act 1986 or other bankruptcy legislation.[32] A trustee in bankruptcy is the person appointed by a general meeting of a bankrupt person's creditors or the court, whose duty is to take over all her/his property, sell the property for cash and distribute the resulting funds among the creditors.

Unoccupied dwelling which cannot be let separately

A dwelling in England and Wales is exempt if it is:
- unoccupied; *and*
- forms part of a single property which includes another dwelling; *and*
- cannot be let separately from that other dwelling without a breach of planning control.

An example of this exemption is an empty 'granny flat'.[33]

Other exempt dwellings

The following other occupied dwellings are also exempt:
- student halls of residence (see below);
- dwellings wholly occupied by students or school or college leavers (see p62);
- armed forces accommodation (see p62);
- visiting forces accommodation (see p63);
- empty caravan pitches or houseboat moorings (see p63);
- dwellings wholly occupied by people under 18 (see p63);
- dwellings occupied by people who are 'severely mentally impaired' (see p63);
- dwellings in which at least one liable person has diplomatic, Commonwealth or consular privilege or immunity (see p63);
- one of at least two dwellings in a single property occupied by a dependent relative of a person living in another dwelling in the property (see p63).

Student hall of residence

A dwelling is exempt indefinitely if it is a hall of residence provided predominantly to accommodate students who would be disregarded for the purpose of a discount (see p108).[34] To qualify for the exemption, the hall must be either:
- owned or managed by a prescribed educational institution (see p110); *or*
- the subject of an agreement allowing a prescribed educational institution to nominate the majority of the people who are to occupy the accommodation.

This exemption also extends to halls of residence, predominantly for the accommodation of students, owned or managed by a body established solely for charitable purposes.[35] The term 'halls of residence' only applies to universities and similar institutions. It does not include boarding school houses for pupils and staff as these are not 'halls of residence' and school children are not classed as 'students' for council tax purposes.[36]

A hall (or hostel) should be exempt even if some non-students (such as wardens, tutors or family members) live there. Any separate, self-contained flat or house provided for a non-student, such as a caretaker, is not covered by this exemption. If a hall of residence is used for more than 140 days a year for commercial purposes, such as conferences, it may be subject to non-domestic rates.

Dwelling wholly occupied by students or 'relevant persons'

To be exempt under this heading, the dwelling must be either:[37]
- occupied by one or more residents, all of whom are 'relevant persons' (see below); or
- occupied only by one or more 'relevant persons' as term-time accommodation.

A **'relevant person'** is a:[38]
- student disregarded for discount purposes (see p108); or
- student's spouse or dependant who is not a British citizen and who is prevented by the terms of her/his leave to enter or remain in the UK from working or claiming benefits; or
- school or college leaver who is disregarded for discount purposes (see p107).

Students of nursing or midwifery who are studying academic courses at universities count as students.[39] If the dwelling has more than one resident, they must all meet the qualifying conditions for the exemption to apply.

A dwelling occupied by a relevant person is regarded as term-time accommodation during any vacation in which s/he:
- holds a freehold or leasehold interest in, or licence to occupy, the whole or any part of the dwelling; and
- has previously used, or intends to use, the dwelling as term-time accommodation.

Example

Three students rent a house as joint tenants. It is exempt from the council tax. The exemption ends when one of the students is dismissed from her course and, therefore, no longer qualifies for a status discount. The three joint tenants are now jointly liable for the council tax on the dwelling. There are three residents, but two of them are disregarded for the purpose of a discount. The bill should be reduced by 25 per cent because there is only one adult resident who is not disregarded.

Armed forces accommodation

Dwellings, either occupied or unoccupied, are exempt indefinitely if they are:[40]
- owned by the Secretary of State for Defence; and
- for the purposes of armed forces accommodation.

This includes, for example, armed forces barracks and married quarters. Contributions in place of the council tax are paid by the Ministry of Defence to local authorities. These contributions should broadly match the amount which would otherwise have been payable.[41]

Visiting forces accommodation

A dwelling is exempt indefinitely if at least one person who would be liable is a member (or dependant) of a visiting force and s/he is neither a British citizen nor ordinarily resident in the UK. A dwelling is exempt under this category 'even if not all of the liable persons have a relevant association with a visiting force'. So, for instance, a dwelling in which the liable persons are a visiting serviceman and his British wife would be exempt.[42]

Unoccupied pitch and mooring

A pitch or mooring not occupied by a caravan or boat is an exempt dwelling for council tax purposes.[43]

Dwelling wholly occupied by someone under 18

A dwelling only occupied by one or more persons under 18 is exempt.[44]

Dwelling occupied by a 'severely mentally impaired' person

A dwelling is exempt if it is only occupied by a person(s) who is 'severely mentally impaired' as defined for the purposes of council tax discount (see p115).[45]

A dwelling is also exempt if it is occupied by at least one severely mentally impaired person and one or more student or 'relevant persons' (see p62).[46]

People with diplomatic immunity

A dwelling is exempt if at least one liable person has diplomatic, Commonwealth or consular privilege or immunity and that person is not a permanent resident of the UK, or a British citizen, British subject or British protected person. This exemption does not apply if that person has another dwelling in the UK which is her/his main residence or if her/his main residence is in the UK.

Dwelling occupied by a dependent relative

This exemption applies to a dwelling, which is one of at least two dwellings in a single property, occupied by a dependent relative of a person living in another dwelling in the property.[47]

A relative is a **'dependant'** if s/he is 65 or over, severely mentally impaired, or substantially and permanently disabled.[48] A **'relative'** is a person's spouse, parent, child, grandparent, grandchild, brother, sister, uncle or aunt, nephew or niece, great-grandparent, great-grandchild, great-uncle, great-aunt, great-nephew or great-niece, great-great-grandparent, great-great-grandchild, great-great-uncle, great-great-aunt, great-great-nephew or great-great-niece. A relationship by marriage (or by living together as husband and wife or by civil partnership[49]) is treated as a relationship by birth and any stepchild of a person shall be treated as her/his child.

2. **Exempt dwellings in Scotland**

In Scotland, the classes of empty dwellings that are exempt from council tax are set out in the Council Tax (Exempt Dwellings) (Scotland) Order 1997 as amended by the Council Tax (Exempt Dwellings) (Scotland) Amendment Order 2012.[50]

Dwellings which were both unoccupied and unfurnished were exempt from council tax liability for a period of up to six months, subject only to a limited transitional provision until 13 May 2013 (see p67).

Dwellings in Scotland which are both unoccupied and unfurnished remain exempt from council tax liability for a period of up to six months. From 1 April 2013, after six months, a second claim for the exemption is only possible after a property has been occupied for a period of at least three months. The dwelling need not have been furnished in the three months and this replaces the requirement of occupation or furnishing for a period of at least six weeks which applied for any earlier financial year.[51]

The property is classed as an unoccupied dwelling (see p53) is exempt if:[52]
- it is recently built and still unfurnished (see below);
- it is undergoing, or has recently undergone, major repair work or structural alteration (see p65);
- it was last occupied by a charity (see p65);
- it is unfurnished (see p65);
- it was last occupied by, and remains the sole liability of, someone in prison or someone living elsewhere to receive or provide care (see p65);
- it is owned by someone who has died (see p66);
- its occupation is prohibited by law (see p66);
- it is owned by a public sector housing authority pending demolition (see p66);
- it is being kept for occupation by a minister of religion (see p66);
- it was last occupied by a student (see p66);
- it has been repossessed following a mortgage default (see p66);
- it was last occupied together with certain agricultural lands (see p67);
- it is held by a trustee in bankruptcy (see p67);
- it is part of the same premises as, or situated within the same 'curtilage' as, another dwelling and is difficult to let separately (see p67);
- the sole liable person is a student (see p68).

Unoccupied new dwelling
A dwelling that is unoccupied and unfurnished is exempt for up to six months if:[53]
- less than six months have elapsed since the effective date of the first entry on the valuation list; *and*
- there was no entry on the valuation list immediately before that effective date.

Unoccupied dwelling undergoing structural repair, improvement or reconstruction

An unoccupied dwelling is exempt if it cannot be lived in because, since the last occupation date, it has been undergoing, or has undergone, structural alteration or major repair work to make it habitable.[54]

The lack of occupation must be because of the work being carried out. If the dwelling is occupied, it is not exempt. The exemption may last for 12 months after the dwelling was last occupied, or (if sooner) for six months after the work or alteration was substantially completed. The property may remain furnished.

Unoccupied dwelling last occupied by a charity

An unoccupied dwelling last occupied by a charitable body is exempt for up to six months if it was last occupied to further the charity's objectives.[55] 'Charitable' has the same meaning as in the Income Tax Acts. Any period of occupation for less than six weeks is disregarded.[56] This disregard is a device to avoid abuse of the exemption. Without the disregard, the liable person could ensure that the building is occupied for a few days near the end of the six-month period and thus trigger the exemption again for a further six months. The property may remain furnished.

Unoccupied and unfurnished dwelling

Unoccupied and unfurnished dwellings are exempt for up to six months from the end of the last period of six weeks or more during which the dwelling was occupied or furnished.[57]

Dwelling last occupied by someone in prison, or living elsewhere to receive or provide care

An unoccupied dwelling is exempt indefinitely if it was last occupied as the sole or main residence (see p77) of someone who continues to be liable for council tax, and since the last day of occupation s/he is:

- disregarded for the purpose of a council tax discount because she is in prison or detention, or is in a hospital, care home or certain care hostels in Scotland, England or Wales (see Chapter 8); *or*
- receiving personal care elsewhere because of her/his old age, disablement, illness, past or present alcohol or drug dependence, or past or present mental illness or disorder; *or*
- providing personal care elsewhere to someone who needs it because of old age, disablement, illness, past or present alcohol or drug dependence, or past or present mental illness/disorder.[58]

Any period of occupation of less than six weeks since the last day of occupation is disregarded. The property may remain furnished.

Dwelling owned by someone who has died

To be exempt, the dwelling must be no one's sole or main residence (see p77). Additionally, any liability to pay council tax must fall under the estate of the deceased person.[59] In such cases, the dwelling is exempt:

- indefinitely if no grant of confirmation to the estate of that person has been made; *or*
- for up to six months from the date such a grant is made.

The property may remain furnished.

Dwelling in which occupation is prohibited

If it is prohibited by law to occupy a dwelling, that dwelling is exempt indefinitely.[60] The property may remain furnished. The fact that such a property is actually occupied should not make it ineligible for the exemption.

It is also exempt if it is being kept unoccupied because legal action is underway to prohibit its occupation or to acquire it under a compulsory purchase order. In these circumstances, if the dwelling is actually occupied, it is not exempt. The property may remain furnished.

Unoccupied dwelling owned by a housing body pending demolition

A dwelling which is owned by a local authority or registered social landlord and is kept unoccupied pending demolition is exempt.[61] The property may remain furnished.

Dwelling held for a minister of religion

A dwelling, such as a manse, which is no one's sole or main residence (see p77), is exempt indefinitely if it is being held by, or on behalf of, any religious body to be available for occupation by a minister of religion as a residence from which to perform the duties of her/his office.[62] The property may remain furnished.

Student's unoccupied dwelling

An unoccupied dwelling which is a student's main residence and which was last occupied by a student(s) is exempt for up to four months from the last day it was occupied for a period of six weeks or more.[63] This applies, for example, to the student's term-time accommodation during vacations if the accommodation remains unoccupied during that period. The property may remain furnished.

Dwelling repossessed by a mortgage lender

A dwelling which is no one's sole or main residence (see p77) is exempt indefinitely if it has been formally repossessed by a mortgage lender.[64] The property may remain furnished.

Dwelling last occupied with agricultural lands

An unoccupied and unfurnished dwelling is exempt indefinitely if it was last used and occupied with the land on which it is situated. The land must be:[65]

- agricultural or pastoral; *or*
- woodlands, market gardens, orchards, allotments or allotment gardens; *or*
- used for the purpose of poultry farming and exceeding one-tenth of a hectare.

Dwelling held by a trustee in bankruptcy

A dwelling which is no one's sole or main residence (see p77) is exempt indefinitely if the only person who would be liable is a bankruptcy trustee.[66]

Unoccupied dwelling that is difficult to let separately

An unoccupied dwelling, such as an empty 'granny flat' or staff accommodation, is exempt indefinitely if:[67]

- it forms part of premises which include another dwelling; *or*
- it is situated within the 'curtilage' of another dwelling; *and*
- it is difficult to let separately from that other dwelling; *and*
- the person who would be liable for it has her/his sole or main residence in that other dwelling.

The property may remain furnished.

Unoccupied dwelling for which the sole liable person is a student

A dwelling which is no one's sole or main residence (see p77) is exempt indefinitely if the person who would be liable is a student for the purpose of a council tax discount (see p108).

If there are joint owners/joint tenants, they must all be students.[68] The property may remain furnished.

Transitional provisions in Scotland

Following the changes from 1 April 2013, a transitional provision applies for dwellings in Scotland whereby the changes do not apply in a case where the dwelling was empty prior to 13 May 2013, where it:

- has been unoccupied and unfurnished during any day in the period of 6 weeks prior to 1 April 2013; *and*
- then becomes occupied or furnished for a continuous period of six weeks that ends before 13 May 2013.

Such a dwelling is awarded an exemption as if it were exempt before 1 April 2013 under the old rules.[69]

Occupied dwellings which are exempt

An occupied dwelling is exempt if it:[70]
- is only occupied by one or more students, school or college leavers or under-18-year-olds (see below);
- is occupied by a student or a student's spouse (see below);
- is a housing association 'trial' property for older people or people with disabilities (see below);
- is a students' hall of residence (see below);
- is armed forces accommodation (see p69);
- is visiting forces accommodation (see p69);
- includes garages, carports and storage sheds (see p69);
- is occupied by a 'severely mentally impaired' person (see p69);
- is 'prescribed housing support accommodation' (see p69).

Dwelling occupied only by students or under-18-year-olds

A dwelling is exempt indefinitely if it is not the sole or main residence (see p77) of anyone other than a student for the purpose of a council tax discount (see p108) or a person under 18, and it is occupied by at least one such person.[71] Also included is a student's spouse or dependant who is not a British citizen and who is prevented by the Immigration Rules from either claiming benefits or working in the UK.[72]

Temporary dwelling for older or disabled people owned by a registered housing association

A dwelling owned by a registered housing association is exempt indefinitely if:
- it is not the sole or main residence (see p77) of any person; *and*
- it is for people over pension age or with a disability who are likely in the future to have their sole or main residences in other dwellings provided by the housing association.

This provides an exemption for trial dwellings for older or disabled people who are likely to live in other property owned by the association in the future. In practice, most local authorities do not charge council tax for the trial period while the person is still liable elsewhere.

Halls of residence

A dwelling is exempt if it is, or is part of, a hall of residence provided predominantly to accommodate students and which:[73]
- is owned and managed by a prescribed educational institution for the purpose of a council tax discount (see p108); *or*
- is the subject of an agreement allowing a prescribed educational institution to nominate the majority of the people who are to occupy the accommodation.

Armed forces accommodation

An occupied or unoccupied dwelling is exempt indefinitely if it is:[74]
- owned by the Secretary of State for Defence; *and*
- held for the purposes of armed forces accommodation.

The local authority receives compensating payments for these dwellings.

Visiting forces accommodation

A dwelling is exempt indefinitely if a member of a visiting force or her/his dependant (but not a dependant who is a British citizen or is ordinarily resident in the UK) would be liable.[75]

Garages, carports and storage sheds

Certain garages, carports, car parking stances and premises used for storing domestic items, including cycles and similar vehicles, are considered to be dwellings (see p16). They are exempt indefinitely from council tax.[76]

Dwelling occupied by a 'severely mentally impaired' person

A dwelling is exempt if it is only occupied by a person(s) who is 'severely mentally impaired', as defined for the purposes of council tax discount (see p115).[77]

A dwelling is also exempt if it is occupied by at least one severely mentally impaired person and one or more students or relevant persons (see p108).[78]

Prescribed housing support accommodation

A dwelling is exempt if it falls into the category of 'prescribed housing support accommodation'.[79] In order to be exempt:
- the dwelling must be the residence of at least one person who is a tenant, sub-tenant or who has a licence to occupy the dwelling; *and*
- a registered prescribed housing support service must be provided to at least one licensee, tenant or sub-tenant of the dwelling; *and*
- all the residents must share the use of a kitchen, bathroom, shower-room or toilet-room, and these must also be shared with at least one other person who is not resident in the dwelling.

A dwelling is not exempt if each resident has exclusive use of a kitchen and a bathroom/shower-room (either containing a toilet or if there is a separate toilet which all the residents can use).

3. **How exempt dwellings are identified**

Local authorities must take reasonable steps each financial year to establish whether any dwellings in their area are exempt from council tax for any period during the year.[80] Most are likely to carry out periodic postal surveys and make use of other sources of information, such as the electoral roll and their benefit records. Most local authorities also carry out regular visits to unoccupied exempt dwellings.

If the local authority has no reason to believe that a particular dwelling will be or was exempt, it will assume it is a chargeable dwelling for council tax billing purposes.[81] Alternatively, if it has reason to believe that a particular dwelling will be or was exempt for a period during the course of the year, it must make that assumption for council tax billing purposes.[82]

4. **Notification of exemption**

If the local authority has assumed that a dwelling is exempt, it must write to the person who would otherwise be liable.[83] The notification must be made as soon as is reasonably practicable.[84] The requirement does not apply in Scotland if:[85]

- the otherwise liable person is a housing body; or
- the dwelling is a separate garage, carport or storage shed.

The local authority should also supply a statement that:[86]

- shows the valuation band for the dwelling;
- summarises how to make a proposal for altering the valuation list;
- in Scotland, specifies for the financial year in question the amounts set as council tax and Scottish Water charges;
- in England and Wales, specifies the local authority's estimate of the amount of council tax (or the actual amount if the year is over) which would have been payable, disregarding any disability reduction, discount, transitional relief (in Wales) or council tax reduction that may have been awarded;
- summarises the most common classes of dwelling which are exempt;[87]
- in Scotland, summarises the individual's obligation to correct any incorrect assumptions the local authority may have made in awarding the exemption, and including the penalty which may be imposed if this obligation is not met (see p71).

The above information need not be given if it was already provided when the scheme was introduced or on any bill ('demand notice').[88] If there is more than one potentially liable person, the local authority only needs to write to one of them.[89]

The duty to correct false assumptions

If you have been notified that the dwelling is, or will be, exempt, you have a duty to tell the local authority if there is reason to believe that this is not the case. The local authority should be notified in writing within 21 days.[90]

If two or more people are jointly liable to pay council tax on a dwelling, they both have a duty to notify the local authority. Only one of them, however, has to supply the information for this obligation to be met.[91]

From April 2013, it is a criminal offence if you obtain, through an act or ommission, a reduction under a council tax reduction scheme which you are not entitled to.[92]

5. **Penalties**

The local authority has the discretion to impose a penalty of £70 (in England) or £50 (in Wales and Scotland) on a liable person who fails to notify it that her/his dwelling is no longer exempt. There are higher penalties for failing to supply information requested by the local authority for council tax purposes.[93]

Such penalties are not criminal convictions or punishments, but if unpaid can be recovered through the magistrates' court (sheriff court in Scotland) in the same way as unpaid sums of council tax.

Each time the local authority repeats the request and the person fails to supply the information, a further £280 penalty (in England) or £200 (in Wales and Scotland) can be imposed.[94]

You can appeal against the imposition of a penalty (see Chapter 12),[95] although English and Welsh local authorities have the discretion to quash the penalty beforehand.[96] In England, you appeal directly to the Valuation Tribunal for England (see p237). In Wales, you should write directly to the appropriate valuation tribunal. In Scotland, an appeal can be made to the valuation appeal committee by writing to the local authority. The local authority should pass the appeal on to the committee. A Scottish local authority may revoke the imposition of a penalty if you have a reasonable excuse for the failure.[97]

In England and Wales, an appeal to a tribunal must normally be made within two months of the penalty being imposed. The president of the tribunal has the discretion to allow an out-of-time appeal if you have failed to meet the time limit because of reasons beyond your control.

In Scotland, the appeal must be made within two months of the penalty being imposed. There is no power to consider out-of-time appeals.

In practice, penalties are relatively little used as they cannot be recovered through the courts while an appeal against the penalty is outstanding. As a result, few local authorities consider enforcement of penalties worth the administrative time and effort involved to recover them.

A local authority may also impose a larger penalty as an alternative to prosecution for a criminal offence of falsely supplying information under offences created following the Local Government Finance Act 2012 (see Chapter 6).[98]

6. Appeals

If the local authority decides that the dwelling is not exempt, you can appeal in writing to the local authority if you are an 'aggrieved person'.[99] There is no time limit for making such appeals. An **'aggrieved person'** is someone who would be liable to pay the tax if the dwelling were not exempt or s/he is the owner (if different). The appeal letter should give the reasons why the dwelling should be exempt. The local authority has two months in which to answer.[100]

Exemptions can be backdated to the date the qualifying conditions for the exemption were first met, the beginning of the scheme or when the particular exemption was first introduced, whichever is the latest. Unlike the provisions for backdating most social security benefits, there is no requirement to show 'good cause' for the backdating.

If an exemption is not granted, or if the local authority fails to answer within two months of receiving the appeal, a further appeal can be made.[101] In theory, the local authority may commence enforcing payment of the original bill while the appeal is outstanding but once a formal appeal has begun the local authority ought to suspend recovery and a court may also order a stay on proceedings (see Chapter 11).

In **England and Wales**, a further appeal can be made by writing directly to the Valuation Tribunal for England or the Valuation Tribunal for Wales. This should normally be made within two months of the date the local authority notified you of its decision, or within four months of the date when the initial written representation was made if the local authority has not responded. The president of the tribunal has the power to allow an out-of-time appeal if you have failed to meet the appropriate time limit because of reasons beyond your control.

In **Scotland**, a further appeal is made by writing again to the local authority. The local authority should pass the appeal on to the secretary of the relevant local valuation appeal committee. The appeal must be made within four months of the date on which the grievance was first raised with the local authority in writing. There is no power to consider an out-of-time appeal.

See Chapter 12 for more information about appeals.

Notes

1 **EW** s4(2) LGFA 1992
   S s72(6)-(7) and Sch 11 para 7(2)-(3)
   LGFA 1992; CT(ED)(S)O 1992
2 **EW** s2(2)(a) LGFA 1992
   S s71(2)(a) LGFA 1992

1. Exempt dwellings in England and Wales

3 para 3.1 *Technical Reforms to Council Tax: Empty homes premium: Calculation of council tax base,* DCLG consultation, September 2012
4 Council Tax (Exempt Dwellings)(England)(Amendment) Order 2012
5 CT(ED)O as amended by art 2 CT(ED)(A)(E)O
6 CT(ED)O as amended by CT(ED)(A)(E)O
7 CT(ED)O
8 CT(ED)O
9 s11B LGFA as inserted by s12 LGFA 2012
10 **E** Reg 2 CT(ED)O
   W CT(ED)(A)(W)O
11 *Summers v Salford Corporation* [1943] AC 283
12 *Edem v Basingstoke and Deane Borough Council* [2012] EWHC 2433
13 *FM Finnieston Ltd (Pursuers) against Kenneth James Gordon Harvey Ross (Defender)* [2009] Scot (D) 19/4
14 Class A CT(ED)O
15 Class B CT(ED)O
16 Class C CT(ED)O
17 Class D CT(ED)O
18 s6 LGFA 1992
19 CT(ED)O
20 Class F CT(ED)O
21 *Valuation in Practice* No.19, November 2010
22 Class G CT(ED)O; CT(ED)(A)(E)O
23 *Watson v Rhondda Cynon Taff Borough Council* [2001] 913 (EWHC)
24 Class H CT(ED)O
25 Class H CT(ED)O
26 Class E CT(ED)O
27 Parliamentary Answer given by Dr Alan Whitehead, Under Secretary of State for Transport, Local Government and the Regions, 24 January 2002
28 Class I CT(ED)O

29 Class J CT(ED)O
30 Class K CT(ED)O
31 Class L CT(ED)O
32 Class Q CT(ED)O, as amended by The Council Tax (Exempt Dwellings) (Amendment) Order 1993 No.150
33 Class T CT(ED)O
34 Class M CT(ED)O
35 Class M CT(ED)O
36 *Stowe School Ltd v Aylesbury Vale District Council* [2012] RA 111
37 Class N CT(ED)O
38 Class N CT(ED)O
39 Practice Note No.2, para 28
40 Class O CT(ED)O
41 Practice Note No.2, para 30
42 Class P CT(ED)O
43 CT(ED)O
44 Class S CT(ED)O
45 Class U CT(ED)O
46 CT(ED)O
47 CT(ED)O
48 CT(ED)O
49 Class W CT(ED)(A)(E)O 2005

2. Exempt dwellings in Scotland

50 CT(ED)(S)(A)O 2012
51 Art 2 CT(ED)(S)(A)O 2012
52 CT(ED)(S)O 1997
53 Sch 1 para 1 CT(ED)(S)O 1997
54 Sch 1 para 2 CT(ED)(S)O 1997
55 Sch 1 para 3 CT(ED)(S)O 1997
56 Art 2 CT(ED)(S)O 1997
57 Sch 1 para 4 CT(ED)(S)O 1997
58 Sch 1 para 5 CT(ED)(S)O 1997
59 Sch 1 para 6 CT(ED)(S)O 1997
60 Sch 1 para 7 CT(ED)(S)O 1997
61 Sch 1 para 8 CT(ED)(S)O 1997
62 Sch 1 para 9 CT(ED)(S)O 1997
63 Sch 1 para 11 CT(ED)(S)O 1997
64 Sch 1 para 13 CT(ED)(S)O 1997
65 Sch 1 para 14 CT(ED)(S)O 1997
66 Sch 1 para 21 CT(ED)(S)O 1997
67 Sch 1 para 19 CT(ED)(S)O 1997
68 Sch 1 para 12 CT(ED)(S)O 1997
69 Art 3 CT(ED)(S)(A)O 2012
70 CT(ED)(S)(A)O

71 Sch 1 para 10(a)(iii) and (iv) CT(ED)(S)O 1997; see also The Education (Graduate Endowment and Student Support) (Scotland) Act 2001
72 Sch 1 para 10(a)(ii) CT(ED)(S)O 1997
73 Sch 1 para 16 CT(ED)(S)O 1997
74 Sch 1 para 17 CT(ED)(S)O 1997
75 Sch 1 para 22 CT(ED)(S)O 1997
76 Sch 1 para 20 CT(ED)(S)O 1997
77 Class U CT(ED)(S)O 1997
78 CT(ED)O
79 The CT(ED)(S)O 1997 was amended by the CT(ED)(S)(A)O 2006. Such a dwelling has the same meaning as accommodation defined by s91(8) Housing (Scotland) Act 2001 and the Housing Scotland Act 2001 (Housing Support Services) Regulations 2002, registered by the Scottish Commission for the regulation of care as a prescribed housing support service under the Regulation of Care (Scotland) Act 2001.

3. How exempt dwellings are identified
80 **EW** Reg 8 CT(AE) Regs 1992
   S CT(ED)(S)O 1992
81 **EW** Reg 9(1) CT(AE) Regs 1992
   S Reg 7 CT(AE)(S) Regs
82 **EW** Reg 9(2) CT(AE) Regs 1992
   S Reg 8 CT(AE)(S) Regs

4. Notification of exemption
83 **EW** Reg 10(1) CT(AE) Regs 1992
84 **EW** Reg 10(2) CT(AE) Regs 1992
   S Reg 9 CT(AE)(S) Regs
85 **EW** Reg 10 CT(AE) Regs 1992
   S Reg 9 CT(AE)(S) Regs
86 **EW** Reg 10 CT(AE) Regs 1992
   S Reg 9 CT(AE)(S) Regs
87 **EW** Reg 10(3) CT(AE) Regs 1992
   S Reg 9 CT(AE)(S) Regs
88 **EW** Reg 10 CT(AE) Regs 1992
   S Reg 9 CT(AE)(S) Regs
89 **EW** Reg 10 CT(AE) Regs 1992
   S Reg 9 CT(AE)(S) Regs
90 **EW** Reg 11 CT(AE) Regs 1992
91 **EW** Reg 11 CT(AE) Regs 1992
   S Reg 10 CT(AE)(S) Regs

5. Penalties
92 **E** The Council Tax Reduction Schemes (Detection of Fraud and Enforcement) (England) Regulations 2013 No.501
   W The Council Tax Reduction Schemes (Detection of Fraud and Enforcement) (Wales) Regulations 2013 No.588 (W.67)

93 Local Government Finance (Substitution of Penalties) Order 2008 No.981
94 **EW** Sch 3 LGFA 1992
   S s97(4) and Sch 3 LGFA 1992
95 **EW** s14(2) and Sch 3 LGFA 1992
   S s97(4) and Sch 3 LGFA 1992
96 **EW** Sch 3 para 1 LGFA 1992
97 **S** s97(4) and Sch 3 LGFA 1992

6. Appeals
98 **EW** s14 LGFA 2012
99 **EW** s16 LGFA 1992
100 **EW** s16 LGFA 1992
    S s81 LGFA 1992
101 **EW** s16 LGFA 1992
    S s81 LGFA 1992

Chapter 6

Liability

This chapter covers:
1. Who is liable (below)
2. Who is a resident (p77)
3. When the owner is always liable (p81)
4. Joint liability (p85)
5. Change of circumstances (p88)
6. Backdating liability (p89)
7. How the liable person is identified (p89)
8. Appeals (p93)

---

1. **Who is liable**

Council tax is payable on any dwelling which is not exempt. See Chapter 5 for more information on exemptions. Normally, the person liable to pay council tax is an adult resident of the dwelling. To be liable, the person must have her/his 'sole or main' residence in the dwelling and have a right to occupy it. To determine who is liable to pay council tax, it is necessary to consult the 'hierarchy of liability' (see p76).[1] This lists different categories of occupier, based on security of occupancy, including owners, tenants, licensees and squatters. Normally, the person(s) whose sole or main residence is in a dwelling and who has the most secure interest in it will be the liable taxpayer(s) and the person to whom the council tax bill will be sent.

Working down the list, as soon as a description is reached which applies to someone in respect of the dwelling in question, that person is the liable person.[2] This will normally be an owner-occupier or a council, housing association or private tenant. A tenant is not liable, however, if the landlord lives in the same dwelling. If no one is solely or mainly resident (see p77) in the dwelling, the non-resident owner is liable. In certain instances, however, the owner is always liable (see p81). If more than one person fits the first description that applies, they will normally be jointly liable (see p85).

For the purpose of determining the liable person on any day, the state of affairs at the end of the day is assumed to have existed throughout that day.[3]

In certain cases, the liable person may also be a person who is disregarded for the purpose of a council tax discount (see Chapter 8). The rules on discounts are separate and do not affect liability, except in some cases where they affect 'severely mentally impaired' people who would otherwise be held jointly liable (see p85).

Following the death of the owner, the deceased's personal representative may become liable in her/his capacity as owner of the estate, but the dwelling is likely to be exempt for some time if left unoccupied. See Chapter 5 for more information.

Note: you do not have to pay council tax unless a bill has been sent with your name on it or, if your name is not known, the 'council tax payer' (see p164), unless (in Scotland) you are jointly liable with someone who has been billed.

Hierarchy of liability in England and Wales

– A resident with a freehold interest in the whole or any part of the dwelling.
– A resident with a leasehold interest (including an assured tenancy or assured shorthold tenancy) in the whole or any part of the dwelling which is not inferior to another such interest held by another resident.
– A resident and a statutory tenant (within the meaning of the Rent Act 1977 or the Rent (Agriculture) Act 1976) or a secure tenant (within the meaning of Part IV of the Housing Act 1985) of the whole or any part of the dwelling.[4]
– A resident with a contractual licence to occupy the whole or any part of the dwelling.
– A resident (including a squatter).
– A non-resident owner – ie, the person who has the inferior (shortest) lease granted for a term of six months or more of the whole, or any part of, the dwelling. If there is no such leaseholder, the freeholder is the owner.[5]

Scotland

In Scotland, in addition to council tax, Scottish Water charges are payable for any dwelling which is not exempt, except if:

- Scottish Water does not provide a supply of water to the dwelling; *or*
- the water is supplied by meter; *or*
- Scottish Water is under an obligation to provide a supply free of charge.

Hierarchy of liability in Scotland

– A resident owner of the whole or any part of the dwelling.
– A resident tenant of the whole or any part of the dwelling.
– A resident statutory tenant (within the meaning of the Rent (Scotland) Act 1984), resident statutory assured tenant (within the meaning of the Housing (Scotland) Act 1988) or resident secure tenant (within the meaning of Part III of the Housing (Scotland) Act 1987) of the whole or any part of the dwelling.[6]
– A resident sub-tenant of the whole or any part of the dwelling.

– A resident of the dwelling or:
  – a sub-tenant of the whole or any part of the dwelling under a sub-lease granted for a term of six months or more;
  – a tenant, under a lease granted for a term of six months or more, of any part of the dwelling which is not subject to a sub-lease granted for a term of six months or more;
  – an owner of any part of the dwelling which is not subject to a lease granted for a term of six months or more.

Caravans and boats in England and Wales

The owner of a caravan or houseboat is liable for council tax except for those days when someone other than the owner is resident and so becomes liable for those days.[7] The normal council tax definitions of 'resident' (see below) and 'owner' apply in the case of residential caravans or boats, but the definition of **'owner'** is extended to include:[8]

- the person who has possession under any hire purchase or conditional sale agreement; *or*
- the person entitled to the property apart from any mortgage or bill of sale which applies to it.

2. **Who is a resident**

Council tax is usually payable by someone who is resident in the dwelling. If no one is resident, the non-resident owner is liable. To count as **'resident'** you must:

- be aged 18 or over; *and*
- be solely or mainly resident in the dwelling (see below).[9]

If everyone who lives in the dwelling is aged under 18, the dwelling is exempt from the tax.

Sole or main residence

If a potentially liable person has more than one home, the local authority must decide which is her/his main residence. The concept of 'sole or main residence' is not defined in the legislation, but has been considered by the courts.

The concept of sole or main residence was originally introduced by the community charge. The (then) Department of the Environment's Community Charge Practice Note No.9 highlighted the *Oxford English Dictionary* definition of 'reside' as 'to dwell permanently or for a considerable time, to have one's settled or usual place of abode, to live in or at a particular place'. In relation to income tax and electoral law, the courts have accepted that:

- residence implies a degree of permanence – temporary presence at an address does not necessarily make a person resident there, unless it is her/his sole residence for that period;
- temporary absence does not deprive a person of residence;
- the lawfulness or otherwise of occupying any home is irrelevant;
- in determining whether or not a person actually present at a given place is legally there, it is necessary to establish whether that person intends to return, whether s/he is free to return, and whether or not s/he could return without breaking any law or contract.

Originally, Council Tax Practice Note No.2 (para 13) pointed out that a person did not need to live in a dwelling all (or even most) of the time for it to be her/his main residence. The Practice Note advised local authorities to take into account all the relevant factors in each case, including the amount of time an individual spends at a dwelling, the place of residence of her/his immediate family, her/his security of tenure and the reason for occupying the dwelling – eg, whether it is occupied solely in relation to a job. The position has been clarified by the Court of Appeal decision in *R (Williams) v Horsham District Council* (see below).

Significantly, the length of time a taxpayer actually spends in a dwelling does not determine residence in itself. For instance, in *Bradford City Council v Anderton*, the appellant was a seafarer who spent most of his life aboard a ship. The Divisional Court ruled that he was solely or mainly resident in Bradford.[10] Similarly, in *Ward v Kingston Upon Hull City Council* an appellant who lived and worked abroad and spent only six weeks a year in the UK was nonetheless held to be resident for poll tax purposes.[11] As a result, sole or main residence in a dwelling could be found on the basis of the most tenuous of connections. Although the High Court stressed that tribunals were required to look at all the relevant facts, the possibility that the taxpayer might ultimately return to the dwelling at some point in the future was often held to be a crucial factor, even if the taxpayer had never actually lived in the dwelling. This approach is no longer correct.

Where the taxpayer lives

The law has been clarified by the Court of Appeal decision in *R (Williams) v Horsham District Council*.[12] The appellant and his wife occupied property provided by an employer between 1993 and 1997. During the same period, they also owned a cottage to which they intended to retire. No one was resident at the cottage in which they stored some belongings and they did not stay overnight. The couple claimed a backdated 50 per cent council tax discount for the four-year period. Horsham District Council refused the application and a valuation tribunal refused their appeal for the discount. The tribunal based its decision on the fact that the couple always intended to return to the cottage, that they enjoyed security of tenure and their absence for four-and-a-half years had been because of work.

The Court of Appeal held that the tribunal's view that local authorities were required to give particular weight to security of tenure and the fact that the couple intended to retire to the cottage was irrelevant. Referring to previous cases might be of assistance when identifying a person's main residence, but because a particular factor was significant in one decided case did not make it important in another.

The Court emphasised that the starting point for deciding sole or main residence should be s6(5) Local Government Finance Act 1992, where 'sole or main residence' refers to premises in which the taxpayer actually resides. Usually, a person's main residence would be the dwelling that 'a reasonable onlooker' with knowledge of the facts would regard as that person's home at the time. The test might not always be easy to apply and the answer would depend on the particular circumstances; it would be a matter of fact and degree.

Establishing a 'reasonable onlooker' principle sets an objective test to be applied in every case and may well differ from what a local authority would conclude. Thus, where a person *actually* lives in any financial year becomes key to determining residence, not a hypothetical question about the right to return in future years.

Following this case, it is clear that the starting point for any appeal is section 6 and the question of who actually lives in the dwelling. By emphasising section 6, the Court of Appeal confirmed that resident tenants, licensees and even trespassers should normally be placed ahead of non-resident owners in terms of liability for council tax. Factors such as voter registration and registration for medical treatment have often been used by valuation tribunals to determine sole or main residence. However, the key question following the *Williams* case is: 'Where does the taxpayer actually live?' Hypothetical questions, such as where a person might move or remain in the event of job loss or serious illness or where s/he might live were tenants to move out, do not, in themselves, determine the answer to this question.

The judgment in *Williams* is particularly important to anyone who has let their principal home to tenants or to someone who normally lives or works abroad. In the case of *Parry v Derbyshire Dales District Council* [2006], the taxpayer lived in Spain and let his cottage to tenants.[13] The High Court held that the taxpayer was resident in Spain for local tax purposes and the fact that the tenant left did not mean that Mr Parry ceased to reside in Spain. The Court followed the approach of the Court of Appeal in the *Williams* case and confirmed s6 Local Government Finance Act 1992: setting out a hierarchy of liability based on who is actually resident in the dwelling rather than security of tenure is crucial to determining the liable person for council tax purposes.

Following the *Williams* case, a person letting a dwelling to tenants should ensure that the calculation of a bill should relate to when s/he actually moves out of a dwelling, not necessarily when tenants move in.

Example

Mr and Mrs Shah live in a house with their 17-year-old daughter. Mrs Shah is the joint owner of the property with her sister, who frequently comes to stay and has a bedroom of her own, but who has her main home elsewhere. At the moment Mr and Mrs Shah are liable for the council tax. The non-resident joint owner is not liable.

If the couple were to separate and Mr Shah to leave the dwelling, Mrs Shah would be liable by herself, but Mr Shah would remain jointly liable for any amount that accrued while living as a couple.

If Mrs Shah were also to leave the dwelling, leaving the daughter as the only person living there, the dwelling may be considered exempt as it is the sole residence of someone under the age of 18. On the daughter's 18th birthday, she would become the sole liable person as the only resident of the dwelling.

Mrs Shah's sister is not liable as her main residence is elsewhere.

Sole or main residence and council tax support

The question of sole or main residence is important when calculating the level of council tax support. Where there is more than one resident adult in a property the amount of council tax support available is likely to be affected, as well as affecting entitlement to discount if only one adult is left living in the property. Inform the local authority when a person moves in or out of the property within 21 days, if it is the case that a change in sole or main residence based upon the test in *Williams* applies.

Merely using a property as a postal address to receive mail or keeping property does not constitute residence for council tax purposes.

Example

Mrs Tims is a pensioner with an adult son Arnie who is homeless. He comes to see her from time to time and receives post at the address but otherwise stays in hostels or with his friends. Arnie does not have sole or main residence with Mrs Tims for council tax purposes.

Establishing sole or main residence

In some cases the local authority does not accept evidence provided by the taxpayer that a person does or does not reside at a particular dwelling. If this the case, all sorts of evidence can be used including bank statements, utility bills, extracts from official registers, forms of identification and statements from neighbours and professionals who know the situation.

If the local authority does not accept the evidence provided, you should make an appeal to the Valuation Tribunal in England or Wales or to the valuation appeal committee in Scotland.

Witness statements may be used where the local authority refuses to accept evidence supplied by the taxpayer. A witness statement must give your name and address and you can set down the relevant facts. It is evidence in courts and tribunals where oral evidence can also be given on oath and must be accepted unless the contrary is proved or the witness is wholly discredited. A local authority which refuses to accept evidence in a witness statement may be liable for breach of statutory duty in civil law. For more on witness statements, see Chapter 13.

Main residence in Scotland

The same approach to residence taken in the *Williams* case (see p78) has been applied in Scotland. In this case, a taxpayer lived during the week and some weekends in a dwelling closer to his job rather than in the dwelling occupied by his wife and family.[14] The Court of Session ruled that the valuation appeal committee was entitled to find that the dwelling where the appellant spent most of his time during the week was his sole or main residence.

3. **When the owner is always liable**

If there are no residents in the dwelling, the non-resident owner is liable. Additionally, the Secretary of State has power to specify circumstances in which, even if there are residents, the owner is always liable.[15] The owner (not the residents) is liable for the council tax on:

- care homes and certain hostels providing care and support (see below);
- houses of religious communities (see p82);
- houses in multiple occupation (see p82);
- second homes with domestic servants (see p84);
- residences of ministers of religion (see p84);
- school boarding accommodation in Scotland (see p85);
- accommodation provided to an asylum seeker under s95 Immigration and Asylum Act 1999 (see p85).

The owner of a house of multiple occupation is liable even if s/he has no beneficial interest in the property.[16]

Care homes and hostels

An owner is liable to pay council tax on care homes and certain hostels providing care and support that are registered under the Care Standards Act 2000.[17]

Religious communities

For the owner to be liable, the dwelling must be inhabited by a religious community whose main occupation consists of prayer, contemplation, education, the relief of suffering, or any combination of these.[18] Monasteries and convents come within this description. Members of such communities may qualify to be disregarded for the purpose of a council tax discount. See p119 for more details.

Houses in multiple occupation

A dwelling is classed as a house in multiple occupation if:[19]
- it was originally constructed, or subsequently adapted, for occupation by more than one household (but see below); *or*
- each person who lives in it is either:
  – a tenant or licensee able to occupy only part of the dwelling; *or*
  – a licensee liable to pay rent or a licence fee on only part of the dwelling.

Examples include some bedsits, hostels, nurses' homes and long-stay wards in hospitals classed as dwellings. In England and Wales, this class can include a dwelling occupied by only one person if the above conditions are met, provided the dwelling was originally constructed, or subsequently adapted, for occupation by multiple households.

From 2003 in Scotland, a dwelling need not have been constructed or adapted for multiple occupation; the fact that the tenant or licensee has the right to occupy or pay rent or a fee for only part of the dwelling is the crucial factor.

The term 'tenant' includes a secure tenant or a statutory tenant and includes leaseholders with leases granted for less than six months. In England and Wales, the normal definition of an owner applies in the case of a house in multiple occupation, except if someone has a leasehold interest. In this case, it must be an interest in the whole dwelling. If this is not the case, the person who has a freehold interest in the whole or any part of the dwelling is liable.[20]

Since April 2006, a landlord of a house in multiple occupation must obtain a licence, as required by the Housing Act 2004. This defines a dwelling as a house in multiple occupation if:
- it consists of one or more units of living accommodation that are not self-contained flat(s);
- the living accommodation is occupied by people who do not form a single household and as their only or main residence (or it is treated as such);
- there is no other use of the accommodation – eg, in the case of a student hall of residence or work-related accommodation;
- at least one person occupying the accommodation pays rent;
- two or more of the households who occupy the living accommodation share one or more basic amenities (eg, a kitchen or bathroom) or the living accommodation lacks one or more basic amenities.

A house in multiple accommodation could therefore be a self-contained flat occupied by people who do not form a single household, or a converted building containing one or more self-contained units, occupied by people who do not form a single household. In *Baker (Listing Officer) v Gomperts,*[21] the High Court held that the correct test to be applied when addressing whether a building had been constructed or adapted for use as separate living accommodation was an objective 'bricks and mortar' test which looked at the reality of what had been constructed and/or how it had been adapted. The test was an objective not a subjective test and therefore the intention of use, whether actual or prospective, was irrelevant to the determination.

The tribunal will look for evidence of adaptation – eg, if separate locks have been fitted to the rooms of residents and they have their own keys and facilities.

Exclusive possession

When deciding the status of residents and the degree of exclusive possession (ie, whether they only occupy part of the dwelling), tribunals can look beyond the tenancy or licence agreement and examine the actual facts.[22] This is very important where the evidence and the accuracy of documents produced at the hearing is challenged. However, they should not decide a property is a house in multiple occupation simply because there are a number of tenants in the dwelling and the owner retains the use of one room – eg, for storing furniture which the tenants do not wish to use. In the case of *R (on the application of Goremsandu) v Harrow London Borough Council,* the High Court ruled that the test to apply was whether the rent paid gave the tenants the right to occupy only part of the dwelling or whether it related to the occupation of the house as a whole.[23] The key issue was whether, ultimately, the tenants had exclusive possession of the whole house.

The tribunal also considered whether the fact that the owner's furniture was kept locked in the conservatory meant the tenants did not occupy the conservatory. It decided that this fact was not sufficient since the statutory test that had to be applied was whether a tenant was a 'tenant of part only of the dwelling'. The tenants remained tenants of the conservatory even though, in fact, they were unable to use or readily gain access to it.

The only items of furniture stored in the conservatory were those that the tenants were paying rent for and, since the terms of the tenancy had not been varied, they were entitled to ask for the key at any time and, if they chose to do so, they could exclude the landlord from the conservatory and also exclude her furniture from that area so long as they stored or used the furniture in another location. They were, therefore, tenants of the whole dwelling, including the conservatory.

In another case, *Watts v Preston*, a key issue was whether the tenants were responsible for paying rent on the dwelling as a whole.[24] The tribunal had erred in finding that they were not, contrary to what was written in the lease.

The question of what a copy of the lease or tenancy agreement says is important but it is not conclusive, in determining exclusive possession, and may not be considered binding on an individual if s/he has not signed it. The lease need not be in writing to be binding but if a written lease has not been signed then a valuation tribunal is entitled consider all the relevant evidence and conclude that the property constitutes a house of multiple occupation.[25] An important question may be whether the occupiers made the agreement together with the landlord or made separate arrangements. If the occupiers did not agree a lease together, the house is more likely to qualify as a house in multiple occupation.

Where residents of a house in multiple occupation are wrongly held liable, evidence from the residents themselves may be crucial. In *O'Shaughnessy v London Borough of Hackney*, the Valuation Tribunal for England (VTE) accepted a witness statement from the appellant as to his whereabouts over a disputed period of liability and his evidence that he never signed any tenancy agreement with other occupiers of a property or lived with them as part of the same household. The tribunal rejected as evidence a purported rent book which contained serious discrepancies and was branded as false by the appellant who had actually been living in a different borough for two of the four-year period of liability in dispute. The VTE accepted the evidence of the appellant given orally and in a witness statement as being consistent and arising from a direct knowledge of the facts and the situation of the dwelling during the material time.[26]

Similar principles apply in Scotland and a valuation appeal committee which applies the wrong tests and makes errors of fact and law may have its decision overturned by the Court of Session.[27]

Second homes with domestic servants

A dwelling fits into this category if it is:[28]

- occupied from time to time by the employer who does not live in it as her/his main residence; *and*
- all the residents are either employed in domestic service in the dwelling or are their family members.

Accommodation for ministers of religion

The dwelling must be inhabited by a minister of religion (of any faith) as a residence from where s/he performs her/his duties of office. If the dwelling is owned by the minister, the minister is liable for council tax. There are exceptions to this rule for English or Welsh dwellings that are owned by a minister of the Church of England who is in receipt of a stipend. In such a case, the liability is transferred to the Diocesan Board of Finance. In Scotland, the body liable for the remuneration of the minister is liable for council tax.[29]

School boarding accommodation

In Scotland, the owner of school boarding accommodation which is specifically included in the definition of a dwelling (see p18) is liable for the council tax.[30]

Accommodation occupied by asylum seekers

Asylum seekers occupying accommodation under s95 Immigration and Asylum Act 1999 are not liable for council tax. The owner is liable.[31]

4. **Joint liability**

If two or more people fall into the liable category (eg, joint owners, joint tenants or simply joint residents), they are jointly and severally liable, except if one is severely mentally impaired or, since 1 April 2004, a student (see p108).[32]

Additionally, the liable person's partner is jointly liable if s/he is:[33]

- married to or in a civil partnership with the liable person; *or*
- living with her/his partner as husband and wife or as if in a civil partnership; *and*
- a resident of the dwelling.

This applies whether or not the partner has a legal interest in the dwelling. The definition of **'couple'** used to establish joint liability for council tax is almost the same as that which applies for many social security benefits. To be a couple under the social security rules, however, both partners must reside in the same *household*. In the case of council tax, it is only necessary to show that they reside in the same *dwelling*. As it is possible for a single dwelling to contain more than one household, there will be some situations when the two definitions do not coincide. For instance, if a married couple are estranged but continue to live in the same house and have separate households, they are still classed as a jointly liable couple for council tax purposes as they remain married and continue to reside in the same dwelling. However, they are not a couple for council tax reduction (CTR) purposes because they reside in different households. This means that both partners are jointly liable, but each can make a separate claims for reductions based on an apportioned (50 per cent) share of council tax liability and her/his own individual circumstances. See Chapter 9 for more information on CTR.

A further complication is that the regulations applicable for CTR define the meaning of a couple in England as:[34]

- a man and woman who are married to each other and are members of the same household;
- a man and woman who are not married to each other but are living together as husband and wife;
- two people of the same sex who are civil partners of each other and are members of the same household; *or*

- two people of the same sex who are not civil partners of each other but are living together as if they were civil partners.

Under the regulations applicable to CTR schemes, two people of the same sex are 'to be treated as living together as if they were civil partners if, and only if, they would be treated as living together as husband and wife were they of opposite sexes'.[35]

In Wales under a CTR scheme a couple is defined as:
- two people who are either married to, or civil partners of, each other and who are members of the same household;
- two people who are living together as if they are a married couple.[36]

In Scotland 'couple' has the same definition as in England with reference to terms including husband and wife.[37]

In terms of joint and several liability for council tax, the meaning of provisions such as these can be difficult to interpret as 'husband', 'wife' and 'married' are not defined in previous council tax law other than by reference to gender. However, there is a substantial body of social security case law on the various criteria that must be considered when attempting to establish whether two people are living together as husband and wife or as married and, arguably, this will be persuasive in establishing a relationship in council tax cases. Simply because two people share accommodation, a local authority should not presume that they are sharing as the equivalent of a married couple or a couple living together as husband a wife, resulting in joint and several liability. Examples where the council may make an erroneous inferences include cases where brothers and sisters who live together and any situation or two people of the same sex (whether related or not) are living or using the same address.

It is difficult to see how the local authority could conclude that two unmarried people are living together as husband and wife unless they were members of the same household (as opposed to merely being resident in the same dwelling) without details of a sexual relationship and the roles assumed in the household. Although there is no established 'right to privacy' in English law, an action[38] may lay for breach of confidence or harassment where private information is released or misused, or improperly demanded. More generally the local authority's power to demand such information is limited in light of Article 8 of the European Convention of Human Rights enshrining a right to privacy and the limits placed in regulations and at law as to what information may be sought.

If the questions that you are asked by the local authority are unreasonable you should make a formal complaint. It is a good idea to involve your Member of Parliament. Complaints may also be taken to the monitoring officer of the local authority, to the Local Government Ombudsman and you may be able to take action through a tribunal or the civil the courts in extreme cases where confidentiality is broken or improper information requested. An erroneous decision on joint and several liability may be challenged before the valuation tribunal (see Chapter 12).

Also, any finding of joint and several liability is displaced and rebutted where the facts show that you do not have sole or main residence in a dwelling with another person. A finding that you do not have sole or main residence in a dwelling will remove you from any liability for council tax altogether from the effective date you ceased to reside. In polygamous marriages, all partners resident in the dwelling are jointly liable[39] and specific provision is made in the regulations for CTR schemes (see Chapter 9).

The significance of joint liability

The local authority has the option of addressing the council tax bill to any one or more of the jointly liable people, or all of them. In Scotland, someone who is jointly liable with the person(s) named on the bill, but whose name is not included, is still liable to make the required payments. See Chapter 10 for more details. In England and Wales, a payment cannot be required from a liable person until s/he has been billed. Practice Note No.2 (para 22) advises English and Welsh local authorities to include the names of as many liable people as possible on their bills. This allows the local authority to take recovery action against any or all of them. If the local authority wants to recover the council tax from someone who is jointly liable but not named on the original bill, a fresh bill (a joint taxpayers' notice) must be issued.[40] In practice, local authorities tend to pursue the first two named persons on a bill.

To be eligible for a reduction under the local authority CTR scheme, you have to be liable for council tax. If someone other than your partner is jointly liable, any reduction is worked out on your apportioned share, even though the local authority may be seeking to recover all of the council tax due from one person. If you are in receipt of a reduction, the late identification of retrospective joint liability may mean an overpayment has been made, and could raise the possibility of a late claim for a reduction from the newly identified jointly liable person. In England and Wales, if the local authority refuses to exercise its discretion to reduce a bill in a case of late billing, you should apply for a discretionary reduction in council tax under section 13(1) of the Local Government Finance Act 2012 (see p48) and you have a right to appeal to a valuation tribunal (see Chapter 12). For more information on CTRs, see Chapter 9.

Joint liability and severe mental impairment

A person who is disregarded for discount purposes because of a 'severe mental impairment' (see p115) is not held jointly liable if there is someone else with the same status and legal interest in the property who is not severely mentally impaired.[41] However, a severely mentally impaired person is liable for the tax if:
- s/he is the only liable person; *or*

- s/he is the only owner, tenant or contractual licensee even if her/his partner is not severely mentally impaired; *or*
- all the jointly liable people are severely mentally impaired.

Dwellings in which all the occupants are severely mentally impaired are exempt (see p63).[42]

- -

Example

A couple are joint owners of a house. The man counts as severely mentally impaired and is disregarded for discount purposes. Normally, the couple (as joint owners and residents) would be liable, but as the man is severely mentally impaired, his wife is liable. If she were no longer to reside in the dwelling, it would become exempt.

- -

If someone goes into a care home, nursing home or hospital, a ruling from the Court of Protection may be required if s/he does not have the mental capacity to determine her/his place of residence. Arguably, 'mental incapacity' is the equivalent of establishing that a person is severely mentally impaired for council tax purposes and may mean s/he is exempt (see p63).

Students

After 1 April 2004, a student who is disregarded for discount purposes (see p108) is not held jointly liable if there is someone else with the same status and legal interest in the property who is not a student. Dwellings occupied solely by students or occupied as term-time accommodation are exempt from council tax. See p62 for more details. If a dwelling is occupied by a student and a non-student, the student is disregarded for discount purposes, attracting a 25 per cent reduction on the amount of council tax payable by the non-student. See p108 for more details.

Before 1 April 2004, a student could have been liable for council tax if s/he occupied a property with a non-student and either had an equal legal interest in the dwelling or was married to, or living together as husband and wife, with a non-student resident.

5. **Change of circumstances**

A change of circumstances may change council tax liability during the year. For example, a liable owner may sell the dwelling or a liable tenant may move to live elsewhere. Liability for council tax arises on a daily basis and the state of affairs at the end of the day is assumed to have lasted all that day.[43] Consequently, the liable person is liable for the first day of residence in the dwelling, but not the last.

If a liable person dies, there is no liability for any part of the day on which s/he dies.

If you fail to declare a change of circumstances, you may be subject to a penalty or prosecuted for an offence. It is an offence not to declare a change of circumstances which you know affects your entitlement to a reduction, and you fail to give a notice of the change as required by the local authority's CTR scheme. It is also an offence to cause or allow a person to fail to give this notification. Knowledge that entitlement is affected is a requirement of the offence in England[44] while in Wales the authority must prove dishonesty.

6. Backdating liability

Liability may be backdated to previous years. The relevant date is the day a person became liable (ie, had her/his sole or main residence in the dwelling), not the date the local authority informed the taxpayer.[45] This may lead to the local authority serving a demand on someone up to six years after s/he may have left a dwelling. However, if a local authority delays serving a demand notice, this may make the demand invalid if it causes prejudice if it seeks to enforce the demand through the magistrates' or sheriff court. See Chapters 10 and 11 for more details. Following the localisation of council tax support, the backdating of reductions in council tax will vary between local authorities but you may apply for a discretionary reduction in council tax under section 13A(1)(c) of the Local Government Finance Act (see Chapters 4 and 9).

If you want to challenge the local authority, you can appeal (see Chapter 12).

7. How the liable person is identified

To establish liability, the local authority has a variety of powers that require people and organisations to provide information. It is also able to use its own information obtained for other purposes. If the local authority is unable to identify a liable person by name, it may serve a bill on the 'council tax payer'. The residents of the dwelling will then need to decide who has to pay the tax.

The local authority's own information

A local authority may use information obtained under any other enactment in England and Wales, provided that it was not obtained in its role as a police authority and, in Scotland, that it is not information obtained through social work activities, unless it consists solely of names and addresses.[46] Thus, local authorities could use their community charge and other records to establish an initial database of liable people. Practice Note No.5 (para 2.2) reminds local authorities, however, to bear in mind data protection law when considering using information held digitally. If a local authority uses data wrongly, any affected person may have a remedy under the Data Protection Act 1998.

Information from residents, owners or managing agents

The local authority has the power to write to anyone who appears to be a resident, owner or managing agent of a particular dwelling, requesting information it requires to identify the liable person or the person who would be liable if the dwelling were not exempt.[47] The rules may place a burden on officials of housing associations and those who manage accommodation for vulnerable individuals. A **'managing agent'** means any person authorised to arrange lettings of the dwelling concerned. If you receive a written enquiry, you must supply the required information within 21 days if it is in your possession or control.

In connection with applications for council tax reduction (CTR) schemes, local authorities may obtain information from qualifying persons, including billings from authorities themselves and those acting on behalf of local authorities.[48] It is an offence to intentionally delay or obstruct an authorised officer in the exercise of her/his powers and a fine of up to £1,000 can be imposed on conviction.[49]

Offences may be committed by corporate bodies such as limited companies, housing associations and charities.[50]

Information from other public bodies

The local authority has the power to request information from:[51]
- any billing authority;
- any levying authority;
- the electoral registration officer for any area in Great Britain.

In Scotland, information may also be requested from the assessor.

Information may also be obtained from HM Revenue and Customs for the authority to:
- make a CTR scheme;
- determine a person's entitlement or continued entitlement to a reduction under a CTR scheme;
- prevent, detect or secure evidence of, or prosecuting the commission of, a council tax offence;
- use in valuation tribunal proceedings.[52]

Penalties

A local authority in England has the discretion to impose a penalty of £70 on someone who fails to respond to a request for information needed to identify the liable person.[53] In Wales and Scotland, the penalty is £50. An English or Welsh authority may quash such a penalty. A Scottish authority may revoke the imposition of such a penalty if the person on whom it was imposed had a reasonable excuse for failing to supply it.[54] Each time the local authority repeated the request and someone fails to supply the information, another £280 penalty (£200 in Wales and Scotland) could be imposed.[55]

The power to impose penalties has since been extended in an attempt to bring the law in line with provisions in welfare benefit security, even though local taxation law is essentially different from social security law. These regulations affect not only taxpayers but also persons who may be providing information on behalf of vulnerable people including owners of houses in multiple occupation, managers of hostels and accommodation for other people and lawyers and advisers who may be acting on behalf of a taxpayer.

The penalty system is designed to operate in conjunction with the system of CTR schemes that each local authority is required to create for pensioners and persons in financial need.[56] New regulations have been made[57] and make provision for powers to require information, the creation of offences and powers to impose penalties in connection with these CTR schemes.

Billing authorities may authorise officers and third parties to discharge these functions for them to individuals with proper authority. These officers can act to collect information for 'detecting and securing evidence of the commission' of offences connected with an application for an award of a reduction of council tax support under a local authority scheme, including access to electronic records.[58]

It is a criminal offence to:
- intentionally delay or obstruct an authorised officer in the exercise of any power to require information;[59]
- refuse or fail (without reasonable excuse) to comply with a requirement to enter into arrangements for access to electronic records, or to fail to provide information when required to do so;[60]
- make a statement or representation which you know to be false for the purpose of obtaining a reduction under a CTR scheme;
- provide or knowingly cause or allow to be provided a document or information which you know to be false in a material particular.[61] (For the information to be material it must actually affect the issue of whether you receive a reduction or not and not simply be any error or mistake.)

A time limit of three months from the date the authority considered evidence justifying a prosecution existed, or 12 months, is placed on bringing proceedings from the commission of the offence whichever period last expires.[62]

Penalties as an alternative to prosecution

You may be offered the opportunity to agree to pay a penalty as an alternative to prosecution. Penalties may be offered as an alternative when a local authority considers that you have committed an offence by obtaining an award of a reduction under a CTR scheme which you were not entitled to, or an offence arising from an act or omission which could have resulted in such an award.[63] The local authority may offer this where it lacks sufficient proof to sustain a conviction or the amount concerned is relatively low and it will cost more to prosecute (where a sum is less than £2,000).

A £70 penalty may be imposed in circumstances such as where you negligently make an incorrect statement in a CTR application or where you fail to notify a change of circumstances when required to do so.

Higher penalties may be imposed, depending on whether a loss has been incurred by the local authority.

Where it appears to the authority that an excess has been awarded, a higher penalty between £100 and £1,000 can be imposed. The authority has to be able to establish that a reduction has been awarded and that this was due to an act or ommission by the person concerned and that there would be grounds for instigating proceedings.[64]

This in fact places a high evidential burden on the authority, as it would have to establish that each of these elements is fulfilled.

Where the authority can establish this, it may, instead of issuing proceedings, offer a minimum penalty, rounded down to the nearest penalty and not be less than £100 or in excess of £1,000.[65]

Where the authority considers false information has been given but no reduction has been awarded, a penalty of £100 may be imposed if the authority considers that proceedings could have been instituted and the act or omission alleged could potentially have been reduced beyond that which you were entitled. This brings a highly subjective test into the issue and it may be hard to say with any certainty at what point the relevant threshold is crossed. A local authority must act reasonably when making such a decision, considering all relevant facts and disregarding irrelevant issues.[66]

If you agree to pay the penalty, it may be recovered through the magistrates' court if you do not pay it like a sum of unpaid council tax. However, no proceedings can begin for the recovery of the amount of the excess reduction. Where you agree to pay the penalty, no criminal proceedings may be commenced against you in the magistrates' court under either council tax legislation or any other law in connection with the act or omission that has given rise to the penalty.[67]

You may withdraw an agreement to pay the penalty within 14 days from the date you agree to pay, by notifying the authority in a prescribed manner. If you do this, any part of the penalty you have already paid is refunded to you. However, the local authority can begin criminal proceedings and an action for the recovery of the amount owed if you withdraw your agreement to pay a penalty, providing the authority does so within the time limit.[68]

Where it is decided by the authority or a valuation tribunal that an excess reduction has not been awarded, the penalty shall be cancelled or quashed and money that has been paid is refunded.[69]

Where the amount of reduction is revised, so that only part is considered excessive, you are repaid the penalty that you have paid so far. However, if a new agreement is made, any amount paid may be treated as recovered and used to pay off a new penalty which applies to the remaining excess reduction.[70]

When the local authority proposes to impose a penalty, a notice must be served upon you explaining what the penalty is for, the type of penalty, the grounds on which it is being imposed and the ways in which it can be recovered.[71]

Failure to serve such a notice may invalidate the imposition of a penalty.

Appeals against penalties

An appeal may be made against the imposition of a penalty.[72] This should be done by writing to the Valuation Tribunal for England or the Valuation Tribunal for Wales. In Scotland, an appeal can be made to a valuation appeal committee by writing to the local authority, which should pass the appeal to the committee. In **England and Wales**, an appeal must normally be made within two months of the penalty being imposed. The president of the tribunal has the discretion to allow an out-of-time appeal if you have failed to meet the time limit because of reasons beyond your control. In **Scotland**, the appeal must be made within two months of the penalty being imposed. There is no power to consider out-of-time appeals. If an appeal has been made, the penalty need not be paid until the appeal has been decided. See below and Chapter 12 for more information about appeals.

8. Appeal procedure

An appeal can be made against a decision on liability by writing to the local authority.[73] There is no time limit for making an appeal. To appeal, you must be an 'aggrieved person' – ie, the person considered liable to pay the tax or the owner (if different). The appeal letter should give the reasons why you believe the local authority has come to the wrong decision. The local authority has two months in which to answer.[74] In the initial appeal letter, it is advisable to refer to the right to take an appeal to the Valuation Tribunal for England (VTE), the Valuation Tribunal for Wales (VTW) or a valuation appeal committee in Scotland if the local authority does not accept the appeal.

If the local authority refuses to alter its decision or fails to answer within two months of receiving the appeal, a further appeal can be made.[75] This is done by writing to the VTE/VTW. In Scotland, a further appeal is made by writing again to the local authority. The local authority should pass the appeal to the secretary of the relevant local valuation appeal committee. If an appeal is served on the local authority, send a copy to the valuation appeal committee for it to be placed on file, in case the letter to the local authority goes astray.

In **England and Wales**, an appeal to a tribunal must normally be made within two months of the date the local authority notified you of its decision, or within four months of the date when the initial written representation was made if the local authority has not responded. The president of the tribunal has the power to allow an out-of-time appeal if you have failed to meet the appropriate time limits for reasons beyond your control.

In **Scotland**, the appeal must be made within four months of the date on which the grievance was first raised with the local authority in writing. There is no power to consider an out-of-time appeal.[76]

The local authority may enforce payment of the original bill while the appeal is outstanding, but if recovery proceedings have been started through the magistrates' court (or a sheriff court in Scotland), you should seek an adjournment of any hearing in the magistrates' court or the sheriff court, pending the outcome of an appeal.[77]

After dealing with an appeal against imposition of a penalty, the VTE may order a penalty to be quashed.[78]

For more information about enforcement action, see Chapter 11 and for more information about appeals, see Chapter 12.

Notes

1. Who is liable
1 **EW** s6 LGFA 1992
 S s75 LGFA 1992
2 **EW** s6(2) LGFA 1992
 S s75(2) LGFA 1992
3 **EW** s2(2)(c) LGFA 1992
 S s71(2)(c) LGFA 1992
4 **EW** s6(6) LGFA 1992
5 **EW** s6(5) LGFA 1992
6 **S** s75(5) LGFA 1992
7 **EW** ss6-7 LGFA 1992
8 **EW** ss6-7 LGFA 1992

2. Who is a resident
9 **EW** s6(5) LGFA 1992
 S s99(1) LGFA 1992
10 *Bradford City Council v Anderton* [1991] RA 45
11 *Ward v Kingston Upon Hull City Council* [1992] RA 71
12 *R (Williams) v Horsham District Council* [2004] EWCA Civ 39, *The Times*, 29 January 2004

13 *Parry v Derbyshire Dales District Council* [2006] RA 25
14 *Highland Council v Highland and Western Isles Region Valuation Committee* [2008] RA 311 Sc

3. When the owner is always liable
15 **EW** s8(1) LGFA 1992
 S s76(1) LGFA 1992
16 *Soor and another v Mayor & Burgesses of the London Borough of Redbridge* [2013] EWHC 1239 (Admin)
17 **E** CT(LO)(A)(E) Regs
 W CT(LO)(A)(W) Regs
18 **EW** CT(LO) Regs
 S CT(LO)(S) Regs
19 **EW** CT(LO) Regs
 S CT(LO)(S) Regs
20 **EW** CT(LO) Regs
21 *Baker (Listing Officer) v Gomperts* [2006] All ER (D) 01 (Jul)
22 *Norris and Norris v Birmingham City Council* [2001] RVR 89

23 *R (on the application of Goremsandu) v Harrow London Borough Council* [2010] EWHC 1873 (Admin)
24 *Watts v Preston City Council* [2009] EWHC 2179 (Admin)
25 *Walsh v Lonsdale* [1882] 21 ChD 9; *Soor v Mayor Burgesses of the Borough of Redbridge* [2013] EWHC 1239 (Admin)
26 *O'Shaughnessy v London Borough of Hackney* [2013] VTE 13 and 20 January 2012 App No.5360M70010/052C/1
27 *Dundee City Council v Dundee Valuation Appeal Committee and another* [2011] CSIH 73
28 **EW** CT(LO) Regs
   S CT(LO)(S) Regs
29 **EW** CT(LO) Regs
   S CT(LO)(S) Regs
30 **S** CT(LO)(S) Regs
31 *R v Hackney LBC ex parte Adebiri and other appeals* [1997] *The Times*, 4 November 1997
   EW Reg 2 CT(LO) Regs
   S CT(LO)(S) Regs

4. Joint liability
32 **EW** s6(3)-(4) LGFA 1992, as amended by s74 LGA 2003
   S s75(3)-(4) LGFA 1992
33 **EW** s9 LGFA 1992
   S s77 LGFA 1992
34 **E** Reg 4 CTRS(PR)(E) Regs
35 **E** Reg 4(2) CTRS(PR)(E) Regs
36 **W** Reg 5 CTRSPR(W) Regs
37 **S** Reg 2 CTR(S) Regs
38 *Wainwright v The Home Office* [2003] UKHL 53; European Court of Human Rights [2006] Application no.12350/04, 26 September 2006
39 para 20 Practice Note No.2
40 **EW** Reg 28 CT(AE) Regs 1992
41 **EW** ss6(4) and 9(2) LGFA 1992
   S ss75(4) and 77(2) LGFA 1992
42 **EW** CT(ED)O

5. Change of circumstances
43 **EW** s2 LGFA 1992
   S s71 LGFA 1992

6. Backdating liability
44 **E** Reg 8(1)(c) CTRS(DFE)(E) Regs
   W Reg 10 CTRS(DFE)(W) Regs
45 *Hammersmith and Fulham Billing Authority v Butler* [2001] RVR 197

7. How the liable person is identified
46 **EW** Reg 6 CT(AE) Regs 1992
   S Reg 5 CT(AE)(S) Regs

47 **EW** Regs 3 and 12 CT(AE) Regs 1992
   S Reg 2 CT(AE)(S) Regs
48 **E** Reg 4 CTRS(DFE)(E) Regs
   W Reg 4 CTRS(DFE)(W) Regs
49 **E** Reg 6 CTRS(DFE)(E) Regs
   W Reg 6 CTRS(DFE)(W) Regs
50 **E** Reg 9 CTRS(DFE)(E) Regs
   W Reg 11 CTRS(DFE)(W) Regs
51 **EW** Reg 3 CT(AE) Regs
   S Council Tax (Administration and Enforcement) (Scotland) Amendment Regulations 2012 No.338
52 Sch 2 para 15A(1)-(4) LGFA 1992
53 **EW** s14(2) and Sch 3 LGFA 1992
   S s97(4) and Sch 3 LGFA 1992
54 **EW** s14(2) and Sch 3 LGFA 1992
   S s97(4) and Sch 3 LGFA 1992
55 **EW** s14(2) and Sch 3 LGFA 1992
   S s97(4) and Sch 3 LGFA 1992
56 s13A LGFA1992 substituted s10 of the LGFA 2012
57 ss14A to 14C LGFA 1992 Act inserted by s14 LGFA 2012 Act
58 **E** Regs 4 and 5 CTRS(DFE)(E) Regs
   W Reg 5 CTRS(DFE)(W) Regs
59 **E** Reg 6 CTRS(DFE)(E) Regs
   W Reg 6 CTRS(DFE)(W) Regs
60 **E** Regs 4, 5 and 6 CTRS(DFE)(E) Regs
   W Reg 6(1)(b) CTRS(DFE)(W) Regs
61 **E** Reg 7 CTRS(DFE)(E) Regs
   W Reg 9(1) CTRS(DFE)(W) Regs
62 **E** Reg 10 CTRS(DFE)(E) Regs
   W Reg 12 CTRS(DFE)(W) Regs
63 **E** Reg 11 CTRS(DFE)(E) Regs
   W Reg 13 CTRS(DFE)(W) Regs
64 **E** Reg 11 (1) CTRS(DFE)(E) Regs
   W Reg 13 CTRS(DFE)(W) Regs
65 **E** Reg 11(4) CTRS(DFE)(E) Regs
   W Reg 13(2) CTRS(DFE)(W) Regs
66 **E** Reg 11(2) and (6) CTRS(DFE)(E) Regs
   W Reg 13(2) CTRS(DFE)(W) Regs; *Associated Provincial Picture Houses v Wednesbury Corporation* [1948] 1 KB 223
67 **E** Reg 11(7) CTRS(DFE)(E) Regs
   W Reg 13(7) CTRS(DFE)(W) Regs
68 **E** Reg 11(8) CTRS(DFE)(E) Regs
   W Reg 13 CTRS(DFE)(W) Regs
69 **E** Reg 9 CTRS(DFE)(E) Regs
   W Reg 13(7) CTRS(DFE)(W) Regs
70 **E** Reg 10 CTRS(DFE)(E) Regs
   W Reg 13(9) CTRS(DFE)(W) Regs
71 Regs 3 and 11 CTRS(DFE)(E) Regs
   W Reg 15 CTRS(DFE)(W) Regs
72 **EW** s14(2) and Sch 3 LGFA 1992
   S s97(4) and Sch 3 LGFA 1992

6

8. Appeals
73 **EW** s16 LGFA 1992
   S s81 LGFA 1992
74 **EW** s16 LGFA 1992
   S s81 LGFA 1992
75 **EW** s16 LGFA 1992
   S s81 LGFA 1992
76 **E** Reg 21(6) VTE(CTRA)(P) Regs
   W Reg 29(5) VTW Regs
77 *R v Ealing Justices ex parte Coatsworth*
   [1980] 126, *Solicitors Journal 128*
78 Reg 38(7A) VTE(CTRA)(P) Regs

Chapter 7

Disability reduction

This chapter covers:

1. What is a disability reduction

Disability reduction schemes apply in England and Wales,[1] and in Scotland.[2] The basic amount of the council tax and, in Scotland, Scottish Water charges,[3] may be reduced if:
- a disabled person lives in the dwelling; *and*
- the dwelling has certain features that are essential, or of major importance, to the disabled person because of her/his disability; *or*
- the disabled person uses a wheelchair in the home.

A reduction can be made on residential care or nursing homes as well as on any other dwelling.

In addition to the disability reduction scheme, the value of fixtures (such as a lift or specially designed kitchen units) designed to make the dwelling suitable for use by a physically disabled person should have been ignored in the valuation of the dwelling if they added to its value. See p27 for more details. If fixtures designed to make the dwelling suitable for use by a physically disabled person reduce the value of the dwelling, they should have been taken into account in the valuation process and, therefore, be reflected in the dwelling's banding.[4]

It is important not to overlook the effect of any entitlement to a reduction in banding in any calculation or claim for a council tax reduction under the local authority's own support scheme (see Chapter 9) or in any issue of disputes over monies owed in enforcement, whether by way of bankruptcy or committal to prison. Because it is possible to backdate an award of a disability reduction for up to six years (see p100), the amount that you may be owed by the local authority can be substantial.

---

2. **When a disability reduction can be made**

The person with a disability

For a reduction to be awarded, the dwelling must be the 'sole or main residence' (see p77) of at least one person with a disability. No additional reduction is made if more than one disabled person lives in the dwelling.

To count as disabled for the purpose of the reduction, a person must be 'substantially and permanently disabled', whether by illness, injury, congenital disorder or otherwise. This means that someone with a learning difficulty or a mental health problem may qualify, as well as someone with a physical disability. The disabled person may be an adult or a child. S/he need not be the person liable to pay council tax on the dwelling.

Social services departments in England and Wales and social work departments in Scotland have a duty to maintain a register of, and provide various services to, people in their area who are substantially and permanently disabled. They have considerably more skills and experience in making assessments of disability than their counterparts in council tax administration. If a person is on the disabled person's register, this should be sufficient to satisfy the criteria of 'substantially and permanently disabled' for the purposes of a disability reduction. However, if someone is not included on the register, this does not necessarily mean s/he is not 'substantially and permanently disabled' as registers are not comprehensive and registering as disabled is not compulsory.

The dwelling

The dwelling must have at least one of the following features:
- a room, but not a sole bathroom, a kitchen or a lavatory, which is predominantly used by the disabled person – eg, a room used for dialysis equipment; *or*
- an additional bathroom or kitchen within the dwelling which is necessary to meet the needs of the disabled person; *or*
- sufficient floor space to permit the use of a wheelchair.

To qualify, the feature must be essential, or of major importance, to the disabled person's wellbeing because of the nature of her/his disability.

Practice Note No.2 (para 40) advises local authorities that, when deciding whether these conditions apply, they should consider whether, if the room or feature were not available:

- the disabled person would find it physically impossible or extremely difficult to live in the dwelling; *or*
- her/his health would suffer or her/his disability would worsen.

Note, however, that this is guidance only and is not contained in the legislation. The High Court has ruled that there must be an appropriate causative link between the disability in question and the need to use the room. Relevant factors to be considered include the nature and extent of the person's disability and whether the use of the room is essential or of major importance to her/him.[5]

A sole bathroom or kitchen, even if specially adapted, is not sufficient to qualify. Additionally, a wheelchair is not considered to be required for meeting the disabled person's needs if s/he does not need to use it in the living accommodation in the dwelling.

Three High Court cases during 2006 clarified the law on rooms attracting a reduction and the meaning of 'major importance'. These were *South Gloucestershire Council v Titley and another [Clothier]*[6] and *Hanson v Middlesborough Council*.[7]

In the case of *Titley*, the taxpayer was a profoundly deaf man living alone in a two-bedroom house. His living room was fitted with a hearing loop box enabling him to hear the television and to communicate with visitors. In the case of *Clothier*, there were two bedrooms occupied by two adults with Down's syndrome who were being looked after by their parents. Both bedrooms were used for therapy and periods of relaxation, which enabled the adult children to cope with their condition. The High Court ruled that a disabled reduction should not be awarded in either case. The Court held that it was necessary to consider whether a room was specifically required for meeting the needs of a disabled person.

The Court stressed that having a disabled resident in a property was not enough. To attract the reduction, the dwelling must have a room that would not be required if the disabled person were not present.

In both these cases, the rooms were not considered additional, since they would be essential or of major importance to almost any household. In the case of *Titley*, the taxpayer would have been using the living room if he were not deaf. Similarly, in *Clothier*, the rooms were not additional; the two adult children would still have required a bedroom if they did not have Down's syndrome.

However, in the *Hanson* case, the appellant succeeded. She was a disabled woman, registered as partially sighted. She had a bedroom converted into an en-suite bathroom in 1996, a few months after she moved into the property, and 19 months before she was registered as blind. In 2004, she became aware of the right to a disability reduction for council tax but was refused. This decision was upheld by Teeside Valuation Tribunal, which rejected her appeal on the basis that the bathroom was not essential to her needs.

The High Court, however, upheld her appeal, concluding that the adaptation was of *major importance* to her because of her disability, as it reduced the risk of tripping or slipping.

The above cases, therefore, confirm that, to obtain a disability reduction, the room used or adapted for a disabled person must be:

- extra or additional to what a person would ordinarily need, whether disabled or not;
- essential or of major importance to the welfare of the disabled person.

3. **Obtaining a reduction**

Who can obtain a reduction

The person liable to pay council tax on the dwelling is entitled to the disability reduction. S/he may be solely liable or jointly liable. If there is joint liability, an application made by one of the liable people is treated as having been made on behalf of both of them. None of the liable people need have a disability.

The local authority may also award a disability reduction to someone who will become liable for council tax on the dwelling – eg, following work on it to meet the needs of a disabled person.

Applications

The local authority cannot award a reduction without a written application for each financial year (April to March) from the liable person or someone acting on her/his behalf. If you are applying on behalf of someone, the local authority normally requires written authorisation or a copy of a power of attorney. There is no prescribed form, but most local authorities have a standard application form. An annex to Practice Note No.2 contains an example form that local authorities may use.

Backdating and repeat applications

The fact that a written application must be made for each financial year does not prevent you from making an application for previous years – ie, backdated to when the qualifying conditions were met. The year(s) in question should be identified on the application. Following the decision in *Arca v Carlisle City Council*,[8] a disability reduction can be backdated for up to six years from the date of making an application. In this case, the tribunal ruled that a taxpayer who applied for a reduction on 3 November 2011 was entitled to a disability reduction dating back to 2 November 2005, six years before the written application was made. The President of the Valuation Tribunal for England Professor Graham Zellick QC held that an application was permissible as a proceeding within the Limitation Act 1980 which places a six year time limit upon civil law claims. While this is a decision of the Valuation Tribunal for England and not of the High Court, Professor Zellick stated that 'until the matter is settled by a higher court...billing authorities would be well advised not only to regard this decision as representing a correct statement of the law but also as the interpretation almost certainly to be applied by this tribunal in any future appeal raising the same issue unless fresh arguments can be made.'[9]

Once a written application has been made, a repeat application is required each financial year. Local authorities should ideally send people receiving the reduction a repeat application form and a reminder at the appropriate time each year, but they are not required to do so. Practice Note No.2 (para 52) suggests that local authorities should not generally require a full application in a second or subsequent year. It will often be sufficient to seek the liable person's confirmation that the circumstances have not changed since the original application.

Information required by the local authority

When considering whether or not the reduction applies, an English or Welsh local authority may make a written request for information it reasonably requires at any time and to anyone. It may also require you to respond within a specified period, but must give you at least 21 days to answer. The local authority may require a supporting letter from a doctor, occupational therapist or social worker, confirming that the disabled person needs the particular qualifying feature of the dwelling because of her/his disability. There is no statutory requirement to seek such letters, however, and local authorities should consider on a case-by-case basis whether verification is necessary. The majority of local authorities also send an officer to visit the dwelling and interview residents or carers.

4. How the reduction is made

If a disability reduction is awarded, the liable person's council tax bill is reduced to that of a dwelling in the valuation band immediately below the band to which the dwelling has been allocated on the valuation list.

The reduction applies for each day that the qualifying conditions are met.

Since 1 April 2000, the amount payable on a dwelling that qualifies for a disability reduction in Band A is reduced by the same proportion of the bill as dwellings in valuation Bands B, C and D, being equivalent to one-ninth of Band D. No reduction is available for dwellings in Band A between 1 April 1993 and 31 March 2000.

Example

Harry's dwelling is shown as being in Band C on the valuation list. Following the award of a disability reduction, the bill that must be paid should be the same as that of someone liable for the tax on a Band B dwelling.

The disability reduction does not alter the actual valuation of the dwelling or its banding on the valuation list. Harry's bill should show both the dwelling's actual band and the reduction.

In Wales, if a dwelling qualifies for transitional relief, the banding reduction for disability is applied after this is taken into consideration – ie, it lowers the transitional band for the years when relief was available by a further band.

The effect of the reduction on other forms of help

Someone entitled to a disability reduction may also be entitled to a discount or council tax reduction (CTR). These other forms of help are calculated on the basis of the council tax liability after the disability reduction has been made. Consequently, the retrospective award of a disability reduction may mean that there has been an overpayment of CTR or the former council tax benefit – seek advice if this applies to you.

5. Change of circumstances

If there is a change in circumstances (eg, if the disabled person moves to alternative accommodation), the liable person may no longer be entitled to a disability reduction. If the liable person believes that s/he has ceased to be eligible for the reduction, s/he must notify the local authority. This obligation extends to all those who are jointly liable for the tax on the dwelling in question.

6. Appeals

If the local authority refuses to award a disability reduction, an appeal can be made in writing to the local authority.[10] An appeal can be made if you are liable to pay the tax or if you are the owner of the property (if different). The appeal letter should give the reasons why you believe the local authority has come to the wrong decision. The local authority has two months in which to answer.[11] If no disability reduction is awarded, or if the local authority fails to answer within two months of receipt of the appeal, a further appeal can be made to the Valuation Tribunal for England, the Valuation Tribunal for Wales or the valuation appeal committee in Scotland. See Chapter 12 for further information about appeals.[12] The local authority may enforce payment of the original bill while the appeal is outstanding (see Chapter 11), but it may agree to a suspension until the matter is resolved. Alternatively, the magistrates' court (sheriff court in Scotland) may agree to an adjournment of any proceedings which may be issued if an agreement to suspend recovery is not reached.

In **England and Wales**, a further appeal can be made by writing to the Valuation Tribunal for England or directly to Valuation Tribunal of Wales. The appeal should normally be made within two months of the date the local authority notified you of its decision, or within four months of the date when the initial representation was made, if the local authority has not responded. The president of the tribunal has the power to allow an out-of-time appeal if you have failed to meet the appropriate time limits for reasons beyond your control.[13]

In **Scotland**, a further appeal can be made by writing again to the local authority. The local authority should pass the appeal to the secretary of the relevant local valuation appeal committee. The appeal must be made within four months of the date on which the grievance was first raised with the local authority in writing. There is no power to consider an out-of-time appeal, so you must make a fresh appeal to the local authority to begin the process again. However, if you fail to appear at a hearing, so that the appeal is dismissed, you can make representations to allow another appeal hearing. You have 14 days from being notified of the dismissal to apply in writing to request another hearing, and the appeal committee has a discretion to allow a longer period. If the appeal committee is satisfied that there was a reasonable excuse for your absence it can recall the decision and fix a date for a further hearing.[14]

Notes

1. What is a disability reduction
1 **EW** s13 LGFA 1992; CT(RD) Regs and CT(RDTA)(W)(A) Regs
2 **S** s80(1)-(4) and (6)-(7) LGFA 1992; CT(RD)(S) Regs
3 **S** CT(RD)(S) Regs
4 **EW** Reg 6 CT(SVD) Regs
  S Reg 2 CT(VD)(S) Regs

2. When a disability reduction can be made
5 *Sandwell Metropolitan District Council v Perks* [2003] RVR 317 Admin 1749 (HC)
6 *South Gloucestershire Council v Titley and another* [2006] EWHC 3117 (Admin)
7 *Hanson v Middlesborough Council* [2006] RA 320 (HC)

3. Obtaining a reduction
8 *Arca v Carlisle City Council* [2013] RA 248
9 *Arca v Carlisle City Council* [2013] RA 248; VTE 29 January and 20 March 2013, per Graham Zellick QC, President.

6. Appeals
10 **EW** s16 LGFA 1992
  S s81 LGFA 1992
11 **EW** s16 LGFA 1992
  S s81 LGFA 1992
12 **EW** s16 LGFA 1992
  S s81 LGFA 1992
13 **E** Reg 21(6) VTE(CTRA)(P) Regs
  W Reg 29(5)VTW Regs
14 Reg 31 ALA(S) Regs; reg 15 Valuation Appeal Committee (Procedure in Appeals under the Valuation Acts) (Scotland) Regulations 1995 SSI 41

Chapter 8

. . . .

Discounts

This chapter covers:
1. When a discount is granted (below)
2. Who is ignored for discount purposes (p105)
3. Who is disregarded for discount purposes (p106)
4. Obtaining a discount (p120)
5. Reduced discounts and increases for long-term empty dwellings and second homes (p121)
6. Miscellaneous discounts (p124)
7. Appeals (p125)

---

1. **When a discount is granted**

As originally designed, the council tax scheme had a system of nationally available discounts, available for certain categories of taxpayer and in respect of certain dwellings.

The council tax (and Scottish Water charges in Scotland) payable on a dwelling is initially based on the assumption that there are at least two adults living in it. The bill does not increase if there are more than two, but should be reduced by:

- 25 per cent if there is only one person solely or mainly resident in the dwelling; *or*
- up to 50 per cent in England and Scotland if no one is solely or mainly resident. This is also normally the case in Wales, but special rules apply in some cases (see p124).

Certain people, however, are ignored or 'discounted' by local authorities when deciding how many people are solely or mainly resident in the dwelling. Effectively, they are not counted as living in the dwelling for council tax purposes when calculating the bill.

For the purpose of deciding whether the council tax is subject to a discount for any day, the state of affairs at the end of the day is assumed to have existed throughout that day.[1]

Discounts can apply to empty dwellings or second homes.

From 1 April 2013, local authorities can change the levels of discount awarded to empty properties, including removing discounts entirely. In many areas, empty properties no longer receive a 50 per cent discount as local authorities may reduce it to zero, and even increase the tax payable on an empty dwelling. For example, Waveney District Council has determined that unoccupied and unfurnished properties (previously exempt under the former Class C) receive a discount of 25 per cent for up to three months and then are to be charged 100 per cent, and properties that are unoccupied, unfurnished and undergoing major repairs (old Class A) receive a discount of 25 per cent for up to 12 months.

Certain empty dwellings are exempt from the tax. See Chapter 5 for more information. A discount may follow at the end of an exemption.

From 1 April 2013, a local authority in England may determine that discounts do not apply in its area, or in part of its area, for any day a dwelling is classed as a long-term empty dwelling.[2]

Discounts and other forms of help

You can be granted a discount in addition to any disability reduction, transitional relief or council tax reduction (CTR) payment. The discount is applied to the tax after granting a disability reduction, but before calculating main CTR. Second adult rebate is worked out on the basis of the council tax liability, ignoring any discount that has been granted. See Chapter 9 for more details on CTR schemes.

2. **Who is ignored for discount purposes**

Only adults solely or mainly resident in the dwelling count for the purpose of working out whether or not a discount applies. Consequently, people under 18 and those solely or mainly resident elsewhere are ignored.[3]

Example
Petra and her 15-year-old daughter live in a property. Thus, there is only one person aged 18 or over residing in the dwelling. A 25 per cent discount is granted.
Petra's friend comes to stay with her but keeps a home elsewhere. If it is decided that the friend is mainly resident elsewhere, the discount should continue. If it is decided that the friend is mainly resident in Petra's house, the discount no longer applies from the day she moved in.

---

3. **Who is disregarded for discount purposes**

In addition to those who are ignored for the purposes of a discount (see p105), certain categories of people are disregarded.[4] They are sometimes described as 'having a status discount', or more simply as 'invisible'. They are:

- people aged 18 for whom child benefit is payable (see p107);
- recent school and college leavers who are under 20 (see p107);
- students under the age of 20 studying up to A level, Scottish Higher National Certificate or equivalent (see p108);
- full-time students attending a college or university (see p108);
- foreign language assistants (see p108);
- student nurses (see p108);
- a person who has diplomatic, Commonwealth or consular privilege or immunity;
- spouses or dependants of foreign students (see p108);
- apprentices (see p114);
- youth trainees (see p114);
- people in prison and other forms of detention (see p115);
- people who are severely mentally impaired (see p115);
- certain carers (see p116);
- hospital patients (see p117);
- people in care homes and hostels providing a high level of care (see p118);
- members of international headquarters and defence organisations and their dependants (see p119);
- members of visiting forces (see p119);
- members of religious communities (see p119);
- in England and Wales, residents in certain hostels and night shelters and other accommodation for those with no fixed abode (see p119).

Personal status discounts and tax bills

If you are disregarded for the purpose of a discount, it does not necessarily mean that the tax bill is reduced. A discount is only awarded if there are fewer than two adults in the dwelling, not counting any who are disregarded. A liable person may be disregarded for the purpose of a discount, but is still liable for the council tax. The exceptions to this last rule concern liable people who are either considered to be severely mentally impaired or students. See Chapter 6 for more details.

Examples

Two adult women are joint owner-occupiers. One is a full-time student and disregarded for the purpose of a discount. The other is in full-time work and is not disregarded. As there are only two residents and one of them is disregarded, a 25 per cent discount should be granted. Although they are both joint resident owners, the student is not jointly liable for the reduced amount of council tax with the one in full-time work.

A couple in their fifties are joint owner-occupiers of a house. Their daughter lives with them. She is aged 20 and a full-time student. Their son, aged 17, also lives with them. He is in full-time work. The daughter, as a full-time student, is disregarded for discount purposes and the son, as someone under 18, is ignored. Nevertheless, no discount is awarded because two adults (the joint owner-occupiers) live in the house and are not ignored or discounted.

A pensioner couple are liable joint tenants. No one else lives with them. One of the couple has Alzheimer's disease and receives the care component of disability living allowance. He is considered to be severely mentally impaired. In these circumstances, a 25 per cent status discount is awarded because there are only two people solely or mainly resident in the dwelling and one of them is disregarded for discount purposes. In this instance, only the joint tenant who is not severely mentally impaired is liable for the tax.

An adult carer, introduced by a charity, comes to live with the above couple. The couple provides free accommodation plus £50 a week to the carer. In these circumstances, the couple lose their discount as there are now two adults living in the dwelling who are not disregarded for discount purposes. If the carer had received £44 a week or less, however, the discount would have continued, as there would still have been only one adult living in the dwelling who was not disregarded.

18-year-olds for whom child benefit is payable

You are in this category if you are aged 18 and someone is entitled to child benefit for you, or would be if you were not in local authority care.[5]

The conditions of entitlement to child benefit are described in CPAG's *Welfare Benefits and Tax Credits Handbook*. A child ceases to qualify for child benefit the week after turning 19 or on the Sunday after the first of the following dates after leaving school or college:

- first Monday in January;
- first Monday after Easter Monday;
- first Monday in September.

School and college leavers

If you are under the age of 20, and have left school or college on or after 1 May in any year after undertaking a qualifying course of education (ie, one no higher than A level, Scottish Higher National Certificate or equivalent) or additionally, in England and Wales, full-time education (see p108), you should be disregarded for the purpose of working out a discount between 1 May and 31 October in the same year.[6] You continue to be disregarded if you go on to some other form of further or higher education.

Students

You are disregarded for discount purposes if you are a student.[7] Dwellings occupied only by students are exempt (see p62).

You count as a **'student'** if you are:[8]
- under 20 and on a 'qualifying course' (see below); *or*
- a full-time student (see below); *or*
- a foreign language assistant.

Students under 20 on a qualifying course

A student must be undertaking a qualifying course of education.[9] You are undertaking such a course on a particular day if:[10]
- you are under the age of 20; *and*
- you are studying for more than three months and for at least 12 hours a week (excluding vacations) for any qualification up to A level or Scottish Higher National Certificate, or equivalent. If two or more courses are being taken at the same establishment, the combined number of weekly hours must exceed 12; *and*
- it is not undertaken as a result of your office or employment; *and*
- tuition, supervised exercises, experiments, project or practical work are normally carried out between 8am and 5.30pm.

You are treated as undertaking a qualifying course throughout both term time and vacations from the date the course begins to the date you complete, abandon or are dismissed from it. You are no longer considered to be undertaking such a course if you become an apprentice or a youth trainee.[11]

Full-time students

To be treated as a full-time student, you must be enrolled on a course with a 'prescribed educational establishment' (see p110) and undertaking a full-time course of education. In Scotland, the course must be a 'specified course' (see p111).[12]

In **England or Wales** a full-time course is one that is for at least 24 weeks in a calendar or academic year, and which normally requires you to undertake periods of study, tuition or work experience (either at the institution's premises or elsewhere) amounting to an average of 21 hours a week over the year. **Note:** from 13 May 2011, you do not need to *attend* a college for at least 21 hours a week, but only to be *undertaking* a course which requires at least 21 hours a week of study, tuition or work experience. Therefore, hours spent studying and working at home or with an employer on a work placement should count towards the definition of being a full-time student, provided you are undertaking activities which form part of the course.

In **Scotland**, the specified course must be for least 24 weeks a year, involving at least 21 hours of study a week during term time.

A course does not count as full time if the combined periods of work experience normally required to be undertaken as part of it exceed the combined periods of study or tuition. This does not apply in the case of a course for the initial training of teachers in schools.[13]

You are treated as undertaking work experience if, as part of the curriculum of the course, you are at:[14]

- your workplace providing services under a contract of employment; *or*
- a place where a trade, business, profession or other occupation which is relevant to the subject matter of the course is carried out in order to gain experience of that trade.

For the purpose of working out the number of weeks of attendance in the year, the following rules apply.

If the course starts at the beginning of an academic year:

- the first calendar year of the course is treated as beginning on the day on which the course begins; *and*
- subsequent calendar years (if any) are treated as beginning on the anniversary of that day.

If the course begins part-way through an academic year:

- the academic year is treated as beginning at the start of the term in which the course begins; *and*
- subsequent academic years (if any) are treated as beginning at the start of the equivalent terms in those years.

The final part of a course which lasts (or is treated as lasting) for other than a number of complete academic or calendar years is disregarded.[15]

You are treated as a full-time student from the date the course begins to the date you complete, abandon or are dismissed from it.

There has been relatively little caselaw from the higher courts on what constitutes a qualifying course for the purposes of student status under council tax legislation but decisions have been made at tribunal level on points concerning student status and treatment for taxation purposes. A number of these decisions are available at www.valuationtribunal.gov.uk.

In *Birmingham City Council v Birmingham VCCT and Adamson*,[16] the High Court considered that the phrase 'normally required to undertake' was a common sense expression and:

'... that as far as the amount of study or tuition is concerned, the timetable will provide the *prima facie* structure against which one justifies whatever conclusion one reaches, supplemented by whatever evidence may be put before the tribunal which establishes that which can properly be considered as the normal expectation of those undertaking the course on the one hand and those providing the course on the other, as to what over and above that which is timetabled should be considered as the requirement of the course for the purpose of its being successfully completed.'

This judgment suggests that a limited amount of extra study outside the full-hours timetable may be taken into account when assessing whether the course constitutes 21 hours or more. The question of whether a course is full-time is a question of fact, with the emphasis being upon whether the 21 hours are a 'requirement' rather than simply a 'recommendation'. If only a recommendation a discount may not be available.[17]

However, it is clear that the High Court expects tribunals to scrutinise such claims and distinguish between how many weeks a student is actually required to attend a place of study and not simply consider how long a course lasts in calendar terms.[18] The 'common sense' approach would also suggest that a student who has special arrangements for her/his course because of illness, disability or childcare arrangements will also come within the definition of a full-time student 'normally required to undertake' the prescribed hours and periods.

Educational establishment

Before 13 May 2011, a 'prescribed educational establishment' included:
- a university (including a constituent college, school or other institution of a university);
- a college or institution providing courses of further or higher education;
- a theological college;
- an institution accredited by the Teacher Training Agency or the Higher Education Funding Council for Wales under regulations in force under s218(2) and (2A) Education Reform Act 1988 – ie, a teacher training college;[19]
- an institution of a research council established by Royal Charter under s1 Science and Technology Act 1965;
- a nursing and midwifery college or a college established under s8 National Health Service Act 1977, or a college of health established by a health board or a regional or district health authority.

From **13 May 2011**, you are treated as a full-time student if you are undertaking a course rather than physically attending a specific institution on the list. A **'prescribed educational establishment'** may be anywhere in the European Union (EU), provided it is solely or mainly for the purpose of providing further or higher education. For this purpose, **'further education'** means:

- any course of education (other than a course of higher education) which is suitable for people over the compulsory school-leaving age in the EU state in which the establishment is situated; *and*
- any organised leisure-time occupation provided in connection with such a course.

'**Higher education**' means any course of education leading to a first degree, a higher degree or a qualification (including a professional qualification) which is regarded by the relevant EU state as equivalent to a first degree or higher degree.

In determining whether a college in an EU state qualifies, local authorities typically refer to the Erasmus Charter – a list of over 4,000 establishments in Europe providing courses which may qualify.[20]

Nursing and midwifery students and those on pre-registration undergraduate courses and undertaking post-registration health visitor training count as students.[21] For discount purposes, a student nurse means a person undertaking a course which, if successfully completed, would lead to a first registration under the Nurses, Midwives and Health Visitors Act 1997.[22]

Student nurses undertaking 'traditional' hospital-based training do not count as students.

Note: a Ministry of Defence training establishment for the armed forces does not count as an educational establishment for discount purposes.[23]

Specified courses in Scotland

The following are 'specified courses' in Scotland:[24]
- a course at undergraduate level leading to a degree, certificate, diploma or licentiateship from a university or theological college, or a degree, certificate or diploma granted by a designated institution, a central institution or any other institution for the provision of any form of further education;
- a course in further education leading to an award of the Scottish National Certificate, the General Certificate of Education, the General Certificate of Secondary Education or the Scottish Baccalaureate;
- a course in further education leading to the National Certificate, the Higher National Certificate or Higher National Diploma of the Scottish Qualifications Authority, or a Scottish Vocational Qualification, or any other course in further education leading to a comparable award;
- a course in further education required by an educational establishment to be undertaken before any other specified course being undertaken;
- a course at undergraduate or postgraduate level for the initial training of teachers, social workers or youth and community workers;
- a course at postgraduate level leading to a certificate or diploma in professional studies or to any other comparable award;
- a course leading to the award of the degree of Doctor of Philosophy, a Master's degree or any other comparable award.

Overlapping courses

With the diverse ways which courses may now be delivered, situations can arise which do not fit into the precise parameters laid down by the regulations. It may be necessary to look in some detail at provisions for study and the relevant periods in which you are required to undertake study or qualifying work and activities. Regard may also be given to statements issued by the Department for Communities and Local Government and its predecessors.

Students undertaking condensed courses that do not fall under the qualifying periods, may not be deemed to satisfy the definition. In the High Court decision in *Merseyside Valuation Tribunal and Wirral Borough Council v Farthing* [2008], a student undertook a course condensed from a one-year course running between October and June to one which commenced in January and finished in June. Because the course did not last either an academic year or a calendar year, it was held to fall outside the qualifying periods. The fact that the student undertook double the number of hours within the condensed period did not alter the position. The Court took the view that had Parliament intended a different period for the purposes of discount and exemption, it would have stated this.

Students on condensed courses may therefore not be 'students' for council tax purposes.

However, a decision of the Valuation Tribunal for England (VTE)[25] shows that in some cases it may be possible for periods of study on different, overlapping courses to be sufficient to qualify as a student for council tax purposes.

The student was enrolled with the Open University, undertaking two part-time and overlapping courses during part of the financial year in question. The first course began on October 2010 and finished in June 2011. The second course commenced on 5 February 2011 and finished on 31 October 2011. Each course involved approximately 16 hours of study each week, delivered by distance learning. A student certificate was obtained from the Open University confirming the details of the courses.

It was argued for the student that both courses required studying a minimum of more than 21 hours a week and that the certificate she sent in established that she was studying 32 hours a week over nine months of the year. The Open University definition of a full time student was 'a student studying 120 credits working the minimum required 32 hours per week over nine months in the year'.

In further support of the appeal, the student produced a statement issued by the then Department of the Environment on 13 September 1997 which states that there is '... no reason why a student on an [Open University] course should not receive a discount' and that following the decision in *R(Feller) v Cambridge City Council*[26] it was no longer essential to physically attend college while writing up a thesis.

The VTE accepted that the two courses, when taken together, exceeded 24 weeks in each academic or calendar year with an average of at least 21 hours a week in attendance. As a result the tribunal allowed the appeal for a full-time student disregard for the period 5 February 2011 to 30 June 2011.

While this is a decision only at tribunal level, it may nonetheless indicate that overlapping courses can qualify for an exemption for periods during a year of study.

Postgraduate students

Before 2011 it was often difficult for a student pursuing a postgraduate course to obtain a discount or an exemption from council tax. This was a particular problem for students who were writing their thesis away from the college to which they were attached. However, this position has now been clarified by the decision in *Feller v Cambridge City Council*.[27] Thus, many PhD students and others (eg, students permitted to work from home, perhaps with childcare responsibilities) are no longer liable for council tax. It is also possible to appeal the question of liability for previous years (see Chapter 12).

Evidence of student status

When considering whether you can be disregarded as a student, the local authority may ask for a student certificate. Except in the case of foreign language assistants and institutions outside England, Wales or Scotland, educational institutions are required to provide certificates when requested to do so by a student or student nurse.[28] Certificates need not be supplied, however, if you stopped following a course at that institution more than a year previously. The former Office of the Deputy Prime Minister issued an advice note, reproduced as Annex E in Practice Note No.2, advising authorities that educational institutions are required, if requested, to provide students and student nurses with certificates, which they may use as evidence of entitlement to student discounts. While it is for authorities to decide what evidence they need, they must act reasonably and a student or a former student has a right of appeal to a tribunal if the evidence is not accepted (see Chapter 12).

The certificate should include the following information:[29]

- the educational establishment's name and address;
- your full name;
- your date of birth, if this is known to the establishment and if you are, or was, under 20 and studying a course no higher than A level or equivalent;
- a statement certifying that you are following, or have followed, a course of education as a student or student nurse;
- the date you became a student or a student nurse at the establishment and the date when your course came, or is expected to come, to an end;
- in Scotland, your home address if different to your term-time one.

If a local authority refuses to accept the evidence offered, the student should submit a sworn witness statement as evidence and any other supporting evidence.

Spouses of foreign students

A foreign student's spouse or dependant who is prevented from working or claiming benefit must be disregarded for discount purposes or may be exempt.[30] To qualify, the spouse/dependant must not be a British citizen and must be 'prevented by the terms of her/his leave to enter or remain in the UK from taking paid employment or from claiming benefits.'

The decision in *Harrow London Borough Council v Ayiku*[31] clarified that the non-British spouse of a student under the 1992 Order was a 'relevant person' exempt from liability to pay council tax, as a student's spouse/dependent, being in either case a person who was not a British citizen and who was prevented, by the terms of her/his leave to enter or remain in the UK, from taking paid employment or from claiming benefits.

A student's spouse who has limited leave to enter the UK is prevented, as a condition of her/his leave to remain in the UK, from claiming benefits or local council tax support (see Chapter 9).

The High Court ruled that the word 'or' in the relevant phrase in Class N had a disjunctive meaning, and that it is sufficient for the non-British spouse of a student to satisfy one or other of the two conditions (either being prevented from taking paid employment or prevented from claiming benefits) so as to qualify under Class N as a relevant person.

Apprentices

An apprentice is someone:
- employed for the purpose of learning a trade, business, profession, office, employment or vocation;
- undertaking a programme of training leading to an accredited qualification;
- receiving a salary or allowance (or both) of no more than £195 a week before any deductions for income tax and national insurance.[32] Guidance to local authorities advises that when calculating earnings, any overtime or bonuses should be ignored.

Before awarding a discount, most local authorities require either a copy of the apprenticeship agreement or a signed copy of an agreement between the apprentice and the employer, together with copies of wage slips.

Youth trainees

Youth trainees are disregarded for discount purposes.[33]

Trainees are usually aged 16 to 21, but the council tax definition includes those under the age of 25 as some trainees (eg, those with disabilities) may need extra time to complete the training or may start training plans late. You are regarded as undertaking training from the day on which the course or programme begins to the day you complete, abandon or are dismissed from it.

People in prison or other forms of detention

In many cases, if you are in prison or some other form of detention, you are considered no longer solely or mainly resident in a dwelling and should therefore be ignored for discount purposes. Dwellings left empty by those in detention are exempt from council tax (see p57). In certain instances, however, detention may be for such a short period that you are still considered mainly to occupy the dwelling. In this case, a disregard for discount purposes applies if you are:[34]

- detained in a prison, a hospital or any other place by a British court;
- detained under the deportation provisions of the Immigration Act 1971;
- detained under the Mental Health Act 1983 or the Mental Health (Care and Treatment) (Scotland) Act 2003;
- imprisoned, detained or in custody (but not in custody under open arrest for the purposes of Queen's Regulations) for more than 48 hours under the Armed Forces Act 2006.

If you are in police custody before your first court appearance, or are detained for non-payment of council tax in England or Wales, or non-payment of a fine, you are not treated as detained for the purpose of a discount.[35] If you are on temporary release, you are treated as being detained.

People who are severely mentally impaired

For council tax purposes, you are considered '**severely mentally impaired**' if you have a severe impairment of intelligence and social functioning (however caused) that appears to be permanent.[36] This includes where you are severely mentally impaired as a result of a degenerative brain disorder such as Alzheimer's disease, a stroke or other forms of dementia. To count as severely mentally impaired, you must have a certificate of confirmation from a registered medical practitioner. Certificates of severe mental impairment issued before the introduction of council tax are acceptable, provided they do not include any information that should only be used for some other purpose – eg, exemption from the community charge. Doctors must issue certificates free of charge.

In addition, to qualify for the discount, you must be entitled to (though not necessarily in receipt of) one of the following benefits:

- short-term or long-term incapacity benefit (IB);
- employment and support allowance;
- attendance allowance (AA);
- severe disablement allowance (SDA);
- the highest or middle rate care component of disability living allowance (DLA);
- an increase in disablement pension for constant attendance;
- the disability element in working tax credit;
- unemployability supplement (this was abolished in 1987 but existing claimants remain entitled);

- constant attendance allowance payable under the industrial injuries or war pension schemes;
- unemployability allowance payable under the industrial injuries or war pension schemes;
- income support including a disability premium because of incapacity for work.

If you would have been entitled to one of the above benefits except for the fact that you have reached pension age, you still qualify for the discount.[37]

You also qualify if your partner is in receipt of income-based jobseeker's allowance (JSA) which includes a disability premium or higher pensioner premium because:[38]

- s/he gets the long-term rate of IB; *or*
- s/he was either in receipt of long-term IB up to pension age and is still alive or is entitled to AA/DLA but has been in hospital for more than 28 days.

Carers

You are disregarded for discount purposes as a carer if you are providing care or support (or both):[39]

- to another person on behalf of a local authority or charitable body (see below);
- to another person, is employed by the person being cared for and was introduced by a charitable body (see below);
- to someone in receipt of certain benefits;
- to someone receiving an armed forces independence payment in England from 8 April 2013, in Wales from 24 May 2013 and in Scotland from 11 June 2013.[40]

Carers providing care on behalf of a local authority or charitable body

You must be:

- providing the care or support in question on behalf of a local authority, the Court of Common Council of the City of London, the Council of the Isles of Scilly, a government department or a charitable body, and be resident in premises provided by, or on behalf of, that organisation, so that the best care can be provided; *and*
- engaged or employed for at least 24 hours a week; *and*
- paid no more than £44 a week.

Carers introduced by a charitable body

You must:

- be employed to provide care or support by the person who needs the care for at least 24 hours a week; *and*
- be earning no more than £44 a week from this employment; *and*
- have been introduced to the person by a charitable body; *and*

- be resident in premises provided by, or on behalf of, the person being cared for to enable the best care to be provided.

Caring for someone in receipt of certain benefits

You must:

- be resident in the same dwelling as the person being cared for; *and*
- be providing care for at least 35 hours a week on average; *and*
- not be the partner of the person being cared for, or, if the person needing care is a child under 18, not be the child's parent; *and*
- be caring for someone entitled to:
  – higher rate AA; *or*
  – the highest rate care component of DLA; *or*
  – an increase in constant attendance allowance under the industrial injuries or war pensions scheme; *or*
  – the highest rate of constant attendance allowance payable on top of full-rate disablement benefit paid for an industrial injury.

More than one person living in the same dwelling can count as a carer.

Example

Mr and Mrs Evans have a son aged 21. He is severely mentally impaired and gets DLA care component at the highest rate. Both parents care for their son for at least 35 hours a week, so they both should be disregarded for discount purposes. As their son is also disregarded, their council tax bill should be reduced by 50 per cent. All three occupiers are disregarded, but cannot claim an exemption.

A dwelling left empty by a carer is exempt, whether or not you meet any of the above criteria. A dwelling left empty by someone who has moved to receive care elsewhere is also exempt (see p59).

For more information on the position of carers and council tax, including sample application letters, see www.carersuk.org.

Hospital patients

If you have a short stay in hospital, it has no effect on council tax liability or the amount of tax that must be paid. If you have been, or are likely to be, in a hospital for so long that you can no longer be considered to be solely or even mainly resident in your home, you should be ignored for the purpose of a discount. A dwelling left empty because you are solely or mainly resident in hospital is exempt from council tax (see p58).

Most hospitals are subject to non-domestic rates, but some types of long-stay hospitals can be considered dwellings for council tax purposes. Patients who are

solely or mainly resident in such a hospital are disregarded for discount purposes.[41] In this context, and for the purpose of exemptions, a **'hospital'** means:[42]
- an NHS hospital; *and*
- a military, air force or naval unit or establishment in which medical or surgical treatment is provided.

People in care homes and hostels

The owners, rather than the residents, of these types of accommodation are liable for the council tax (see p81). The owners may be eligible for a disability reduction (see p98). If you are solely or mainly resident in such accommodation, you are disregarded for discount purposes if you are receiving care or treatment (or both) in the home or hostel.[43] If you have left your own home empty, it may be exempt from the council tax. See p58 for more details.

For the purposes of a discount, a **'care home'** is:
- a care home within the meaning of the Care Standards Act 2000 – ie, it provides accommodation with nursing or personal care to people:
  - who have been ill;
  - who have had a mental disorder;
  - with a disability or infirmity;
  - dependent on alcohol or drugs; *or*
- a building, or part of a building, in which residential accommodation is provided under s21 National Assistance Act 1948.

In **England and Wales**, a **'hostel'** refers to bail and probation hostels and hostels that provide:[44]
- mainly communal residential accommodation; *and*
- personal care for people who need it because of old age, disablement, past or present alcohol or drug dependence, or past or present mental disorder.

In **Scotland**, a **'hostel'** is an establishment in which residential accommodation is provided and whose sole or main function is to provide personal care or support to people who have their sole or main residence there.

'Personal care' includes providing appropriate help with physical and social needs and **'support'** refers to counselling or other help provided as part of a planned programme of care. To qualify, the hostel must be:[45]
- managed by a registered housing association or a voluntary organisation within the meaning of s94(1) Social Work (Scotland) Act 1968; *or*
- operated other than on a commercial basis and for which funds are provided wholly or in part by a government department or agency, or a local authority.

Members of international headquarters and defence organisations

A member (or dependant) of certain international headquarters or defence organisations listed in s1 International Headquarters and Defence Organisations Act 1964 is disregarded for discount purposes.[46]

Members of visiting forces

Members of visiting forces and any of their dependants who are neither British citizens nor ordinarily resident in the UK are disregarded for the purposes of a discount.[47] A dwelling is exempt from council tax if one of the liable people has a relevant association with a visiting force. See p63 for more details on exemptions. Consequently, this disregard only applies if none of the liable people have a relevant association. This would be the case, for example, if a member of a visiting force lodges with a British citizen.

Members of religious communities

You are a member of a religious community if:[48]
- the principal occupation of the community consists of prayer, contemplation, education, the relief of suffering, or any combination of these; *and*
- you have no income or capital of your own and are dependent on the community to provide for your material needs.

In considering whether or not you have any income, the local authority should disregard any pension(s) from former employment.

The owner, rather than the residents, is liable for the tax on a dwelling occupied by a religious community. See p82 for more details.

Residents in hostels and night shelters for homeless people

In England and Wales, you are disregarded for discount purposes if you are living in a hostel for homeless people, such as those run by the Salvation Army or Church Army. Most of the accommodation must be communal (ie, not divided into self-contained units) and most agreements to occupy the accommodation must be under licences which do not constitute tenancies. The disregard applies to resident staff as well as residents, provided the accommodation is predominantly for those with no fixed abode on the terms and conditions specified.

4. **Obtaining a discount**

Before calculating the council tax liability of any dwelling, a local authority should take reasonable steps to establish whether any discount should be granted.[49]

If the local authority has reason to believe that a discount applies, this should be assumed when calculating the council tax liability for the dwelling.[50] Practice Note No.2 (para 70) points out that a local authority may have reason to believe that a discount applies (and hence may be required to apply one) even if it does not have conclusive evidence.

Applications

To enquire about discounts available in a particular area, first contact your local authority taxation office. If the local authority has not granted a discount, a liable person may write and request one on the council tax bill. Any relevant evidence supporting the request should be included. In the case of a student, a student's certificate may prove useful but is not necessary. In the case of someone who is severely mentally impaired, a certificate from a GP is required. Practice Note No.2 (para 74) reminds authorities that anyone who presents information which they know to be false in order to reduce their council tax bill may be subject to a civil penalty. It advises them to pass any evidence of such deception to the police.

Backdating discounts

Many local authorities have claim forms for council tax discounts. Although filling in such a form may speed up the award of a discount, you can obtain a discount without making a claim. Authorities must therefore grant discounts for a past period if the appropriate conditions were met. Unlike the provisions for backdating most social security benefits, there is no requirement to show 'good cause' before a discount is backdated. If a discount should not have been granted for a past period, it may be withdrawn and you may have to appeal to the valuation tribunal if the council does this. There is no time limit on how much backdating you can apply for (ie, you can apply for a discount to be backdated further than the six years imposed by the Limitation Act 1980) but it is likely that a valuation tribunal will follow the decision in *Arca v Carlisle City Council*[51] (see Chapter 7). At the same time, it is arguably wrong for a local authority to try and reverse a discount decision that is more than six years old, and problems would also arise with respect to enforcement.

The duty to correct false assumptions

If a discount has been granted, the local authority must inform the liable person in writing, normally on the tax bill. If that person, or any jointly liable person, has reason to believe that the discount should not have been awarded, s/he should write and advise the local authority within 21 days of first having reason to believe the discount was incorrect.[52] This obligation only arises before the end of the financial year following the financial year in respect of which the local authority's assumption about the discount was made.[53]

Penalties

The local authority has the discretion to impose a penalty of £70 (in England) and £50 (in Wales or Scotland) on a liable person who fails to notify it that a discount should not have been granted.[54] An English or Welsh authority may quash such a penalty. A Scottish local authority may revoke the imposition of such a penalty if the person on whom it was imposed had a reasonable excuse for the failure.[55] Each time the local authority repeats the request and the person continues to fail to supply the information, a further £280 penalty in England, or a further £200 penalty in Wales or Scotland, can be imposed.[56]

An appeal against the imposition of a penalty may be made.[57] This is done by writing to the Valuation Tribunal for England or to the Valuation Tribunal for Wales. In Scotland, an appeal can be made to a valuation appeal committee by writing to the local authority. The local authority should pass the appeal to the committee. An appeal should be made within two months of the imposition of the penalty. If you appeal, the penalty need not be paid until the appeal has been decided. See Chapter 12 for more information about appeals.

From 2013, the civil penalties the billing authority may offer as an alternative to a criminal prosecution have been extended (see Chapter 6).

The £70 penalty may be imposed on someone who, through negligence, fails to promptly notify the billing authority of a relevant change in circumstances or who makes an incorrect statement. The level of the penalty offered as an alternative to criminal prosecution varies between £100 and £1,000 and is based on the excess reduction awarded or applied for.

5. Reduced discounts and increases for long-term empty dwellings and second homes

From 1 April 2013, the powers of local authorities in England and Wales to reduce the amount of discount awarded for certain classes of unoccupied dwellings (ie, in which no one has sole or main residence) are extended.

Under changes introduced in 2012, a discount can be reduced to zero as the local authority sees fit, including as part of its local council tax reduction scheme (see Chapter 9).

A local authority may determine that the normal 50 per cent discounts laid down on a national basis for certain classes of dwelling may not apply in its area or in respect of certain types of dwelling as it may decide. Such a determination may apply in just part of the local authority's area.[58]

Where it makes such a determination, the local authority must also increase the amount of tax payable, by up to 50 per cent, for a property which is classed as a 'long-term empty dwelling'.[59] A billing authority which makes a determination to increase the amount payable on an empty dwelling must publish a notice of it in at least one newspaper circulating in its area within 21 days from the date of the determination – however, failure to do this does not affect the validity of the determination.[60] A billing authority may make a determination varying or revoking a determination under this section for a financial year, but only before the beginning of the year.[61]

A dwelling is 'long-term empty' on any day if for a continuous period of at least two years it has been unoccupied and substantially unfurnished.[62]

In determining whether a dwelling has been empty for two years or more, no account is to be taken of any one or more periods of less than six weeks during which either the dwelling is not empty or was furnished (or both) are not counted.[63] Thus short periods of occupation do not affect the running of the two-year period.

As originally established, the council tax allowed a 50 per cent discount to second homes which were not occupied. In 2003 the position was changed so that a local authority could reduce the discount to 10 per cent of the annual council tax bill payable on a property if it falls into one of the following classes.

- **Class A.** Dwellings which are unoccupied and are furnished, but occupation of which is prevented by a planning condition for at least 28 days a year – eg, holiday chalets.
- **Class B.** Dwellings which are unoccupied and furnished and which are not subject to a planning condition restricting occupancy for at least 28 days – eg, potential second homes.

A discount may be reduced to 0 per cent of the annual council tax bill payable on a property if it fell into:

- **Class C.** Dwellings which are unoccupied and substantially unfurnished. **Note:** dwellings in Class C are those which have been substantially unfurnished and unoccupied for more than six months. If they are substantially unfurnished and have been unoccupied for *less* than six months, they are normally exempt from council tax. See p53 for more information.

This leaves 100 per cent of the bill payable.

From **1 April 2013**, a local authority has powers to determine different levels of discounts in its area for all such dwellings or certain classes of such dwellings.[64] A local authority may determine whatever percentage of discount it wishes to a class of dwellings but may not specify a class by reference based wholly upon the length of time or shorter period for which any discount applies.[65] Details of discounts in a particular area are published by the local authority.

As well as increasing the amount of revenue for local authorities, the reduction in discount serves to encourage property owners who own more than one dwelling to let a second home. For some taxpayers who do not want to let a dwelling on a commercial basis, it may be an option to allow a relative (such as a son or daughter over 18) to occupy the property, thus qualifying the property for a 25 per cent discount. If the person occupying the property is under 18, the property will be exempt (see p63).

Local authorities cannot reduce the amount of discount applicable to properties which fall outside the definitions in Classes A and B. These dwellings continue to receive a discount of 50 per cent.

Dwellings not included in Class A or B include those which consist of a pitch occupied by a caravan, a mooring occupied by a boat, job-related dwellings, and unoccupied dwellings left empty because a person is required to occupy another dwelling because of her/his job.

Job-related dwellings and discounts

For reduced discount purposes a job-related dwelling is one provided to you or your spouse because of your or her/his employment and which:
- is necessary in order to do the job properly; *or*
- has been provided so that duties are performed better and where it is customary for employers to provide accommodation to employees; *or*
- is part of special security arrangements.

Job-related dwellings include any accommodation provided as a second home as part of your employment (eg, a live-in teacher or caretaker), and property owned as a second home if you are required by your employment to occupy another dwelling – eg, you are a publican who is required to live in other licensed premises as a tenant of a brewery.

If you also have a second home in England on which council tax is payable, the local authority in which the second home is situated is prevented from reducing the 50 per cent discount.

Company directors and partnerships

If the dwelling is provided by a company and you are either a director (as defined by ss67 and 69 Income Tax (Earnings and Pensions) Act 2003) of it or an associated company, the local authority may reduce the discount unless:[66]
- you are employed as a full-time director; *or*
- the company is non-profit making; *or*
- the company is established for charitable purposes.

Ministers of religion

Ministers of any religious denomination who are required to live in premises in England to perform their duties of office come within the definition of those with a job-related dwelling. This means that if a minister of religion also has a second home in England on which council tax is chargeable, the local authority is prohibited from reducing the council tax discount below 50 per cent.[67]

Wales

Originally in Wales, most classes of unoccupied dwelling qualified for a 50 per cent discount, but each Welsh local authority could decide that a 25 per cent discount, or no discount at all, applied if a furnished dwelling had been no one's sole or main residence for six months. Following changes introduced by the Local Government Act 2003, the Welsh Government now has wider powers to change the amount of discount available on an unoccupied property – eg, a second home.[68] Local authorities in Wales may reduce the amount of discount for dwellings of a particular class by at least 10 per cent or remove the discount altogether. Such a decision lasts for one financial year.

If the local authority makes a decision using the latest power, it must apply it to all such dwellings in its area. It cannot, however, apply it to a pitch occupied by a caravan or a mooring occupied by a houseboat. Additionally, it does not apply if:[69]

- someone is liable for the tax on a dwelling only in her/his capacity as a personal representative (ie, the executor of a will) and either no grant of probate or letters of administration have been made, or less than 12 months have elapsed since the day on which such a grant was made; *or*
- the liable person is also a liable person of another job-related dwelling.

If a Welsh authority has made a decision to alter the discounts available on second homes, it must publicise it in at least one newspaper circulating in its area within 21 days of the decision. Failure to comply with this requirement, however, does not make the decision invalid.[70] If such a decision has been made for any financial year, it may be varied or revoked at any time before the beginning of that year.

A Welsh authority's decision about applying a discount to a class of dwelling cannot be appealed. It may, however, be challenged via judicial review.[71] You may appeal in the normal way (see p125) against the local authority's decision that a dwelling is within a prescribed class.

6. **Miscellaneous discounts**

Local authorities have the power to give discretionary discounts.[72] In a Parliamentary Answer given in the House of Commons by John Healy, Minister for Local Government, on 2 February 2009, at least 23 local authorities were mentioned as having granted some kind of discount in particular cases. These included discounts for:

- people over pension age;[73]
- hard-to-sell property;
- newly unfurnished property;
- property affected by a wind turbine;
- occupied and unoccupied property without the benefit of mains services – eg, beach chalets;
- problems with a chalk mine;
- property that is no one's sole or main residence and with restricted access;
- single occupiers called up for 28 days or more as members of the reserve forces;
- taxpayers who cannot comply with the council's mooring policy;
- members of the Royal Air Force whose redundancy was delayed because of events abroad.

Precise details of which authorities had awarded which discounts were not given, however, on the grounds that individual properties or individual taxpayers might be identified.

You should, therefore, check with your local authority whether additional discounts are available.

7. **Appeals**

If the local authority refuses to grant a discount, you can appeal in writing if you are an **'aggrieved person'**.[74] There is no time limit for making such an appeal. You are an 'aggrieved person' if you are liable to pay the council tax or you are the owner (if different). The appeal letter should give the reasons why the discount should be granted. The local authority has two months in which to answer.[75] If no discount is granted, or if the local authority fails to answer within two months of receiving the appeal, you can make a further appeal. See Chapter 12 for further details.[76]

In a case where a local authority reduces the amount of discount available and a person experiences hardship, an application may be made to reduce the amount of council tax payable. The local authority must consider the application to reduce the sum on an individual basis.

The local authority may enforce payment of the original bill while the appeal is outstanding (see Chapter 11). The local authority may be prepared to agree to suspend recovery action while awaiting the outcome of the appeal. Alternatively, an adjournment may be sought from the magistrates' court or sheriff court if recovery proceedings are commenced.

In **England and Wales,** the further appeal is made by writing to the Valuation Tribunal for England or the Valuation Tribunal for Wales. The appeal should normally be made within two months of the date the local authority notified you of its decision, or within four months of the date when the initial representation was made if the local authority has not responded. The president of the tribunal has the power to allow an out-of-time appeal if you have failed to meet the appropriate time limit because of reasons beyond your control.

In **Scotland,** a further appeal is made by writing again to the local authority. The local authority should pass the appeal to the secretary of the relevant local valuation appeal committee. The appeal must be made within four months of the date on which the grievance was first raised with the local authority in writing. There is no power to consider an out-of-time appeal.

Notes

1. When a discount is granted
1 **EW** s2(2)(d) LGFA 1992
  S s71(2)(d) LGFA 1992
2 s11B(1)(a) LGFA 1992 inserted by s12 LGFA 2012

2. Who is ignored for discount purposes
3 **EW** s6 LGFA 1992
  S s99(1) LGFA 1992

3. Who is disregarded for discount purposes
4 **EW** s11 and Sch 1 LGFA 1992; CT(DD)O; CT(APDD) Regs
  S CT(D)(S)O; CT(D)(S) Regs
5 **EWS** Sch 1 para 3 LGFA 1992
6 **EW** CT(APDD) Regs
  S CT(D)(S)CAO
7 **EWS** Sch 1 para 4 LGFA 1992
8 **EW** CT(DD)O, as amended
  S CT(D)(S)O, as amended
9 **EW** CT(DD)O
  S CT(D)(S)CAO
10 **EW** CT(DD)O
  S CT(D)(S)CAO
11 **EW** CT(DD)O
  S CT(D)(S)CAO
12 **EW** CT(DD)O
  E CT(DD)(A)(E)O
  W CT(DD)(A)(W)O

S CT(D)(S)CAO
13 **EW** CT(DD)O
14 **EW** CT(DD)O
15 **EW** CT(DD)O
16 *Birmingham City Council v Birmingham VCCT and Adamson* [1993] CO365/92 (QBD)
17 *Hakeem v Enfield London Borough* [2013] EWHC 1026 (Admin)
18 *R (Carmarthenshire CC) v West Wales Valuation Tribunal* [2004] EWHC 223
19 **EW** CT(DD)O
20 Art 7 The Council Tax (Discount Disregards) (Amendment) Order 2011 No.948
21 Practice Note No.2, para 28
22 **EW** CT(DD)O
  S CT(D)(S)CAO
23 **EW** CT(DD)O
24 **S** Schs 3 and 4 CT(D)(S)CAO; The Education (Recognised Bodies)(Scotland) Amendment Order 2009 No.61
25 Appeal ref: 0121M73910/212C, available on the Valuation Tribunal website
26 *R(Feller) v Cambridge City Council* [2011] EWHC 1252 (Admin)

27 *Feller v Cambridge City Council* [2011] All
ER 349 [2011] EWHC 1252 (Admin)
28 CT(D)(S)CAO
29 **EW** CT(DD)O
S Reg 9 CT(D)(S)CAO
30 CT(DDED)(A)O, as amended. See also
CT(ED)(S)(A)O 1995 and CT(D)(S)(A)
Regs
31 *Harrow London Borough Council v Ayiku*
[2012] EWHC 1200
32 **E** Amended by Art 2(2) CT(DD)(A)(E)O
W Amended by CT(DD)(A)(W)O
S CT(D)(S)CAO
33 **E** CT(DD)O, as amended by
CT(DD)(A)(E)O
EW Reg 3 CT(EDDD)(A)O
S CT(D)SO
34 **EWS** Sch 1 para 1 LGFA 1992
EW CT(DD)O
S Reg 3 CT(D)(S)CAO
35 **EWS** Sch 1 para 1 LGFA 1992
EW CT(DD)O
36 **EWS** Sch 1 para 2 LGFA 1992
EW CT(DD)O
S CT(D)(S)CAO
37 **EW** CT(DD)O
38 **EW** CT(DD)O
S CT(D)(S)O
39 **E** CT(APDD) Regs, amended by The
Council Tax and Non-Domestic Rating
(Amendment) (England) Regulations
2006 No.3395
W The Council Tax (Additional
Provisions for Discount Disregards)
(Amendment) (Wales) Regulations 2007
No.581
S The Council Tax (Discounts) Scotland
Amendment Order 2007
40 **E** Council Tax (Additional Provisions for
Discount Disregards) Regulations 1992
No.552 as amended by Art 5 Sch Armed
Forces and Reserve Forces
Compensation Scheme (Consequential
Provisions: Subordinate Legislation)
Order 2013 No.591
W Council Tax (Additional Provisions for
Discount Disregards) (Amendment
No.2) (Wales) Regulations 2013
No.1049
S CT(D)(S)O as amended by the Welfare
Reform (Consequential Amendments)
(Scotland) (No.3) Regulations 2013
No.142
41 **EWS** Sch 1 para 6 LGFA 1992
42 **EWS** Sch 1 para 6 LGFA 1992
43 **EWS** Sch 1 paras 7-8 LGFA 1992
44 **EW** CT(DD)O
45 **S** CT(D)(S)O

46 **EWS** Sch 1 para 11 LGFA 1992; The
European Union Military Staff
(Immunities and Privileges) Order 2009
No.887; The International
Organisations (Immunities and
Privileges) (Scotland) Order 2009 No.44
EW CT(APDD) Regs
S CT(D)(S) Regs
47 **EW** CT(APDD)(A) Regs
S CT(D)(S)(A) Regs
See also The Visiting Forces and
International Headquarters (Application
of Law)(Amendment) Order 2009
No.705 and The European Union
Military Staff (Immunities and Privileges)
Order 2009 No.887
48 **EW** CT(APDD) Regs
S CT(D)(S) Regs

4. **Obtaining a discount**
49 **EW** Reg 14 CT(AE) Regs 1992
S Reg 12 CT(AE)(S) Regs
50 **EW** Reg 15 CT(AE) Regs 1992
S Reg 13 CT(AE)(S) Regs
51 *Arca v Carlisle City Council* [2013] RA
248; VTE 29 January and 20, March
2013, per Graham Zellick QC, President
52 **EW** Reg 16 CT(AE) Regs 1992
S Reg 15 CT(AE)(S) Regs
53 **EW** Reg 16 CT(AE) Regs 1992
S Reg 15 CT(AE)(S) Regs
54 **EW** s14(2) and Sch 3 LGFA 1992
S s97(4) and Sch 3 LGFA 1992
55 **EW** s14(2) and Sch 3 LGFA 1992
S s97(4) and Sch 3 LGFA 1992
56 **EW** s14(2) and Sch 3 LGFA 1992
S s97(4) and Sch 3 LGFA 1992
57 **EW** s14(2) and Sch 3 LGFA 1992
S s97(4) and Sch 3 LGFA 1992

5. **Reduced discounts and increases for
long-term empty dwellings and second
homes**
58 s11(4A)LGFA 1992 as inserted by LGFA
2012
59 s11B(1)(b) LGFA 1992 inserted by s12
LGFA 2012
60 s11B(6) and (7) LGFA 1992 inserted by
s12 LGFA 2012
61 s11B(5) LGFA 1992 inserted by s12
LGFA 2012
62 s11B(8) LGFA 1992 inserted by s12
LGFA 2012
63 s11B(9) LGFA 1992 inserted by s12
LGFA 2012
64 s11A(4A) LGFA 1992 as inserted by
LGFA 2012

65 s11A(4B) LGFA as inserted by LGFA
    2012
66 Sch paras 2 and 3 CT(PCD)(E) Regs
67 Regs 2 and 6 CT(PCD)(E) Regs
68 **W** s12 LGFA 1992, as inserted by s75
    LGA 2003
69 **W** CT(PCD)(W) Regs
70 **W** s12 LGFA 1992, as inserted by s75
    LGA 2003
71 **W** s66 LGFA 1992

6. Miscellaneous discounts

72 s13A LGFA 1992
73 A further answer indicated that special
    discounts for pensioners had been
    recognised by Bury, Hillingdon, Kirklees
    and Wirral Councils

7. Appeals

74 **EW** s16 LGFA 1992
    S s81 LGFA 1992
75 **EW** s16 LGFA 1992
    S s81 LGFA 1992
76 **EW** s16 LGFA 1992
    S s81 LGFA 1992

Chapter 9

. . . .

Council tax reduction schemes

This chapter covers:
1. The operation of local council tax reduction schemes (below)
2. Who can apply for a council tax reduction (p132)
3. The amount of council tax reduction (p140)
4. Alternative maximum council tax reduction (p152)
5. Applying for a reduction (p154)
6. Appeals about council tax reductions (p158)
7. Discretionary reductions (p159)
8. Future schemes (p160)

1. The operation of local council tax reduction schemes

The introduction of council tax reduction schemes

If you need help to pay your council tax, you might be able to get a council tax reduction (CTR). CTR replaced council tax benefit (CTB) from 1 April 2013. Instead of a nationwide system of benefit or support, the level of support is now decided by each local authority. CTR may be referred to by your local authority as council tax 'support' or 'rebate'.

Local schemes must follow broad principles laid down within a framework of statutory principles.[1] Local CTR schemes must apply means tests controlled by national and local rules. In most cases, CTR reduces the sum of the weekly amount payable on the property, but not the complete amount. The maximum amount available under a local authority scheme is 100 per cent, which is awarded to low-income pensioners with capital under £16,000. If you have reached pension age, your local authority should provide support that mirrors that previously available under CTB. Separate schemes operate in England, Wales and Scotland.

In **England and Wales**, local authorities may devise their own local schemes which must meet minimum 'prescribed' requirements (see p131). However, if a local authority does not adopt its own scheme, a default scheme applies.[2] As a result there are potentially as many as 326 different localised systems of support each with its own rules in England and 22 in Wales. Local schemes vary between areas; the reduction that you receive may be different to that given in another borough. Crucially, local authorities may set a percentage of the council tax bill which claimants of working age must pay, whether or not they are on any benefit. A person of working age may be required in some boroughs to pay 10 or 20 per cent of the annual council tax bill, which was previously covered by full CTB. It is estimated that 3.1 million people who previously did not have to pay now do. The amounts vary between authorities, and it is a general presumption that any non-dependants (see p143) are also be expected to pay. All local authority reduction schemes are required to protect pensioners on low incomes, but there are no guarantees to protect the position of anyone of working age.

In Wales, a further prescribed and default scheme regulations have been set for 2014/15.[3]

In England and Scotland, there are two types of CTR:

- **main CTR,** based on your council tax liability and your (and any partner's and dependants') needs and resources (see p140); *and*
- **alternative maximum CTR,** known as second adult rebate, to help you if you share your home with anyone on a low income, and lose your 'single occupier discount' as a result. This is not based on your needs or resources, but on the circumstances of certain other adults ('second adults') living with you (see p152).

In Wales, there is no second adult rebate, only main CTR.

Second adult rebate can be paid instead of, but not in addition to, main CTR. If you are eligible for both, you are paid whichever is the higher.

If you are entitled to income support (IS), income-based jobseeker's allowance (JSA), income-related employment and support allowance or universal credit (UC), you may qualify for maximum main CTR. Otherwise, your CTR is calculated using a special formula. Maximum CTR in your area might not cover 100 per cent of your council tax bill.

If you are of working age in England and Wales, you need to check the details of the scheme operated by your local authority. To determine how much support may be available to you, the first step is to contact your local authority and make an application as soon as possible. Many local authorities use the same online application form as for housing benefit, and have online calculators you can use to see if you might qualify. You should always make a claim, if your income is low, or you are having difficulty paying your council tax bill. Making an application for CTR is an essential step for receiving it (see p154).

Scotland

One CTR scheme applies throughout Scotland, with no local variations. The Scottish government has absorbed the cost of the abolition of CTB for 2013/14, so if you were previously entitled to CTB you should, in theory, be awarded CTR.[4]

The entitlement criteria, wherever possible, are identical to those used under the previous CTB scheme.

The scheme, set out in the Council Tax Reduction (Scotland) Regulations 2012, makes provision for a reduction in liability for council tax people who have not reached the qualifying age for PC. There are separate rules for people over state pension age.[5] If you are over this age, but still claim IS, income-based JSA or UC you are assessed under the main scheme.

Prescribed matters

Certain key requirements which every local authority scheme must include for each financial year are laid down by the Secretary of State in prescribed regulations.[6] Apart from following these requirements, local authorities are free to set the particular details of their CTR schemes with respect to identifying particular classes of individuals who are in financial need. In England and Wales, if a local authority failed to produce its own scheme or its scheme was ruled invalid by 31 January, a default scheme prepared by the Secretary of State applies.

Under the prescribed requirements, the only dwellings automatically entitled to a 100 per cent reduction (as existed with CTB) are those occupied by certain classes of pensioners.[7]

Following consultation, all local authorities in England and Wales were required to create schemes for 'persons whom the authority considers to be in financial need' or 'persons in classes consisting of persons whom the authority considers to be, in general, in financial need'.[8] However, the size of any reduction varies from area to area and there is no fixed definition in the legislation of how the local authority is to determine 'financial need' although the phrase has been considered in some court decisions by the higher courts (see p49). In most cases, the amount of reduction is less than that provided by the former CTB system. Transitional relief for local authorities was available to councils for the year 2013/14 if a proposed CTR scheme meets certain requirements. These include that those who previously paid no council tax because of CTB are not made to pay more than 8.5 per cent of their council tax liability, that the taper rate does not increase above 25 per cent (see p149 for an explanation of the taper) and that there is no sharp reduction in support for unemployed people entering work.

In addition to CTR schemes, a local authority in England and Wales also has discretionary powers to reduce a sum in council tax (see p159), but this does not apply in Scotland.[9]

The operation of CTR reduction schemes

The reduction available under a local CTR scheme comes into operation once the banding and the amount of tax on a dwelling, and the person(s) liable to pay it, are ascertained (see Chapters 3–6).

CTR schemes take into account any disability reduction (see Chapter 7) or discount (see Chapter 8) and apply it to the amount of council tax after either or both have been awarded.

A reduction in council tax may be awarded in a number of ways:[10]

- as a discount on the dwelling calculated as a percentage of the bill payable on the dwelling;
- as a discount of an amount set out in your council's scheme or to be calculated in accordance with provisions laid down in your council's scheme;
- as a part reduction in the council tax bill payable on your property;
- as a reduction of the entire council tax bill payable on the property(so that the amount payable is nil).

In most cases, CTR is awarded as a reduction on the weekly amount payable on the dwelling, but not the complete amount.

Contents of a council tax reduction scheme

A CTR scheme must state the classes of person entitled to a reduction under the scheme, with particular reference to reductions for pensioners.[11] The classes may be determined by assessing the income or capital of any person liable to pay council tax.[12] Local authorities can have different rules as to how they treat your income and savings, as long as they are within the boundaries set by the regulations.

A local authority scheme must also set out the procedure for applying for a reduction,[13] together with details of the right of appeal (see Chapter 13).

2. **Who can apply for a council tax reduction**

Council tax reduction (CTR) schemes operate as means tests. Entitlement to CTR is available to the person liable to pay the council tax (see Chapter 6).

If you are liable to pay council tax, your entitlement to a reduction is based on your income and capital and the circumstances of the people living with you.

The amount of CTR is affected by the number of people in your household, your income and your personal circumstances, including levels of savings, pensions and the income of any spouse or partner. It is also affected by any other adults who live with you other than your partner.

What is your family

For the purposes of a CTR scheme, 'family' means:
- a couple;
- a couple and a child or a young person living in your household for whom one (or both) of you are responsible; *or*
- a person who is not a member of a couple and a child or young adult who is a member of the same household for whom that person is responsible.

A 'child' or 'young person' includes a child for whom child benefit is payable but does not include a young person on income support, jobseeker's allowance or a person to whom section 6 of the Children (Leaving Care) Act 2000 (exclusion from benefits) applies.[14]

A **'couple'** means:
- a man and woman who are married to each other and who are members of the same household;
- man and woman who are not married to each other but are living together as husband and wife;
- two people of the same sex who are in a civil partnership and are members of the same household; *or*
- two people of the same sex who are not civil partners of each other but are living together as if they were civil partners.

Note: the Marriage (Same Sex Couples) Act 2013 provides for same sex marriages in England and Wales. Same sex marriages in Scotland are expected to be possible at some point in 2014. References to marriage made throughout this chapter also apply to members of a same sex marriage.

Two people of the same sex are to be treated as living together as if they were civil partners if, and only if, they would be treated as living together as husband and wife were they of opposite sexes.

Provision is also made in the regulations for polygamous marriages.[15]

Who is included your household

CTR schemes consider all those who live with you as being part of your **'household'**.[16] Any children or young people who live with you, and for whom you have responsibility, may entitle you to a special premium which will apply in calculating your applicable amount. The presence of children and young people as part of your household could also affect the amount of CTR you get, depending on the details of your local authority scheme. The temporary absence of a child or young person does not affect her/his position part of your household.

Your local authority must treat a child or young person as a member of your household in any reduction week where:
- s/he lives with you for part or all of that reduction week; *and*

- the authority considers that it is reasonable to do so, taking into account the nature and frequency of her/his visits to you.[17]

You are treated as being responsible for a child or young person who normally lives with you. Where a child or young person spends equal amounts of time in different households, or where there is a question as to which household s/he is living in, s/he is treated as normally living with the person who is receiving child benefit for her/him.[18]

A child or young person is not usually treated as a member of your household if s/he is being fostered by you or your partner or s/he is placed or boarded with you prior to adoption.

Joint liability

Where you are jointly liable for council tax with one or more other people, the amount of maximum CTR is divided by the number of liable people.[19] The entitlement of each liable person is then calculated based on the applicable amount and resources appropriate to her/him (and her/his household if s/he has one).

Where you are resident

For CTR purposes, you are resident in the home where you live: your normal 'sole or main residence' (see Chapter 6).[20]

If you are not yet liable for the council tax on the property (eg, because you have not yet moved in) but are likely to be eligible for a CTR when you become liable, you can make your application in advance. You can apply up to 13 weeks in advance, or 17 weeks if you, or your partner, are 17 weeks younger than the qualifying age for PC (see p136).[21]

Owners not resident in a dwelling, or those whose main residence is elsewhere, are not entitled to CTR for that dwelling – ie, for a second home.

Temporary absence from home

Where you are entitled to a CTR, a property can count as your sole or main residence even if you spend substantial periods of time away from it, if you consider it to be the main place where you live. You can argue that you count as temporarily absent from home even if you have not yet stayed there – eg, you move your furniture and belongings in but then have to go into hospital.[22]

You can get CTR for up to **13 weeks** for your normal home while you are away, whatever the reason, provided you have not let or sub-let your dwelling to someone else.[23] You must be unlikely to be away for longer than this.

You can get CTR for up to **52 weeks** providing you intend to return to the dwelling (normally within 52 weeks but, exceptionally, if you are unlikely to be absent for substantially longer), have not let or sub-let it and fulfil certain conditions.

The circumstances in which you can remain eligible for longer than 13 weeks include:

- you are detained in custody on remand pending trial or sentence;
- you are on bail and required, as a condition of bail, in a bail hostel or in premises approved under section 13 of the Offender Management Act 2007;
- you are a patient in a hospital or similar institution;
- you, your partner or a dependent child under 16 is undergoing, in the UK or elsewhere, medical treatment, or medically approved convalescence, in accommodation other than residential accommodation;
- you are on (in the UK or elsewhere) a training course which will help you secure employment;
- you are undertaking medically approved care of a person residing in the UK or elsewhere;
- you are undertaking the care of a child whose parent or guardian is temporarily absent from the dwelling normally occupied by that parent or guardian for the purpose of receiving medically approved care or medical treatment;
- you are in the UK or elsewhere, receiving medically approved care provided in accommodation other than residential accommodation;
- you are a student;
- you are away from home as a result of a fear of violence;
- you are in residential accommodation for a trial period and intend to return home if it is not suitable. You can only get a reduction for 13 weeks in any one trial period. If the accommodation is not suitable, you may have further trial periods, as long as they do not exceed 52 weeks.[24]

Pensioners on low incomes

Reductions are given to all pensioners on low incomes under all CTR schemes in England, Wales and Scotland. Pensioners who have capital or savings above £16,000 are excluded from support and must not be included in the local authority's scheme, unless they receive the guarantee credit of PC, in which case all their capital in income is disregarded.[25]

Who is a pensioner

You are a pensioner for CTR purposes if:[26]

- you have attained the qualifying age for state pension credit (PC) – see p136; *and*
- you or your partner are not in receipt of income support, income-based jobseeker's allowance (JSA), income-related employment and support allowance (ESA) or universal credit.

The qualifying age for pension credit

The qualifying age for PC for a woman is the minimum age she can receive state retirement pension. The qualifying age for a man is the minimum age a woman born on the same day as him can receive state retirement pension.

If your date of birth is before 6 April 1950, your qualifying age is 60.

If your date of birth is between 6 April 1950 and 5 December 1953 inclusive, see CPAG's *Welfare Benefits and Tax Credits Handbook* or check www.gov.uk/calculate-state-pension to find your qualifying age.

If your date of birth is after 5 December 1953, your qualifying age is 65 or over. To check your pension age, see www.gov.uk/calculate-state-pension.

The qualifying age for men and women is rising steadily to 66 (by 2020) and will eventually go up to 68.

Categories of pensioner support

All CTR schemes must make three types of provision for pensioners on low incomes. Pensioners are divided into three groups referred to as Class A, Class B and Class C (some local authorities refer to them as Class 1, Class 2 and Class 3).[27]

With all three classes, you must make an application to receive a reduction (see p154). The class into which you are placed is determined by your income and applicable amount.

Applicable amounts for pensioners

The applicable amount for a pensioner is made up of:[28]
- a personal allowance;
- an amount for any child or young person who is a member of your family;
- any premiums which may be applicable.

Class A: income is less than the applicable amount

Income is the key element for determination of support for Class A. If your income is less than your applicable amount, you qualify for 100 per cent CTR, less any non-dependant deductions.[29]

If you are in Class A and get the guarantee credit of PC, your income and capital are disregarded. This means that your income is automatically less than your applicable amount and you automatically qualify for 100 per cent CTR wherever you live, less any non-dependant deductions for persons who live with you.

Class B: income is greater than the applicable amount

You are in Class B if your income is greater than your applicable amount.[30] If your total net income exceeds your applicable amount, your full CTR is reduced by 20p for every pound you receive above the applicable amount.

Example

John, 70, and has a council tax liability of £18.50 a week. His total weekly income is £132.69 state pension and £37.23 private pension, totalling £169.92. His applicable amount is £163.50.

Total income £169.92 *minus* £163.50 applicable amount = £6.42

20% of £6.42 excess income = £1.28

£18.50 – £1.28 = £17.22 basic CTR

John is entitled to a weekly £17.22 CTR on his weekly council tax liability.

Class C: entitled to an alternative maximum council tax reduction

You may be entitled to a Class C reduction where you are liable to pay council tax in respect of a dwelling which is shared with one or more adults on a low income who is not your spouse or partner and who does not pay rent.[31] This person may be known as a 'second adult' (see p153).

It is the income of the second adult that determines what level of reduction is awarded. The reduction awarded can be 7.5, 15, 25 or 100 per cent (see p153).

In determining a second adult's gross income, a number of benefits must be disregarded from the calculation. This includes any attendance allowance, disability living allowance or personal independence payment.[32]

Adults of working age

Those not defined as pensioners are by default defined as 'working age'. It is left to individual authorities to decide which classes of working age adults are eligible to receive support and how much is provided. Local authorities are entitled to set a lower level of CTR for persons of working age than that which existed until 1 April 2013 under council tax benefit (CTB). There is no obligation on the council to provide a maximum CTR for persons of working age as there is for pensioners. This power has not been interpreted by the courts but appears to give the local authority broad powers to make provisions, so the support available varies from area to area. In some local authority areas, those who are unable to work receive CTR in the same way as they received CTB. However, in most areas some of the amount in council tax payable on a dwelling is passed on to the person liable to pay.

If you are of working age you may be eligible for some CTR if you are over 18 years of age and are in receipt of a benefit such as JSA, or have a low income and are employed or self-employed.

Check the details of the scheme for your area. If the authority has set a minimum figure for the amount of support and your award falls below it, you have to pay the whole council tax bill or apply for a discretionary reduction (see p159).

Levels of reduction for working age adults

The maximum amount of CTR is calculated using a maximum figure and the percentage of support given by the local authority.

Until you reach pensionable age (see p136), you may not be entitled to a full 100 per cent reduction. Some local authorities have set a figure of 80 per cent for working-age adults to pay, while others have set a different percentage. For example, Waveney District Council in Suffolk grants a 91.5 per cent reduction to persons of working age.

Example

George, 45, is single and gets income-based JSA. He lives in a local authority area where the maximum CTR allowed for persons of working age is 80 per cent.

Annual council tax bill on the property	£854.10
Less discount of 25%	£640.57
Divided into 52 weeks = council tax weekly liability	£12.32
Maximum eligible CTR (80% x £13.14)	£9.86

George is required to pay council tax of £2.46 for each week in each week he qualifies for CTR.

Reducing local support for working age adults

Local authorities may adopt the following measures to reduce the support given by a CTR scheme to an amount that is less than the maximum possible for working age adults.

- **Introducing a property banding cap.** Some authorities may limit the support they give to properties in the lowest bands. This may be done by way of the imposition of a banding cap whereby properties higher than band D do not receive a reduction.
- **Limits on the amount of eligible CTR.** Some authorities have a policy of only granting a reduction above a minimum figure, such as £2, £4 or £5. Any amount of reduction that might theoretically be awarded to you below this figure is not paid and you have to pay the balance.
- **Minimum payments.** Some CTR schemes may require you to pay at least some council tax each month if you are of working age.
- **Lowering of savings cap.** Pensioners with savings over £16,000 are not eligible for help. However, with working-age adults, the saving cap can be lowered. Some local authorities place their savings cap at £6,000. If your savings fall below this level because you pay your council tax or other essential bills, you may be able to claim CTR.

- **Change the income taper.** Under the 'default scheme', the amount of CTR that you receive falls by 20 per cent or 20p for every extra £1 of income above your applicable amount (see p149). This rate of reduction or 'taper' can be increased – eg, to 25p or 30p for each pound of excess income.
- **Disregards of earnings for certain groups.** Some schemes protect those who the Department for Work and Pensions considers are unable to work or do not need to be available to work. These include lone parents with pre-school children and disabled people and their carers, and those who receive disability living allowance, attendance allowance, ESA, or the severe disability element of working tax credit.

Example

For 2013/14, Birmingham City Council provides a maximum CTR to claimants who are entitled to a disability premium or disabled child premium, claimants or their partners who are entitled to ESA and also receive a disability related benefit; claimants and their partners who receive carer premiums; claimants and their partners who receive war disablement pensions, war widow's pension or war widower's pension; and claimants or their partners who have dependent children under six.

- **Disregarding additional income.** In calculating income for CTR, certain benefits and other forms of income are disregarded. However, local authorities may change these amounts if you are of working age. For example, some authorities may give more support to households with children and allow certain forms of benefit.
- **Removal or reduction of the second person rebate.** If you are of working age and share your home with someone on a low income, the entitlement to second adult rebate may be changed.
- **Change non-dependant deductions.** This entitlement could be altered.

Who is excluded from council tax reduction

You are excluded from CTR if you:
- are a pensioner with over £16,000 capital;[33]
- are subject to immigration control;[34]
- are not habitually resident in the UK.[35]

See CPAG's *Welfare Benefits and Tax Credits Handbook* for more about who is a person subject to immigration control and who is habitually resident.

3. **The amount of council tax reduction**

Contact your local authority for information about the council tax reduction (CTR) scheme for your area.

The amount of CTR you get depends on:
- whether you are a pensioner or an adult of working age; *and*
- your 'maximum CTR' allowed under your local scheme (see below); *and*
- your 'applicable amount' (see p141). This is made up of personal allowances as well as premiums and components for any special needs. It may also include a transitional addition if you or your partner were transferred to contributory employment and support allowance (ESA) from income support (IS) 'on the grounds of disability', incapacity benefit (IB) or severe disablement allowance (SDA);[36] *and*
- how much income and capital you have (see pp146 and 149); *and*
- how many people live with you in the dwelling.

If you get the guarantee credit of pension credit (PC), you are automatically passported to maximum CTR (once you have made a claim). You do not, therefore, need to work out applicable amounts, income or capital.

Online calculators

Information about the local CTR scheme should be available on the local authority's website or you can ask for a copy of the scheme to be sent to you. Most local authorities have an online benefit calculator on their websites. If you cannot use the internet yourself, you can authorise another person to do this for you.[37] A benefit calculator should enable you to put in your details and those of your partner to determine the amount of support for the property which you occupy. If you are not able to access the local authority's online service, contact the CTR section and make an application in writing as soon as possible. Do not delay in doing this as there may be restrictions on backdating (see p157).

Maximum council tax reductions

Most schemes calculate CTR in terms of percentages, with maximum council tax reduction being 100 per cent of daily council tax liability.[38]

100 per cent is the maximum amount for all pensioners entitled on grounds of income. Until you reach pension age, you may not be entitled to 100 per cent CTR (see p138).

The amount of CRT that you receive depends on:
- national levels of applicable amounts for pensioners and working age adults;
- details of the local scheme (which vary for adults of working age);
- your circumstances and any income and capital;
- the number of persons residing the property, their status and income.

Your income	Amount payable*	Availability
Your income is less than your applicable amount	100 per cent of maximum council tax liability is payable depending your age	All eligible pensioners in England, Wales and Scotland and some adults of working age depending on the authority's scheme
Your income is greater than applicable amount	20 per cent of the value of the excess income above the applicable amount is deducted from the maximum council tax liability to give the amount of CTR	All eligible pensioners in England, Wales and Scotland and persons of working age unless the authority reduction scheme has set a different taper

* However, a further 'non-dependent deduction' may be made from your CTR if you have adults living with you who do not pay you rent (see p143).

An 'alternative' reduction based upon the income of any second adults living with you may apply (see p152).

Applicable amounts

CTR is calculated with reference to your applicable amount and whether your income is below or above this amount.

Your applicable amount is made up of:
- a personal allowance (which is based on whether you are single, part of a couple and whether you have dependents); *and*
- any 'premiums' which you or other members of your family (see p133) qualify for because of your circumstances, or the benefits you receive.

See CPAG's *Welfare Benefits and Tax Credits Handbook* for more information about applicable amounts. Normally the rules for calculating applicable amounts for CTR are the same as those used in calculating housing benefit.

Depending on the details of your local authority scheme, if your income is less than the applicable amount you may be entitled to up to 100 per cent reduction based upon your maximum council tax liability and depending upon your circumstances, and whether or not you have a partner.

Applicable amounts for 2013/14 and 2014/15

Personal allowances		2013/14	2014/15
Single	Under 25	£56.80	£57.35
	Under 25 (on main phase ESA)	£71.70	£72.40
	25 or over	£71.70	£72.40
Lone parent	Under 18	£56.80	£57.35
	Under 18 (on main phase ESA)	£71.70	£72.40
	18 or over	£71.70	£72.40
Couple	Both under 18	£85.80	£86.65
	Both under 18 (claimant on main phase ESA)	£112.55	£113.70
	One or both 18 or over	£112.55	£113.70
Dependent children	Under 20	£65.62	£66.33
Over qualifying age for pension credit	Single under 65	£145.40	£148.35
	Single 65 or over	£163.50	£165.15
	Couples both under 65	£222.05	£226.50
	Couple one or both 65 or over	£244.95	£247.20
Components			
Work-related activity		£28.45	£28.75
Support		£34.80	£35.75
Premiums			
Carer		£33.30	£34.20
Disability	Single	£31.00	£31.85
	Couple	£44.20	£45.40
Disabled child		£57.89	£59.50
Enhanced disability	Single	£15.15	£15.55
	Couple	£21.75	£22.35
	Child	£23.45	£24.08
Severe disability	One qualifies	£59.50	£61.10
	Two qualify	£119.00	£122.20
Family	Ordinary rate	£17.40	£17.45
	Some lone parents	£22.20	£22.20

Depending on your income and whether you fall below the applicable amount figures, you may be entitled to CTR based on your income and that of your household, with the level or reduction set by the local authority.

Income less than applicable amount

Pensioners

Where your income is less than your applicable amount, 100 per cent of your maximum council tax liability can be covered by CTR (see p140). If you get the guarantee credit of PC, your income and capital are counted as zero.

Working age adults

If your income in any week is at or below your applicable amount it does not preclude you from being liable for some of the council tax in your area, although certain groups may receive a 100 per cent reduction under a local scheme.

Income is greater than the applicable amount

Where your income is greater than your applicable amount, you may receive some support but your CTR is reduced by 20 per cent of the excess income which takes you over the applicable amount figure (known as the 'taper'). For pensioners and some working age adults, the 20 per cent reduction in excess income is deducted from the maximum council tax liability on a sliding scale.

In some areas a higher taper of 25 or 30 per cent may be applied by the local authority under its scheme.

Joint and several liability

Where two adults (other than spouses or partners) are jointly liable for council tax under the principle of joint and several liability, the maximum CTR is divided between them.[39] This does not apply in the case where a student would be the person jointly or severally liable.[40]

Non-dependent deductions

If other people normally live with you in your home who are not part of your 'family' (see p133) and are not also liable for council tax (called 'non-dependants'), a set deduction may be made from the amount of your CTR. These are non-liable adults who are normally expected to contribute to helping you pay the council tax bill but do not come within the hierarchy of liability imposed by section 6 of the Local Government Finance Act 1992 (see p76). This is because it is assumed the non-dependant makes a contribution towards your outgoings, whether or not s/he does so in practice. Examples of non-dependants are adult sons or daughters, or older relatives who share your home. You may, therefore, need to ask your non-dependant(s) for a contribution. A person can only be treated as living with you if s/he shares some accommodation with you. A person does not normally live with you if s/he has not been there long enough to regard your home as her/his normal home.

Students and partners are not included, along with those who are disregarded for the purposes of discount (see Chapter 8).

Many reduction schemes expect non-dependants to make a contribution to council tax whether they are working or not.

A 'non-dependant' means any person who normally resides with you, *except* someone who is:

- a member of your family for benefit purposes;
- if you are in a polygamous marriage, your partner and any child qualifying young person in your household for whom you or a partner are responsible;
- a child or young person who is living with you but is not a member of your household;
- a person who makes payments of rent to you or your partner. **Note:** although no non-dependant deduction can be made for him/her, the rent s/he pays can count as your income.

Example

Sara is a lone parent receiving IS and child tax credit in for a child under five and also has a non-dependant son who is in receipt of contribution-based JSA.

Weekly council tax liability	£23.36
Maximum eligible council tax	£23.36
Less non-dependant deductions	£5.00
Weekly entitlement to CTR	£18.36

Sara is awarded £18.36 CTR and her son has to pay £5 towards the council tax liability.

Exceptions to rules on non-deductions for pensioners

No non-dependent deduction is to be made if you are a pensioner and you or your partner are:[41]

- blind or treated as blind;
- receiving attendance allowance (AA);
- receiving the care component of disability living allowance (DLA);
- receiving the daily care component of personal independence payment (PIP);
- receiving an armed forces independence payment.

Non-dependants residing with pensioners

If you are a pensioner entitled to CTR, no deduction is made for a non-dependant if:[42]

- although s/he resides with you, her/his normal home is elsewhere;
- s/he is on IS, PC, income-based JSA or income-related ESA;
- s/he is receiving a training allowance paid for doing youth training;
- s/he is a full-time student; *or*
- s/he has been in hospital for more than 52 weeks. Separate stays which are not more than 28 days apart are added together when calculating the 52 weeks.

Residence and non-dependant deductions

No deduction is made if, although the non-dependant resides with you, it appears to the authority that her/his normal home is elsewhere (see also sole or main residence, p77).

Amount of non-dependant deduction

The amount of a non-dependant deduction is applied to reduce the amount of CTR you are awarded.

If you are a pensioner or of working age and entitled to maximum CTR, the amount of non-dependant deduction to be applied each day is set out in regulations.[43]

Circumstances of the non-dependent	Deduction
Working 16 or more hours a week with a weekly average gross income of:	
below £188	£3.70
£188 – £325.99	£7.25
£326 – £405.99	£9.40
£406 or more	£11.25
Not working or working less than 16 hours a week	£3.70

Note: the level of non-dependant deductions for people of working age may be varied by the local authority. However, most local authorities have kept within the amounts set down by the prescribed scheme or the deductions which apply for housing benefit (HB).

Certain sums may be disregarded when calculating the income of a non-dependant. In the case of non-dependants living with a pensioner the following are disregarded from the non-dependant's weekly gross income:

- AA;
- DLA;
- PIP;
- armed forces independence payment;
- certain charitable funds, such as the independent Living Fund or the Macfarlane Trust.

Example

Geraldine, 47, is single and gets income-related ESA. She lives alone in a band D property. Local support is set at a maximum of 80 per cent for adults of working age by her authority, meaning that Geraldine has to pay 20 per cent. Her son, 21, comes to live with her.

Weekly council tax liability   £23.36
Applicable amount   £71.70

If she lives alone as a single person or with dependants aged under 18 Geraldine's maximum council tax will be:

Maximum eligible council tax	£18.69
Non-dependant deductions	£5.00
Weekly entitlement to CTR	£13.69

£23.36 – £13.69 = £9.67

Geraldine has to make up the shortfall of £9.67 a week herself if payment is not forthcoming from her son.

Calculation of income

If you are of working age, your local authority scheme determines how your income is calculated.

If you a pensioner (see p136), the prescribed regulations lay down what counts as your income.[44]

The rules here apply to pensioners, although if you are of working age, the rules in your scheme may be similar.

Income is calculated on a weekly basis.[45] In calculating your applicable amount and whether you can potentially qualify for CTR, the local authority looks at both earned and unearned income – eg, social security benefits or payments from a trust or a charity. 'Tariff income' is also included. This is the deemed income you are presumed as obtaining from any money-raising assets you may own or which pay you a benefit of some kind. In the case of tax credits where an award is subject to a deduction relating to any overpayment, the amount counted towards income is the amount of working tax credit (WTC) or child tax credit (CTC) awarded less the amount of that deduction.[46]

If you get pension credit

There is special treatment of income and capital if you are in receipt of PC. If you get the PC **guarantee credit**, the whole of your income and capital is disregarded and you automatically qualify under Class A for 100 per cent CTR, less any non-dependant deductions (see p140).[47]

If you get the PC **savings credit** but not the guarantee credit, the local authority uses the Pension Service's assessment of your income and capital to calculate your CTR.

If you do not get pension credit

If you are a pensioner but you are not in receipt of PC, the amount you get is means-tested by the local authority. Your income is compared to your applicable amount (see p141) to determine how much CTR you get. See the table on p142. **Note**: if you have capital of £16,000 or more, you are not entitled to CTR.

The following are counted as income:

- earnings;
- WTC;
- retirement pension income;
- income from annuities;
- war pensions;
- armed forces independence payment;
- AA;
- DLA;
- PIP;
- increases in disablement pension;
- child benefit or guardian's allowance;
- social fund payments;
- Christmas bonus;
- HB;
- council tax benefit from a past period;
- bereavement payments;
- statutory sick pay;
- statutory maternity, adoption and paternity (ordinary and additional) pay;
- certain other payments.[48]

Earnings

Earnings are income from employment, self-employment or any office or position you hold. This includes all bonuses and commissions, payments in lieu of notice where employment ends, holiday pay and retainers.[49]

Self-employed average weekly earnings are based on either a yearly amount if your business is established or a different period if you have recently started your business. If there is a change in the pattern of the business, the period can be adjusted to provide the weekly amount which most accurately reflects your income.[50]

Expenses counted as earnings

Expenses that are not wholly incurred for performance of a job, including travelling expenses between home and place of employment, are included as income. However, travel costs provided as part of the Mandatory Work Programme are not paid under a contract of employment but a payment made to help you find work. Some local authorities, such as Newcastle Under Lyme, have made specific provision disregarding travel expenses which are paid as part of the Mandatory Work Programme.

Amounts not included as earnings

The following amounts are *not* included as income for CTR purposes:[51]

- any payment in kind – eg, a free meal;
- payments in respect of expenses wholly, exclusively and necessarily incurred in the performance of your job or employment;
- redundancy payments;
- occupational pensions;
- any lump sum payment made under the Iron and Steel Employees Re-adaptation Benefits Scheme;
- compensation awarded by an employment tribunal for unfair dismissal or unlawful discrimination;
- any payment of expenses arising from being involved with a service user group – eg, NHS or social work;
- non-cash vouchers.

Your earnings are considered net of tax and national insurance. Depending on your circumstances, disregards of varying amounts may also be allowed by some authorities from the net amount. For example, childcare costs may be included.

Sums disregarded from earnings

Sums may be disregarded from earnings, for example:[52]

£25 disregard	You are a lone parents (unless claiming IS, income-based JSA or income-related ESA).
£20 disregard	You are a lone parent on IS or income-based JSA.
	You or your partner quality for a disability premium, severe disability premium, carer premium or the work-related activity or support component.
	You are employed as a part-time firefighter, lifeboat crew, auxiliary coastguard or a member of any territorial or reserve force.
	You or you partner get main phase ESA, long-term incapacity benefit, SDA, AA, DLA, PIP, armed forces independence payment or the disability or severe disability element of WTC.
£17.10 disregard	You or your partner gets the 30-hour element of WTC.
	You or your partner are aged over 25 and work 30 hours a week or more.
	You or your partner work 16 hours a week or more and get a family premium.
£10 disregard	None of the above apply and you are a member of a couple.
£5 disregard	None of the above apply and you are single.

However, you need to check that the scheme allows any disregard for adults of working age. You may also able to have certain childcare costs disregarded.[53]

The income taper

The amount of CTR your household is entitled to is subject to an income taper which applies if your income goes above the applicable amount. The threshold set by the regulations for pensioners in England and Wales, and all claimants in Scotland, reduces the amount of CTR 20p for every extra £1 of income that is received.

If you are of working age in England and Wales, the amount of the taper varies between local authorities and can be increased. This rate of withdrawal or taper could be increased in the future.

Calculating income

All income figures are calculated on a weekly basis, so your earnings and other income have to be converted into a weekly amount if necessary.

- In a case where the payment is for a month, by multiplying the amount of the payment by 12 and dividing the product by 52.
- In a case where the payment is for three months, by multiplying the amount of the payment by 4 and dividing the product by 52.
- In a case where the payment is for a year, by dividing the amount of the payment by 52.
- In any other case, by multiplying the amount of the payment by 7 and dividing the product by the number of days in the period in respect of which it is made.[54]

Calculation of capital

CTR is only available to people with capital below certain fixed limits. The capital limit for a pensioner is £16,000 and any pensioner who has capital above this is excluded, unless they receive the guarantee credit of PC.[54]

A pensioner's capital includes any payment of arrears of CTC, WTC or PC if the payment was made for of a period for the whole or part of which a reduction under an authority's scheme was allowed before those arrears were paid.

Where income or capital cannot accurately be determined, the local authority may estimate a figure.

The capital rules for a reduction are set out in detail in the regulations and must be the whole your capital and include any arrears of benefit owed from an earlier claim.[55]

Where you have two accounts with the same bank, one of which is in credit and the other is overdrawn, the amount of the overdraft should be deducted from the account in credit to determine the actual figure of capital.[56]

Sums that are excluded from the definition of capital

Certain sums are excluded from the definition of capital and should not be used to determine your capital. Excluded capital includes:[57]

- any personal possessions;
- amounts paid under an insurance policy for loss or damage to your home and to your personal possessions;
- assets from a former business which are in the process of being disposed of;
- any premises acquired which you intend to occupy as your home within 26 weeks of the date of acquisition (or longer period if reasonable);
- any premises which you intend to occupy as your home but which need essential repairs or alterations to render them fit for such occupation, for a period of 26 weeks from the date repairs begin, or so long as is needed for them to be completed;
- any premises occupied in whole or in part by a disabled relative who has reached the qualifying age for PC (see p136);
- any premises occupied by a former partner as her/his home unless you are estranged or divorced from her/him or the partnership is dissolved;
- any case where you are taking 'reasonable steps' to dispose of an interest in capital – eg, selling your home to pay for care costs or entering sheltered accommodation;
- certain business assets.

Rules differentiate between capital in the UK and outside it. See CPAG's *Welfare Benefits and Tax Credits Handbook* for more information.

Notional capital

In certain circumstances, the council may treat you as having capital that you do not actually have. You are treated as possessing capital of which you have deprived yourself for the purpose of securing entitlement to CTR or increasing the amount of CTR. Cases where this occurs are likely to be rare and the local authority needs to have evidence for such a claim, although it may claim you have done this where there is evidence that your savings have been reduced prior to an application.

However, if you dispose of capital as a means of:

- reducing or paying debts you owe; *or*
- purchasing goods or services if the expenditure was reasonable in the circumstances,

you are not treated as not depriving yourself of it.

For example, if you spend your savings to have special medical treatment this would be reasonable.[58]

Where you hold capital jointly with another person, it is presumed that you have equal shares unless you provide evidence to contrary.[59]

Extended reduction on entering work

If you have been continuously getting IS, income-based JSA, income-related or contributory ESA, incapacity benefit or SDA for 26 weeks and it stops because you or your partner start work or your hours or earnings in your existing job increase, you may be entitled to an extended reduction of CTR for four weeks.[60] The change must be expected to last for at least five weeks. If you qualify, you receive the same amount in CTR as you did before you started work or changed hours.

Local authorities in England and Wales can vary the conditions for extended payments; in Wales, this includes making them more generous.[61] Contact your local authority to report the change in your circumstances and it will assess if you are entitled to an extended reduction.

After the extended reduction period, you may still qualify for CTR if you meet the qualifying conditions – check with your local authority.

Example
Deanna, 34, has been getting income-related ESA for 32 weeks. She starts a full-time job on 3 March 2014.
She receives an extended reduction for four weeks to 30 March 2014.
From 31 March 2014, if she still qualifies for CTR under her local authority's scheme, Deanna is entitled to a new amount of CTR. She does not need to make a new application, but does need to provide the information the local authority needs to calculate her new CTR.

Continuing reduction on claiming pension credit

To avoid problems caused by delays in reassessing your CTR when you move from IS, income-based JSA or income-related ESA onto PC, provided you otherwise continue to qualify for CTR, you continue to receive it, normally at the same rate as before this happened.[62] You qualify for continuing payments if:
- your partner has claimed PC and the DWP has certified this; *or*
- your IS, income-based JSA or income-related ESA ceased because you reached the qualifying age for PC (see p136) or, if you were getting income-based JSA or income-related ESA beyond that age, this ceased because you turned 65. The DWP must certify this and that you are required to claim or have claimed PC (or are treated as having done so).

You get continuing payments for four weeks.

4. Alternative maximum council tax reduction

In England and Scotland, 'alternative maximum council tax reduction', known as '**second adult rebate**', is a council tax reduction (CTR) designed to help you if you share your home with anyone on a low income who does not share liability for council tax with you and who does not pay rent to you (referred to as a 'second adult').[63]

Second adult rebate is an alternative type of CTR that can be paid instead of, but not as well as, main CTR. When you apply for CTR, the local authority must assess you for both types and award whichever is the higher – sometimes referred to as the 'best buy'.[64]

The second adult rebate rules:
- apply to all eligible pensioners in England and Scotland;[65]
- apply to working-age adults in Scotland;[66]
- vary for working-age adults in England, with some local authorities choosing not to award a second adult reduction;[67]
- are not available in Wales.

You qualify for a second adult rebate if:[68]
- you are liable for council tax in respect of the home where you are 'resident' (see p75); *and*
- you are the only person liable for the council tax on the home (with certain exceptions – see p75); *and*
- no one living in your home is liable to pay you rent; *and*
- you have one or more 'second adult(s)' living with you who are on a low income; *and*
- you satisfy the 'right to reside test' and the 'habitual residence test' and are not a 'person subject to immigration control' for benefit purposes.

Note: second adult rebate is based on the circumstances of the 'second adult(s)' living with you. The whole of *your* income and capital is ignored. Therefore, you can get second adult rebate even if you have a high income and/or capital worth more than £16,000, and if you are student who is liable to pay council tax.

Example
Lorraine owns her own home and earns £40,000 a year. She is liable for council tax of £750 a year. Lorraine's adult son Barry, who receives income support (IS), moves in with her. Lorraine loses her 25 per cent single person's discount and her council tax liability is now £1,000. Barry is a second adult. Lorraine is entitled to a second adult rebate of £250.

Who counts as a second adult

You must have at least one 'second adult' residing with you to qualify for alternative maximum CTR. In practice, residents classified as second adults are mainly the same people as those treated as non-dependants (see p143). However, someone residing with you does not count as a second adult if s/he:

- is aged under 18;[69] *or*
- has a status discount – ie, s/he is disregarded for council tax purposes (see p106);[70] *or*
- is your partner with whom you are jointly liable for council tax;[71] *or*
- is jointly liable to pay the council tax on the dwelling with you – eg, because s/he is a joint owner or tenant.[72] Although you cannot get second adult rebate for her/him, s/he may be able to claim main CTR for her/his own share of the bill (see p134).

Examples

Jason's elderly widowed mother lives with him. Jason is liable for council tax and can claim alternative maximum CTR as his mother is a second adult.

Dorinda is the tenant of a three-bedroom house. She lives with her partner, who is a full-time student and is disregarded for the purpose of a council tax discount. Their 20-year-old daughter and 25-year-old son live with them. The daughter is unemployed and in receipt of income-based jobseeker's allowance. The son is in low-paid employment. Dorinda may claim the alternative maximum CTR as the adult daughter and son are second adults.

Phoebe is a lone parent who lives with her two children aged 10 and 14. She is not entitled to alternative maximum CTR as there are no second adults in the dwelling.

You cannot qualify for alternative maximum CTR if a second adult who lives with you is liable to pay you rent for occupying your home.

It is important to check that the local authority has not confused a non-dependant deduction situation with a case where a second adult reduction should be applied.

Calculating alternative maximum council tax reduction

The amount of second adult rebate you get is a percentage of your council tax liability based on the gross income of the second adult.[73] If there is more than one second adult, their combined gross income is used.

Income of second adult(s)	Second adult rebate
Second adult (or all second adults) on IS/income-based JSA/ income-related employment and support allowance (ESA)/ pension credit (PC)	25 per cent
Second adult(s) total gross weekly income:	
Below £183	15 per cent
£183–£239	7.5 per cent
Over £239	Nil
Student dwellings	
Occupiers are either students excluded from entitlement to main CTR or on IS/income-based JSA/income-related ESA/PC. At least one must be a student and at least one on IS/income-based JSA/income-related ESA/PC.	100 per cent

For the 100 per cent rebate, someone counts as a student excluded from entitlement to main CTR if s/he would be excluded if s/he were under the qualifying age for PC (see p136).

Unless you qualify for a 100 per cent rebate, the maximum second adult rebate you can get is always 25 per cent of your council tax liability, even if you would have received a 50 per cent council tax discount, or would have been exempt from council tax altogether, were it not for the presence of two or more second adults in your home.

Examples

Liam is a student who lives alone in a home he owns, so he is exempt from paying council tax. His friend Brian, who is on income-related ESA comes to lodge with him, so Liam is now liable for council tax. Liam claims second adult rebate. This is 100 per cent of his council tax liability.

Ravi is the tenant of his flat. He is in a very well-paid job so lets his friend Carl stay with him without charging him rent. Carl earns £190 per week. Ravi's second adult rebate is 7.5 per cent of his council tax liability.

---

5. **Applying for a reduction**

You should apply for council tax reduction (CTR) as soon as you think you might be entitled. If you are not yet liable for the council tax on the property (eg, because you have not yet moved in) but are likely to be eligible for CTR when you become liable, you can make your application in advance (up to eight weeks in England[74] and Scotland[75] and up to 13 weeks in Wales[76]).

The procedure for making an application must meet certain criteria, including giving details of your right of appeal if you do not agree with its decision or its calculations.[77]

If you are not eligible, you may still apply for a discretionary reduction (see p159).

Making an application

An application for CTR must normally be made:[78]
- in writing on a properly completed claim form. Claim forms are available from your local authority, or you may be able to download one from its website;
- online;
- by telephone, if the local authority has published a number for this purpose.

You must provide any information and evidence required. You can claim in some other written form (eg, by letter), as long as the written information and evidence you provide is sufficient.[79]

Check with the local authority that any application you make has been received. If you are claiming CTR in writing, keep a copy of your claim in case queries arise.

An application made on a form provided by an authority is properly completed if it is completed in accordance with the instructions on the form, including any instructions to provide information and evidence in connection with the application.

Supply of further information

Where possible, your claim should be accompanied by all the information and evidence needed to assess it, but you should not delay your claim just because you do not have all the evidence ready to send. Even if you provide all the information required with your claim, the local authority might ask you for further evidence or information. If the local authority requests further information, the supply of information must normally be within one month of a request being made, or such longer time as the local authority considers reasonable.[80]

If you think the local authority has made a wrong decision, you should appeal (see p158 and Chapter 12) and also make a formal complaint to the council.

The local authority must act reasonably, if it acts unreasonably, appeal on the basis that the local authority has wrongly concluded that an appeal has not been validly made.

Applications by couples

If you are part of a couple or polygamous marriage (see p133), your application for CTR is to be made by you or your partner as agreed between yourselves. If you do not agree between yourselves, the local authority may pick the person who is required to make the application.[81]

Amendment and withdrawal of applications

Your application may be amended at any time before a decision has been made on it.[82] This gives an opportunity to include new information, changes in circumstances or correct any errors. Following the amendment, this must be treated as backdated to the time the application was made, as if amended in the first instance.

You may withdraw your application at any time before a decision has been made on it. A notice of withdrawal has effect from when it is received by the local authority.[83]

Where you make you amendment or withdrawal by telephone, you may be required to confirm your amendment or withdrawal in writing.[84]

Notification of decision

Your local authority must make its decision within 14 days or as soon as practicable thereafter. It must notify you and any other person affected the decision in writing within 14 days of the application.[85]

When your entitlement begins and ends

In **England and Scotland**, the general rule is that your first day of entitlement to CTR is the Monday following your date of claim.[86] If your date of claim is a Monday, you have to wait until the following Monday. In **Wales**, your first day of entitlement is the exact date of your claim.[87]

In England and Scotland, if you become liable for the first time for a dwelling in which you are resident, you are entitled from that reduction week.[88] This may arise where the circumstances of the liable person changes – eg, where s/he ceases to be a student.

If your application is not treated as valid, you are not paid until the week after the authority decides that your application is properly made. During this period you are denied CTR and are expected to pay the council tax as if no reduction has been awarded.

You do not have to reapply for CTR, your award continues indefinitely. However, your entitlement to CTR ends if your circumstances change in a way that means you no longer satisfy the rules described in this chapter. **Note:** if you stop claiming income support, income-based jobseeker's allowance or income-related employment and support allowance, your entitlement to CTR continues without you having to make a fresh claim, but your new circumstances could affect the amount of CTR you get.

Backdating

If you are working age, the backdating of your CTR is limited to what is provided in your local authority's scheme.

If you are a pensioner, CTR can be backdated for up to three months from the date you were entitled to claim.[89] No backdating can be made any earlier than three months if you have made a claim for the guarantee credit of PC.[90]

Reporting changes in circumstances

It is your duty to report any change in your circumstances which you might reasonably be expected to know might affect your right to, or the amount of, CTR.[91] You, or a person acting on your behalf, must notify the authority of any changes between the making of an application and a decision being made on it. Similarly, changes must be reported after the decision is made, including at any time you are in receipt of a reduction.

Examples of changes that you must inform the local authority about
Whenever you have a change of address.
Whenever any person joins or leaves your household.
Whenever the income or capital for anyone in the property changes so as to affect benefit or reduction.
Changes in the amount of tax credits or benefits received.
Whenever anyone in the property starts or finishes employment.
Whenever there is a change of ownership of the property in which you live.

In England and Wales, you must report the change within 21 days of when the change occurs, or as soon as reasonably practicable after the change occurs.[92] In Scotland, there is no set time limit to report changes. Do this promptly to the office handling your claim. You can do this in writing, or by telephone if your local authority has published a number for that purpose. If your local authority authorises it, you can also report changes by electronic means, such as email or an online form. However, it is always best to report a change in writing and to keep a copy in case of a dispute in the future. If you do not report a change promptly, any resulting overpayment may be recoverable from you.

There is also a special rule (sometimes call 'Tell Us Once') for births and deaths. You can report such a change to the local authority (and, in England, to a county council) office, if such an office has been specified for reporting these changes. Check with your local authority (eg, at the registrar's office) to see if it provides this service.

If you fail to report a change in circumstances, your CTR may be quashed and you become liable to pay the tax for the period concerned. If you are considered to have deliberately acted falsely or dishonestly, you may also be guilty of an offence.

If you move to a new local authority area, report this change to your old authority and apply for CTR in your new local authority.

Note: what is reasonable may vary from person to person and from area to area, in the same way that CTR schemes vary between different local authorities. For instance, it may not be reasonable in an area where English is not a first language to be expected to report changes. Similarly, where a class of reductions is aimed at assisting certain persons with particular disabilities, it may not be reasonable to expect them to act as promptly as an able-bodied person.

6. **Appeals about council tax reductions**

Challenging the local authority's scheme

If you want to challenge the local authority's council tax reduction (CTR) scheme itself (eg, because you think it is unlawful), you can only do so by way of judicial review.[93] For more on judicial reviews, see Chapter 12.

Challenging a decision about your council tax reduction

England and Wales

You have a right of appeal against decisions made by the local authority about your CTR. Your local authority scheme should contain details of your right of appeal, and the decision notification the local authority issues you about your CTR award should explain how to appeal.[94]

You can appeal decisions about your entitlement or the amount of reduction awarded.[95]

Your appeal must be writing and is commenced by serving a notice on the local authority stating why you are aggrieved – eg, because the local authority has established the wrong facts or has misapplied the law. The authority must consider the matter raised in your notice and inform you in writing either that your ground of grievance is not well founded, and give its reasons, or state the steps it will take to deal with your grievance – eg, look at the matter again, or award the reduction to which you are entitled.[96]

If you are not satisfied with the response of the local authority, or if it fails to respond within two months, you may appeal to the Valuation Tribunal for England (VTE) or the Valuation Tribunal for Wales (VTW) (see Chapter 12).[97]

It is advisable to refer to the right of appeal in the initial letter you send to the local authority. In the case of a dispute over entitlement to a reduction, a calculation or an exemption, a letter can, for example, include the following line: 'In the event that you do not accept my submission, please treat this letter as notice of appeal established under section 16 of the Local Government Finance Act 1992.'

Thus, if the authority does not accept your submission, it must refer the appeal to the VTE or the VTW.

Check with both the local authority and the valuation tribunal to ensure that the local authority has done this. If the local authority does not refer the appeal, contact the tribunal yourself within four months of the appeal.[98]

Appeals about CTR involving income, capital and right of residence or any novel point of law may be heard by a judge from the First-tier Tribunal (Social Entitlement Chamber) if s/he is likely to have particular expertise that is relevant to the determination of the appeal.[99] The High Court may also consider claims concerning the failure of local authorities to properly consider and review applications in exceptional circumstances.[100]

Scotland

If you disagree with the local authority's decision on your CTR application, you can request that the local authority reviews its decision on your CTR application in the same way as described above for England and Wales. You must make the request within two months of the decision, stating why you are aggrieved.[101]

The authority must considered the matter and inform you in writing within two months of its decision.[102]

From October 2013, if you are still dissatisfied with the local authority's decision following its review, you can request in writing within 42 days that your appeal be sent to the Council Tax Reduction Review Panel for further review.[103] See p242 for more information.

7. **Discretionary reductions**

In addition to reductions under its scheme, each local authority in **England and Wales** has a discretionary power to reduce a bill.[104]

Even if your local authority has a scheme which does entitle you to support, it still has a discretion to grant you a reduction – eg, on the grounds of general hardship.

Councils have been given wide scope to reduce bills. The reduction is calculated with reference to an existing discount on a dwelling – eg, a 25 per cent discount might be increased to a 50 per cent discount when calculating a bill, or a 10 per cent discount increased to 20 per cent (see Chapter 8). The power to apply a discretionary reduction includes the power to reduce the bill to zero.[105]

Each scheme must explain how a discretionary reduction can be applied for.[106]

The power to award discretionary relief can be exercised with respect to persons of a particular class.[107] You may appeal if a local authority makes an error in failing to include you in the correct class.

8. Future schemes

Each financial year, a local authority must consider whether to revise or to replace its scheme.[108] It must consult with any major precepting authority such as county councils, the Greater London Authority, police authorities and Metropolitan county fire and rescue authorities. The authority is also required to publish a draft scheme and consult with such 'other persons as the authority considers to be likely to have an interest in the operation of the scheme.' The Secretary of State has power to make provision for the procedure for preparing a scheme or a revision to an individual council scheme, though the government has stated that it does not intend to make regulations under this power. The Secretary of State retains the ultimate power to prescribe classes of people who must be included in a scheme, and those who are not, together with any reductions that may be applied to them.

If a reduction is to be reduced or removed, the billing authority must make such transitional provision as it thinks fit.

Review of council tax support by the Secretary of State

A review of all local reduction schemes by the Secretary of State is required after three years.[109] The terms of the review will be to consider the effectiveness, efficiency, fairness and transparency and their impact on the localism agenda, and to determine whether the schemes should be brought within the universal credit (UC) scheme. The words 'effectiveness, efficiency, fairness and transparency' are not defined in the legislation, so the review is open to influence from political rather than just administrative considerations.

Universal credit

With the introduction of UC, the income and capital of people who receive UC will be treated in accordance with the default scheme if not otherwise covered in a local authority scheme.

Notes

1. The operation of local council tax reduction schemes

1 s13A LGFA 1992 inserted by s10 LGFA 2012
   E CTRS(PR)E Regs
   W CTRSPR(W) Regs
   S CTR(S) Regs; CTR(SPC)(S) Regs
2 **E** CTRS(DS)(E) Regs; CTRS(PR)(E) Regs
   W CTRS(DS)(W) Regs; CTRSPR(W) Regs
3 The Council Tax Reduction Schemes and Prescribed Requirements (Wales) Regulations 2013 No.3029; The Council Tax Reduction Schemes (Default Scheme) (Wales) Regulations 2013 No.3035
4 Statement by the Scottish Government Council Tax Reduction (Scotland) Regulations 2012
5 CTR (SPC) (S) Regs
6 **E** CTRS(PR)(E) Regs
   W CTRSPR(W) Regs
   S CTR(S) Regs; CTR(SPC)(S) Regs
7 **E** Reg 14 and Sch 1 paras 2-4 CTRS(PR)(E) Regs
   W Regs 15 and 20-23 CTRSPR(W) Regs
8 **EW** s13A LGFA 1992
9 s13A LGFA 1992 as amended by LGFA 2012
10 Sch 1A para 2(4) LGFA 1992 as inserted by Sch 4 LGFA 2012
11 **E** Reg 14 CTRS(PR)(E) Regs
   W Regs 20-22 CTRS(PR)(W) Regs
   S Regs 2-6 CTR(S) Regs; regs 2-6 CTR(SPC)(S) Regs
12 Sch 1A para 2(2) LGFA 1992 as inserted by Sch 4 LGFA 2012
13 Sch 1A para 2(5) LGFA 1992 as inserted by Sch 4 LGFA 2012

2. Who can apply for a council tax reduction

14 **E** Reg 6 CTRS(PR)(E) Regs
   W Reg 6 CTRSPR (W) Regs
   S Regs 2, 9 and 11 CTR(S) Regs; regs 2, 9 and 11 CTR(SPC)(S) Regs
15 **E** Reg 5 and Sch 1 paras 4, 8 and 11 CTRS(PR)(E) Regs
   W Regs 5 and 9 and Sch 1 CTRSPR(W) Regs

S Regs 8 and 24 CTR(S) Regs; regs 8 and 21 CTR(SPC)(S) Regs
16 **E** Reg 8 CTRS(PR)(E) Regs
   W Reg 8 CTRSPR(W) Regs
   S Reg 11 CTR(S) Regs; reg 11 CTR(SPC)(S) Regs
17 **E** Reg 8(4) CTRS(PR)(E) Regs
   W Reg 8 CTRSPR(W) Regs
   S Reg 11 CTR(S) Regs; reg 11 CTR(SPC)(S) Regs
18 **E** Reg 7(1) and (2) CTRS(PR)(E) Regs
   W Reg 7 CTRSPR(W) Regs
   S Reg 10 CTR(S) Regs; reg 10 CTR(SPC)(S) Regs
19 **E** Sch 1 para 7(3)-(5) CTRS(PR)(E) Regs
   W Sch 1 para 2(3)-(5) CTRSPR(W) Regs
   S Reg 66(2) and (3) CTR(S) Regs; reg 47(2) and (3) CTR(SPC)(S) Regs
20 *R(on the application of Williams) v Horsham District Council* [2004] *The Times*, 29 January
21 **E** Sch 8 para 5(6)-(7) CTRS(PR)(E) Regs
   W Sch 13 para 2(6)-(7) CTRSPR(W) Regs
   S Reg 85(3),(5) and (6) CTR(S) Regs; reg 65(2)-(3) CTR(SPC)(S) Regs
22 R(H) 9/05
23 **E** Sch 1 para 5 CTRS(PR)(E) Regs
   W Reg 24 CTRSPR(W) Regs
24 **E** Sch 1 Para 5(2) CTRS(PR)(E) Regs
   W Reg 24(2)(a)(iii) CTRSPR(W) Regs
25 **E** Sch 1 para 13 CTRS(PR)(E) Regs
   W Sch 1 para 7 CTRSPR(W) Regs
   S Reg 24 CTR(SPC)(S) Regs
26 **E** Reg 3 CTRS(PR)(E) Regs
   W Reg 3 CTRSPR(W) Regs
   S Reg 12 CTR(S) Regs; reg 12 CTR(SPC)(S) Regs
27 **E** Sch 1 paras 1-4 CTRS(PR)(E) Regs
   W Regs 20-22 CTRSPR(W) Regs
28 **E** Sch 1 para 6(1) CTRS(PR)(E) Regs
   W Sch 1 para 1 CTRSPR(W) Regs
   S Sch 1 CTR(SPC)(S) Regs
29 **E** Sch 1 para 2 CTRS(PR)(E) Regs
   W Reg 20, Sch 1 para 2 and Sch 6 para 4 CTRSPR(W) Regs
   S Sch 1 CTR(SPC)(S) Regs
30 **E** Sch 1 para 3 CTRS(PR)(E) Regs
   W Reg 21 CTRSPR(W) Regs
   S CTR(SPC)(S) Regs
31 **E** Sch 1 para 4 CTRS(PR)(E) Regs

W Reg 22 CTRSPR(W) Regs
S CTR(SPC)(S) Regs
32 **E** Sch 1 para 16(j) CTRS(PR)(E) Regs
W Schs 1 para 10(j) CTRSPR(W) Regs
S CTR(SPC)(S) Regs
33 Reg 11(2) CTRS (PR)(E) Regs
W Reg 28 CTRSPR(W) Regs
S Reg 40 CTR(SPC)(S) Regs
34 **E** Reg 13 CTRS (PR)(E) Regs
W Reg 27 CTRSPR(W) Regs
S Reg 19 CTR(S) Regs
35 **E** Reg 12(5) CTRS (PR)(E) Regs
W Reg 26(5) CTRSPR(W) Regs
S Reg 16(5) CTR(S) Regs
36 **E** Sch 3 para 25 CTRS(DS)(E) Regs
W Sch 3 para 25 CTRS(DS)(W) Regs
S Sch 3 para 25 CTR(S) Regs
37 **E** Sch 8 para 4(2) CTRS(PR)(E) Regs
W Sch para 107(2) CTRS(DS)(W) Regs
38 **E** Sch 1 para 7 CTRS(PR)(E) Regs
W Sch 1 para 2 CTRSPR(W) Regs
S Reg 47 CTR(SPC)(S) Regs
39 **E** Sch 1 para 7(3) and (2) CTRS(PR)(E) Regs
W Sch 1 para 2 and Sch 6 para 4 CTRSPR(W) Regs
S Reg 66(2) and (3) CTR(S) Regs; reg 47(2) and (3) CTR(SPC)(S) Regs
40 **E** Sch 1 para 7(5) CTRS(PR)(E) Regs
W Sch 1 para 2(5) CTRSPR(W) Regs
S Reg 66(2) and (3) CTR(S) Regs; reg 47(2) and (3) CTR(SPC)(S) Regs
41 **E** Sch 1 para 8 CTRS(PR)(E) Regs
W Sch 1 para 3 CTRSPR(W) Regs
S Reg 48(6) CTR(SPC)(S) Regs
42 **E** Sch 1 para 8 CTRS(PR)(E) Regs
W Sch 6 para 5(8) CTRSPR(W) Regs
S Reg 48 CTR(SPC)(S) Regs
43 Sch 1 para 8 CTRS(PR)(E) Regs as amended by reg 2 Council Tax Reduction Schemes (Prescribed Requirements) (England) (Amendment) Regulations 2013 No.3181
44 **E** Sch 1 para 16(3) CTRS(PR)(E) Regs
W Schs 1 and 9 CTRSPR(W) Regs
S Regs 27-33 CTR(CPS)(S) Regs
45 **E** Sch 1 para 17 CTRS(PR)(E) Regs
W Sch 1 paras 11 and 18 CTRSPR(W) Regs
S Reg 28 CTR (CPS)(S) Regs
46 **E** Sch 1 para 16(3) CTRS(PR)(E) Regs
W Sch 6 para 17(5) CTRSPR(W) Regs
S Reg 27(4) CTR(CPS)(S) Regs
47 **E** Sch 1 para 13 CTRS(PR)(E) Regs
W Sch 1 para 7 CTRSPR(W) Regs
S Reg 24 CTR(SPC)(S) Regs
48 **E** Sch 1 para 16 CTRS(PR)(E) Regs
W Sch 1 para 10 CTRSPR(W) Regs

S Reg 27(1) CTR(SPC)(S) Regs
49 **E** Sch 1 para 18 CTRS(PR)(E) Regs
W Sch 1 para 12 CTRPR(W) Regs
S Regs 32 and 34 CTR(SPC)(S) Regs
50 **E** Sch 1 Para 20 CTRS(PR)(E) Regs
W Sch 1 para 14 CTRSPR(W) Regs
S Regs 34-37 CTR(SPC)(S) Regs
51 **E** Sch 1 para 18 CTRS(PR)(E) Regs
W Sch 1 para 12 CTRPR(W) Regs
S Reg 34 CTR(SPC)(S) Regs
52 **E** Sch 4 paras 1-3 CTRS(PR)(E) Regs
W Sch 3 CTRSPR(W) Regs
S Sch 3 CTR(S) Regs; Sch 2 CTR(SPC)(S) Regs
53 **E** Sch 1 para 25 CTRS(PR)(E) Regs
W Sch 1 para 19 and Sch 6 para 21 CTRSPR(W) Regs
S Reg 28 CTR(S) Regs; reg 29 CTR(SPC)(S) Regs
54 **E** Reg 11(2) CTRS(PR)(E) Regs
W Reg 28 CTRSPR(W) Regs
S Reg 40 CTR(SPC)(S) Regs
55 **E** Sch 1 para 31(1) CTRS(PR)(E) Regs
W Sch 1 para 25 CTRSPR(W) Regs
S Reg 43 CTR(S) Regs; reg 41 CTR(SPC)(S) Regs
56 *Lloyd v Secretary of State for Work and Pensions* [2011] UKUT
57 **E** Sch 6 Part 1 CTRS(PR)(E) Regs
W Schs 5 and 10 CTRSPR(W) Regs
S Sch 5 CTR(SPC)(S) Regs
58 **E** Sch 1 para 34 CTRS(PR)(E) Regs
W Sch 1 para 28 CTRSPR(W) Regs
S Sch 5 para 44 CTR(SPC)(S) Regs
59 **E** Sch para 36 CTRS(PR)(E) Regs;
W Sch 1 para 30 CTRSPR(W) Regs
S Reg 51 CTR(S) Regs
60 **E** Sch 1 para 38 CTRS(PR)(E) Regs
W Sch 1 para 32 and Sch 6 para 34 CTRSPR(W) Regs
S Reg 73 CTR(S) Regs; reg 49 CTR(SPC)(S) Regs
61 **W** Reg 31(3) CTRSPR(W) Regs
62 **E** Sch 1 para 43 CTRS(PR)(E) Regs
W Sch 1 para 37 CTRSPS(W) Regs
S Reg 55 CTR(SPC)(S) Regs

4. **Alternative maximum council tax reduction**
63 **E** Sch 1 para 4 and Sch 3 para 1 CTRS(PR)(E) Regs
S Reg 78 and Sch 2 CTR(S) Regs; reg 56 and Sch 5 CTR(SPC)(S) Regs
64 CH/48/2006
65 **E** Sch 3 CTRS(PR)(E) Regs
S Reg 56 CTR(SPC)(S) Regs
66 Reg 78 CTR(S)Regs
67 Regs 15 and 18 CTRS(DS)(E) Regs

68 **E** Sch 1 para 4 CTRS(PR)(E) Regs; regs 15 and 18 CTRS(DS)(E) Regs
   S Reg 78 CTR(S)Regs; reg 56 CTR(SPC)(S) Regs
69 s6(5) LGFA 1992
70 Sch 1 LGFA 1992
71 **E** Sch 1 para 9 CTRS(PR)(E) Regs
   S Reg 78 CTR(S) Regs; reg 56 CTR(SPC) Regs
72 **E** Sch 1 para 9 CTRS(PR)(E) Regs
   S Reg 78 CTR(S) Regs; reg 56 CTR(SPC)(S) Regs
73 **E** Sch 3 CTRS(PR)(E) Regs
   S Sch 2 CTR(SPC)(S) Regs

5. Applying for a reduction
74 Sch 8 para 5(6) CTRS(PR)(E) Regs
75 Reg 85(3) CTR(S) Regs
76 Sch 13 para 2(6) CTRSPR(W) Regs
77 Sch 1A para 2(5) and (6) LGFA 1992
78 **E** Sch 7 para 2 CTRS(PR)(E) Regs
   W Sch 12 para 2 CTRSPR(W) Regs
   S Regs 83 and 84 CTR(S) Regs; regs 63 and 64 CTR(SPC)(S) Regs
79 **E** Sch 7 para 4(b) CTRS(PR)(E) Regs
   W Sch 12 para 4(1)(b) CTRSPR(W) Regs
   S Reg 83(1)(b) CTR(S) Regs; reg 63(1)(b) CTR(SPC)(S) Regs
80 **E** Sch 8 para 5(5)(c) CTRS(PR)(E) Regs
   W Sch 13 para 2, 5(4) CTRSPR(W) Regs
   S Reg 83(5) CTR(S) Regs; reg 63(5) CTR(SPC)(S) Regs
81 **E** Sch 8 para 4(1) CTRS(PR)(E) Regs
   W Sch 13 para 1 CTRSPR(W) Regs
   S Reg 82 CTR(S) Regs; reg 61 CTR(SPC)(S) Regs
82 **E** Sch 8 para 8(1)-(3) CTRS(PR)(E) Regs
   W Sch 13 para 6(1)-(3) CTRSPR(W) Regs
   S Reg 87 CTR(S) Regs; reg 67 CTR(SPC)(S) Regs
83 **E** Sch 8 para 8(4)-(6) CTRS(PR)(E) Regs
   W Sch 13 para 6(4)-(6) CTRSPR(W) Regs
   S Reg 88 CTR(S) Regs; reg 68 CTR(SPC)(S) Regs
84 **E** Sch 8 para 8(7) CTRS(PR)(E) Regs
   W Sch 13 para 6(7) CTRSPR(W) Regs
   S Reg 87(2) CTR(S) Regs; reg 67(2) CTR(SPC)(S) Regs
85 **E** Sch 8 para 11 CTRS(PR)(E) Regs
   W Sch 13 para 8 CTRSPR(W) Regs
86 **E** Sch 1 para 45(1) CTRS(PR)(E) Regs; Sch para 106 CTRS(DS)(E) Regs
   S Reg 80(1) CTR(S) Regs; reg 58(1) CTR(SPC)(S) Regs
87 **W** Sch 1 para 39 CTRSPR(W) Regs; Sch para 104 CTRS(DS)(W) Regs
88 **E** Sch 1 para 45(2) CTRS(PR)(E) Regs
   S Reg 80(2) CTR(S) Regs

89 **E** Sch 8 para 6(2) CTRS(PR)(E) Regs
   W Sch 13 para 3(1) CTRSPR(W) Regs
   S Reg 62(1) CTR(SPC)(S) Regs
90 **E** Sch 8 Reg 6(3) CTRS(PR)(E) Regs
   W Sch 13 para 3(2) CTRSPR(W) Regs
   S Reg 62(2) CTR(SPC)(S) Regs
91 **E** Sch 8 para 9 CTRS(PR)(E) Regs
   W Sch 13 para 7 CTRSPR(W) Regs
   S Reg 89 CTR(S) Regs; reg 69 CTR(SPC)(S) Regs
92 **E** Sch 8 para 9(2) CTRS(PR)(E) Regs
   W Sch 13 para 7(2) CTRSPR(W) Regs

6. Appeals about council tax reductions
93 s66(ba) LGFA 1992 as amended by LGFA 2012
94 **E** Sch 8 para 12(4) CTRS(PR)(E) Regs
   W Sch 14 para 3 CTRSPR(W) Regs
95 **E** Sch 7 para 8(1)CTRS(PR)(E) Regs
   W Sch 12 para 8 CTRSPR(W) Regs
96 **E** Sch 7 para 8(2) CTRS(PR)(E) Regs
   W Sch 12 para 9 CTRSPR(W) Regs
97 **E** Sch 7 para 8(3) CTRS(PR)(E) Regs
   W Sch 12 para 10 CTRSPR(W) Regs
98 s16 LGFA 1992
99 Sch 11 para A18A LGFA 1988 inserted by Sch 4 para 2 LGFA 2012
100 *Norman and another v East Dorset District Council* [2012] EWHC 3696 (Admin)
101 Reg 90A(3) CTR(S) Regs; reg 70A(2) CTR(SPC)(S) Regs
102 Reg 90A(4) CTR(S) Regs; reg 70A(4) CTR(SPC)(S) Regs
103 Reg 90B(5) CTR(S) Regs; reg 70B(5) CTR(SPC)(S) Regs
104 s13A(1)(c) LGFA 1992
105 s13A(6)LGFA 1992
106 s13A(1)(c) LGFA 1992
107 s13A(7) LGFA 1992
108 Sch 1A para 5(1) LGFA 1992 as amended by LGFA 2012
109 s9(1) and (2) LGFA 2012

Chapter 10

Bills and payments

This chapter covers:

1. Who must pay the bill

Chapter 6 identified the people who are liable for council tax, but in most cases no one need actually pay the tax until a bill has been issued.[1] If the name of a liable person cannot be established after reasonable enquiries have been made by the local authority, the bill may be addressed to the 'council taxpayer'.[2] Bills may be issued to both individual taxpayers or a company if it is liable – eg, as an owner of a dwelling. The Secretary of State prescribes the form that bills take.

Local authorities should ensure that their computer systems do not issue bills in the name of taxpayers who have died. These should normally be sent to the 'personal representatives of deceased' or the 'executors of the deceased'.

In Scotland, a bill need not be issued if the only liable person is a housing body (eg, a local council or new town development corporation) or an owner who has agreed with the local authority that a bill need not be served.[3]

The liable person's spouse or partner, and anyone who has the same degree of legal interest in the dwelling, is jointly liable for the bill (see p85). In Scotland, but not England and Wales, someone who is jointly liable with the person(s) named on the bill but whose name is not included on the bill is still liable to make any payments required.[4]

In England and Wales, no payment can be required of someone who is jointly liable who has not previously been included on a bill until a 'joint taxpayers' bill' has been issued.[5] This must be served within six years of the first day of the financial year to which it relates. The liable people themselves must determine how exactly they share the responsibility for the bill.

Joint liability means that both or all jointly liable taxpayers can be held individually or collectively liable to pay the whole amount. A decision on 'joint and several liability' can be appealed (see Chapter 12).

2. **When bills should be issued**

The local authority should serve a council tax bill on each chargeable dwelling each financial year. In England and Wales, this should be done 'as soon as practicable' after the local authority first sets a council tax for the year.[6] In Scotland, a local authority should serve the bill as soon as practicable after it has first set a council tax and knows the water charge for the year.[7]

Separate bills must be sent for different financial years and for different dwellings, even if the same person is liable for both.[8] This rule is sometimes breached by outsourced companies acting for local authorities who may issue repeated bills for the same periods, each with differing amounts. In such a case, problems may arise at the enforcement stage as it can be unclear which bill is to be treated as valid and difficult for the local authority to show it has complied with the rules on billing. In England and Wales, however, one council tax bill may also cover the current and preceding financial years if it is for the same dwelling.[9]

Local authorities will want to ensure that bills are produced promptly to maximise their cash flows. Most local authorities aim to send out council tax bills in mid-March, with the payment falling due from 1 April. People paying by direct debit may be given several dates in April on which to make their first payment. In Scotland, local authorities have two options for starting annual billing. The established method of 10 annual instalments can be used, or the local authority may allow payment by 12 instalments.

Late bills

A local authority must issue a bill (or 'demand notice') 'as soon as reasonably practicable'. If there has been a long delay, the local authority may not be able to recover the money if it has been in breach of this requirement. In one case concerning non-domestic rates, the local authority delayed seven years before serving demand notices for the years 1990–1997.[10] When the ratepayers failed to pay, the local authority obtained liability orders. The High Court, however, quashed the liability orders as the delay in serving the demand notices was 'inexcusable'.

The High Court has indicated, however, that late bills may be valid, even if they are sent several years after the tax fell due, but invalid if they cause 'prejudice' to the taxpayer. In three cases involving North Somerset District Council, the High Court considered the effect that serving a bill late had on validity.[11] Ordinarily, mere delay is not sufficient to invalidate a notice. The High Court ruled that the test was to look at the length of the delay and the impact on the taxpayer. The key test is whether 'prejudice' has been caused. '**Prejudice**' is different from inconvenience and must be substantial and can be caused in a number of ways. The Court also said that there was also a public interest in ensuring that local taxes were collected, which had to be weighed in the balance. In all three cases, the defendants were found to have suffered prejudice.

Prejudice could arise for an individual on a low income who is sent council tax bills for previous financial years that do not take into account any past entitlement to council tax benefit (CTB) that might have existed at the time. Indeed, any application for CTB for earlier financial years will be thwarted by the benefit backdating rules. Arguably, prejudice is caused to anyone who effectively loses a right to claim CTB which might have covered the total liability for the year concerned. Similarly, from 1 April 2013, if you are unable to claim under the local authority's council tax reduction scheme because of failure to supply a demand notice in time, it is possible to challenge the bill as invalid as it has caused prejudice.

If you want to challenge the late issue of a bill, do so before a liability order is issued by a magistrates' court. In theory, this should also be the case before the sheriff court in Scotland[12] but the difficulty is the Scottish summary procedure does not give notice to the council taxpayer (see Chapter 11).

Another remedy might be to lodge an appeal with the Valuation Tribunal for England, the Valuation Tribunal for Wales or valuation appeal committee in Scotland under s16 (s81 in Scotland) of the Local Government Finance Act 1992, which allows appeals on 'any calculation' in respect of a sum of council tax (see p240). The right to appeal arises as soon as you become aware of the bill.

Reducing council tax if a bill is late

A local authority has the power to reduce an individual council tax bill (see p48). If a bill is served late, perhaps years after the original liability arose, you can apply to the local authority to reduce the sum concerned by way of a discretionary reduction.

Late service of a bill may amount to maladministration (see Chapter 13) and cause hardship. Although a bill being served late does not automatically make it invalid, a local authority is expected to act sympathetically and reasonably if you are prejudiced through official error, including giving you time to pay. A failure to respond properly if a late bill causes hardship to a vulnerable person may amount to maladministration. If a council has an anti-poverty strategy, it is expected to act in accordance with it.

3. **How the bill is calculated**

Liability for council tax is calculated on a daily basis. Council tax is payable for each day a dwelling is a chargeable dwelling which is the sole or main residence of the taxpayer, with the taxpayer being liable for each day s/he lives in the dwelling. As soon as s/he ceases to have sole or main residence, liability to tax will end. In some cases, the owner of the empty dwelling may be entitled to a discount (see p104) or exemption (see p53). However, the bill issued at the beginning of the financial year is for the full year. The local authority is required to use certain assumptions to estimate what it thinks the council tax will be for the whole year and correct it later, if necessary (see p168).

The local authority must estimate the 'chargeable amount' by taking the relevant amount of council tax for that dwelling (depending on its valuation band), and then make the following assumptions.

- The person will be liable for every day.
- The dwelling's valuation band will not change and it will remain a chargeable dwelling throughout the year.
- Any reduction under the disability reduction scheme has been properly calculated and applies throughout the year.
- The bill is either eligible or not eligible for a discount throughout the year.
- Any council tax reduction (CTR) which applies does so throughout the year.[13]
- Liability for Scottish Water charges applies throughout the year in Scotland.[14]

If more than one reduction applies to the council tax for the band, they should be applied in the following order:
- disability reduction;
- discount;
- any reduction under the local authority's CTR scheme and/or any discretionary reduction.

The local authority must ensure that if 100 per cent CTR is awarded, this is equal to your liability.

The bill can also take into account any credits from past periods, penalties due and any alleged overpayment of council tax benefit (CTB).

The question of whether an amount of excess CTB from more than one year earlier may be subject to recovery action through the magistrates' court remains an unsettled question.

Special rules apply if a bill is for a period earlier in the financial year, and if, on the day it is issued, you are no longer liable for council tax at that address. The bill will either:
- require payment of the amount due up to the last day of liability (calculated as described above but based on the actual, not estimated, circumstances); *or*

- if you are due a credit, require the amount payable (if any) after the credit has been offset against the chargeable amount.[15] This could apply, for example, following a delay in re-calculating a reduction or where a referendum is held.

If a bill is issued after the end of the year to which it relates, it must require payment of the amount due for the year, calculated as described above, but based on the actual circumstances and after taking into account any credits carried over from earlier years.

If the estimated amount has been based on incorrect assumptions

It may become clear during the course of a year that an estimated amount has been based on an incorrect assumption – eg, your entitlement to a discount may change part way through the year. If so, the local authority should calculate the appropriate amount that currently appears due for the year.[16] If:

- the new amount is **greater than** the estimated amount, the local authority should bill you and give you at least 14 days to make the interim payment;
- the new amount is **less than** the estimated amount, the local authority should notify you accordingly and make an interim repayment (but see below).

Further rules apply about changes in the tax payable as a consequence of any local referendum (see p46).

In England and Wales, if an overpayment of council tax has occurred because you are no longer liable to make payments on one dwelling but become immediately liable to make payments to the same local authority on another dwelling, the local authority may credit the overpayment against your new liability, rather than make you a repayment. This is likely to be done unless you specify otherwise to the authority. If you overpaid a lump-sum payment, the local authority should make an interim repayment in the usual way.[17]

If you have made payments under the statutory instalment scheme or, in England and Wales, the council tenant instalment scheme, see pp173 and 176.

Incorrect payments

The actual amount owed to the local authority will be known for certain only at the end of the financial year or when your liability ends. Another bill is therefore required if a previous bill was issued for a financial year (or part of a financial year) and the payment(s) required was, in fact, more or less than the actual liability and there has been no appropriate adjustment. The local authority should, as soon as practicable after the end of the year (or the part of a year), serve a new bill on the liable person. This should state the actual amount due and adjust the amount(s) required to be paid under the previous bill.[18]

If the amount stated in the new notice is greater than the amount previously required, you must pay the difference within a period specified by the local authority. This period must be at least 14 days following the issue of the new bill.[19]

If there has been an overpayment of council tax and you require a refund, this must be given. In any other case, the local authority may decide either to repay the amount in question to you or credit it against any future council tax liability.[20] However, if the overpayment has arisen because you are no longer liable to make payments on one dwelling, but are immediately liable to make payments to the same local authority on another dwelling and you have not made a lump-sum payment, the local authority may require the amount of any overpayment to be credited against the new liability.[21]

In England and Wales, if the local authority is required to repay a sum but does not do so, you can take recovery action using the civil debt procedure in the county court.[22] The small claims procedure of the county court can be used for sums up to £5,000. A similar procedure exists in Scotland for sums up to £3,000.

See also excessive amounts of council tax on p172.

4. **How bills are served**

Before you are required to pay council tax, a bill must be served. This does not mean that you necessarily must know it is served, only that the bill was served in such a way that you could be expected to know about it. Bills may be served by:
- post; *or*
- being delivered to the liable person at her/his usual or last known address; *or*
- being delivered to some other person at the chargeable dwelling; *or*
- being fixed to some conspicuous part of the dwelling; *or*
- email.

In the case of a limited company, the bill should be addressed to the company's registered office and, in the case of a partnership, to the principal office of the partnership.

If a bill has been served in one of the above ways, the date of issue is the date the bill was posted or left at the address. In all other cases, it is the date of actual service of the notice. The bill should include the date of issue, which determines such matters as when payments become due.[23] Practice Note No.5 (para 5.4) reminds local authorities to ensure that when a bill is sent by post, the first instalment due is payable at least 14 days after the day on which it is delivered to a post office. Practice Note No.5 (para 5.5) suggests that local authorities should maintain records of the days on which bills are delivered to the post office so that they can present evidence of the date of issue for any particular bill. If the bill has not arrived at the appropriate address, the local authority must serve it again if it wishes to start enforcement proceedings (see Chapter 11). Under the Interpretation Act 1978, a document is deemed served two days after it is sent by first-class post. Some local authorities use outsourced providers who organise specially arranged deliveries with the post office. In such a case the local authority must still be able to provide evidence that demands have been served correctly (see Chapter 11).

5. Information the bill should contain

The bill must contain certain prescribed information. This includes comparative information relating to areas that are subject to local government restructuring.[24] There are minor variations between England, Wales and Scotland. Local authorities can decide the exact wording and how the information appears on the bill.

Information contained on council tax bills[25]

- The name of the person to whom the bill is addressed. If not known, the bill may be addressed to the 'council taxpayer'.
- The day of issue.
- The period covered by the bill.
- The address of the chargeable dwelling.
- The dwelling's valuation band.
- The amount of council tax (and Scottish Water charges in Scotland) per chargeable dwelling for the relevant valuation band for each tier of local government (eg, district and county council) including, where applicable, a specified amount to cover parish or community council expenditure.
- A reference to the billing authority's discretionary power to reduce bills under section 13A(1) of the Local Government Finance Act.[26]
- How the amount of the council tax (and Scottish Water charges in Scotland) payable has been calculated, showing separate amounts of any disability reduction, discount and variation of discount or council tax reduction under the local authority scheme and the period they cover.
- In England, the percentage change in council tax from the previous year expressed to one decimal place.
- The gross expenditure of each billing and precepting authority for the year and the previous year, and the reasons for any difference between the figures for the previous and current year.
- The opinions of the billing authority and precepting opinion of the effect that its gross expenditure has on the level of council tax set for the relevant year.[27]
- The reason for any discount, reduction or premium and a statement of the person's duty to inform the local authority of anything that affects entitlement to a discount and the fact that if s/he does not comply with this duty, without a reasonable excuse, the local authority may impose a financial penalties in England Wales and Scotland.

- The amount (if any) to be credited against the amount of council tax which would otherwise be payable for the relevant year.
- The amount of any penalty.
- Council tax arrears from the preceding year(s), but only to the extent that they have not already been billed for.
- The amount of council tax payable and how it should be paid.
- The address, telephone number and email to which enquiries may be made.
- A statement on any reduction applicable under a local council tax reduction (CTR) scheme, explaining the amount of the reduction and the reasons for it.
- An explanation of the duty to report changes of circumstances[28] and an explanation of the possible consequences of failing to notify relevant changes in circumstances.

Bills served after the end of the year in question or with another bill for another period are not required to contain all of the above information.[29]

Explanatory notes and accompanying information

The bill should be accompanied by a set of explanatory notes that provide key points of information on: valuation and banding, exempt dwellings, disability reductions, discounts, appeals and the local CTR scheme. The billing regulations distinguish between information which a demand notice is required to contain and information which it is required to supply with a demand notice.[30]

Additionally, in England and Wales, the bill, if issued before the end of the financial year to which it relates, must be accompanied by information explaining the local authority's income and expenditure. Bills served on or after 1 April 2010 in England must also include details of efficiency savings made by the local authority in the preceding year.[31] Bills that are served after the end of the financial year concerned or with another bill are not required to contain all the specified information.[32]

A local authority may publishing the information on its website rather than including the information with a demand notice.[33] The website address must be provided in the demand notice's explanatory notes and state where on the website the information may be accessed. To prevent discrimination against people who do not have access to the internet or cannot use it, it must also be stated that there is a right to request, in writing, a free of charge printed copy of that information[34] and that the authority must supply it as soon as reasonably practicable.[35]

Local authorities are also required to include information about the annual percentage changes in council tax between the previous year and the relevant year. If the valuation band of a dwelling has changed, the bill must show the percentage difference between the amounts calculated in the relevant year and the previous year.[36]

Invalid bills

A bill is invalid if it does not contain all the required information. Nevertheless, if the failure to comply with these requirements arose because of a mistake and the amount to be paid is demanded correctly, the bill is treated as valid. The local authority must issue a correction and a statement of the matter omitted from the bill as soon as practicable after the mistake has been found and send it to you.[37] However, there may be situations where the details contained in the bill are confusing or contradicted by amounts stated in other demands. It may be that the bill is a nullity and should be treated as invalid. If the amount stated in the bill is incorrect, it should be challenged immediately with the local authority and an appeal commenced (see Chapter 12).[38] If the local authority or an outsourced company acting on its behalf does not respond, make a formal complaint.

Excessive amounts of council tax and referendums

If an authority's relevant basic amount of council tax is excessive, the local authority is required to include details as a footnote and give notice that a referendum will be held with further information to be supplied in due course. The demand notice continues to be valid in spite of the inclusion of the additional amount identified as excessive but, importantly, the local authority cannot take recovery action in respect of the additional amount until a referendum is held.

No liability order may be issued and no enforcement action (eg, sending in bailiffs or attachment of earnings) may be taken for an additional amount, unless it is approved by a referendum. The 'additional amount' is the difference between the amount on the bill and any substituted amount which is applicable following a referendum.[39]

If the excessive amount is not approved in a referendum, a referendum is held to be void or if no referendum is held, a substitute non-excessive amount takes effect, and a local authority may issue a further revised demand notice.[40] Thus, no recovery action can be taken in respect of the amount on a demand that has been declared excessive following a referendum.

If you request that a fresh bill is issued, the local authority must provide it. This also appears to have consequences for enforcement as, if the local authority does not issue a fresh bill, then the sum cannot be enforced as the local authority will be unable to prove it has followed the rules on billing that are essential for applying for a liability order (see Chapter 11).[41]

Where an authority's excessive relevant basic amount is not approved in a referendum, its substitute calculations have effect. However, an election court may subsequently overturn the result on the basis that it is not in accordance with the votes cast.

Where the result of the referendum is to approve the level of council tax originally set by the local authority, the original demand notice is enforceable.[42]

However, an election court may subsequently overturn the result on the basis that it is not in accordance with the votes cast. Any demand notices originally issued for the excessive amount continue to have effect, and have effect as if they include the difference between the excessive amount and the substituted amount.[43]

6. **Payment arrangements**

Most taxpayers have a right to pay by instalments. The 'normal' method of payment is by 10 monthly instalments between April and January (see below).[44] From 2013 if you are in England, this can be spread over 12 instalments if you inform the local authority before 15 April, or over as many months of the year as remain up until 31 March. The local authority may, however, adopt a variety of different payment arrangements, including:

- in England and Wales, the council tenant instalment scheme (see p176). In Scotland, the local authority may establish an agency arrangement with a housing body which then establishes its own payment arrangements;[45]
- special arrangements (see p178);
- discounted lump-sum payments (see p179);
- discounts for non-cash payments (see p179).

Instalments

In **England and Wales**, if the bill is issued:[46]
- on or before 30 April in the relevant year, payments under the statutory scheme are made in 10 monthly instalments;
- from 1 May onwards, the monthly instalments must equal one less than the number of whole months remaining in the financial year (see p174);
- between 1 January and 31 March in the relevant year, the total amount due is payable in a single instalment on the day specified on the bill.

The instalments must be made in consecutive months, but the local authority may choose the month in which to start and state this on the bill.[47]

Note: from 1 April 2013 in **England**, you also have a legal right to request to pay your council tax bill in 12 monthly payments, rather than a maximum of 10, in the course of the year.[48] Information on how to arrange this should be given with the explanatory notes which accompany the demand notice sent at the beginning of the financial year.[49]

In **Scotland**, a local authority cannot demand the first instalment in the same month as the bill was issued. If the bill is issued:[50]
- before 1 April in the relevant year, the local authority determines when the first of the 10 instalments is due – this can be either in April or May;

- from 1 April onwards, the monthly instalments must equal one less than the number of whole months remaining in the financial year (see below);
- between 1 December and 31 March in the relevant year, the total amount due is payable in a single instalment on the day specified on the bill.

Some Scottish councils allow 12 monthly instalments at their own discretion if you pay by direct debit – eg, Edinburgh City Council has done this in the past.

Number of instalments

Month in which demand notice is issued	Number of instalments
April (or before)	10
May	9
June	8
July	7
August	6
September	5
October	4
November	3
December	2
January	1
February	1
March	1

Amount of the instalments

The amount of the instalments is worked out by dividing the total amount of the bill by the number of instalments. If this gives an amount which is a multiple of a pound, the instalments will be of that amount.[51]

Example

The council tax is £500 and payments are to be by 10 instalments. The amount of each instalment is £50.

If the total amount due, divided by the number of instalments, does not give an amount which is a multiple of a pound, the amount payable is divided by the number of instalments and rounded to the nearest pound. Amounts ending in 50p should be rounded up. This amount is the amount of the instalments other than the first. This first amount is multiplied by the number of instalments less one, and the resulting amount is subtracted from the total amount payable. The amount remaining is the amount of the first instalment.[52]

Example

The council tax is £500 and payments are to be by nine instalments.
The amount of all but the first instalment will be £56.
(ie, £500 ÷ 9 = £55.5555)
The first instalment will be £52.
(ie, £500 − (£56 x 8 instalments))

If you only have a small amount of council tax to pay, the instalment method is an expensive way for the local authority to collect it. Consequently, local authorities have the power not to accept any instalment for less than £5. If the calculation of instalments would produce an instalment of less than £5, the local authority may require that the second instalment be added to the first and that the number of instalments be reduced by one. If the total amount payable is less than £10, the local authority may request payment of that amount in a single instalment. If the total amount payable is £10 or more, the local authority may reduce the number of instalments to the greatest number that allows individual instalments of at least £5.[53]

Where the annual amount is divided into 12 instalments, the annual amount is payable over 12 months unless otherwise specified or agreed. The onus is on you to begin the process by requesting this from the local authority. Your request may be made either before or after a demand notice is issued and may be made in relation to the relevant year, or the year following the relevant year.

If you make a request during the financial year, the local authority must issue an instalment notice 'as soon as reasonably practicable'.[54]

Local authorities in England are encouraged to make provision for payment of council tax in 12 monthly instalments as an alternative to the statutory 10 instalment scheme.[55] Where your request to arrange payment in 12 monthly instalments is made between 1 January and 15 April in the year in which the financial year begins, the number of instalments is 12. If your request is made on or after 16 April of the year in question, the number of monthly instalments is the number of whole months remaining in the relevant year after the issue of the notice.[56] Effectively, in any case arising after 16 April, you are able to spread the remaining year's liability over as many months as remains which also means treating February and March as instalment months.

Example

Eliza wants to pay in 12 monthly installments in 2014/15. She must request this from the local authority between 1 January and 15 April 2014.
However, if Eliza does not make her request until 6 June, she will have nine instalments to pay (July – March).

In England, where the total amount is calculated by reference to a determination involving a discount which varies during the course of the year (ie, where the Secretary of State or the local authority changes the classification of dwelling entitled to discount), the monthly instalments do not need to be equal amounts but shall be as specified in the notice.[57]

Instalment scheme for council tenants

In **Scotland**, the local authority may establish an agency arrangement with a housing body. It is then for that housing body to establish appropriate payment arrangements.[58]

In **England and Wales**, a local authority may have an instalment scheme for its council tenants to pay their council tax on the same day as they pay their rent but these have become increasingly rare. This means that if you pay your rent weekly, for example, the local authority may also allow you to pay your council tax weekly.[59] The scheme may also continue to apply during any period in the year in which rent is not payable, provided such a period follows a period in which rent was payable.

The scheme must:
- apply to all council tenants;
- apply to all financial years following the introduction of the scheme unless varied or revoked;
- only be varied in its operation if this is agreed before the local authority first sets its council tax for the relevant year;
- not be revoked later than 31 December of the year immediately preceding the beginning of the financial year in which it will no longer apply;
- have at least 10 instalments, but no more than 52;
- require the first instalment no earlier than 14 days after the day on which the bill is issued;
- specify the interval of instalments to be payable on such a day in each interval as is specified in the scheme;
- require the last instalment to be paid before the end of the relevant year;
- provide for how the amount of any instalment will be determined if the total amount, when divided by the number of instalments, does not give an amount which is a multiple of 10 pence.[60]

Instalments when liability ends

No further instalments under either the statutory schemes or, in England and Wales, the council tenant's scheme are due once you are no longer liable for council tax (and for Scottish Water charges in Scotland). If more than one person is jointly liable, whether named on the original bill or not, this only applies if both or all of them are no longer liable. In England and Wales, if the only person(s) who is liable is someone not named on the original bill, the local authority must issue a joint taxpayers' notice on her/him.[61]

If the original liable person(s) is no longer liable, the local authority must serve a notice on the former liable person or, if there was joint liability, on at least one of the jointly liable people. The notice should state the actual amount due up to the day liability ended. This should be done as soon as practicable after liability ends.[62]

If the amount due is less than the total amount paid, the liable person may require the local authority to repay the overpayment. If no request is made, the local authority may decide either to repay it or to credit it against a subsequent council tax debt on another property for which the same person is liable.[63] It cannot be used to meet any other debt recoverable by the local authority, such as an overpayment of housing benefit.

If the amount due is greater than the total amount paid, the local authority will issue a bill requiring the liable person to pay the outstanding amount to the local authority. The local authority must allow at least 14 days from issuing the bill for this amount to be paid.[64]

If the former liable person becomes, once again, liable for the tax to the local authority in the same financial year, the matter is dealt with afresh. Any previous overpayment of tax by the liable person may, however, be credited against the subsequent liability.

Instalments when liability changes

The instalment schemes are based on the assumption that your circumstances will remain the same throughout the year. Liability may change, however, because:
- the council tax changes as a result of budgets being capped by central government; *or*
- the dwelling becomes exempt; *or*
- the dwelling's valuation band changes; *or*
- entitlement to a discount changes; *or*
- entitlement to a disability reduction changes; *or*
- entitlement to a council tax reduction (CTR) under the local authority scheme changes; *or*
- liability to pay Scottish Water charges in Scotland changes.[65]

The local authority must adjust the remaining instalments (if any) as soon as practicable after the change of circumstances.[66] As many adjustments may be made as the circumstances require. The local authority must also serve a revised bill (an adjustment notice) each time an adjustment is made. This should state the:
- revised estimated liability for the relevant year, assuming no further changes; *and*

- amount of any instalments that remain 14 or more days after the issue of the notice.

In **England and Wales**, if instalments are payable under the statutory scheme and additional amounts are now due as a result of a change, the payments must be fixed in accordance with the rules for that scheme (see p173). In **Scotland**, the local authority has the discretion to set the amount of each remaining instalment. If no further instalments are due, the additional amount must be paid as a lump sum within a period set by the local authority. The local authority must give you at least 14 days from the date the bill was issued to pay the amount owing. In Scotland at least two instalments must fall to be paid under the demand notice concerned in accordance with the statutory instalment scheme or any agreement with the council.[67]

If the revised amount is less than the combined amounts of the instalments payable before the change, you should request that the overpayment is refunded. If you do not make such a request, the local authority may decide either to repay it or credit it against your subsequent liability.[68]

If a local authority revises its estimate of your council tax liability, when adjusting the remaining instalments it must take into account any amounts paid before the day on which the adjustment takes effect which were due to be paid after that day.[69]

Special payment arrangements

If you owe council tax for a previous year and want to repay it by instalments, the local authority must agree to this. If you try to top up your instalments for the current year with a payment towards previous years and the computer system is not expecting it, the total payment may be allocated to the oldest bill owing while the current year's bill remains unpaid. The result could be that you lose the right to pay the current year's council tax by instalments. See below and Chapter 11 for more details.

A local authority may agree that you can pay your council tax in a particular manner.[70] These special payment arrangements may be entered into either before or after a bill has been issued, although in England and Wales if there is joint liability, the arrangement can only be entered into with someone named on the bill. Special payment arrangements may prove useful if you are facing financial problems. These may allow payments to be ended or adjusted. They may also allow for a fresh estimate to be made if the original estimate turns out to be wrong. If the special arrangement is entered into after the bill has been issued, it may make provision for dealing with any sums paid by instalments.

A bill issued under a special arrangement requires payment of the amount concerned:
- within a set period of not less than 14 days after the day the bill is issued; *or*
- by instalments and payable at intervals and on days as specified on the bill.

The normal enforcement procedures (see Chapter 11) do not apply to special agreements. Practice Note No.9 (para 1.11) advises local authorities to ensure that the agreement sets out the procedures to be followed in the event of non-payment.

Discounts for lump-sum payments

The local authority may decide to encourage payment of council tax by lump sums as this improves its cash flow and reduces its collection costs. The benefits and costs of such an arrangement, not only to the local authority but to all taxpayers, need to be considered carefully. To encourage lump-sum payments, the local authority can offer a discount.[71]

If the local authority has discount arrangements it must:
- decide to operate such a scheme and the amount to be discounted on or before the day it first sets its council tax for the year; *and*
- apply the scheme in the same way to people who pay the same number of instalments in the year. For example, if a 5 per cent reduction is offered to everyone who is liable to pay 10 instalments, it must be offered to everyone who is liable.

Furthermore, for a lump sum to qualify for a discount:
- at least two instalments of council tax must be payable under the statutory instalment scheme or, in England and Wales, the council tenant instalment scheme; *and*
- the single lump-sum payment must be made on or before the day on which the first instalment would have been due.

Discounts for non-cash payments

Various methods are available to pay the council tax, but some are more cost-effective for local authorities than others. From the local authority's point of view, direct debit has the most advantages and direct debit mandate forms are often sent with demand notices to encourage the use of this payment method. In addition, the local authority is able to offer a discount to taxpayers if they use such non-cash methods of payment.[72]

The local authority should consider the costs and benefits of such arrangements. The size of the discount and when non-cash payments are to be accepted must be decided by the local authority on or before the day it first sets the council tax for the year.

If an adjustment is needed to the amount paid and the amount has been paid by a discounted non-cash payment, the instalment or other payment on which the discounted amount was accepted must be treated as having been paid in full. Any sum to be repaid, or credited against any subsequent liability, however, is reduced by the same proportion as was allowed for the discount.

If you have debts from previous years

If you make a payment to a local authority when you have an existing debt (eg, if you have a council tax liability for a previous year), you should specify the period of liability that the payment is to cover. You must do this, even if the local authority has suddenly issued a bill for an earlier period of liability. If you are paying towards this earlier period, indicate this when making your current payment, to avoid the local authority only using your payment for the current year. If you pay by cheque, mark the back of the cheque with details of the year for which payment is made and also enclose a written note. If you do not, you could face enforcement action, as the local authority's computer system is unlikely to distinguish between payments for particular years, and will continue to record a debt for the earlier year.

If liability orders have been obtained in earlier years, the local authority is likely to include sums in costs. You should challenge the sums in costs as it is unclear on what basis a local authority will have calculated or imposed these and whether they are reasonable (see Chapter 11).

If the local authority repeatedly allocates payments to different years so as to create or allow indebtness to continue, make a complaint as this is likely to be maladministration (see Chapter 13).

Reductions and changes of circumstances

In **England and Wales**, council tax bills served on or after 1 April 2013 contain a statement that anyone receiving a council tax reduction (CTR) under the local authority's scheme (or prescribed scheme) is under a duty to report a change in circumstances and explain the consequences of failing to do so, including that the taxpayer may be liable to prosecution.[73] Given that many vulnerable taxpayers are unlikely to understand a complex and technically worded bill, it should not be presumed that this notice is read or understood simply because the demand is served. In an absence of a copy of the bill, it is insufficient for the local authority to state that this information is on its website if a person did not, or could not have had, access to the website.

Where you are entitled to a premium in your applicable amount for CTR purposes, the demand notice must state the reasons for the premium and that, if at any time before the end of the following year, you have reason to believe that the amount of council tax payable:

- is not subject to a premium; *or*
- is subject to a premium of a smaller or larger amount,

you must notify the billing authority within 21 days beginning on the day on which you 'first had that belief'.[74] If you fail to do this without 'reasonable excuse', the local authority may impose a penalty.[75] What is reasonable depends upon the facts and a tribunal will not readily infer that you should be subject to a penalty in circumstances where there is no criminal intent or recklessness. The words 'reasonable excuse' should be given their plain and ordinary meaning without unnecessary embellishment and include whether there are circumstances beyond your control or not.[76]

7. Penalties

In certain circumstances, a civil penalty may be imposed by the local authority if you:
- fail to respond to a request for information to identify the liable person (see Chapter 6); *or*
- fail to notify the local authority that a dwelling is no longer entitled to an exemption (see Chapter 5); *or*
- fail to notify the local authority that you are no longer entitled to the same level of discount (see Chapter 8) or premium (Chapter 9).

A penalty may be collected by the local authority by including it on your council tax bill (see p170) or sending a separate bill.[77]

If the local authority sends a separate bill, it must allow at least 14 days for it to be paid. If the imposition of a penalty is subject to an appeal or, in England and Wales, arbitration:
- no bill can be issued for the recovery of a penalty;
- no amount is payable in respect of the penalty.[78]

You may not be liable to a penalty if you have a reasonable excuse for not notifying the local authority. Each case will turn on its facts and individual circumstances of the taxpayer.

In this case, the proportions of the instalments on the bill attributable to the penalty are not payable until the appeal or arbitration is finally disposed of, abandoned or fails for non-prosecution.[79]

If a penalty is paid and is later quashed either by the local authority or following an appeal, the local authority must repay it. This can be done by deducting an amount from any other penalty, council tax and, in Scotland, Scottish Water charges that are owed to the local authority and repaying any balance.[80]

8. Appeals against the amount of the bill

If you do not agree with the calculation of the amount you are liable to pay, you should write to the local authority. This includes both actual and estimated amounts.[81] Explain which decision you believe to be incorrect and why – eg, because a disability reduction or discount has not been awarded.

The local authority has two months in which to consider the representations made. If it fails to respond in writing within the two-month period, or if you are still dissatisfied with the response, an appeal can be made to the Valuation Tribunal for England, the Valuation Tribunal for Wales or via the local authority to a valuation appeal committee in Scotland. This should normally be done within four months of the date the grievance was first raised with the local authority.

An appeal cannot be made on the basis that any assumption the local authority is required to make about the future may prove to be inaccurate.[82]

The council tax bill must still be paid while the appeal is outstanding, subject to any agreement made with the local authority. However, if the local authority has applied for a liability order in the magistrates' court, you should apply for an adjournment of the liability order hearing (see Chapter 11).

For the special rules on appeals against a council tax reduction under the local authority scheme, see Chapter 9.

Notes

1. Who must pay the bill
1 **EW** Reg 22 CT(AE) Regs 1992
   S Reg 18 CT(AE)(S) Regs
2 **EW** Reg 2(3) CT(AE) Regs 1992
   S Reg 19(2) CT(AE)(S) Regs
3 **S** Reg 17 CT(AE)(S) Regs
4 **S** Reg 18 CT(AE)(S) Regs
5 **EW** Reg 28 CT(AE) Regs 1992

2. When bills should be issued
6 **EW** Reg 19 CT(AE) Regs 1992
7 **S** Reg 17 CT(AE)(S) Regs
8 **EW** Reg 18 CT(AE) Regs 1992
   S Reg 19 CT(AE)(S) Regs
9 **EW** Reg 18 CT(AE) Regs 1992
10 *Encon Insulation Ltd v Nottingham City Council* [1999] RA 382

11 *North Somerset District Council v Honda Motor Europe Ltd; North Somerset District Council v Chevrolet United Kingdom Ltd; North Somerset District Council v Martin Graham* [2010] EWHC 1505 QB
12 *Regentford Ltd v Thanet District Council* [2004] 246 (HC QBD)

3. How the bill is calculated
13 **EW** Reg 20 CT(AE) Regs 1992
    S Reg 20 CT(AE)(S) Regs
14 **S** Reg 20 CT(AE)(S) Regs
15 **EW** Reg 20 CT(AE) Regs 1992
    S Reg 20 CT(AE)(S) Regs
16 **EW** Regs 24 and 25 CT(AE) Regs 1992
    S Regs 23 and 24 CT(AE)(S) Regs
17 **EW** Reg 24 CT(AE) Regs 1992
18 **EW** Regs 24, 25 and 31 CT(AE) Regs 1992
    S Regs 23, 24 and 27 CT(AE)(S) Regs
19 **EW** Regs 24, 25 and 31 CT(AE) Regs 1992
    S Regs 23, 24 and 27 CT(AE)(S) Regs

20 **EW** Regs 24, 25 and 31 CT(AE) Regs
1992
S Regs 23, 24 and 27 CT(AE)(S) Regs
21 **EW** Reg 24 CT(AE) Regs 1992
S Reg 23 CT(AE)(S) Regs
22 **EW** Reg 55 CT(AE) Regs 1992

4. How bills are served
23 **EW** Reg 17(4) CT(AE) Regs 1992

5. Information the bill should contain
24 **E** Schs 1 and 2 CT(DN)(E) Regs 2011 as
amended by CT(DN)(E)(A) Regs
W CT(DN)(W) Regs; CT(DN)(E) Regs
S Reg 28 and Sch 2 CT(AE)(S) Regs
25 **E** Schs 1 and 2 CT(DN)(E) Regs 2011 as
amended by CT(DN)(E)(A) Regs
S CT(AE)(S) Regs as amended by
Council Tax (Administration and
Enforcement) (Scotland) Amendment
Regs 2012 No.338
26 Para 18 Sch 1 CT(DN)(E) Regs 2011 as
amended by reg 2 CT(DN)(E)(A) Regs
27 Sch 2 paras 2-6 CT(DN)(E) Regs
28 **E** Reg 19A CT(DN)(E) Regs 2011
inserted by reg 2(4) CT(DN)(E)(A) Regs
W Schedule 1 para 8A CT(DN)(W) Regs
1993 as amended by reg 2(4) Council
Tax (Demand Notices) (Wales)
(Amendment) Regulations 2013 No.63
29 Reg 5 and 6 CT(DN)(E)Regs 2011
30 Schs 1 and 2 CT(DN)(E) Regs 2011
31 **E** Sch 3 Part I CTNDR(DN)(E) Regs;
CT(DN)(E) Regs
W Sch 2 Part II CT(DN)(W) Regs
32 **E** Reg 5(2) CT(DN)(E) Regs 2011
33 Reg 2(4)A CT(AE) Regs as amended by
Reg 2(3)(b) CT(AE)(A)(No2)(E) Regs
34 Reg 27(e)(i) and (ii) CT(DN)(E) Regs
2011
35 Reg 2(4C) CT(AE) Regs as inserted by
reg 2(3) CT(AE)(A)(No2)(E) Regs
36 Reg 6(1) CTNDR(DN)(E) Regs; reg 8
CT(DN)(E) Regs
37 Reg 7 CT(DN)(E) Regs 2011
38 s16 LGFA 1992
E Reg 4C CTNDR(DN)(E) Regs
W Reg 5 CT(DN)(W) Regs
S Reg 29 CT(AE)(S) Regs
39 **E** Reg 21A(5) CT(AE) Regs as inserted by
CT(AE)(A)(No2)(E) Regs
40 Reg 21A(3)(a) CT(AE) Regs
41 **E** Reg 21A(3)(b) CT(AE) Regs as inserted
by CT(AE)(A)(No2)(E) Regs
42 **E** Reg 21(B) CT(AE) as inserted by
CT(AE)(A)(No2)(E) Regs
43 **E** Reg 21 CT(AE) Regs as inserted by
CT(AE)(A)(No2)(E) Regs

6. Payment arrangements
44 **EW** Reg 21 and Sch 1 Part I CT(AE) Regs
1992
S Reg 21 and Sch 1 CT(AE)(S) Regs
45 **S** Sch 2 para 19 LGFA 1992
46 **EW** Sch 1 Part I CT(AE) Regs 1992
47 **EW** Sch 1 Part I CT(AE) Regs 1992
S Sch 1 CT(AE)(S) Regs
48 **EW** Reg 21(1A) CT(AE) Regs as
amended by reg 2(13) and (14)
CT(AE)(A)(No2)(E) Regs
49 Sch 1 para 27 LGFA 1992 as amended
by reg 2(5) CT(DN)(E)(A) Regs 2012
50 **S** Sch 1 Part I CT(AE)(S) Regs
51 **EW** Sch 1 Part I CT(AE) Regs 1992
S Sch 1 Part I CT(AE)(S) Regs
52 **EW** Sch 1 Part I CT(AE) Regs 1992
S Sch 1 Part 1 CT(AE)(S) Regs
53 **EW** Sch 1 CT(AE) Regs 1992
54 **E** CT(AE) 21(1C) Regs as amended by
reg 2(13) CT(AE)(A)(E) Regs 2013
55 Part 2 CT(DN)(E) Regs 2011
56 s11A LGFA; para 2(3A) and Sch 1 CT(AE)
Regs inserted by reg 2(14)
CT(AE)(A)(No2)(E) Regs
57 Sch 1 para 2(3B) CT(AE) Regs as inserted
by reg 2(14) CT(AE)(A)(No2)(E) Regs
58 Sch 2 para 19 LGFA 1992
59 **EW** Sch 1 Part II LGFA 1992
60 **EW** Sch 1 Part II LGFA 1992
61 **EW** Reg 28 CT(AE) Regs 1992
62 **EW** Sch 1 Part III CT(AE) Regs 1992
S Sch 1 Part II CT(AE)(S) Regs
63 **EW** Sch 1 Part III CT(AE) Regs 1992
S Sch 1 Part II CT(AE)(S) Regs
64 **EW** Sch 1 Part III CT(AE) Regs 1992
S Sch 1 Part II CT(AE)(S) Regs
65 **EW** Sch 1 Part III CT(AE) Regs 1992
S Sch 1 Part II CT(AE)(S) Regs
66 **EW** Sch 1 Part III CT(AE) Regs 1992
S Sch 1 Part II CT(AE)(S) Regs
67 **S** Reg 24 CT(AE)(S) Regs as amended by
reg 4 Council Tax (Administration &
Enforcement)(Scotland)Amendment
(No.2) Regs 2000 No.261
68 **EW** Sch 1 Part III CT(AE) Regs 1992
S Sch 1 Part II CT(AE)(S) Regs
69 **EW** Sch 1 CT(AE) Regs 1992
70 **EW** Reg 21 CT(AE) Regs 1992
S Reg 21 CT(AE)(S) Regs
71 **EW** Reg 25 CT(AE) Regs 1992
S Reg 24 CT(AE)(S) Regs
72 **EW** Reg 26 CT(AE) Regs 1992
S Reg 25 CT(AE)(S) Regs
73 **E** Reg 19A CT(DN)(W) Regs 1993 as
amended by reg 2(4) CT(DN)(W)(A)
Regs

W Sch 1 para 8A CT(DN)(W) Regs 1993 as amended by CT(DN)(W)(A) Regs 2013

74 Reg 19B(a) and (b) CT(DN)(W) Regs 1993 as amended by reg 2(4) CT(DN)(W)(A) Regs 2013

75 Reg 19B(c CT(DN)(W) Regs 1993 as amended by reg 2(4) CT(DN)(W)(A) Regs

76 TC01556: *World of Enterprise Ltd First Tier Tribunal (Tax)* case: TC/2011/03815, 9 Nov 2011

7. Penalties

77 **EW** Reg 29 CT(AE) Regs 1992
   S Reg 26 CT(AE)(S) Regs

78 **EW** Reg 29 CT(AE) Regs 1992
   S Reg 26 CT(AE)(S) Regs

79 **EW** Reg 29 CT(AE) Regs 1992
   S Reg 26 CT(AE)(S) Regs

80 **EW** Reg 29 CT(AE) Regs 1992
   S Reg 26 CT(AE)(S) Regs

8. Appeals against the amount of the bill

81 **EW** s16 LGFA 1992
   S s81 LGFA 1992

82 **EW** Reg 30 CT(AE) Regs 1992

Chapter 11

Enforcement

This chapter covers:
1. Introduction (below)
2. Statutory enforcement in England and Wales (p186)
3. Liability orders (England and Wales) (p188)
4. Recovery methods (England and Wales) (p200)
5. Statutory enforcement in Scotland (p225)

1. Introduction

This chapter describes the statutory enforcement process. This is the way in which the local authority can recover unpaid amounts of council tax. The process in Scotland is different from the one in England and Wales. Some elements, however, such as the ability to make deductions from certain benefits, are common to both systems.

The local authority can agree a special payment arrangement with you (see p178). The rescheduling of payments under such an arrangement may often be the most appropriate response if you are in arrears. Non-payment of any amount due under a special payment arrangement is also covered by the statutory enforcement procedure.

Note: at any point in the enforcement process, recovery action must stop if the outstanding amount (including costs) is paid.

Council tax collection protocol

Launched in 2009 and refreshed in 2013, a protocol on council tax collection was jointly issued by the Local Government Association and Citizens Advice.[1] This aims to promote good practice in the recovery of council tax and co-operation between billing authorities and advice agencies. The full protocol can be found at www.local.gov.uk and www.citizensadvice.org.uk.

---

2. **Statutory enforcement in England and Wales**

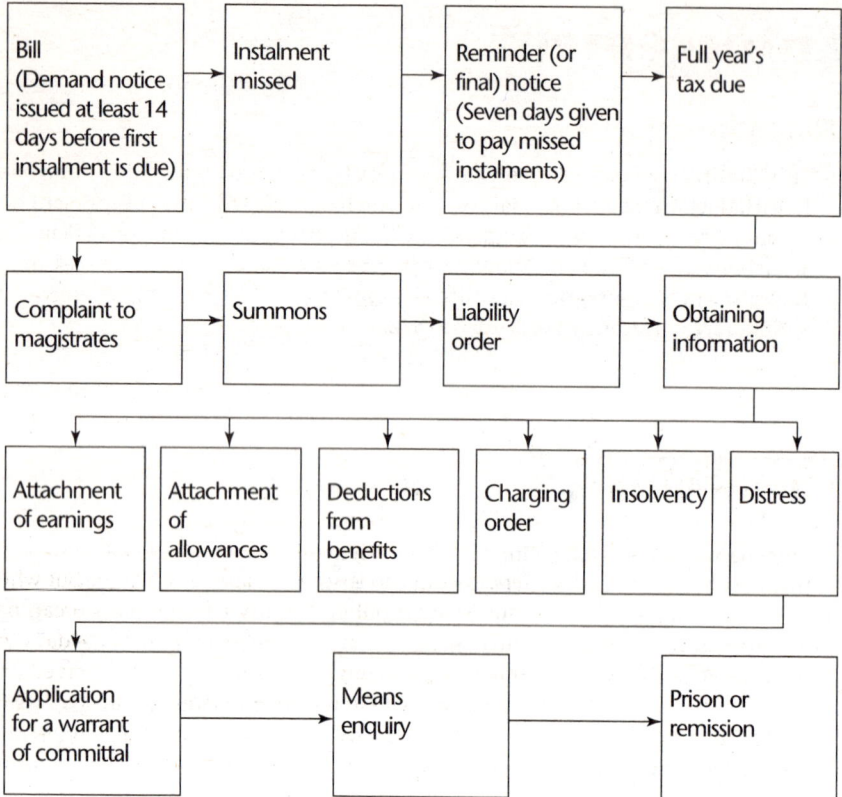

```
┌─────────────────┐   ┌─────────────┐   ┌──────────────────┐   ┌──────────────┐
│ Bill            │   │ Instalment  │   │ Reminder (or     │   │ Full year's  │
│ (Demand notice  │ → │ missed      │ → │ final) notice    │ → │ tax due      │
│ issued at least │   │             │   │ (Seven days given│   │              │
│ 14 days before  │   │             │   │ to pay missed    │   │              │
│ first instalment│   │             │   │ instalments)     │   │              │
│ is due)         │   │             │   │                  │   │              │
└─────────────────┘   └─────────────┘   └──────────────────┘   └──────────────┘

┌─────────────────┐   ┌─────────────┐   ┌──────────────────┐   ┌──────────────┐
│ Complaint to    │   │ Summons     │   │ Liability        │   │ Obtaining    │
│ magistrates     │ → │             │ → │ order            │ → │ information  │
└─────────────────┘   └─────────────┘   └──────────────────┘   └──────────────┘

┌───────────┐ ┌───────────┐ ┌───────────┐ ┌──────────┐ ┌──────────┐ ┌──────────┐
│Attachment │ │Attachment │ │Deductions │ │Charging  │ │Insolvency│ │Distress  │
│of earnings│ │of         │ │from       │ │order     │ │          │ │          │
│           │ │allowances │ │benefits   │ │          │ │          │ │          │
└───────────┘ └───────────┘ └───────────┘ └──────────┘ └──────────┘ └──────────┘

┌─────────────────┐   ┌─────────────┐                   ┌──────────────┐
│ Application      │   │ Means       │                   │ Prison or    │
│ for a warrant    │ → │ enquiry     │ →                 │ remission    │
│ of committal     │   │             │                   │              │
└─────────────────┘   └─────────────┘                   └──────────────┘
```

Reminder notice

If the council tax bill has been correctly issued but you fail to pay an instalment (see p173), the local authority issues a reminder notice.[2] The reminder notice requires payment to be made within seven days.[3] It must include:

- a note of the instalment, or instalments, that have not been paid;
- a statement informing you that if no, or insufficient, payment is made to cover any instalments that are overdue, together with any which will become due within seven days, the right to pay by instalments is lost and the full year's tax becomes payable after a further seven days.

This reminder also acts as a notice of impending enforcement action. If a reminder is issued and you fail to pay within seven days, the local authority does not need to issue another notice before it applies for a liability order (see p188).

If two reminders are issued during the financial year, the next time you miss a payment you automatically become liable for the whole of the outstanding amount. No further reminder is required.[4] You should be informed of the consequences of a third failure to pay on the second reminder notice.[5]

Final notice

A final notice is required if the local authority has issued a reminder notice on two occasions in the same financial year and you have failed to pay an instalment on time. A final notice is also required if only one payment is due under a demand notice. It should state every amount that the local authority would seek on a liability order (see p188), unless that amount is the same as that on the second reminder.[6] In the case of joint taxpayers, a final notice may be addressed to all of them.[7] In all cases, once the outstanding amount has become payable following a reminder, or after seven days following a final notice, the local authority may seek a liability order from the magistrates' court (see p188).[8]

Joint liability

If a bill has been issued in joint names, the local authority can seek to recover the unpaid amount from anyone who is jointly liable. If a joint bill has not been issued, the authority must send a notice to those who are jointly liable but who have not previously been issued with a bill before any recovery action can be taken against them. The jointly liable person must be given at least 14 days in which to pay the bill. If payment is not received, a reminder must be served on the jointly liable person. If payment is not received after seven days, an application may be made to a magistrates' court for the issue of a summons a liability order and a further 14 days must be given between any summons and hearing where a liability order may be granted (see p188).

It is possible to apply for a liability order solely against the person to whom the bill was originally sent (even if a joint bill has not been sent), or against both that person and another person(s) who is (or are) jointly and severally liable with that person. It is not, however, possible for a summons to cover more than one person – separate summonses are needed.

Write-offs and payments

While local authorities normally pursue debts until they are recovered, in certain instances it may be appropriate for a local authority to consider writing off a debt which is not cost effective to pursue or in a case of particular financial hardship.

Practice Note No.9 (para 16.1) reminds authorities that they can write off small amounts. Para 16.3 advises that it may be appropriate to write off liability if a person dies soon after the start of the financial year and so only had a small liability.

Some local authorities may deny they have any power to write off a council tax debt, but s13A (1)(c) of the Local Government Finance Act 1992 allows an authority to reduce a sum that may be owed in council tax as it thinks fit. This power can be used where a reduction has already been awarded under the local authority's scheme.[9]

3. Liability orders (England and Wales)

A liability order issued by a magistrates' court provides a local authority with a variety of options to recover the amount of council tax owed (see p200). A local authority must follow the rules on billing, as an order cannot be obtained if it has not issued a reminder or final notice, as described on p187. Before seeking a liability order, the local authority should, as a matter of good practice, carry out checks to see whether you:

- are entitled to a reduction under your local authority's council tax reduction (CTR) scheme (see Chapter 9);
- have made a claim for CTR which has yet to be processed;
- have appealed or are seeking a review (see Chapter 12);
- are owed a refund for previous period.

Many local authorities in London and Metropolitan Boroughs, however, fail to carry out sufficient checks and there are frequently failures by local authorities to communicate adequately between the council tax department and the section handling CTR. The problem is particularly acute in the cases of council taxpayers who move in and out of low-paid jobs, relying on benefit during periods of unemployment. Delays in awarding discounts or CTR, stoppages and delays by the Department for Work and Pensions awarding social security benefits, can all result in many people being wrongly recorded as council tax debtors. Because the enforcement process is effectively governed by a computer program, a failure to award CTR or an exemption – however caused – results in the automatic commencement of enforcement proceedings.

If any of the above circumstances apply, the local authority may suspend recovery action until benefit entitlement has been determined or an appeal decided.

If you are in such a situation, make an appeal in writing (see Chapter 12).

Considerable effort may be needed to persuade relevant officers of the local authority to suspend recovery proceedings. Where necessary, you should appeal, although it can take time to obtain a hearing. The local authority may be willing to make an alternative payment arrangement with you in return for withdrawing proceedings. Many local authorities will still wish to obtain a full liability order, however, as this gives them the ability to enforce payment if the arrangements are broken. If the local authority does not act reasonably and a summons is issued, go into court and tell the magistrates what has happened.

If your council tax reduction has yet to be determined

If you receive a summons before your application for CTR has been determined, apply to the magistrates' court for an adjournment of the hearing (see p194).

Under the previous council tax benefit (CTB) system, the view of some local authorities was that a person was liable for the full amount of the council tax demanded by the local authority, and a magistrates' court can order payment. In a community charge (or poll tax case), *R v Bristol Magistrates' Court ex parte Willsman and Young*, it was decided that the magistrates' court could grant a liability order, despite the fact that a claim for community charge benefit had been made and despite the fact that the local authority had failed to determine the claim within the statutory period. In court, local authorities often seek to rely on this case.[10]

The decision to seek a liability order, however, is a discretionary one.[11] Consequently, the local authority must consider the relevant facts of the individual case and not act in an unreasonable manner.[12] The legality of the local authority's action was not tested under the council tax system as originally established with a system of 100 per cent CTB between 1993 and 2012. Following the localisation of council tax support from April 2013, each local authority must establish a local support system to provide help to pensioners on low incomes, with a further discretion that can be exercised to alleviate liability for persons in financial need (see Chapter 9).

The decision to issue a summons is also a discretionary matter which has to be exercised reasonably in a local tax case; even though the process is controlled by computer programs, it remains a legal decision not a technical operation. If a local authority seeks a liability order knowing that a CTR claim is pending, it is therefore possible to argue that this constitutes an unreasonable exercise of the local authority's discretionary power. Furthermore, as pensioners on low incomes should receive a maximum 100 per cent of their liability covered by CTR, and a degree of help should be given to those on low incomes, it is arguable that Parliament did not envisage that such support systems should be undermined by the making of liability orders in the magistrates' courts with the imposition of costs, particularly where the basis of those costs is unclear (see p192). Such a case can clearly be made in the case of pensioners – eg, a pensioner who is entitled to pension credit guarantee. Arguably, the function of the local support system is to provide support for local taxpayers, not to create debt.

Support for this view is given in *Hardy v Sefton Metropolitan Council* where the High Court decided '… that the magistrates' court must enquire into questions as to whether the taxpayer is entitled to set off monies owed by the billing authority, or is entitled to say in law that the billing authority is precluded from asserting any liability to pay.'[13]

A test of 'substantial prejudice' to the taxpayer caused by delays by the local authority has also been applied in cases of bills and summons which are issued late, as in the High Court case of *North Somerset District Council v (1) Honda Motor Europe Ltd (2) Chevrolet United Kingdom Ltd and (3) Martin Graham*.[14] This was a case involving business rates, but the same principles apply to council tax. Arguably substantial prejudice may arise to a council taxpayer where a summons is sent early, before CTR has been determined, as well as when a bill and summons that has been sent out late and it is no longer possible to apply for any CTR under the local authority scheme. Loss of CTR, or a refusal to pay CTB in a previous year because of the rules preventing backdating, which would otherwise have been payable, is also an example of prejudice. Other examples of prejudice include losing a right of appeal or having to move home or being unable to meet other payment demands.

It may also be possible to use human rights law to object to a liability order if a sum has yet to be calculated. The European Court of Human Rights considers that there must be certainty in orders and judgments issued by courts. If a liability order is made, but CTR entitlement is still to be determined for the year ahead, the amount ultimately due is uncertain, and may be revised. However, the matter has yet to be tested.

Readjusted bills

It is often unclear on what basis a readjusted bill has been issued, particularly if it is several years after the initial period of liability. This may cause particular problems for people who may have been entitled to CTB before April 2013 or who are entitled to CTR but whose circumstances change.

If a readjusted bill is served, you should request an explanation for the readjustment. Experience suggests this may cause the local authority (or often an outsourced company) to re-examine the amount being claimed. Be prepared to take an appeal to a valuation tribunal to challenge any readjustment, particularly if CTR has already been awarded.

If a lawful basis for the bill cannot be provided or it is too late to apply for either CTB (before 1 April 2013) or CTR because of the rules on backdating, apply for a discretionary reduction of council tax (see p159). If the local authority persists in trying to enforce the bill and issues a summons, you should attend court and challenge the bill before the magistrate and argue that either you have paid your liability for the year in question or you are caused prejudice.

The issue of a late bill which has caused prejudice is a defence to an application to make a liability order. In *North Somerset District Council v (1) Honda Motor Europe Ltd (2) Chevrolet United Kingdom Ltd and (3) Martin Graham*,[15] the local authority delayed sending out bills for local taxes payable between 2002 and 2007. The High Court accepted the argument that the failure to serve the business rates as soon as practicable after 1 April in the relevant financial year rendered the notices invalid.

The Court held that no duty existed on the taxpayer to discharge rates until a correct demand notice was served. Relevant factors to be considered are the length of the delay and the prejudice to the taxpayer which could arise in any number of ways.

Prejudice is considered different from inconvenience and must be 'substantial' and certainly not technical or contrived. There was also countervailing public interest in the collection of taxes, the interests of other taxpayers and the revenues of the local authority concerned which had to be examined by the court.

The judgment shows that the courts will look beyond the simple failures to serve notices and consider both the overall conduct of the local authority and the impact that defects in procedure may have on taxpayers.

Significantly, the Court recognises (para 34) that the defendants are entitled to raise an issue of invalidity by way of defence at both the magistrates' court and as an administrative decision: 'Had the Council sought to enforce the notices by way of complaint in the Magistrates' Court the same defence could have been raised'.[16]

Time limits

An application for a liability order from the magistrates' court must be made within six years from the date the bill was issued.

Once a liability order has been made, there is no time limit on how long the local authority may take to enforce it. In *Bolsover District Council and another v Ashfield Nominees Ltd and another*, a local authority was allowed to use insolvency proceedings against a company where a liability order had been obtained more than six years earlier. However, it is possible that an attempt to enforce a liability order that is more than six years old might be considered an abuse of process and unreasonable in law if the taxpayer is an individual.

If a local authority is seeking to enforce liability from an earlier year, the Valuation Tribunal for England or the Valuation Tribunal for Wales still has jurisdiction to determine the matter. If there have been extensive delays, this may be considered maladministration and so you should complain to the Ombudsman (see Chapter 13). If bills and reminder notices are served late, liability order proceedings based on them may be dismissed by the magistrates' court if prejudice to the taxpayer can be shown (see p165).

Obtaining a liability order

To obtain a liability order, the local authority must apply to the magistrates' court for a summons to be issued to the debtor. In practice, this is issued by computer and endorsed with a facsimile signature of a justice of the peace. The decision to seek a summons must be in accordance with the regulations and be a reasonable one.[17]

Regulations state that a summons may be addressed to two or more joint taxpayers in joint names, but natural justice would require that separate summonses should be issued against each defendant, in order to give each person notice of the hearing. If a single reminder is issued to two or more people who are jointly and severally liable, the local authority should produce separate summonses for each person against whom a liability order is to be sought.

The summons instructs the debtor to attend the court to show why s/he has not paid.[18] No warrant may be issued for the arrest of someone who does not appear and, in practice, most people who have been summonsed do not attend. The 'hearing' takes place in their absence. You should have reasonable notice of the hearing as there must be at least 14 days between serving the summons and the hearing at which the liability order is made.[19]

The summons is not a prescribed form, but should set out the amount outstanding. It may also include the costs reasonably incurred. A Parliamentary answer obtained in February 2009 from Bridget Prentice, Minister for Justice, indicated that the cost of issuing a liability order through the magistrates' court system was £3. This represents the court's administration costs and also the costs associated with the local authority's action. While it is likely that local authorities will have discussed a level of costs with the clerk to the court, Practice Note No.9 (para 12.1) points out that the court should be satisfied that the amount claimed in costs is no more than that reasonably incurred by the local authority. It is unclear how costs are currently calculated, and there is every reason to believe that debtors are being overcharged. Given the lack of certainty there are grounds for challenging the costs incurred since no proper explanation is being provided. Furthermore, costs vary dramatically around England and Wales for what is essentially an identical and almost fully automated procedure.

It appears that many local authorities may use liability order costs as a form of revenue raising.

From a study conducted in 2011, it appears that London Boroughs were receiving around £1 million pounds each per year on issuing summonses for liability orders.[20]

This is likely to be in breach of the intention of the regulations, which allow only permitted costs which are 'reasonable'. For costs to be reasonable, it is necessary that an explanation as to how they have been calculated is available. The inflated sums being charge are likely to be a breach of the legal and constitutional requirement that statutes must precisely set out the basis for charging any sum or amount. Furthermore, it appears that the sum in costs goes into the local authority's revenue account and therefore is being treated as a form of tax income rather than a legitimate attempt to set costs necessary for a legal proceeding. In *R (on the Application of Curzon Berkeley Ltd) v Bliss (VO),*[21] the High Court stated:

'There is a strong constitutional convention which maintains an exclusive Parliamentary control over the levying and the expenditure of public money. In particular, it is well established that nothing less than clear, express and unambiguous language is effective to levy a tax.'

Given that the costs in many liability order applications do not appear to relate to any realistic scheme set down by Parliament and appear to be set by unidentified officials in circumstances which are unclear and according to principles not laid down in statute, there is an arguable case that costs could offend against this principle and could be unlawful.

You should, therefore, query other amounts included in the costs on a summons to establish why they have been incurred. You can do this before the hearing, and if the local authority does not agree to reduce or drop the costs, the matter may be raised in court.

Serving the summons

A summons may be served on someone by:
- posting it to her/his usual or last known place of abode;
- delivering it to the person;
- leaving it at her/his usual or last known address;
- in the case of a company, leaving it at, or posting it to, its registered office;
- leaving it at, or posting it to, an address given by the person as an address at which service will be accepted.[22]

If you do not receive a summons for a liability order hearing and the magistrates' court makes the order in your absence, the order may be quashed by the High Court on judicial review.[23] If a summons is not served, any liability order based upon it is invalid.[24]

Withdrawal of the summons

Once a summons has been issued, it can only be withdrawn by the court. The power to withdraw a summons is inherent in the powers of the court and a summons, once issued, cannot be withdrawn by the local authority which is a party to the case.[25] A summons may be withdrawn by the clerk or justices' chief executive if both you and the council agree. If a party does not agree to the withdrawal of the summons, it can only be withdrawn by a magistrate after both parties have been heard in court.

Payment of the outstanding amount

If the outstanding amount, plus costs, is paid, the local authority cannot continue with the application for a liability order.[26] If the amount outstanding has been paid but the costs have not, a liability order can still be made for the costs alone, although the local authority may be prepared to forego these.[27] The costs claimed by a local authority on a summons can sometimes be up to £125 or more and the legal basis of these costs is unclear. You should demand to know the legal basis of, and calculation of, any costs above £3.

Payment of liabilities for previous years

If you have existing liabilities (eg, you owe money for several years), always specify the year for which you are making the payment, and include a letter or cheque endorsed with the relevant financial year. This will avoid the problem of the local authority applying the sum to different years and leaving outstanding debts.

Adjournments

You can apply to the court for an adjournment if, for instance, you have an arguable case that you should be exempt, if you should be receiving CTR or if there is a matter that should go as an appeal to a valuation tribunal (see p239). This is done by writing to the Justices' Chief Executive Clerk.

In some courts, the task of listing and adjourning proceedings is carried out by the local authority for reasons of administrative convenience. This raises questions of what is known as natural justice since there is no power in law to delegate the functions and duties of the court to a party to the case.

If a court fails to consider a proper application for an adjournment because of administrative problems, any decision made may be open to challenge by way of judicial review. A complaint should also be lodged with the court concerned and it is advisable to contact a Member of Parliament as ultimately responsibility for maladministration lies with Her Majesty's Court Service and the Ministry of Justice. If a court fails to consider an application for an adjournment, any decision may be quashed by judicial review to the High Court.[28]

A sample letter for applying for an adjournment can be found in Appendix 3.

If you do not receive a reply from the magistrates' court, telephone the listing department of the court to enquire about what is being done.

Attending court

If the matter cannot be adjourned, you will have to attend court. Before this, however, the local authority may try to reach an agreement or settlement with you. In some cases, the local authority will agree to withdraw the application, but it is more common for it to insist on getting a liability order to rely on if the agreement is not kept. This also enables the local authority to obtain more in costs.

Most local authorities normally send officials to court to negotiate with taxpayers outside the court room. This can provide an opportunity to discuss any problems that have arisen and to negotiate and reach a solution. In some cases, the local authority may agree to withdraw the liability order application, but any agreement should be in writing. It may be advisable to go into the court room following such an agreement to ensure that this is done formally with notice given to the court. You will be in a stronger position to negotiate if you have already applied for an adjournment in writing to the court. In some cases, the local authority will agree to withdraw the sum in costs, though it may insist on obtaining a liability order. Sometimes a local authority will agree to suspend the liability order on terms that require you to repay the money. This agreement should be obtained in writing.

The hearing

If it is not possible to reach a settlement or you wish to challenge the basis of the local authority's case, there must be a hearing where you must show why you have not paid the council tax.

You are entitled to be present and hear the case against you. The burden of proof is on the local authority to demonstrate that it has complied with the rules of billing, not upon you to show why you have not paid.

The procedure for the hearing follows rule 14 of the Magistrates' Courts Rules 1981. You should be allowed an opportunity to examine all the evidence produced by the local authority and ask questions in cross-examination. The court normally must comprise two justices of the peace or a single magistrate, now known as a district judge.[29] You may make a submission of 'no case to answer' if the local authority has failed to prove an essential part of its case. If the submission of 'no case to answer' succeeds, the local authority is not entitled to a liability order.

Representatives

You can represent yourself without a legal representative. In addition, you have the right to have the assistance of a friend – eg, an adviser, who is not a lawyer.[30] Such a person can sit with you in court and help by taking notes, prompting and giving you advice on the conduct of the case. S/he is known as a 'McKenzie friend'. It is sensible to mention to the court or the clerk that such an adviser is present at the earliest opportunity.

McKenzie friends have become more common in magistrates' court proceedings in the last 20 years, but some restrictions operate on what they can do. McKenzie friends may not sign court documents or normally make oral submissions or examine witnesses as of right, but courts have a discretion to allow a McKenzie friend to address the court. Magistrates' courts have a discretion at common law to allow a lay person to be an advocate.[31] Guidance indicates that a court must consider carefully whether a person should be allowed a right of audience to address the court, but certain situations have been recognised in which it may be appropriate:[32]

- if a person is a close relative of the litigant;
- if health problems preclude the litigant from addressing the court and s/he cannot afford representation;
- if the litigant is relatively inarticulate and cannot address the court without considerable prompting which would delay proceedings.

A magistrates' court should ensure, as far as possible, that someone who is representing her/himself 'is not disadvantaged in any way and indeed the court will provide him with every reasonable means of assistance'.[33] A court retains the power to refuse a McKenzie friend if it is satisfied that the interests of justice and fairness do not require the person's assistance, but this will be rare with a system as complicated as council tax. Refusal of a McKenzie friend without good cause would be grounds to have the proceedings quashed on appeal by way of judicial review to the High Court. The court may, however, exclude such a 'friend' from giving assistance if there is good reason to believe that s/he is interfering with the proper administration of justice. The clerk is also able to provide assistance if this can be done without prejudicing her/his impartiality. You are also entitled to bring books, papers, pens, pencils and any other appropriate material.[34]

Grounds for granting a liability order

An order must be made if the magistrates are satisfied that:
- the sum is payable by the person concerned; *and*
- it has not been paid.[35]

The local authority must satisfy the court that:
- the council tax has been fixed by the local authority;
- the sums have been demanded in accordance with the regulations;
- full payment of the amount due has not been made by the required date;
- a reminder, second reminder or a final notice has been issued;
- the sum has not been paid within seven days of the reminder or final notice being issued and the full amount has become payable;
- the summons has been served for the amount outstanding at least seven days after the reminder or final notice; *and*
- the full sum claimed has not been paid.

The defences available to you include:
- the amount has not been demanded in accordance with the regulations – eg, the local authority failed to follow the correct time periods in serving bills and reminders;
- the authority has issued two bills for the same amount;
- bills have been issued late (see Chapter 10);
- instalments have not been calculated in accordance with the regulations (see Chapter 10);
- the amount has been paid;

- you are not the person named on the summons;
- the level of council tax is not in accordance with the sum set by the local authority;
- the hearing is being held less than 14 days following the issue of the summons.[36]

Any matter concerning liability that could be the subject of an appeal to a valuation tribunal (see p240) cannot be raised in liability order proceedings – eg:[37]

- whether or not you are a liable person;
- whether or not the dwelling is a chargeable dwelling;
- entitlement to a disability reduction;
- entitlement to a discount or exemption.

However, if there is an issue concerning liability, proceedings may be adjourned. Most courts will do this if an issue within the jurisdiction of the local authority is raised.

Practices can vary greatly between courts, but if there is evidence of a serious objection to liability, many courts will adjourn the proceedings. The case for an adjournment may be strengthened if you have lodged an appeal with a valuation tribunal. Unless agreed in advance, an application for an adjournment must be made in the courtroom directly to the bench on the return day of the summons. Wherever possible contact the court in writing to seek an adjournment, and also inform the local authority.

Evidence

Most of the evidence used by a local authority at a hearing will have been generated electronically. The local authority can use any statement contained in a document, including a computer-generated statement, provided:

- the document forms part of a record compiled by the authority;
- direct oral evidence of any fact stated in it would have been admissible;
- if the document has been produced by a computer, it is accompanied by a certificate which:[38]
  - identifies the document and the computer from which it was produced;
  - includes a statement that the computer was operating properly or, if not, that the defect did not affect the production of the document or its accuracy;
  - explains the content of the document;
  - is signed by a person occupying a responsible position in relation to the operation of the computer.

The local authority officer presenting the case should be asked to produce the certificate for inspection. Failure to do so will make the computer evidence inadmissible and the local authority will be unable to prove its case in court.[39]

Your direct evidence, given on oath, is admissible, together with any other documents or statements.[40] Notice of any document used or any other hearsay statement[41] (ie, a statement made by any person not called as a witness in court) must be given to the clerk and the local authority. These rules are complicated and place a debtor at a disadvantage, as they require notice to be given to the clerk at least 21 days before a hearing, whereas a debtor may only receive 14 days' notice of a summons. However, one possible way around this problem is to serve copies of any documents on the local authority so that they become records held by the local authority (which are acceptable). Alternatively, in many cases the local authority will have had notice of the documentary evidence more than 21 days before a hearing – eg, where correspondence has been ongoing over a matter of CTB entitlement before April 2013 or CTR after. If there has been a history of maladministration of billing and reminder notices by the local authority, the magistrates' court may order staff from the billing authority to explain what has happened. The High Court may also order the local authority to reconsider a benefit application from an earlier year on judicial review in exceptional circumstances.[42]

The liability order

The court may make a liability order for one person for one amount. It can also make one liability order for more than one person and more than one amount in the form of a schedule.[43] However, in nearly all cases the court fails to draw up an order in accordance with these regulations, which can lead to problems in the future. In either case, the liability order is meant to identify the aggregate amount that can be recovered. If the full sum claimed has been reduced (eg, because CTR has been awarded), the liability order will be for a greater sum than the amount payable. In such cases, the order remains in force and the excess amount should be treated as paid. If, following the issue of an order, you owe more than the amount specified, the local authority can only enforce up to the limit stated in the order. It must seek a new order to enforce the outstanding balance. However, if no proper stamped and sealed order is issued by the court then effectively the local authority may not be able to establish that an order exists.

In practice, the court seldom issues an individual liability order; the judge or chair of the magistrates normally just signs a certificate attached to the list of non-payers, but in a form that does not comply with the regulations without the stamp or seal of the court.

This is a serious flaw in proceedings identified by the Court of Appeal.[44] Until 2012, many courts did not keep any proper record of liability order hearings or the orders issued, leaving local authorities to maintain records which could be wrong and incapable of independent verification. This has also been identified as a serious flaw in enforcement by the High Court.[45] Together with the fact that liability orders are open to recalculation, the lack of an adequate and independent record may be a breach of the human rights of the debtor under Article 6 regarding the process of determining the civil rights and obligations of a citizen.[46]

Appealing against a liability order

Sometimes a liability order may be wrongly issued by a magistrates' court, often in a debtor's absence. If this is the case, you can appeal to the High Court on a point of law within 21 days of a decision or apply for judicial review within three months. Professional legal advice should be sought. Public funding is available for certain appeals to the High Court for people on low incomes, although this has been more difficult to access since April 2013 with government restrictions on legal aid.

It is possible for a liability order to be 'set aside' – ie, the court quashes or cancels the order and the local authority cannot take enforcement action. A local authority can apply to a magistrates' court to have a liability order quashed, on the basis that it should not have been made.[47] If the court decides that it would have granted an order for a lesser sum, it may make a liability order for a lesser sum together with the costs reasonably incurred in obtaining the order. The local authority must issue a summons for a new amount within six years.

One potential drawback for the council taxpayer is that the right to quash the order is wholly reliant on the local authority being willing to make the application. Unreasonable refusals to quash liability orders could be challenged by judicial review. A complaint of maladministration may also be made (see Chapter 13). In the meantime, you remain subject to the order.

Caselaw has also established that magistrates can set aside liability orders if there has been a mistake.[48] For example, the High Court ruled that magistrates were wrong not to have quashed three liability orders made between 1996 and 1998 against an applicant who was unaware of the proceedings until January 2004.[49]

Guidance on setting aside liability orders is contained in *R (on the application of Newham London Borough Council) v Stratford Magistrates' Court*, in which the High Court ruled that the following apply when deciding to set aside a liability order.

- There must be a genuine and arguable dispute about the liability to pay.
- There must have been substantial procedural error, defect or mishap for the liability order to have been made.
- The application to set aside was made promptly after the defendant had notice of its existence.[50]

There is no prescribed form for making an application to set aside a liability order. A letter should be sent to the court's clerk or justices' adviser identifying the liability order and requesting a hearing to consider setting it aside. This is crucial if a local authority is seeking to enforce a liability order through bankruptcy proceedings (see p215). It may also be necessary in order to lodge an appeal with the Valuation Tribunal for England or the Valuation Tribunal for Wales. See Chapter 12 for more information on appeals.

4. **Recovery methods (England and Wales)**

The liability order gives the local authority the power to:

- obtain information about the financial circumstances of the debtor and thus assess the best course of recovery action (see below);
- make an attachment of earnings order (see p201);
- make an attachment order on an elected member's allowances (see p204);
- apply to the Department for Work and Pensions (DWP) for deductions to be made from the debtor's income support (IS), jobseeker's allowance (JSA), employment and support allowance (ESA), pension credit (PC) or universal credit (UC)[51] (see p205);
- use bailiffs to seize the debtor's goods (known as 'distress') (see p206);
- apply for a charging order against the dwelling in respect of which the debtor's liability arose (see p214);
- apply to bankrupt the debtor (if s/he is an individual) or to wind up the company (if the debtor is a corporate body) (see p215).

The local authority may decide which recovery method it wishes to use in each case and may use it more than once, but it may not pursue more than one method at any one time.[52] In the case of joint liability, it may pursue only one person at a time.[53] So, if, for example, one of the joint taxpayers is the subject of an attachment of earnings order (see p201), the local authority cannot seize the goods of the other.

Information from the debtor

Once the liability order has been made and, for as long as the amount in question remains unpaid,[54] the local authority may request you to provide the following information:

- the name and address of your employer;
- your earnings or expected earnings;
- statutory deductions from pay (these must be disregarded when calculating the amount to be deducted under an attachment of earnings order);
- the work or identity number used by your employer;
- details of existing attachment of earnings orders;
- details of other sources of income – eg, occupational pension, benefits, councillor's allowance;
- whether there is anyone jointly liable for the whole, or any part, of the amount for which the order was made.[55]

You do not have to supply the information if the request is not made in writing, or if the information is not in your possession or control.[56] Similarly, you are not required to provide any information which is not prescribed by the regulations –

eg, the number plate of a vehicle you may own. Otherwise, you must provide the information within 14 days of the request being made.[57] You do not, however, have to advise the local authority of a change of circumstances unless it makes a fresh request for the relevant information but you do have to inform it about any change in your circumstances as regards your ongoing liability and entitlement to council tax reduction (CTR – see Chapter 9). If a liability order has been granted against people who are jointly liable, the local authority can require this information from any, or all, of them. If you fail, without a reasonable excuse, to supply the requested information, you are guilty of a criminal offence and may be fined by the magistrates' court up to a maximum of level 2 (£500).[58] If you 'knowingly or recklessly' supply false information, you could be found guilty of a criminal offence and fined up to a maximum of level 3 (£1,000).[59]

Attachment of earnings order

A local authority which has obtained a liability order against a person who is employed may arrange to have standard deductions made from her/his earnings.[60] This is known as an 'attachment of earnings order'. Practice Note No.9 (para 5.2) advises that attachment of earnings orders are a practical and, in many cases, preferable alternative to seizing a person's goods (see p206). The decision to use this method of recovery, however, is a discretionary one and the local authority must consider all the relevant factors before deciding to adopt this method. Certain costs arising from unsuccessful enforcement activity may also be recovered by an attachment of earnings order.

In practice, however, relatively few attachment of earnings orders are made. As many people who have liability orders against them are not in regular or stable employment, this method of enforcement is impracticable. Also, the local authority often does not know where debtors are employed.

A local authority cannot have more than two council tax attachment of earnings orders against a person at one time.[61]

The order

The form of the attachment of earnings order is specified in the regulations.[62] A Welsh language version has also been issued.[63] The order should be addressed to, and may be served on, 'any person who appears to the authority to have the debtor in his employment; any person on whom it is so served, who has the debtor in his employment, shall comply with it'. It does not have to be addressed to a person by name. A copy should also be sent to you. The order must specify:

- the fact that a liability order has been obtained against you and the outstanding sum;
- the rate at which deductions are to be made from net earnings (see p203);
- the period within which each deduction made is to be paid to the local authority – ie, within 19 days of the end of the month in which the deduction is made.

The order must be signed by the proper officer at the local authority. Practice Note No.9 (para 5.6) advises that a facsimile signature is acceptable.

Once an attachment of earnings order has been made, it remains in force until:

- the whole amount to which it relates has been paid; *or*
- it is cancelled by the issuing authority.[64]

The local authority may cancel the order on its own initiative or following an application by you or your employer.[65]

The debtor's duties

While an attachment of earnings order is in force, you must notify the local authority in writing if you:[66]

- leave a job; *or*
- become employed or re-employed.

The notification must include:[67]

- the name and address of your employer;
- your work or identity number in the employment; *and*
- a statement of earnings or expected earnings from the job, and the deductions or expected deductions for income tax, Class 1 national insurance (NI) contributions and contributions to an occupational pension scheme.

This notification must be given within 14 days of the day on which you leave, start or recommence the employment, or (if later) the day on which you are informed by the local authority that the order has been made.[68] If you do not comply, without a reasonable excuse, you commit an offence[69] and may be fined.[70] If you make a statement which you know to be false, you may also be found guilty of an offence.[71]

Employers must also tell the local authority within 14 days of the date a debtor enters their employment and they become aware that an attachment of earnings order is in force, or on the day on which they become aware that an attachment of earnings order exists.[72] An employer is guilty of an offence and liable to a fine if s/he fails to provide the required notification without reasonable excuse, or if s/he makes a false statement.[73]

In addition to each amount deducted under the attachment of earnings order, the employer can deduct a further £1 towards administration costs each time a deduction is made.

The deductions to be made

The deductions under an attachment of earnings order are made from your net earnings (see p203).[74] The amount deducted depends on the payment period. If you are not paid weekly or monthly or are paid on an irregular basis, a daily rate is used. Special rules cover more unusual payment arrangements. You can agree with the local authority and employer a lower deduction than the statutory amount. The employer should alter the deductions if your earnings change.

'**Earnings**' include any fees, bonus, commission, overtime pay or other emoluments payable in addition to wages or salary, or payable under a contract of service. They also include statutory sick pay.[75] The following are not treated as earnings:[76]

- sums payable by any public department of the government of Northern Ireland or of a territory outside the UK;
- pay or allowances payable to a member of the armed forces;
- social security benefits;
- tax credits;
- allowances payable for disablement or disability;
- wages paid to a seaman, other than of a fishing boat.

'**Net earnings**' are defined as the gross earnings minus:[77]

- income tax;
- Class 1 NI contributions;
- amounts deducted towards a superannuation scheme; *and*
- tax credits.

Deductions from weekly net earnings[78]	Deduction rate %
Below £75	0
£75.01 to £135	3
£135.01 to £185	5
£185.01 to £225	7
£225.01 to £355	12
£355.01 to £505	17
£505.01 and over	17 for the first £505 and 50 for the remainder

Deductions from monthly net earnings	Deduction rate %
Below £300	0
£300.01 to £550	3
£550.01 to £740	5
£740.01 to £900	7
£900.01 to £1,420	12
£1,420.01 to £2,020	17
£2,020 and over	17 for the first £2,020 and 50 for the remainder

Deductions from daily net earnings	Deduction rate %
Below £11	0
£11.01 to £20	3
£20.01 to £27	5
£27.01 to £33	7
£33.01 to £52	12
£52.01 to £72	17
£72.01 and over	17 for the first £72 and 50 for the remainder

Priority of attachment of earnings orders

There is a priority for attachment of earnings orders if more than one has been made against the same individual.[79] Council tax attachment of earnings orders should be dealt with one at a time and in the order in which they are made. If an order is already in force (eg, for child support arrears), a council tax order is applied to the balance of pay remaining after the other deductions have been made. If an order for of council tax is in effect when another order is made, the council tax order should continue to be met and the balance considered attachable for the other order.[80]

Elected members' allowances

If you are a local authority councillor (but not a member of the Common Council of the City of London or the Receiver for the Metropolitan Police District), the local authority can make an order to deduct 40 per cent from your allowances – eg, for attending conferences and meetings and for special responsibilities. The decision to use this method of recovery is a discretionary one. The local authority must consider all the relevant factors before deciding to adopt this method.

Once an order has been made, it remains in force until:
- the whole amount to which it relates has been paid; *or*
- it is cancelled by the issuing authority, either on its own initiative of following an application from the debtor.[81]

Restrictions on voting

If an elected member fails to pay an amount of council tax within two months of the due date, s/he cannot vote on any matter which influences the setting of the local authority's council tax.[82] You must disclose this fact at any meeting where this rule applies. If you fail to comply with this rule you are, on summary conviction, liable to a fine not exceeding level 3 on the standard scale unless you prove that you did not know that it applied to you at the time of the meeting or the matter in question was the subject of consideration at the meeting. In England

and Wales, prosecutions may only start with the permission of the Director of Public Prosecutions.[83]

Deductions from benefits

In England, Wales and Scotland, if a liability order has been obtained, the local authority may apply for deductions to be made from your IS, JSA, income-related ESA, PC or UC.[84] The decision to use this method of recovery is a discretionary one. The local authority must take all the circumstances of the case into account before deciding to pursue it.

Although if you are on IS, income-based JSA, income-related ESA, PC or UC you should be able to receive up to the maximum allowed under the local support scheme, if you are working age the maximum may not be available if:

- you are jointly liable with someone other than your partner; *or*
- there is a non-dependant in the household.

Deductions from IS/JSA/ESA/PC/UC may also be pursued by the local authority if you were liable to pay council tax before being entitled to one of these benefits.

There are maximum weekly amounts that can be deducted from your benefits. In the case of income-related benefits, this is generally the equivalent of 5 per cent of the IS/JSA personal allowance for a single claimant aged 25 or over. There are also restrictions if deductions are being made for other debts. See CPAG's *Welfare Benefits and Tax Credits Handbook* for details about the rules.

To obtain the deduction, the local authority must supply to the DWP the:[85]

- name and address of the debtor;
- name and address of the local authority making the application;
- name and place of the court which made the liability order;
- date on which the liability order was made;
- amount specified in the liability order;
- total sum which the local authority wishes to have deducted.

Deductions from IS/JSA/ESA/PC/UC can only be made in respect of one application from the local authority at any given time. If a second application is made before the sum specified in the first application has been fully recovered, the second has to wait until the first has been cleared.[86]

As far as is practicable, you and the local authority should be notified of the decision in writing within 14 days. You should also be notified of your right to appeal against the decision. Deductions should be made provided:

- you are entitled to IS/JSA/ESA/PC/UC throughout any benefit week; *and*
- no deductions are being made for council tax arrears under any other application.[87]

Payments deducted from IS/JSA/ESA/PC/UC should be made to the local authority concerned, as far as is practicable, at intervals not exceeding 13 weeks.[88]

Deductions should end if:

- there is no longer sufficient entitlement to IS/JSA/ESA/PC/UC to enable a deduction to be made; *or*
- the local authority withdraws its application for deductions to be made; *or*
- the debt is discharged.[89]

If the whole of the amount to which the deductions relate has been paid, the local authority must notify the local Jobcentre Plus office within 21 days, or as soon as practicable after that.[90]

The DWP must notify you in writing of the total amount deducted under any application if:

- you request this information in writing; *or*
- the deduction end.[91]

Distress

'**Distress**' is a remedy that enables a local authority to use bailiffs to seize a debtor's possessions anywhere in England or Wales and sell them, usually by auction, to pay off the debt. Since the enactment of the Tribunals, Courts and Enforcement Act 2007, the term 'enforcement agent' has been increasingly used for individuals who carry out seizures of goods, but the term 'bailiff' remains in common use, including by bailiffs themselves.

The billing authority may employ its own bailiffs, but increasingly, private companies of bailiffs undertake the seizure of goods as part of the range of enforcement services carried out by private companies. If the local authority employs the firm Capita for its council tax collection services, the bailiff firm Equita, a subsidiary company of Capita, is used to recover council tax debts.

Distress can be prevented if all amounts due have been paid.[92] Once distress has been levied, a sale can be prevented by paying the full amount due.[93] Practice Note No.9 (para 4.3) advises that, while distress can be an effective recovery method, local authorities should consider other methods (such as attachment of earnings or deductions from benefits) in preference to distress as an initial enforcement option. If some other method of recovery is in force, the local authority has no power to levy distress.[94]

Distress cannot be attempted by a local authority unless the debtor has been sent a written notice[95] at least 14 days before any first visit to her/his home. The written notice must mention the following specified matters:

- the fact that a liability order has been made;
- the amount for which the liability order was made and the amount which remains outstanding, if this is different;
- a warning that unless the amount specified is paid within 14 days distress may be used;
- a warning that further costs may be incurred;

- a copy of the fees payable;
- the local authority's address and telephone number.

Codes of practice

The local authority is responsible for ensuring that the activities of its bailiffs comply with the law. Local authorities must ensure their bailiffs have a certificate from a county court. Bailiffs who apply for a certificate must undergo a standard security check, regardless of whether they are applying for a first certificate or a renewal. As well as national enforcement standards issued originally by the former Lord Chancellor's Department (now the Ministry of Justice), local authorities may also have their own codes of practice, setting out rules for the use of distress, to which they are expected to adhere. If a local authority fails to observe its code of practice (eg, it decides to use bailiffs and a member of a household has a disability, or if it has failed to calculate council liability correctly), this may amount to maladministration and may be grounds for a complaint to the Ombudsman (see Chapter 13).[96]

Vulnerable households

National enforcement standards indicate that care should be taken with vulnerable households.

The standards require bailiffs and the local authority to recognise they have a role to protect vulnerable and socially excluded households. Local authorities are expected to have agreed procedures on how vulnerable people should be treated during the recovery process. Bailiffs encountering a vulnerable situation are expected to contact the local authority and exercise discretion which is 'appropriate' to the situation. The guidance is seen as a measure to protect debtors, but also helps bailiffs to avoid action which could lead to accusations of inappropriate behaviour.

Examples of when a local authority might be expected to exercise discretion include the following:

- older people;
- people with a disability;
- people who are seriously ill;
- people who are recently bereaved;
- lone parents;
- pregnant women;
- unemployed people; *and*
- people who have obvious difficulty in understanding, speaking or reading English.

For the full text, see Appendix 2.

Goods that cannot be seized

The local authority cannot seize goods which do not belong to you. The council tax rules make it clear it is only the goods of the debtor that can be taken.[97] The local authority cannot seize:

- goods on lease or hire purchase;
- goods belonging to a landlord or other members of the household.

The following goods are also exempt:[98]

- tools, books, vehicles and other items of equipment that you need for your employment, business or vocation;
- clothing, bedding, furniture, household equipment and provisions necessary for your and your family's basic needs;
- items the law classes as 'fixtures' – ie, things which are attached to the property, including anything which is plumbed in or forms part of the property. This includes light and electrical fittings, baths, hobs, stoves, shelves and built-in wardrobes.

General powers of bailiffs

Distress must be carried out by a certificated bailiff who has the written authorisation of the local authority. The written authorisation of the local authority must be shown if a person asks to see it.[99]

Lawful entry to premises

At common law, bailiffs have no power to force initial entry or break open an outer door which is locked or bolted.[100] This is known popularly as 'an Englishman's home is his castle', dating back to 1604. As the law stands, it protects households from forced or violent entry and is also a safeguard against bailiffs entering the wrong property by mistake – eg, if a debtor has moved out of the property.

To be a lawful entry, the bailiff must enter a property peacefully through an unlocked door or through an open window. S/he may not open a closed window (even if it is not locked). Bailiffs cannot obtain a court order to gain entry to any property, nor can an occupier be sent to prison merely for refusing to allow bailiffs to enter. A householder is entitled to refuse entry to bailiffs without a warrant and also to use reasonable force in resisting bailiffs who try unlawfully to push their way in.[101]

The use of force and the powers of the police

At common law, bailiffs cannot use force against a person, so a bailiff cannot apply force to push into a property, or to remove clothing, items of jewellery or watches which are being worn by a person once peaceful entry to a property has taken place. The power contained in the Tribunals, Courts and Enforcement Act 2007 to make regulations allowing the use of force against debtors was removed from the law in April 2013.[102] Regulations to provide a fixed code on the powers of bailiffs and enforcement have been promised.

A bailiff is only empowered on entry to a property by the regulation to act as a bailiff in making a levy and for no other purpose. For example, the bailiff is not entitled to enter a property and refuse to leave until the debt is paid. A bailiff has no entitlement to remain on a property following lawful entry and should leave as soon as the levy is complete. If a situation occurs where a bailiff ceases to act as a bailiff, you are entitled to eject the bailiff or call the police.

The police should play no part in the actual levy of distress as non-payment of council tax is a civil not criminal matter. The police should only attend a levy of distress to prevent a breach of the peace, or where there is the threat or use of violence by you or a bailiff. The police have a power to enter private premises to prevent a breach of the peace.[103]

Once the bailiffs gain entry

If a bailiff is able to gain peaceful entry to the building, s/he can enter and search any room for a debtor's goods and seize them. For a seizure of goods to be lawful, the bailiff must have entered the property.

Once inside, the bailiff can force any inner door which is locked. This applies even to rooms which the debtor does not occupy. It also applies to any building in which her/his goods are located, not just the one s/he occupies as a main residence. Once the bailiff has gained peaceful entry, with or without the consent of the occupier, withdrawing consent or refusing permission to enter other parts of the property are of no effect. This applies even if the occupier was misled into believing that the bailiff only wanted to discuss the situation and not levy distress on that occasion.

There are a number of different ways of possessing goods.[104]

- **'Walking possession'** is where the debtor signs an agreement to keep the goods on the premises without physical supervision by the bailiff until payment is made or the goods are eventually removed for sale.
- **'Close possession'** is similar to walking possession, except that the bailiff stays on the premises for most of the day to supervise the goods.
- **'Removal'** is where the bailiff takes the goods away with a view to selling them.

In cases of council tax arrears, actual removal of goods is becoming increasingly rare because of difficulties with transportation and the low prices which goods typically raise if sold. The most common form of possession in council tax arrears cases is walking possession. Having taken walking possession of a debtor's goods, the bailiff cannot be refused entry if s/he has to return to remove them at a later date. The bailiff is entitled to force entry under these circumstances, but reasonable notice should be given to the householder before any forcible entry to remove the goods is made.[105]

The bailiffs must leave:
- a copy of regulation 45 and Schedule 5 (charges connected with distress) of the Council Tax (Administration and Enforcement) Regulations 1992 (as amended); *and*
- a memorandum setting out the appropriate costs (see below).

Additionally, a copy of any close or walking possession agreement entered into must be handed to the debtor.[106]

In the past, bailiffs who were unable to gain entry to a debtor's home claimed that they could carry out what was referred to as 'constructive distress'. This involved posting a 'notice of distress' through the letterbox claiming that (usually unspecified) goods on the premises had been seized. In *Evans v South Ribble District Council*, it was held that it is not possible to carry out constructive distress in this way.[107]

Charges

Matter	Charge[108]
Visiting premises with a view to levying distress (where no levy is made):	
– the first or only visit	£24.50
– the second visit	£18.00
Levying distress	The lesser of:
	– the costs and fees reasonably incurred; *and*
	– if the sum due at the time of the levy does not exceed £100, £24.50; *or*
	– if the sum due at the time of the levy is more than £100, 24.5% on the first £100 of the sum due, 4% on the next £400, 2.5% on the next £1,500, 1% on the next £8,000 and 0.25% on any additional sum
Attending once with a vehicle to remove the goods (where goods are not removed)	Reasonable costs and fees incurred
Removing and storing goods for sale	Reasonable costs and fees incurred

Possession of goods:	
– close possession (the person in possession to provide her/his own board)	£15 a day
– walking possession	£12
Appraising an item distrained, at the written request of the debtor	Reasonable fees and expenses of a broker (no charge is payable unless the debtor has been first advised of the charge and how it was calculated)
Other expenses of a sale by auction:	
– held on the auctioneer's premises	The auctioneer's commission fee, out-of-pocket expenses (but not more in total than 15% of the sum realised), together with reasonable advertising costs and fees
– held on the debtor's premises	The auctioneer's commission fee (but not more than 7.5% of the sum realised), together with the auctioneer's out-of-pocket expenses and reasonable advertising costs and fees
If no sale takes place because of payment or tender If goods have been seized but not sold	Either: – £24.50; or – the actual costs incurred, to a maximum of 5% of the amount for which the liability order was made, whichever is the greater

In practice, the sums raised at auction will seldom even cover the bailiff and auctioneer fees.

Bailiffs can only impose the above charges, plus the outstanding amount due under the liability order. The bailiff or the local authority cannot charge for other matters, such as writing letters, making arrangements to pay or for any costs associated with bounced cheques or failed card payments.[109]

It is also not unknown for bailiffs to seek to make a charge for attending with a van at the same time as conducting the levy. Although the higher courts have not ruled on this issue, it is clear from the table of charges that the so-called 'van call' is intended to take place on a different occasion from that on which the levy has been made.

Some bailiffs may also impose a charge when entering into a walking possession and making an arrangement to pay. They do this on the basis that the goods are seized when distress is levied, on the assumption that the debtor will make the payments agreed under the walking possession agreement, and that the goods will be freed from the levy and seizure at that time. This is clearly wrong in that each event listed in the schedule of charges is intended to involve some action on the part of the bailiff. If no action takes place (ie, the bailiff no longer pursues the debtor for payment because the debt is then cleared), there can be no lawful imposition of a further charge.

If a bailiff visits to enforce more than one liability order at a time but does not seize goods, the bailiff is only entitled to one visit fee, not one for each liability order.

A charge is due if goods have been removed by the bailiff and are later released as a result of payment, or (in very rare circumstances) if the auction sale is to take place on the debtor's premises, but if it is later cancelled as a result of payment.

Any spurious charges should be challenged, first with the bailiffs concerned and, if that fails, with the local authority, if necessary using the local authority's formal complaints procedure. If neither succeeds, a complaint may be made to the Ombudsman (see Chapter 13).

If you think you have been overcharged, an application may also be made to a county court judge – a process known as 'taxation'.

Sale of goods

In practice, bailiffs do not want to seize goods as the amounts raised at auction are invariably low and may not even cover the costs of the auction sale.

Practice Note No.9 (para 4.12) advises local authorities to ensure that they obtain the best price for the goods seized but, in practice, the seizure and sale of goods never raises sufficient money to discharge the liability order. Consequently, a levy of distress only adds to the costs of enforcement which ultimately has to be paid by the local authority or the bailiff firm if the debtor has no money. Goods are usually sold by auction which should not normally take place until at least five days after the removal of the goods. You or an adviser should try to prevent the sale of goods wherever possible, since it is not a cost-effective way of clearing the debt from a debtor's point of view; nor is the local authority likely to recover any more than a small part of the debt. The proceeds from the sale usually only represent a fraction of the goods' replacement value. If a sale does take place and raises more money than was owed, the balance, minus the costs associated with the sale, should be returned.

Delays in levying distress

It is not unknown for debtors to receive letters from bailiffs relating to periods of liability going back several years. If a local authority has delayed unreasonably in using bailiffs to recover an old debt, a complaint of maladministration may be made. See Chapter 13 for more details.[110]

Return of the council tax debt to the local authority

Some local authority finance departments claim that, once a bailiff is instructed, it is not possible to return the debt to the local authority. This is wrong in law as the bailiffs are the servants of the local authority and subject to its direction, since the liability order grants a range of options to be pursued. The only power of the bailiffs set down in the legislation is to levy distress on goods, not to make decisions on behalf of the authority. Furthermore, the enforcement regulations make it clear that money may be paid to the local authority at any time.[111] The Ombudsman has indicated that local authorities must act appropriately and in a proportionate way when enforcing debts. If a local authority refuses to consider taking back a particular debt from the bailiffs, this can be challenged by way of judicial review. It may also be a matter for investigation by the District Auditor, and informing the local authority that the matter will be sent to the auditor for investigation invariably results in the local authority reconsidering its policy and action.

Complaints against bailiffs

If a bailiff behaves wrongly, a complaint can be made to the firm concerned and to the professional body of bailiffs and enforcement agents, the Civil Enforcement Association. Legal action can also be taken against the bailiff company or the bailiff as an individual. The procedure on complaints can be found at www.civea.co.uk. A complaint should normally be made first to the bailiff company concerned. If the response is unsatisfactory or there is no response, a complaint may then be made to the Civil Enforcement Association. Failure to answer the initial complaint will be taken into consideration. The complaint should also be copied to the local authority.

A complaint may also be made to the local authority using its complaints procedure for any wrongful action by its own bailiffs or bailiffs it employs. A complaint can also be made to the county court which issued the bailiff's certificate. Such a complaint should normally only be made in extreme cases, but the certificate which the bailiff needs to practice may be cancelled or declared void by the district judge.

Appealing against distress

If you are unhappy about the use of distress, it is possible to appeal to a magistrates' court.[112]

Legal advice is essential before commencing an appeal, not least because of the risk of costs if the appeal fails. In more complex cases, the county court or the High Court may also be used to bring an action against the local authority or the bailiffs concerned.

Distress is not unlawful simply because of a defect in the liability order.[113] However, more commonly, the bailiffs cannot produce any copy of a liability order when requested to do so. The most common ground of appeal is when bailiffs have seized goods belonging to a non-liable person.[114]

If the court is satisfied that a levy was irregular, it may:

- order any goods taken to be returned if they are still in the local authority's possession; *and*
- award the aggrieved person an amount of money for any goods seized and sold.

The award is equal to the amount which, in the opinion of the court, would be awarded as damages for the goods if proceedings were brought in connection with trespass.[115] If the court is satisfied that the levy was irregular, it may also make an order requiring the local authority to stop levying in such a manner.[116] In practice, however, appeals to the magistrates' court are rare because of the obscurity of the procedure and the risk of costs.

If harm or damage caused by a bailiff is valued below £5,000, a claim may be pursued through the small claims court. For example, if you are owed money or should be paid compensation, a claim can be commenced through the county court. The small claims court is a more attractive option as neither side can claim for legal costs.

Leaflets explaining how to bring a claim in the county court can be obtained from your local county court or at www.justice.gov.uk/global/forms/hmcts.

Charging orders

This method of recovery is available if the debtor is the owner or part-owner of the dwelling. It cannot be used if s/he is a tenant or licensee. If the local authority has obtained one or more liability orders and the total debt outstanding is at least £1,000, it can apply to the county court for a charging order against the dwelling, provided it is the one that gave rise to the council tax arrears.[117] **Note:** a charging order cannot be used against any other property owned or occupied by the debtor. The decision to use this method of recovery is a discretionary one. In practice, local authorities may use a charging order if a person has £5,000 or more in council tax arrears. The local authority must consider all the relevant factors before deciding to adopt this method and a local authority is likely to attract criticism if it seeks to obtain a charging order for a relatively small amount.

In deciding whether to grant a charging order, the county court must consider all the circumstances of the case including:[118]

- the personal circumstances of the debtor; *and*
- whether any other person would be 'unduly prejudiced' if an order were granted.

A charging order effectively 'mortgages' the property with the debt. If the debt remains unpaid, the local authority may apply to the court for the property to be sold to pay the debt. In practice, the court rarely orders the property to be sold.

Obtaining a charging order does mean, however, that if the property is sold or remortgaged, the local authority is potentially entitled to receive the outstanding amount from the proceeds of the sale. This is only the case, however, if there are sufficient funds remaining after any charge with a higher priority, such as a mortgage, has been met. If you have negative equity with an existing mortgage lender, the use of a charging order will not result in any recovery.

Bankruptcy proceedings

If a liability order has been obtained, the (outstanding) amount on it is a debt for the purposes of bankruptcy (if the debtor is an individual) or winding-up proceedings (if the debtor is a registered or unregistered company).[119]

This means that the local authority can apply to bankrupt an individual or wind up a company, provided s/he owes at least £750 (the local authority can combine all the debts owed to it – eg, rent and council tax). The court may make an order following a hearing or series of hearings if there is an appeal or any challenges to the procedure. In the event of bankruptcy or winding-up proceedings, no other recovery action can be taken. This does not affect the bankrupt individual's ongoing council tax liability.

The only advantage to a bankruptcy order being made against a debtor is that no other enforcement measure can be used thereafter, including imprisonment,[120] and it will clear other debts.

If you are facing bankruptcy proceedings, you should obtain professional advice as quickly as possible. The implications for homeowners are serious because bankruptcy can result in the loss of your home. The bankruptcy process also adds heavy legal costs which will be added to the money owed. However, bankruptcy proceedings provide a last chance to dispute council tax liability or local authority calculations.

A useful guide to bankruptcy is produced by the Insolvency Service (part of the Department for Business, Innovation and Skills). It is available at www.bis.gov.uk/insolvency.

In 2011, the Local Government Ombudsman highlighted flaws in the way councils decide to pursue bankruptcy for council tax debts,[121] and concern about the practice has also been raised by the higher courts.[122] The Local Government Ombudsman report summarises its experience of complaints so that councils can avoid maladministration and advice agencies can identify suitable cases to refer on to the Ombudsman. It also highlights the devastating consequences that bankruptcy can have for a debtor – in one case study, an original council tax debt of just under £840 escalated to over £67,000 by the end of the proceedings.

In 2009/10, councils initiated at least 4,700 bankruptcy proceedings to recover council tax debts. Although the total number of complaints to the Ombudsmen is relatively small there has been an unusually high proportion of formal reports with findings of maladministration. The report says that the Ombudsman is likely to find maladministration if a council:

- does not have a formal, published debt recovery policy;
- has not gathered and considered information about a debtor's circumstances;
- does not include in its debt recovery policy the steps officers must take before deciding on bankruptcy, committal to prison or charging orders; or
- pursues bankruptcy without clearly recording that each of these steps has been taken.

The report draws attention to the importance of councils considering whether the debtor may be mentally ill and taking account of their duties under the Equality Act. For example, one case study involves a woman with long-term, severe mental illness against whom the council would not have used bankruptcy if the officers responsible for the decision had known of her circumstances.

The use of bankruptcy proceedings against a person lacking mental capacity may be a breach of the Disability Discrimination Act 1995. While the duty of a public authority to collect a tax cannot be classed as discrimination.[123]

Procedure

Bankruptcy proceedings are complex, and specialist advice should be sought if any can be found. Only a basic outline of the procedures is given here. The most important consideration is for the debtor to engage in the process; otherwise there is a risk that a bankruptcy order will be imposed automatically. In practice, it may not be worth pursuing a council tax debtor who has assets and capital (including a property) which amount to less than £20,000 since legal costs and fees have to be paid first, with any money left going towards the unpaid council tax debt and other debts that s/he may owe. However, it is not unknown for local authorities to begin bankruptcy proceedings for relatively small amounts, a practice which has been criticised by the Ombudsman.

Bankruptcy proceedings are started by serving a document known as a 'statutory demand' on the debtor. This must comply with the Insolvency Rules.[124] The demand must:

- be dated and signed by the proper officer of the local authority;
- state the amount of the debt and how it has arisen;
- specify whether it is a debt payable immediately or not;
- give details of the liability order and when it was granted by a magistrates' court;
- state details of any other charge or costs.

The demand must also give details about the rights of the debtor and ways of complying with the demand. It must include an explanation of why bankruptcy proceedings must be started if the demand is not complied with, details of how the demand may be complied with and details of how to contact the local authority. The demand must inform you of your right to apply to the county court or High Court to have the demand set aside. This must be done within 18 days of service.[125] If the local authority fails to comply with the rules (eg, it starts proceedings on the wrong form), this will not automatically invalidate the demand.[126] For this to happen, 'prejudice' must be caused to the council tax debtor.[127]

Response by the council tax debtor and appeals to a valuation tribunal

On receipt of the statutory demand, you may pay the debt, provide a security against it, or settle or adjust the debt to the satisfaction of the local authority. If you reduce the amount owed to below £750, a bankruptcy petition cannot be presented. Alternatively, you can apply to 'set aside' (see below) the demand through the High Court (in London) or the county court (elsewhere).

Note: in particular, consider whether there are grounds for an appeal to a valuation tribunal. This step is often overlooked by debtors and advisers. It is possible that the claim is based on an error or miscalculation – eg, if an exemption on the dwelling should have been awarded or you were not liable or you were not awarded any CTR to which you are entitled. See Chapter 12 for more on appeals.

While a formal appeal is outstanding, the local authority should not pursue recovery action and bankruptcy proceedings should not be used.

Setting aside a statutory demand

Setting aside a demand suspends its legal effect, so that no bankruptcy proceedings can be taken until a court has ruled on the validity of the demand that has been sent to you.

An application to set aside a statutory demand may be made on Form 6.4, available from the county court. The application must be supported by a copy of the demand and a witness statement of truth. A letter to the local authority requesting that a demand is set aside is not sufficient.[128] The statement should specify the date the demand was served and the grounds on which it is to be set aside (see below). You must make the application within strict time limits.

When a court can set aside a statutory demand

The application to set aside the statutory demand may be granted if:[129]

- you appear to have a counterclaim, which equals or exceeds the amount of the statutory demand; *or*
- the debt is disputed on substantial grounds; *or*
- the local authority holds some security in respect of the debt and the value of this equals or exceeds the full amount of the debt; *or*
- the court is satisfied that there are other grounds to set aside the demand.

You may be able to make a case if the local authority has failed to award CTR, has miscalculated the year's council tax liability, has failed to award a discount or grant an exemption, or has failed to repay money owed from an earlier year. In such cases, try to rely on grounds which appear to be substantial.[130] Seek to put all your arguments as to why the statutory demand is invalid in at this stage, as in any appeal (which goes to the High Court) you are not normally allowed to raise fresh arguments or points.[131]

If you raise questions about entitlement to CTR under the local authority scheme, you may need to show that you are also appealing to the Valuation Tribunal for England (VTE) or the Valuation Tribunal for Wales (VTW) about any award, or any entitlement to a discount or a disability reduction.

To succeed, it may be necessary to show that the disputed part of the debt would reduce the overall level of council tax debt to below £750.

The practice directions for insolvency proceedings issued by the courts indicate that a statutory demand may be set aside if a 'triable issue' can be shown. This means that there is a possible defence to the debt claim which needs to be examined by the court. However, equally, the court may refuse to set aside a liability order if it is founded on a judgment or order.[132] This can cause problems if a liability order has been granted by a magistrates' court, but you have a bona fide case which should be heard by the VTE/VTE. You will need to explain that an issue for a tribunal (eg, a question of liability or entitlement to a discount) is dealt with separately and that, until a tribunal has ruled on the matter, the debt and the order should not pursued.

Under the Insolvency Rules, the court also has a discretion to set aside a statutory demand if satisfied that it ought to do so – eg, if there has been maladministration or harassment by the creditor.[133]

Although the use of bankruptcy proceedings to recover unpaid council tax has been held to be compatible with human rights,[134] it is possible that human rights principles could be used if bankruptcy is disproportionate to the size of the debt. The Court of Appeal has held that bankruptcy is not a more severe enforcement method than imprisonment,[135] and an objection may only exist where a local authority has other options to recover the money and the use of bankruptcy is unreasonable. The courts have yet to consider the human rights of those living with a debtor, such as dependent relatives or people with disabilities.

An argument may exist against the use of bankruptcy proceedings if officers of the council involved with starting proceedings have not been given proper delegated authority to do so, although failure to publicise the arrangements has been held not to be sufficient to invalidate the process.[136]

Suspension of the time limit

Once documents are 'filed', the court will review their content. The effect of filing is to suspend the time limit for compliance, giving you time to negotiate or settle the debt.

If the application to set aside the statutory demand is dismissed at this stage, the three-week period for compliance with the demand begins to run again.[137] If, on reviewing the document, the court is satisfied that the application to set aside should be heard, a hearing date is set with at least seven days' notice.

Proving the bankruptcy debt

It is essential that the local authority be required to produce a copy of the liability order or prove that it exists. The High Court has indicated that it is prepared to look at whether the debt can be proved, and this may be the only option for the debtor in many cases. The problem for the local authority is that liability orders are often not properly recorded by the magistrates' court which issues them and no properly signed or sealed judgment is obtained proving that it was the court which issued the order.

This is a major flaw in the whole enforcement process and is a point that needs to be resolved on appeal to the higher courts.

Often the computerised bulk summonsing procedures used by local authorities may not actually result in a hard copy of an individual order against a debtor being signed or endorsed by a court.

If you have had no notice of liability order proceedings, request that the local authority produces the liability order.[138] If no liability order can be produced in a correct form which is endorsed by a signature of a justice of the peace or other court stamp, the application may fail on the grounds that the order was not properly obtained from the magistrates' court.

In the case of *London Borough of Lambeth v Simon*,[139] the local authority alleged non-payment of council tax debts and sought to present a bankruptcy petition against the debtor in the High Court. The local authority had obtained three liability orders for council tax amounting to £2,258 for 1997/98, 1998/99 and 2004/05. A statutory demand had been served, but the debtor had made no attempt to set aside either the demand or the liability orders. The debtor contested the petition on the basis that a previous bankruptcy order which post-dated the three liability orders had been annulled in May 2005 as all his debts had been paid. At the hearing of the petition, the debtor presented a letter from the local authority which tended to confirm his claim that the liability orders had been paid in full. The petition was dismissed, as the local authority had made errors and the Court of Appeal was not satisfied that the statements in the petition were true.

The Court also referred to the fact that, in other cases, liability orders were shown not to exist or they could not be proved by the production of a sealed order or a statement from the clerk to the magistrates that an order had been made. In some cases, no credit for payments was shown. Thus, the integrity of the debt on which bankruptcy petitions were based was in question. The Court stated that, in future, petitions by local authorities relying on liability orders should set out a full history of the account at both the statutory demand and the petition stages, properly showing all debts and credits. If a liability order is being relied on, the local authority must be able to prove its existence to the satisfaction of the court.

Paying the debt

You can avoid bankruptcy by paying the debt at the stage of the final bankruptcy order, and the court may adjourn proceedings if there is a realistic chance of your raising the money. However, repeated adjournments are unlikely, and you may still be liable for the costs of the bankruptcy proceedings even if the council tax is paid.

The bankruptcy petition

If a debtor fails to set aside a statutory demand, the local authority may then present a bankruptcy petition against her/him. Normally, the High Court or county court accepts the liability order as validly issued and may refuse to examine the grounds on which it was granted. If the statutory demand is not set aside, the local authority may seek a bankruptcy hearing at the county court, present a bankruptcy petition and the court decides whether to make you bankrupt.

It is essential to attend any hearing, otherwise you risk being made bankrupt in your absence. You are entitled to help from a McKenzie friend (see p195) at such a hearing, and evidence should be given by witness statement and you may raise arguments in law against being made bankrupt. The local authority evidence can be tested and cross-examined. The court may dismiss the bankruptcy petition. The county court may dismiss the petition if it is satisfied that you are able to pay all your debts or is satisfied:

> that you have made an offer to secure or compound the amount and that the acceptance of the offer would have required the dismissal of the petition, *and* the offer has been unreasonably refused by the council. An example might be where a relative or friend might lend you the money to cover the council tax debt but the council refuses it. In determining for the purposes of this subsection the court will consider your means and liabilities.[140]

By the time the bankruptcy petition reaches court, it is usually too late to challenge the liability order by applying to the magistrates' court or the High Court. However, in *Mohammed v Southwark Borough Council*,[141] the Court indicated that there were circumstances in which it would look at issues regarding liability for, or the amount of, council tax.[142] In particular, the Court considered itself entitled to deal with the argument intended to be the subject of a valuation tribunal appeal. You should also try to raise reasonable arguments previously put forward at a hearing to set aside a statutory demand.

You may raise any arguments as to why you consider the liability order to be wrong in law if you have not raised them at the statutory demand stage.

An adjournment of proceedings might be obtained if there is a realistic prospect of settling the debt.

Appeals against a bankruptcy order

Where a bankruptcy order is made by the county court, an application must be made to the High Court.[143] Legal aid is available where your home is at risk but you may have to take the initial steps by yourself, such as serving the Notice of Appeal on the High Court at the Royal Courts of Justice in London within 14 days of the bankruptcy judgment. A Practice Direction about bankruptcy proceedings is published by the Ministry of Justice (available at www.justice.gov.uk/courts/procedure-rules/civil/rules/insolvency_pd).

You have to provide details of the county court which made the order, as well as details of the local authority and a copy of any judgment. You are required to obtain a transcript of the hearing and a skeleton argument and chronology (the requirement to serve these with the Notice of Appeal may be waived if you are unrepresented, although you will be required to do this later).[144]

The High Court may grant a stay on the bankruptcy proceedings until your appeal is heard. If you have already been made bankrupt in the county court and your home is at risk, you may be eligible for legal aid assistance. The appeal should provide grounds of appeal, explaining where the county court judge erred in law by granting the bankruptcy petition. Grounds of appeal may include that the local authority could not produce a valid liability order or the evidence is not probative or there has been a material irregularity during the proceedings.

Imprisonment

England and Wales remain the only countries in Europe in which a person can be sent to prison for not paying a local tax. There is no imprisonment for failure to pay council tax in Scotland.

In certain circumstances, English or Welsh local authorities can apply to the magistrates' court for a warrant committing a debtor to prison.[145] This is a coercive measure designed to extract payment from someone who has the means to pay the debt. It is not a punishment for failure to pay or imposed as a deterrent.[146]

The maximum period of imprisonment is three months,[147] but this should be reserved for only the most extreme cases, such as deliberate non-payment.[148]

If you are unable to pay and are threatened with imprisonment, contact the local authority immediately in writing, setting out the financial problems which you are experiencing, and ask the local authority to use its power under s13A(1)(c) of the Local Government Finance Act 1992 to reduce or remit the debt where there is poverty.

However, the threat of imprisonment is still used to coerce payment.

If either before or after a warrant is issued the amount in question is paid or offered to the local authority, it must accept the amount concerned and no further action should be taken.[149]

If you pay the amount due after the local authority has applied for a warrant but before it is issued or a term of imprisonment fixed and the issue of a warrant is postponed, a local authority may recover reasonable costs in connection with the committal proceedings. However, no further steps can be taken once you have been committed to prison and have served your term.

The local authority is required to pay court fees of £75 for a warrant of arrest and £250 for an application for a warrant of commitment to the court. Whether they are recoverable from the debtor depends on the order of the court, which may remit the debt or order that the fees are not recoverable if wilful refusal or culpable neglect is not established. The maximum costs that can be recovered from a debtor on a successful application are as follows.

Maximum costs[150]

Application for a warrant to be issued	£305
Application for an arrest warrant	£145

If you have been committed to prison and the whole of the amount outstanding is paid, you should be released.[151] If part of the amount outstanding is paid, your sentence should be reduced on a proportionate basis.

After a warrant has been issued, any liability, including that of someone who is jointly liable,[152] must be written off as no further recovery action can be taken.[153]

Applying for a warrant of commitment

An application for a warrant can only be made if:[154]
- the debtor is aged 18 or over; *and*
- the local authority has sought to levy distress; *and*
- the bailiff attempting to levy was unable (for whatever reason) to find any or sufficient goods.[155] This includes cases where a bailiff has been unable to obtain entry. If a liability order has been made against joint taxpayers, a warrant may not be applied for, unless the local authority has sought to levy distress against all of them and the bailiff has been unable to find any or sufficient goods belonging to all of them.

Practice Note No.9 (para 14.1) advises that a local authority which has not attempted any remedy other than distress should satisfy itself that none of the other available remedies would prove more effective. Magistrates are required to consider alternative enforcement methods before issuing a committal warrant as part of the process.[156]

Means inquiry

The court must examine the debtor's means before issuing a warrant (a 'means inquiry'). This involves questioning you in court about your circumstances, income, outgoings, debts and savings to discover the reason for your failure to pay and your means. To enable such an inquiry to take place, you may be summoned to appear before a magistrates' court.[157]

You may qualify for legal aid for advice and representation. The court should be able to provide a duty solicitor or ensure that you have the opportunity for assistance.

A warrant to commit you to prison is only issued if the court is satisfied that failure to pay is due to:

- your wilful refusal; *or*
- your culpable neglect;[158] *and*
- you have the means on the day of the hearing to pay the debt.[159]

If magistrates do not conduct a proper means inquiry, the proceedings are unlawful and any order committing you to imprisonment may be quashed on appeal to the High Court. Magistrates are expected to assess properly your means and not to make irrational assumptions. A typical error of many means inquiries is to fail to ask the debtor if s/he has any savings or capital. A lack of accessible savings or capital is likely to mean that the debtor lacks the ability to pay the sum immediately.

Only a failure by the debtor to pay council tax which is 'blameworthy' is considered to be wilful refusal or culpable neglect. If you are unable to pay council tax because you are too poor, or the failure arose through illness, job loss, a domestic disaster such as a fire or flood, unexpected pregnancy, being forced from a property as a result of domestic violence, or a failure to pay benefit, you should not be at risk of imprisonment. In such cases, an application should be made by the court to remit the debt (see p224).

If wilful refusal or culpable neglect is found, the decision to issue a warrant must still be a reasonable one. A debtor is often asked to make an offer of payment. If a viable offer has been made, magistrates should accept it and not issue the warrant.[160]

Mothers with young children

The provisions of the Human Rights Act 1998 apply to imprisonment for debts recoverable in magistrates' courts. In *R (Stokes) v Gwent Magistrates' Court*, the High Court held that the decision to jail a young mother for 12 days for owing £455 was an infringement of Article 8 of the European Convention on Human Rights (right to family life).[161] Magistrates' courts, therefore, have to consider whether the proposed interference with the rights of the children is in proportion to the amount of debt involved.

Committal proceedings for default on local taxes have often involved mothers with young children and the disproportionate nature of imprisonment has been expressed in other cases. Arguably, in every case where someone could be imprisoned, the effect on family life must be considered. In some cases, for instance, there could be a loss of accommodation if a person is committed to prison for a long term.

There would seem to be very few cases where a warrant of commitment would be justified or proportional, particularly with the availability of deductions from benefit and attachment of earnings orders. The courts have also indicated that imprisonment is inappropriate where the amounts concerned are small.[162]

Postponing the issue of a warrant

Immediate imprisonment should be a rare situation and is difficult for a court to justify. A magistrates' court normally postpones or suspends issuing a warrant for such time and on such conditions as it decides.[163] These conditions normally include the debtor's being ordered to pay the amount outstanding by instalments. The conditions imposed must be reasonable ones[164] and should be in proportion to the size of the debt. The court should avoid a repayment rate which would take more than three years to clear the debt. If a reasonable repayment rate cannot be achieved to clear the debt over three years, the court should remit a portion of the debt (see below).

In *R v Faversham and Sittingbourne Justices ex parte Ursell*, it was held that the court, which had fixed a term of imprisonment for wilful refusal to pay the community charge but postponed issuing a warrant on condition of future instalments, must hold a further hearing before issuing a warrant of commitment to prison following breach of the condition.[165] The magistrates' court must be satisfied that the debtor has been served with proceedings and knows about the hearing.[166] You must therefore be given notice of the date and time of that further hearing and an opportunity to attend. You may wish to require the local authority to prove non-payment, and are entitled to draw the court's attention to any change of circumstances since the decision to fix a term of imprisonment was made. In *R v Mid-Hertfordshire ex parte Cox*, it was held that magistrates must examine events which have happened since the previous court fixed a term of imprisonment and postponed the issue of the warrant.[167] When a debtor goes back to court, the magistrates must consider all the circumstances that have happened and decide whether to issue the warrant of commitment, postpone it again or make some other order.[168]

The case of *R v Northampton Magistrates' Court ex parte Newell* confirmed that a warrant could be issued committing someone to prison for breach of the conditions when s/he is not present in court, providing that s/he had been given notice of the hearing.[169]

Special care should be taken if a debtor is illiterate.[170]

Remission of the debt

If you are unable to pay or the debts are very old, the magistrates' court can remit the debt, in part or in full.[171] The council tax debt is extinguished for the financial year in question, but liability remains for subsequent years.

Magistrates should remit part of the debt if an order to pay instalments would result in an unreasonably long repayment period.[172] Any period in excess of three years is considered unreasonable.[173] However, the court may choose to postpone the warrant to a specific date (if it appears that the payment level will not achieve payment within three years) and conduct a review at that time to see if repayment should be increased or reduced.

Once the magistrates have set a term of imprisonment, however, there is no power to remit. Therefore, if your circumstances deteriorate and you can no longer pay the amounts ordered, you should tell the court, which can simply postpone the issue of the warrant indefinitely, without any payments being ordered. Alternatively, a warrant may be quashed by the High Court if the means enquiry has been defective so that a warrant based on it is invalid.[174]

Use of handcuffs

In two cases involving the imprisonment of people over pension age in 2008, it was reported that both had handcuffs applied. Normally, a civil prisoner should not be handcuffed unless there is a risk of violence or escape.

Challenging a decision to imprison

A decision to imprison can be challenged by appealing (within 21 days) or by judicial review (within three months). In practice, if the warrant of commitment has been issued and you are already in prison, judicial review is the preferred route of appeal as the High Court can grant immediate bail to an imprisoned debtor, pending the full appeal hearing. Public funding by way of legal aid is available. You will need to have a solicitor who can arrange an application to the High Court via a barrister. The application for leave and bail can be made directly to a High Court judge outside normal court hours in emergency cases.

If imprisonment is quashed on judicial review, the magistrates or the local authority may be liable to pay costs.[175]

5. **Statutory enforcement in Scotland**

The enforcement system for local taxes in Scotland varies greatly from that in England and Wales. Enforcement in Scotland has been subject to far less scrutiny and clarification by the higher courts and council tax debtors have suffered a wide range of difficulties.

Individuals may be unaware that local tax debts are owed and are suddenly faced with large bills with no apparent warning.

Unlike in England and Wales where a six-year limitation applies, the limitation in Scotland is treated by some authorities as up to 20 years, whereas other local authorities treat it as less. Problems with local taxation have included:
*   being faced with sudden demands for large sums from many years before;

- local authorities erroneously claiming individuals are in arrears when payment has been made or they did not reside in the property at the time;
- difficulty in disproving liability for debts that are 15 or 20 years old;
- individuals in receipt of benefits at the relevant time are unable to prove this due to records no longer being kept by the Department for Work and Pensions for the relevant time period;
- the implementation of severe recovery action, such as bankruptcy;
- arrestments, with little or no prior warning.[176]

Reminders and losing the right to pay by instalments

If an instalment under the statutory instalment scheme or any special agreement has not been paid by the due date, the local authority must serve a reminder notice on the liable person. The reminder notice requires payment to be made within seven days.[177] It must include a:
- note of the instalment(s) required to be paid and the remainder to be paid for the year;
- statement that if no, or insufficient, payment is made to cover any instalments that are, or will become, due within seven days of the issue of the reminder, the right to pay by instalments is lost and the remaining balance for the year becomes payable after a further seven days.

If two reminders have been issued during the financial year, even if you pay what you owe, you become liable for the whole of the outstanding amount following a third failure to pay, without the need for another reminder.[178] On the second reminder notice, you should be informed of the consequences of a third failure to pay.[179]

The local authority may take recovery action if any sum, including the 10 per cent statutory surcharge and civil penalties, which has become payable to the local authority has not been paid.[180] Additionally, if an elected member of a local authority is in at least two months' arrears, there are restrictions on her/his ability to vote on specific matters (see p204).[181]

Summary warrant or decree

If council tax, Scottish Water charges or a civil penalty is owed, the local authority can apply to the sheriff court for a 'summary warrant' or seek a 'decree' for payment. The summary warrant allows for a special accelerated enforcement procedure.

The sheriff must grant a summary warrant if the local authority provides a certificate.[182] The certificate must contain the following statements:
- that the person specified in the application has not paid the sums due;

- that the local authority has served a reminder notice on the person requiring her/him to pay the amount due within 14 days from the day on which the notice was served;
- that this period has expired without full payment;
- that, in respect of each person on the application, either:
  - a period of 14 days has passed without her/him initiating an appeal because s/he disagrees with the local authority's decision that the dwelling is a chargeable dwelling, or that s/he is liable to pay the tax, or with the calculation of the amount which must be paid, including her/his entitlement to a disability reduction or a discount; *or*
  - the local authority has notified the person that it believes the grievance is not well founded, or steps have been taken to deal with the grievance, or two months have passed since the service of the aggrieved person's notice;
- the amount unpaid by each person.[183]

If two or more people are jointly liable, the local authority may seek a warrant which shows them as jointly or individually liable for the outstanding sum.[184]

The application for a warrant differs to the procedure in England for a liability order in that there is no requirement for the council or the sheriff court to give notice to the debtor or allow an opportunity for the debtor or any other person to make representations.

Consumer Focus Scotland (now Consumer Futures) and a number of legal opinions consider that the summary warrant procedure may be in breach of human rights law and open to challenge under the Human Rights Act 1998.[185] Article 6 of the European Convention on Human Rights guarantees a fair and impartial tribunal and the right to be represented in courts and tribunals in the determination of civil rights and obligations,[186] but no opportunity is given to the debtor to be heard in a summary warrant application. The issue was raised in the Enforcement of Local Tax Arrears (Scotland) Bill 2010 presented by John Wilson MP but this legislation failed to be passed by the Scottish government. In a summary warrant application, the debtor is prevented from any opportunity to present evidence that may show the rules on billing have not been followed, that the sums has been paid or make any application to postpone proceedings where an appeal may lie to a valuation committee (see Chapter 12).

Information from the debtor

If a summary warrant or decree for payment has been granted, you must provide specified information required by the local authority.[187] The obligation lasts for as long as any part of the relevant amount remains unpaid. You must provide:
- the name of your employer;

- the address of the employer's premises where you work;
- if there are no such premises in Scotland, the address of any one place of the employer's business in Scotland;
- your national insurance number;
- details of your bank account;
- the name and address of any other person(s) who is jointly liable to pay the whole or any part of the amount in respect of which the warrant or decree was granted.

The information must be supplied in writing within 14 days of the day on which the request is made by the local authority.[188] Failure to comply could result in a civil penalty being imposed.[189]

Recovery methods

The summary warrant or decree of payment authorises the local authority to recover the unpaid council tax, Scottish Water charges and civil penalties, plus a surcharge of 10 per cent of the amount owed (see p230), by either:

- an earnings arrestment (see p229); *or*
- deductions from benefits (see p205); *or*
- an arrestment and action of furthcoming and sale (see p229);[190] *or*
- sequestration of the debtor's assets (an equivalent to bankruptcy in England and Wales) where the debt exceeds £3,000; *or*
- attachment and exceptional attachment orders. **Note:** special permission is needed from the sheriff for a special attachment to seize goods.

The summary warrant is enforced by sheriff officers or messengers at arms. Their fees and expenses in connection with the warrant are charged to the debtor.[191]

When sheriff officers serve a document by leaving it at a household or place of business, it must be appropriately addressed and placed in a sealed envelope.

Note: sheriff officers cannot demand entry to your home unless a court order known as an 'exceptional attachment order' has been obtained. Forced entry cannot take place unless there is a person present who is at least 16 and is not, because of her/his age, knowledge of English, mental illness, mental or physical disability or otherwise, unable to understand the consequence of the procedure being carried out.

Assistance in court

The right to a McKenzie friend does not exist in Scotland. However, if you cannot afford a lawyer, you are entitled to be represented by another person who need not be legally qualified.[192] A lay representative can appear in both the Court of Session and at a sheriff court and can speak on your behalf.

Earnings arrest

A sheriff officer serves an 'earnings arrestment' schedule on your employer. This requires the employer to deduct a prescribed amount from your net earnings on every payday. The arrestment remains in force until either the debt has been paid in full or you stop working for the employer.

The amounts that can be seized by way of a diligence against earnings are similar to those for an attachment of earnings in England and Wales. The amounts are currently set out in The Diligence Against Earnings (Variation) (Scotland) Regulations 2012 No.308. These figures do not apply to any existing diligence made before 6 April 2013, unless an employer chooses to apply them after being informed about them.[193]

Net weekly earnings	Deduction
Not exceeding £106.17	Nil
Exceeding £106.17 but not exceeding £383.74	£4 or 19% of earnings exceeding £106.17, whichever is the greater
Exceeding £383.74 but not exceeding £576.92	£52.74 plus 23% of earnings exceeding £383.74
Exceeding £576.92	£97.17 plus 50% of earnings exceeding £576.92

Net monthly earnings	Deduction
Not exceeding £460.06	Nil
Exceeding £460.06 but not exceeding £1,662.88	£15.00 or 19% of earnings exceeding £460.06, whichever is the greater
Exceeding £1,662.88 but not exceeding £2,500	£228.54 plus 23% of earnings exceeding £1,662.88
Exceeding £2,500	£421.07 plus 50% of earnings exceeding £2,500

Net daily earnings	Deduction
Not exceeding £15.12	Nil
Exceeding £15.12 but not exceeding £54.68	£0.50 or 19% of earnings exceeding £15.12, whichever is the greater
Exceeding £54.68 but not exceeding £82.19	£7.52 plus 23% of earnings exceeding £54.68
Exceeding £82.19	£13.84 plus 50% of earnings exceeding £82.19

An arrestment and action of furthcoming or sale

'**Arrestment**' is the process by which money or goods held by a third party for a debtor may be frozen. It could be applied, for example, to money held in your bank account. If your bank account details are unknown, usually bank arrestments are initiated by serving letters on the main banks. If money is identified as being held by a third party (eg, a letting agency), an arrestment is served by an officer of the court in the presence of one witness and it freezes the funds. They cannot be withdrawn until the debt has been settled. Usually, the debtor is asked to sign a mandate authorising the release of funds equal to the arrears and costs to the local authority. Any money that remains in the account is released. If a mandate is not signed, the local authority must raise an action of **'furthcoming'** to allow arrested funds to be transferred. You cannot defend the action by disputing the debt, but you can defend it by showing that the arrestment was invalid, procedurally irregular or gained nothing.

Time to pay orders

From April 2008, you can apply to a sheriff court for a **'time to pay order'**. If granted, the local authority cannot seek to enforce a council tax debt while the order is in force.

The court must grant the order if it is satisfied that it is reasonable in all the circumstances to do so. It must take into account:
* the nature of and reasons for the debt;
* any action taken by the local authority to assist you in paying the debt;
* your financial circumstances;
* the reasonableness of your proposal;
* the reasonableness of any refusal or any objection from the local authority.

Enforcement costs

The amount added to the debt is 10 per cent of the outstanding balance. The sheriff officer's fees set by the court, together with costs incurred in connection with the execution of a summary warrant, can also be charged to you once formal recovery proceedings begin through a summary warrant.

Notes

1. Introduction

1 *Collection of council tax arrears good practice protocol*, Citizens Advice and the Local Government Association, October 2013

1. Statutory enforcement in England and Wales

2 Reg 23 CT(AE) Regs 1992
3 Reg 23 CT(AE) Regs 1992
4 Reg 23 CT(AE) Regs 1992
5 Reg 23 CT(AE) Regs 1992
6 Reg 33 CT(AE) Regs 1992
7 Reg 54 CT(AE) Regs 1992
8 Reg 34 CT(AE) Regs 1992
9 s13A(1)(c) LGFA 1992 inserted by s10 LGFA 2012

2. Liability orders (England and Wales)

10 *R v Bristol Magistrates' Court ex parte Willsman and Young* [1991] RA
11 Reg 34 CT(AE) Regs 1992
12 *Associated Provincial Picture Houses Ltd v Wednesbury Corporation* [1948] 1 KB 223
13 *Hardy v Sefton Metropolitan Council* [2006] EWHC 1928
14 *North Somerset District Council v (1) Honda Motor Europe Ltd and (2) Chevrolet United Kingdom Ltd and (3) Martin Graham* [2010] EWHC 1505 (QB)
15 *North Somerset District Council v (1) Honda Motor Europe Ltd and (2) Chevrolet United Kingdom Ltd and (3) Martin Graham* [2010] EWHC 1505 (QB)
16 *North Somerset District Council v (1) Honda Motor Europe Ltd and (2) Chevrolet United Kingdom Ltd and (3) Martin Graham* [2010] EWHC 1505 (QB)
17 *Ratford and Hayward (Receivers and Managers) v Northavon District Council* [1986] RA 137
18 *Ratford and Hayward (Receivers and Managers) v Northavon District Council* [1986] RA 137
19 Reg 35(2A) CT(AE) Regs 1992
20 Study by Zacchaeus 2000 Trust and Nucleus Legal Advice, Earls Court
21 *R (on the Application of Curzon Berkeley Ltd) v Bliss (VO)* [2001] All ER(D) 314

22 Reg 35 CT(AE) Regs 1992
23 In *R (on the application of Clark-Darby) v Highbury Corner Magistrates' Court* [2001] All ER (D)229 the High Court quashed a liability order where the person had not received the notice of the hearing as it was unjust to allow the order to stand.
24 *Chowdhury v Westminster City Council* [2013] EWHC 1921
25 *DPP v Porthouse* [1988] 153 JP 57
26 Reg 34 CT(AE) Regs 1992
27 Reg 34 CT(AE) Regs 1992
28 *Liverpool City Council v Pleroma Distribution Ltd* [2002] All ER(D) 302
29 Reg 2 CCCTNR(E)(MC) Regs
30 *R v Leicester City Justices ex parte Barrow and another* [1991] 3 All ER 935; *Practice Guidance: McKenzie friends*, issued by Lord Neuberger, Master of the Rolls, 12 July 2010
31 *O'Toole v Scott* [1965] 1 AC 939
32 *Practice Guidance: McKenzie friends*, issued by Lord Neuberger, Master of the Rolls, 12 July 2010, paras 19-21
33 *R v Burnley Justices ex parte Ashworth* [1992] 32 RVR 27
34 *R v Leicester City Justices ex parte Barrow and another* [1991] 3 All ER 935
35 Reg 34 CT(AE) Regs 1992
36 Reg 35(2A) Council Tax (Administration and Enforcement) (Amendment) Regulations 1998 No.295
37 Reg 57 CT(AE) Regs 1992
38 Reg 53(4) CT(AE) Regs 1992
39 *Sutton v Islington London Borough Council* [1997] CO/1784/94, 17 October 1997, unreported
40 The Magistrates' Courts (Hearsay Evidence in Civil Proceedings) Rules 1999 No.681
41 rr3-6 The Magistrates' Courts (Hearsay Evidence in Civil Proceedings) Rules 1999 No.681
42 *Norman and another v East Dorset District Council* [2013] All ER (D) 153
43 Regs 35 and 48 and Sch 2 Forms A and B CT(AE) Regs 1992

44 *R (On the application of Mathialagan) v London Borough of Southwark and another* [2005] RA 43
45 See *London Borough of Lambeth v Simon* [2007] BPIR 1629, 6 June 2007
46 Article 6 ECHR; see also *Rommelfanger v Germany* (1989) 62 DR 151 and *Diennert v France* (1996) 21 EHRR 554
47 *s82 LGA 2003; reg 5 CT(AE) Regs 2004*
48 *Liverpool City Council v Pleroma Distribution Ltd* [2002] All ER(D) 302
49 *R (on the application of Tull) v Camberwell Green Magistrates' Court and another* [2005] RA 30
50 *R (on the application of Newham London Borough Council) v Stratford Magistrates' Court* [2008] All ER(D)

4. Recovery methods (England and Wales)

51 Reg 56 Universal Credit (Consequential, Supplementary, Incidental and Miscellaneous Provisions) Regulations 2013 No.630
52 Reg 52 CT(AE) Regs 1992
53 Reg 54 CT(AE) Regs 1992
54 Reg 36 CT(AE) Regs 1992
55 Reg 36 CT(AE) Regs 1992
56 Reg 36 CT(AE) Regs 1992
57 Reg 36 CT(AE) Regs 1992
58 Reg 56 CT(AE) Regs 1992
59 Reg 56 CT(AE) Regs 1992
60 Reg 37 CT(AE) Regs 1992
61 Reg 37(4) CT(AE) Regs 1992
62 Sch 3 CT(AE) Regs 1992
63 CT(AE)(AEO)(W) Regs
64 Reg 37a(2) CT(AE) Regs 1992
65 Reg 41 CT(AE) Regs 1992
66 Reg 40 CT(AE) Regs 1992
67 Reg 40 CT(AE) Regs 1992
68 Reg 40 CT(AE) Regs 1992
69 Reg 56 CT(AE) Regs 1992
70 Reg 56 CT(AE) Regs 1992
71 Reg 56 CT(AE) Regs 1992
72 Reg 39(6) and (7) CT(AE) Regs 1992
73 Reg 56 CT(AE) Regs 1992
74 Reg 38 and Sch 4 CT(AE) Regs 1992
75 Reg 32 CT(AE) Regs 1992
76 Reg 32 CT(AE) Regs 1992
77 Reg 32(1) CT(AE) Regs 1992; CT(AE)(A)(E) Regs
78 Inserted into Sch 4 CT(AE) Regs 1992 by The Council Tax and Non-Domestic Rating (Amendment) (England) Regs 2006 No.3395, The Council Tax and Non-Domestic Rating (Amendment) (England) Regs 2007 No.501; and CT(AE)(A)(W) Regs

79 Reg 42 CT(AE) Regs 1992
80 Reg 42 CT(AE) Regs 1992
81 Reg 42 CT(AE) Regs 1992
82 s106 LGFA 1992
83 s106 LGFA 1992
84 CT(DIS) Regs as amended by the Fines, Council Tax and Community Charges (Deductions from Universal Credit and Other Benefits) Regs 2013 No.612
85 Reg 4 CT(DIS) Regs
86 Reg 8(4) CT(DIS) Regs
87 Reg 8 CT(DIS) Regs
88 Reg 8(5) CT(DIS) Regs
89 Reg 8(3) CT(DIS) Regs
90 Reg 8(6) CT(DIS) Regs
91 Reg 8(7) CT(DIS) Regs
92 Reg 45 CT(AE) Regs 1992
93 Reg 45 CT(AE) Regs 1992
94 Reg 52 CT(AE) Regs 1992
95 Reg 45a(1) and (2) CT(AE) Regs 1992
96 Local Government Ombudsman Report 96/A/3626
97 Reg 45 CT(AE) Regs 1992
98 Reg 45(1a) CT(AE) Regs 1992
99 Reg 45 CT(AE) Regs 1992
100 *Semayne's Case* [1603] 5 CO Rep 91(a); *Southam v Smout* [1963] 3 All ER 104
101 *Vaughan v McKenzie* [1969] 1 QB 557
102 Sch 12 TCEA 2007 amended by s25(5) of the Crime and Courts Act 2013
103 *Thomas v Sawkins* [1935]
104 Sch 5 para 2(2) CT(AE) Regs 1992
105 *Khazanachi v Faircharm Investments Ltd and others* and *McLeod v Butterwick* [1998] EWCH Civ 471
106 Reg 45(5) CT(AE) Regs 1992
107 *Evans v South Ribble District Council* [1991] 12 July 1991 (QBD)
108 Change in the table put into place by The Council Tax and Non-Domestic Rating (Amendment)(England) Regs 2007 No.501
109 The principle that a council is not empowered to impose further costs generated of its own volition is established in a complaint to the Ombudsman against Thurrock Council: 09/006/694, 3 February 2010. The decision confirms that charging must be strictly in accordance with regulations.
110 Complaint against Tameside Metropolitan Borough Council 98/C/4810 reported at [1999] RVR 283
111 Reg 45 CT(AE) Regs 1992
112 Reg 46(1) CT(AE) Regs 1992
113 Reg 45(7) CT(AE) Regs 1992
114 Reg 45(1) CT(AE) Regs 1992
115 Reg 46(3) CT(AE) Regs 1992

116 Reg 46(4) CT(AE) Regs 1992
117 Reg 50(1)-(3) CT(AE) Regs 1992
118 Reg 51(1) CT(AE) Regs 1992
119 Reg 49 CT(AE) Regs 1992
120 *Re: Smith (a bankrupt) ex parte Braintree District Council* [1990] AC 215
121 Local Government Ombudsman press release 6 October 2011
122 *Lonegran v Gedling Borough Council* [2009] EWCA Civ 745
123 *Haworth v Cartmel and another* [2011] EWHC 36
124 r6.1 Insolvency Rules 1986, as amended by The Insolvency (Amendment) Rules 1987 No.1919
125 r6.2(1)(d) Insolvency Rules 1986
126 *Cartwright v Staffordshire and Moorlands DC* [1998] BPIR 328
127 *Re: a Debtor* (No.1 of 1987) [1989] 1 WLR 271 (CA)
128 *Ariyo v Sovereign Leasing plc* [1998] BPIR 177
129 r6.5(4) Insolvency Rules 1986
130 r6.5(4)(b) Insolvency Rules 1986
131 *Sharab v Al-Suad* [2009] EWCA Civ 353
132 *Morley v IRC (re a Debtor)* [1996] BPIR 452
133 r6.5(4)(d) Insolvency Rules 1986
134 *Lonegran v Gedling Borough Council* [2009] EWCA Civ 1569
135 *Griffin v Wakefield MBC* [2000] (CA); *Lonegran v Gedling Borough Council* [2009] EWCA Civ 1569
136 *Lonegan v Gedling Borough Council* [2009] EWCA Civ 1569
137 r6.5(1) Insolvency Rules 1986
138 *Smolen v Tower Hamlets LBC* [2006] RVR 296
139 *London Borough of Lambeth v Simon* [2007] BPIR 1629, 6 June 2007
140 s271 Insolvency Act 1986
141 *Mohammed v Southwark Borough Council* [2006] RVR 124
142 See also *HMRC v Chamberlain* [2011] EWCA Civ 271 para 20 per Sir Andrew Morritt
143 r52.4 Civil Procedure Rules 1998
144 Civil Procedure Rules 1998; Practice Direction on Insolvency Proceedings, para 17.22(7B)
145 Reg 47(1) CT(AE) Regs 1992
146 *Stevenson v Southwark Borough Council* [1993] RA 113
147 Reg 47(7) CT(AE) Regs 1992
148 *R v Highbury Corner Magistrates' Court ex parte Uchendu* [1994] RA
149 Reg 47(6) CT(AE) Regs 1992
150 Sch 6 CT(AE) Regs 1992

151 Reg 47(6)-(8) CT(AE) Regs 1992
152 Reg 54 CT(AE) Regs 1992
153 Reg 52(1) CT(AE) Regs 1992
154 Reg 54 CT(AE) Regs 1992
155 Reg 47(1) CT(AE) Regs 1992
156 *R v Birmingham Magistrates' Court ex parte Mansell* [1988] RVR 112; *R v Alfreton Justices ex parte Gratton* [1993] *The Times*, 8 December 1993; *R (on the application of Wandless) v Halifax Magistrates' Court and Calderdale Metropolitan Borough Council* [2009] EWHC (Admin) 1857 (QBD)
157 Reg 48(5) CT(AE) Regs 1992
158 Reg 47(2) CT(AE) Regs 1992
159 *R v Poole Justices ex parte Benham* [1992] 156 JP 157
160 *R v Alfreton Justices ex parte Gratton* [1993] *The Times*, 8 December 1993
161 *R (on the application of Stokes) v Gwent Magistrates' Court* [2001] All ER(D) 125
162 *R v Worthing Justices ex parte Waller* [1988] COD 69
163 Reg 47(3)(b) CT(AE) Regs 1992
164 *R v Alfreton Magistrates ex parte Gratton* [1993] *The Times*, 8 December 1993; *R v Leicester Justices ex parte Wilson* [1993] 16 December 1993, unreported
165 *R v Faversham and Sittingbourne Justices ex parte Ursell* [1992] *The Times*, 18 March 1992
166 *R v Newcastle-Upon-Tyne Justices ex parte Devine* [1998] RA 97
167 *R v Mid-Hertfordshire Justices ex parte Cox* [1995] ALR 205
168 *R v Mid-Hertfordshire Justices ex parte Cox* [1995] ALR 205
169 *R v Northampton Magistrates' Court ex parte Newell* [1992] RA 283
170 *R v Barnet Justices ex parte Ribbans* [1997] CO/2757-96, 18 June 1997, unreported
171 Reg 48(2) CT(AE) Regs 1992
172 *R v Newcastle-Upon-Tyne Justices ex parte Devine* [1998] RA 97
173 *R v Newcastle-Upon-Tyne Justices ex parte Devine* [1998] RA 97
174 See *R (on the application of Wandless) v Halifax Magistrates' Court and Calderdale Metropolitan Borough Council* [2009] EWHC (Admin) 1857 QBD, 2 April 2009, RVR [2010] 6
175 *R v Newcastle Under Lyme Magistrates' Court ex parte Massey* [1995] 1 All ER 125
176 John Wilson MSP in *ScoLag* Journal issue 391 pp97-98, May 2010

5. Statutory enforcement in Scotland

177 Reg 22 CT(AE)(S) Regs
178 Reg 22 CT(AE)(S) Regs
179 Reg 22 CT(AE)(S) Regs
180 s97 and Sch 8 para 1 LGFA 1992
181 s112 LGFA 1992
182 Sch 8 para 2 LGFA 1992
183 Reg 30 CT(AE)(S) Regs
184 Reg 30 CT(AE)(S) Regs
185 Consumer Focus Scotland response to
     the consultation document on the
     proposal for the Enforcement of Local
     Tax Arrears (Scotland) Bill, June 2010
186 *Rommelfanger v Germany* (1989) 62 DR
     151 and *Diennert v France* (1996) 21
     EHRR 554
187 Reg 31 CT(AE)(S) Regs
188 Reg 31 CT(AE)(S) Regs
189 Sch 8 para 5 LGFA 1992; reg 31 CT(AE)
     Regs 1992
190 Sch 8 para 2 LGFA 1992
191 Sch 8 para 4 LGFA 1992
192 ss126 and 127 Legal Services (Scotland)
     Act 2010 inserts s5A into Court of
     Session Act 1988 and s32 inserts s32A
     into Sheriff Courts (Scotland) Act 1971
193 Explanatory Note, The Diligence Against
     Earnings (Variation) (Scotland) Regs
     2012 No.308

12

Chapter 12

Appeals

This chapter covers:
1. Valuation tribunals and valuation appeal committees (below)
2. Matters that can be appealed (p237)
3. How appeals are dealt with (p246)
4. Appeal hearings (p249)
5. Reviews of tribunal and committee decisions (p259)

1. Valuation tribunals and valuation appeal committees

In England and Wales, appeals are dealt with by valuation tribunals. In England appeals are heard by the Valuation Tribunal for England (VTE) and in Wales by the Valuation Tribunal for Wales (VTW). In Scotland, appeals are heard by valuation appeal committees.

Valuation tribunals and valuation appeal committees determine disputes about:
- the banding of a property;
- liability and the amount of council tax;
- exemptions and discounts.

Disputes over entitlement to a council tax reduction (CTR) in England and Wales may also be taken on appeal to the valuation tribunals but, from 1 October 2013, there is no right to appeal a CTR decision to a valuation appeal committee in Scotland (see p159).[1]

Both tribunals and appeal committees should conduct themselves in a more informal and less intimidating way than a court of law and provide a free mechanism to review and correct any erroneous decisions affecting taxpayers. They are designed to be independent of both the local authority and the Valuation Office Agency (VOA).

Note: it is possible to negotiate with a local authority to settle a dispute if you are prepared to appeal.

Until 19 August 2013, valuation tribunals and valuation appeal committees were supervised by the Administrative Justice and Tribunals Council. This comprised the Parliamentary Commissioner for Administration, and 10–15 members chosen by the Lord Chancellor and Scottish and Welsh Ministers. The Administrative Justice and Tribunals Council also had a Scottish and Welsh Committee. New bodies will be established by the Scottish and Welsh governments, but details have not yet been announced.[2] The abolition of the Administrative Justice and Tribunals Council has raised concerns that the valuation tribunal and appeals committee systems is left without effective oversight and co-ordination as to its administration,[3] while the Scottish government was left with the creation of a separate appeals panel for CTR from October 2013.[4] Appeals about CTR do not go to committees but are heard by a separate panel, the Council Tax Reduction Review Panel. In England and Wales, the Lord Chancellor appoints the tribunal president, vice president, members and person chairing the tribunal. The national clerk or registrar provides advice and support to the president and gives professional guidance to staff.

Since 1 October 2009, valuation tribunals in England come under the general administrative title of 'the Valuation Tribunal for England' which is under the direction of a single president who has worked to streamline and standardise procedures throughout with the aim of achieving decisions of a consistent quality and consistency.

Tribunal members are local people serving in a voluntary capacity unless they are excluded because of age or other prescribed circumstances.[5] Members do not necessarily have any particular professional qualifications, but from 2013 judges from the First-tier Tribunal may sit with the chairs of tribunals to hear appeals which involve CTR (see Chapter 9).[6] The administration of the tribunal is done by Valuation Tribunal Service staff.

In Scotland, a valuation appeal committee is made up of local people appointed by the appropriate sheriff principal. A committee consists of a chairperson and three to six ordinary members. Members are unpaid and independent of the assessor and the local authority. The committee is assisted by a paid secretary who is usually a lawyer. Tribunals and committees are advised on matters of law and procedure by clerks, employed by the tribunal or committee. The clerk is the taxpayer's point of contact and should be able to respond to requests for advice on procedures in advance of the hearing. S/he cannot, however, advise on the substance or merits of the appeal.

Information on valuation matters and appeals can be found at the VOA website (www.voa.gov.uk) or the Valuation Tribunal Service website (www.valuationtribunal.gov.uk or www.valuation-tribunals-wales.org.uk).

Tribunals in England and Wales sometimes sit at an administrative centre but more often may sit in a local authority building or in rooms or suites booked at hotels, conference centres and church halls.

The Valuation Tribunal for England

Created in October 2009, the Valuation Tribunal for England (VTE), replaced the 56 valuation tribunals, which had been operating on a local basis since 1992.

In 2011, the VTE was centralised and now delivers its services from two administrative centres in Doncaster and London. These administer all appeals and allocate cases to 80 different hearing centres around England. There is a national telephone number (0300 123 2035) which recognises your geographical location and transfers you to the correct office.

More information about appeals in England is available at www.valuationtribunal.gov.uk. This is regularly updated, with summaries given in recent valuation tribunal decisions.

The VTE issues a number of booklets and guidance notes which can help you with an appeal.

The Valuation Tribunal for Wales

From July 2010, the Valuation Tribunal for Wales replaced the four tribunals which previously operated in Wales. More information on appeals in Wales can be found at www.valuation-tribunals-wales.org.uk.

2. Matters that can be appealed

Appeals can be on:
- council tax reduction (CTR) decisions in England and Wales (p158);
- valuations (see p238);
- liability (see p240);
- discounts (see p240);
- disability reductions (p240);
- exemption (see p240);
- calculations on the amount of tax, other than CTR decisions (see p240);
- completion notices (see p243);
- penalties (see p243);
- discretionary reductions (see p244).

A number of matters are excluded, including those for which there is some other route of appeal – eg, to the First-tier Tribunal, the magistrates' court or the High Court.

Also, in England and Wales, the following matters can only be dealt with by the High Court:
- the classes of dwellings that qualify for an exemption;
- a determination by the local authority when exercising its discretion to prescribe a class of dwellings where the owner, rather than the resident, is liable;

- the failure of an authority to include prescribed classes or discounts or any other particular matters in its CTR scheme;
- any determination made by a Welsh local authority to give a smaller or no discount on certain furnished property that is no one's sole or main residence;
- the setting of the council tax.

If an appeal raises any topic which is outside of the jurisdiction of the tribunal, it will be struck out.[7]

Valuations

England

Chapter 3 describes the way in which you can make a proposal to the listing officer to alter the valuation list. Standard forms for making proposals are available from the Valuation Office Agency.

Since 2007, you are expected to play a greater role in taking a valuation appeal to the Valuation Tribunal for England (VTE) than in the past. Listing officers are no longer obliged to refer appeals automatically to the tribunal. Not every person who makes a proposal to alter her/his property banding wants a full tribunal hearing, and the system gives you the choice of whether or not to proceed. The number of appeals reaching the tribunal stage is also reduced, enabling resources to be concentrated where a dispute cannot otherwise be settled by negotiation.

On receipt of a proposal, the listing officer has four months to decide whether or not to alter the list and to issue you with a decision notice. During this four-month period, you can negotiate and reach an amicable solution on the banding. The listing officer should discuss the proposal with you and any interested parties before issuing a decision notice. The notice states either that the listing officer agrees to alter the valuation list or that s/he rejects the proposal and no alteration is made. A letter is sent with the notice, explaining that you and any interested party have a right of appeal. This must be done within two months of the date of the decision letter.

You and any interested party have three months from being notified of the listing officer's decision to appeal to the VTE.[8] If you fail to commence an appeal within three months, the tribunal president has the discretion to allow the appeal if satisfied that the delay arose because of circumstances beyond or your control.[9]

The VTE should aim to list the appeal within six months of receiving the appeal notice and give you not less than four weeks' notice of the hearing.

If you decide to appeal, the listing officer prepares a presentation pack. This typically includes background information relating to the case, accompanied by evidence of comparable property values. You can also present your valuation evidence.

If a listing officer believes that a proposal has not been validly made and serves an 'invalidity notice' (see p36) on you, you can appeal against the invalidity notice (within four weeks) directly to VTE. You must serve a notice of appeal to the clerk of the tribunal (sometimes known as the 'tribunal officer') with a copy of the notice. The notice must include a written statement of the following if they are not included on the invalidity notice:[10]

- the address of the dwelling;
- the reasons for the appeal against the invalidity notice;
- the names and addresses of the proposer and the listing officer.

If the listing officer reconsiders the matter and withdraws an invalidity notice after an appeal has been started, s/he must inform the tribunal.[11]

If the listing officer agrees to the proposal or decides to alter the list, whether or not an agreement has been reached, the list will be altered within six weeks.[12]

Wales and Scotland

In Wales and Scotland, the listing officer or the regional assessor must refer appeals to the Valuation Tribunal for Wales (VTW) or valuation appeal committee.

The closing date for appeals in Wales against new valuations was 31 December 2005; thereafter, only limited rights of appeal are possible until the next revaluation.

Deciding which valuation applies

When determining a council tax banding, the VTE, VTW or valuation appeal committee in Scotland applies the same valuation assumptions that were applied in the original valuation (see p26). You must show that, on applying the new valuation assumptions to your dwelling, a different sale price to that which the listing officer or assessor reached would be obtained. An appeal is only likely to succeed, therefore, if you can show that a mistake was made in the way the assumptions were originally applied to the individual dwelling, indicating that a different value should have been reached and the difference in value is sufficient to justify moving the dwelling into another valuation band.

The mistake may include, for instance, an error about the number of rooms in a property, or the size of its garden or the existence of something in the locality which would have an effect on the valuation of a property – eg, it is next door to an industrial or commercial building, the nature of which is likely to bring down the value of a neighbouring property.

The VTE/VTW or valuation appeal committee is bound to follow the valuation assumptions and cannot consider whether they are wrong in law or that the regulations themselves are defective.

If your appeal covers a particularly complex, novel or contentious point of law (including principles of valuation), the case may be listed for hearing by the president or a vice-president of the tribunal.[13]

Liability, exemptions, reductions, discounts and amounts

You can appeal if you disagree with the local authority's decision that:
- someone is, or is not, a liable person (Chapter 6);
- a dwelling is not exempt (Chapter 5);
- a disability reduction should not be granted (Chapter 7);
- a discount should not be granted (Chapter 8);
- whether you should or should not be entitled to CTR (see Chapter 9);
- the amount payable is correct.

There are two stages to appeals on liability and calculation issues. The first stage involves writing to the local authority.[14] The letter should state the decision that is in dispute and the reason(s) for the disagreement. The local authority has two months in which to consider these matters and may ask for additional information. A further appeal may be made to the VTE/VTW or valuation appeal committee in Scotland if the local authority:[15]
- rejects the appeal;
- makes some changes, but fails to satisfy you; *or*
- fails to make a decision within the two-month period.

Tactically, it is advantageous to mention your right of appeal in the early stages of correspondence. In the case of a dispute over liability, a calculation or an exemption, a letter can, for example, include the following line: 'In the event that you do not accept my submission, please treat this letter as notice of appeal established under section 16 of the Local Government Finance Act 1992.'

As a precaution against the loss of relevant correspondence by the local authority, it may also be advisable to send a copy to the relevant tribunal or committee, with an accompanying letter stating that you wish an appeal to be listed in the event that a negotiated settlement cannot be reached with the local authority. Such a copy should be marked 'for information' and dated clearly. In the event that the local authority loses the appeal, this will provide a record to establish it was made within the time limits.

If you do not get a reply or acknowledgement from the local authority, proceed with your appeal. Also send copies of all documents you intend to use to the local authority even though it does not reply (see p241). You can make also make a formal complaint about the failure of the authority to respond.

England and Wales

An appeal to the VTE/VTW must normally be made:[16]
- within two months of the date the local authority notified you of its decision; *or*
- within four months of the date when the initial representation was made if the local authority has not responded.

The tribunal president has the power to allow an out-of-time appeal if you have failed to meet the appropriate time limit because of reasons beyond your control.[17]

It is important to distinguish between appeals to the VTE/VTW and appeals that go to the First-tier Tribunal for other social security benefits, such as Department for Work and Pensions benefits, and for decisions about entitlement and calculations which were made for the council tax benefit (CTB) system before 1 April 2013.

Form and contents of appeals

Your appeal must be in writing. You, or someone on your behalf, must write directly to the clerk of the relevant tribunal. The appeal letter should state a number of prescribed matters, including:[18]

- the reasons for the appeal;
- the date on which the first letter about the matter was served on the local authority;
- the date, if any, when you were notified by the local authority of its decision.

If your appeal arises under section 16 of the Local Government Finance Act 1992 regarding liability, exemption or discount or from a decision about your entitlement to CTR, it must include the following:

- your full name and address;
- the address of the property (if different to your home address);
- the name of your local authority and the date you first wrote to it;
- the date on which the authority refused your appeal (if it replied);
- brief reasons why you consider the decision or calculation to be wrong;
- details of any other appeal relating to CTB (pre-1 April 2013) or housing benefit which arises from the same facts and which you made to the First-tier Tribunal for social security matters.[19]

If you fail to supply the information, you are informed in writing by the VTE and required to provide it. If you do not supply the information within the time specified, your appeal will not be admitted.[20]

If it is discovered at the hearing that you have omitted information which should have been supplied, the tribunal can apply a 'common sense test' so the appeal is not struck out. The appeal should not be struck out if the error or omission is merely technical or the result of a clerical error and no difficulty or prejudice has been caused to the billing authority. If the appeal is struck out, you may bring a new appeal.

Documents and evidence

England and Wales

When a local authority receives notice of your appeal it may send further information and documents to the tribunal about your reduction if it wishes to challenge your appeal. The local authority must supply these documents to you and the tribunal at least four weeks before the hearing, providing key documents for the tribunal.[21]

You are required to provide the documents and materials you rely on and any response to the arguments of the local authority at least two weeks before the hearing.[22] It is important that the local authority is supplied with a copy of all the evidence you intend to use.

Forms on which the required information is requested are available from the relevant tribunal's office. The clerk should notify you within two weeks that the appeal request has been received. The clerk should also send a copy of the appeal letter or form to the local authority.[23]

Scotland

In Scotland, an appeal to a valuation appeal committee must be made by writing to the local authority within four months of the date on which the grievance was first raised with it in writing.[24] There is no power to consider out-of-time appeals. The letter should state:[25]

- the reasons for the appeal; *and*
- the date on which the first letter disputing the matter(s) was served on the local authority.

The local authority must pass the appeal to the secretary of the relevant valuation appeal committee.[26]

Appeals on council tax reductions in Scotland

To appeal a determination by a local authority about an amount of CTR, you must first seek a review by the local authority which made the determination. This must be requested from the authority in writing within two months of the determination and takes the form of an internal review.[27]

If you are still dissatisfied by the decision following a review, you have a further right of appeal to the Council Tax Reduction Review Panel (CTRRP) within 42 days of the date of the local authority notification.[28] You may also request for further review of a determination on an application where your local authority has not notified you of a decision on your first request for review, and more than two months have gone by.[29]

Review panels are drawn from a judicial panel appointed by the Cabinet Secretary for Finance, Employment and Sustainable Growth. Members of panels are normally solicitors or legally qualified individuals of at least five years' or more standing.[30]

A further review of a determination on an application is heard by one member of the panel. It is an oral hearing unless you, the local authority and the member of the panel undertaking the review agree that the review is to be dealt with by written representations.[31]

An application for a review before a panel must be made in writing and:

- include a copy of your CTR decision letter;
- give your reasons for the request of the review;
- be signed by you, unless a court has appointed someone else to act on your behalf;
- be sent within 42 days of the local authority review decision notification.

Completion notices

In England and Wales, the local authority and, in Scotland, the assessor, may issue a completion notice that states the date on which a newly erected or structurally altered property is considered to be a dwelling. While the matter can be discussed with the local authority or the assessor, an appeal can be made to the VTE/VTW or valuation appeal committee in Scotland.

England and Wales

An appeal on a completion notice must normally be made within four weeks of the notice's having been sent.[32] The president of the tribunal may, however, allow an out-of-time appeal if you have failed to meet this time limit for reasons beyond your control.[33]

You, or someone on your behalf, should write directly to the clerk of the relevant tribunal.[34] The letter should:

- state the reasons for the appeal; *and*
- be accompanied by a copy of the completion notice.

Appeal forms on which the information is requested are available from the relevant tribunal office. The clerk should notify you within two weeks that the appeal request has been received. The clerk should also acknowledge and send a copy of the appeal letter or form to the local authority.[35]

Scotland

In Scotland, an appeal to the valuation appeal committee must be made in writing to the assessor within 21 days of receiving the completion notice.[36] There is no power to consider out-of-time appeals. The letter should state the reasons for the appeal and be accompanied by a copy of the completion notice.[37] The assessor must pass the appeal to the secretary of the relevant valuation appeal committee.[38]

Penalties

The local authority has the power to impose a penalty in certain instances where someone is required to provide information but fails to provide it, or provides information which s/he knows to be false. While the matter may be discussed with the local authority, and it has the power to withdraw the penalty, an appeal can be made to the VTE/VTW or a valuation appeal committee in Scotland. For more on penalties, see p181. Grounds on which a penalty may be quashed include where:

- the local authority already has the information;
- you have valid reasons for withholding the information – eg, on grounds of confidentiality;
- the amount of information being sought is excessive or the demand is impossible to comply with;
- the information is irrelevant or it is not within the remit of the local authority to seek.

England and Wales

An appeal must normally be made within two months of the penalty's being imposed.[39] The president of the tribunal has the discretion to allow an out-of-time appeal if you have failed to meet the time limit for reasons beyond your control.[40] The appeal is made by you, or someone acting on your behalf, by writing directly to the clerk of the relevant tribunal. The letter should state:[41]

- the reasons for the appeal; *and*
- the date, if any, you were notified by the local authority of the penalty.

Appeal forms on which the required information is requested are available from the relevant tribunal office. The clerk should notify you within two weeks that the appeal request has been received. The clerk should also send a copy of the appeal letter or form to the local authority.[42]

Scotland

In Scotland, an appeal to a valuation appeal committee must be made by writing to the local authority within two months of the penalty being imposed.[43] There is no power to consider out-of-time appeals. The letter should state:

- the reasons for the appeal; *and*
- the date, if any, you were notified by the local authority of the penalty.[44]

The local authority must pass the appeal to the secretary of the relevant valuation appeal committee.[45]

Discretionary reductions and appeals

You have a right of appeal to the VTE against the billing authority's discretionary decision to refuse a reduction or in respect of the amount awarded.[46]

The tribunal will not simply substitute its decision for that of the local authority but will consider whether the local authority has used its powers correctly and lawfully when deciding whether to grant a discretion. The tribunal applies principles that operate in judicial review hearings in the High Court, and considers whether the local authority has made an error of law, which means its decision should be quashed.

Principles on which the tribunal may quash a decision to refuse a discretionary reduction include the following.

- **The authority has got the facts wrong.** This applies where the authority has made fundamental mistakes of fact that completely alter the nature of the decision and the way it approached the question of using its discretion.
- **The authority fails to follow due process** – eg, it failed to follow proper procedures determining a discretionary reduction or to look at the application properly. The authority also is expected to follow its own rules and guidance on discretionary reductions.
- **The authority fails to consider the hardship test properly.** The discretionary reduction is meant to include tackling hardship, and a local authority errs when it fails to give sufficient weight to this purpose.
- **The authority fails to make an individual decision on your case.** The local authority should look at individual circumstances and not simply apply a general policy.
- **The authority fails to follow its own guidance.**[47]
- **The authority has acted unreasonably.**[48] An authority may act unreasonably by:
  - failing to consider relevant facts;
  - considering irrelevant facts;
  - acting perversely or irrationally.

Failing to consider relevant facts occurs where the authority has ignored matters it should have considered when looking at your application. For example, the local authority may fail to consider your income properly or fail to apply a means test or ignore the effect on any disability.

Taking irrelevant facts into consideration may occur where an authority refuses you a reduction over an irrelevant issue, such as your having just moved into a property, that you are unemployed or have been bankrupt, or you have rent arrears.

The authority has acted irrationally and perversely where it has refused an application for a discretionary amount and has made a decision that no authority, properly directing itself would have reached. An example where an authority might act unreasonably in refusing a discretionary reduction is where the authority has created a liability by its own failure to award you a reduction, due to its own errors.

The tribunal may remit the matter to the billing authority to be reconsidered.[49]

Council tax payments if there is an outstanding appeal

A person who has been served a bill must make the payments required by either the bill or by any subsequent special agreement reached with the local authority. The fact that an appeal has been made does not affect this obligation, though some local authorities are willing to suspend recovery action until an appeal has been dealt with. If an appeal is upheld, any overpayment of tax should be refunded or credited against future liability.

In England and Wales, if the local authority seeks a liability order through the magistrates' court, the magistrates' court may also agree to an adjournment if an appeal about liability has started. An adjournment should always be granted if there is the prospect of a successful appeal in a case in which a local authority is seeking a committal order against a debtor (see p221).

However, the authority may have already obtained a liability order against you through the magistrates' court (see Chapter 11). In such a case, the local authority should suspend recovery action until the appeal has been determined.

A further exception is if an appeal has been made against a penalty imposed by the local authority (see p243). In such cases, the penalty does not have to be paid until the appeal has been decided. If a sum in council tax relates to a previous year, it could also be argued that the matter should wait for a determination by the VTE/VTW or a valuation appeal committee in Scotland.

If, following the initiation of an appeal against the imposition of a council tax penalty, the local authority decides to remit the penalty, it notifies the VTE/VTW or valuation appeal committee in Scotland and the appeal is treated as withdrawn on the date on which the notice is served.[50]

3. **How appeals are dealt with**

While there are many similarities in the way in which the Scottish valuation assessment committee and the English and Welsh valuation tribunals deal with appeals, different rules apply in Scotland from those which apply in England and Wales.[51] Additionally, in England and Wales there are a number of differences in the way in which tribunals deal with appeals on valuation matters and the way in which they deal with appeals on other council tax issues.

An appeal is normally dealt with by an oral hearing (see p249) but, if all the parties agree, it can be dealt with by written representation (see p247).[52] In most cases, it is advisable to request an oral hearing.

There is likely to be a wait of some months between the acknowledgment of your appeal and the actual hearing. Use this time to prepare for the hearing.

In an appeal under section 16 of the Local Government Finance Act 1992 on liability, exemptions, discount or any calculation, the tribunal normally contacts you about two weeks before the hearing, and you must make sure you send copies of any documents you intend to use at the hearing well in advance to the tribunal and other parties to the appeal (see p240).

Pre-appeal agreement

From 1 October 2009 in England, the parties may reach an agreement before the appeal hearing (see p249) or before written representations are considered (see below). The agreement will include how the valuation list is to be altered and the listing officer must serve a copy of this on the Valuation Tribunal for England (VTE) and on all the parties to the agreement. The appeal is treated as withdrawn and there is no need for you to do anything further. The alteration to the list must take place within six weeks.[53]

Written representations

Before 2007, Practice Note No.6 (para 7.1) described the ability to deal with disputes by written representations as a relatively quick and effective procedure for resolving straightforward appeals. For an appeal to be dealt with in this way, all the parties (normally you, the listing officer/assessor and the local authority) must give their written agreement.[54]

There is no maximum time limit in which the tribunal or committee must determine the appeal on the basis of written representations. Once it is agreed that the appeal is to be dealt with in this way, the clerk must serve notice on the parties, and they have four weeks in which to send their written representations. Copies are sent to the other parties. There is then a further four-week period in which comments may be made. At the end of this last period, the clerk or secretary sends the available material to the tribunal or committee within four weeks. The tribunal or committee may:[55]

- require any party to provide additional material;
- order that the appeal be dealt with by a hearing; *or*
- go on to reach a decision.

If additional information is required, copies of that material must be provided to all the other parties. Each party may, within four weeks of receiving the additional material, supply a further statement in response.[56]

In **Scotland**, permission to deal with the appeal by written representation can be withdrawn by any of the parties at any time before a decision is reached. This might happen, for example, if the other party's arguments are not as expected. If permission has been withdrawn, the appeal must be dealt with by an oral hearing.[57]

Pre-hearing review

In **England and Wales**, a tribunal chair may order a pre-hearing review to clarify the issues to be dealt with at the hearing, such as the procedure to be followed, evidence and time limits.[58] This may be done either at the request of the appellant, any other party, or on the chair's own initiative. At least four weeks' notice must be given of a pre-hearing.

Extension of time limits

If you cannot meet one of the time limits that applies in any of the steps of an appeal, ask for it to be extended. Time limits can be extended in appeals concerning liability, completion notices, penalties and council tax valuation bands.[59]

A request for an extension of time should be made to the president using the prescribed form.

An appeal can be pursued out of time if the president is satisfied that you were unable to appeal by the normal deadline because of circumstances beyond your control. You must therefore provide a reason for why you need an extension. More information may be requested from you and other parties to the appeal in order for a decision to be made. In some cases, a hearing may be held.

The president considers the following when deciding whether an extension should be granted:[60]

- when the notice was actually received;
- whether you were informed of the right of appeal and the 28-day limit;
- whether you have acted with all reasonable speed in the circumstances;
- your reasons (and any proof) for the delay, such as illness, absence from home or bereavement;
- whether it would be contrary to the interests of justice not to permit the appeal to be heard or heard fairly.

A decision is sent to you, with copies sent to all other parties (or potential parties). There is normally no further right of appeal against the decision to reject an application to extend time limits. A further application may be made only on the basis of completely new information that was not available or known at the time of the earlier application.[61]

Withdrawing an appeal

In **England and Wales**, you may also withdraw an appeal on a valuation matter by either sending or delivering a notice to the VTE/VTW.[62] The relevant tribunal must notify each party in writing that an appeal has been withdrawn.

In England, you can withdraw an appeal at any time before a hearing by writing to the relevant tribunal or orally at a hearing. If you give notice to withdraw the appeal at the hearing, the tribunal must give its formal consent. In Wales your appeal may be withdrawn by the clerk if received in writing before the hearing, and at the hearing itself by the appeal panel after considering written representations.[63]

In **Scotland**, an appeal may be withdrawn by writing to the secretary of the valuation appeal committee, or at the hearing by asking the permission of the committee. If the assessor decides, after the appeal has been initiated, to agree to the original proposal or the local authority decides not to contest the appeal, it is considered to be withdrawn.[64]

Reinstatement of an appeal

In **England**, it is possible to apply to reinstate an appeal after you have given notice to withdraw it. This might be appropriate, for instance, if an appeal has been withdrawn by mistake, if new advice or evidence has been obtained or if a ruling of another tribunal or the High Court might affect the position.

An application must be made in writing to the VTE and within one month of either the date:[65]

- on which the VTE received the withdrawal notice; *or*
- of the hearing at which the appeal was withdrawn.

You should provide any supporting documentation and give your reasons.

4. **Appeal hearings**

Practice statements in England and Wales

The president of the Valuation Tribunal for England (VTE) has issued a series of Practice Statements for the conduct of proceedings. These help interpret the procedural regulations and the steps which must be taken when appealing, and give an idea of the approach of the tribunal in specific situations. The Practice Statements apply whenever problems arise and are worth consulting when making an appeal. They are available at www.valuationtribunal.gov.uk/Attending_A_Hearing/PracticeStatements.aspx.

There are Practice Statements to cover:

– extensions of time limits for making appeals;

– adjournments and postponements;

– summoning witnesses;

– decisions without a hearing;

– sending and delivering documents;

– procedures at hearings;

– duties and responsibilities of the clerk/tribunal officer at the hearing;

– hearings in private;

– non-attendance by an appellant at a hearing;

– appeals where parties have reached agreement;

– reviewing and setting aside decisions;

– applications for re-instating proceedings on strike-out;

– professional representatives.

In Wales, Valuation Tribunal for Wales (VTW) Best Practice Protocols cover the same areas. They can be found at www.valuation-tribunals-wales.org.uk/en/best-practice-protocols/index.php.

Notice

In **England**, the VTE must give each party 'reasonable notice' of the date and time of the hearing. This normally means 14 days, unless parties consent or there are urgent or exceptional circumstances. In **Wales**, if the appeal is to be dealt with at a hearing, the clerk to the tribunal must give at least four weeks' written notice of the date, time and place of the hearing.[66] In **Scotland**, the secretary to the committee must give at least 35 days' written notice.[67]

There is no maximum time limit in which the tribunal or committee must hear the appeal.

In **Wales**, the clerk must advertise the date, time and place of the hearing:[68]
- at the tribunal's office; *and*
- outside an office earmarked by the local authority for this purpose; *or*
- in another place within the local authority's area.

In **Scotland**, the secretary must advertise the details at a local authority office and the place at which the hearing will be, if different.[69]

In all cases, the advert must name a place where a list of the appeals to be heard may be inspected by members of the public.[70]

People disqualified from participating in the hearing

Natural justice refers to the rules and procedures to be followed by any body, including a tribunal or committee, which has the duty of adjudicating disputes. One of the principles of natural justice is the rule against bias. This requires that someone should not take part in a hearing if a reasonable person would think that her/his participation is likely to lead to bias. In **Wales**, the following people may be excluded from participation as a member, clerk or officer of a tribunal in relation to a particular appeal:[71]
- an elected member of the local authority in which the dwelling is situated; *or*
- the appellant's spouse or civil partner; *or*
- someone who supports the appellant financially.

A person is not disqualified, however, simply because s/he is a member of a local authority (eg, a county council), which derives its revenue directly or indirectly from council tax payments that may be affected by exercising her/his functions.[72] In Wales, if the appellant is a current or former employee or member of the relevant tribunal, her/his appeal is dealt with by another tribunal.[73] As tribunals have to act impartiality it is considered essential to avoid giving any impression that the respondent's representative is a member of, or has a special relationship with, the panel. S/he should therefore be treated in exactly the same way as the appellant. In particular, s/he must withdraw at the end of each case and may only return to the hearing room when the next appellant enters. There must be no signs of familiarity between the panel and the respondent's representative.[74]

Representatives

On the day of the hearing, any party may:[75]
- represent her/himself; *or*
- be represented by a lawyer; *or*
- be represented by anyone else.

In **England and Wales**, where you are representing yourself, you may have the assistance of someone else – eg, a friend, a relative or an adviser.[76] In **Scotland**, you may be represented by another person, whether legally qualified or not. However, if there are good and sufficient reasons for doing so, the committee may refuse to permit a particular person to represent a party at a hearing.[77] Members of the tribunal or the panel from which the valuation committee is drawn are not permitted to represent parties at its hearings.[78] Additionally, in England and Wales, employees of the tribunal are also barred from acting in that capacity.

How the hearing is conducted

In **England and Wales**, the appeal is heard by three members, one of whom must be the chair and who must preside. If all parties who attend the hearing agree, the appeal may be decided by two members in the absence of a chair.[79]

A council tax reduction (CTR) appeal must have a First-tier Tribunal judge as one of the panel if it involves:[80]
- an assessment of income or capital;
- a right of residence (whether you are from the UK or not, so far as it is relevant).

In **Scotland**, the minimum number of people who can constitute a valid committee is three.

Putting documentary evidence to the tribunal

Written statements are encouraged from appellants, and you should produce relevant documents concerning your appeal. The VTE states on its website and in the booklet *Preparing for your Valuation Tribunal Hearing*: 'The other party's evidence can appear fairly formal, but we do not expect people presenting their own case to give their evidence in the same way as them. However, you may find it useful to prepare a written statement.' This remains good advice because although the tribunal allows you to give oral evidence to establish the facts, it often wants whatever you say to be confirmed by documentary evidence.

Serving documents on the local authority or listing officer

The VTE advises that you should aim to bring five copies of any written documents that you want to present in evidence (a copy for each of the three members, and one each for the clerk and the other party).

It is very important that the local authority or listing officer is sent the copies of any evidence in advance, even if s/he does not read it.

In an appeal about CTR, send the local authority copies of any documents you wish the tribunal to consider at least 14 days in advance of the hearing.

In an appeal about liability, a discount, an exemption or any calculation, you should also send copies of the written evidence and documents in advance to the local authority. Ideally, this should be at least 14 days, and at the very least five days, before the hearing, or otherwise there may have to be a postponement of the case. However, in the case of documents that may become available at a late stage, the tribunal has the discretion to admit or exclude such evidence.[81] In Wales, the VTW expects parties to have discussed and exchanged evidence at least two weeks before the hearing day.[82]

The tribunal may give directions to produce what is known as a 'bundle'[83] and this is often the best way to present your evidence, whether the tribunal gives a direction or not.

A **'bundle'** is a collection of all the documents attached together, with each page given a number. The simplest way to produce a bundle is to put the documents together in date order, although there is no specific rule that documents have to be in this order. You can also add your own statement or witness statement to the documents, which you can place at the beginning of the bundle. You should add a front page to the bundle. This should be marked 'In the Valuation Tribunal for England' and give the appeal number and your name as the appellant and that of the local authority or listing officer as the respondent. The purpose of the bundle is to help the tribunal pinpoint the key evidence, and speeds up the tribunal process where all parties have copies of the documents in the same order.

Other evidence that may be difficult to copy, such as photographs and large plans, can be shared on the day, but you should let the other parties know in advance.

You can send copies of information by electronic means as well as physical copies, but the VTE cannot accept electronic documents of more than 10 megabytes.[84]

Public hearing

The hearing normally takes place in public. This means you can attend another hearing as an observer to see how a tribunal works. However, in **England and Wales**, a tribunal can decide to hold the hearing in private if any of the parties request it and the tribunal considers that the interests of that party would be prejudicially affected if the hearing were held in public. In this case, the panel decides who should be present.[85] Someone who might disrupt a hearing or who is likely to prevent another person giving evidence may be excluded.

In **Scotland**, the committee may, if it has reasonable cause, hold the hearing in private.[86]

Failure to appear and striking out of appeals

In England and Wales, if you (in Scotland, you or your representative) fail to appear at the hearing, the appeal may be dismissed or struck out, including where a party fails to follow a direction from the tribunal. This power may be exercised in England by a clerk or any other member of VTE staff. In **England and Wales**, an appeal on a valuation matter may also be struck out if any party other than the listing officer fails to attend, and in Wales the VTW may also strike out an appeal or part of an appeal related to CTR where the reduction awarded is the maximum that the authority can award under its scheme. If the appeal relates to more than one issue, only that part which relates to the reduction can be struck out by the tribunal under this power, although the tribunal must give you an opportunity to be heard.[87]

In **England and Wales**, if a party can show reasonable cause for not appearing, s/he may request the tribunal to review its decision (see p259). The request must be made within four weeks of the notice of the decision being given.[88]

In **Scotland**, if you have a reasonable excuse for your absence, the committee may set a new date, time and place for the hearing.[89] It must give all parties at least seven days' notice. For a hearing to be recalled in this manner, you must write to the committee (normally within 14 days of being notified that the original appeal was dismissed) requesting a new hearing date and setting out the reason for the original absence. If the committee considers that there are special circumstances, it may allow an out-of-time request.

If any party does not appear at the hearing, the tribunal or committee may hear and determine the appeal in her/his absence.[90] Local authorities vary in their willingness to appear. Whether the local authority sends a representative or not, always send it a copy of the documents you plan to use in an appeal well before the hearing.

Order of the hearing

The VTE/VTW or a valuation appeal committee may determine the order of the hearing – ie, which party puts its case first.[91] The 'model procedure' practice statement 'provides that usually you are to open your case first, explaining the reasons for the appeal, what you are asking the tribunal do, and advancing argument and evidence in support.[92] However, if you are unrepresented, the panel is entitled to invite the local authority or listing officer to go first where it is thought that to do so will result in a fairer hearing. The panel must, however, ensure that the local authority or listing officer is not prejudiced and is given the opportunity to respond to the your case. In all cases, you must be given the final opportunity to address the panel.[93] You are given an opportunity to put questions to the local authority. Parties at the hearing may examine and cross-examine any witness and call witnesses. Evidence can be given in written submissions, including in witness statements.[94] Where you are unrepresented and are having difficulty in formulating questions, the clerk (or the chair) may assist you, but not to the point where s/he becomes your advocate.[95] At the end of the hearing, the tribunal or committee will normally retire to consider its verdict or the parties to the appeal will be asked to leave the room. The clerk can advise the tribunal or committee, but no other person should be present while it is engaged in deliberations. If any other person is present, the decision may be challengeable on grounds of breach of natural justice.[96]

Adjournment and dismissal

A hearing may be adjourned for such time, to such a place and on such terms (if any) as the tribunal or committee thinks fit. Reasonable notice of the time and place to which the hearing has been adjourned must be given to every party.[97]

In **England**, an application for an adjournment must be made in writing to the clerk of the VTE. The clerk considers the request and takes into account relevant factors including:

- the reasons;
- the other parties' comments on the request;
- the length of notice that was given for the hearing;
- the preparation for the hearing that the parties have undertaken;
- the time remaining before the hearing;
- whether the appeal has previously been listed for hearing.

If the clerk refuses the adjournment, an application can be made to a member or to the VTE itself on the day. Adjournments will only be rarely granted at the hearing, however, as parties are expected to be prepared.

In **Scotland**, a valuation appeal committee may request representations from both parties and then adjourn as it sees fit.

In some cases, an appeal may be dismissed if the listing officer or assessor fails to show that you have been properly served with notices and documents.

Witnesses

The VTE may summons a person to attend as a witness and order her/him to produce any documents or answer any questions relating to the proceedings.[98] A summons must normally be given with 14 days' notice (or a shorter period if the tribunal directs). A summons or order must state that a person may apply to vary or 'set aside' the summons or order if s/he has not had the opportunity to object to it and must state the consequences of non-compliance. There is currently no equivalent rule in Wales or Scotland.

Evidence

Where facts such as the value of a dwelling are in dispute, each party to the hearing should provide evidence that supports her/his view of the facts. The rules relating to evidence are different in Scotland from those that apply in England and Wales.

England and Wales
Tribunals are not bound by any rules on the admissibility of evidence before courts of law; rather, they are concerned with the weight of any evidence.[99] For example, what someone else has been heard to say (hearsay) would be admissible at a hearing, but given less weight than the direct evidence of a witness.

Evidence can be given orally or in written form, such as valuation reports. Make sure that you have multiple copies of any documents wherever possible. If the valuation of a dwelling is in question, evidence could include photographs or even a video. Occasionally, physical evidence may even be produced. In *Morgan v Dew*, damaged pillowcases and sheets were produced to prove local pollution existed which the appellants contended had an adverse effect on house valuation.[100]

However, since the appeal in *Tilly v Listing Officer for Tower Hamlets LBC*, it seems that the High Court expects a stricter approach to valuation evidence.[101] In this case, the appellant sought a judicial review of the dismissal of a second valuation tribunal appeal. She alleged that the value of her property had been adversely affected by chemical pollution arising from developments in London's Docklands. She was successful at her first hearing and later lodged a second appeal to secure a further reduction in banding from D to C. She produced a report from the South East Institute of Public Health on chemical pollution and argued such pollution affected the value of her home. The tribunal dismissed her appeal on the basis that pollution was already known at the time of the first alteration.

On appeal to the High Court it was held that, although the tribunal had erred in concentrating on the date the pollution was first discovered, it refused to interfere with the decision. No substantial wrong or miscarriage of justice had been caused. The High Court considered that the evidence produced was wholly inadequate for the tribunal to form an opinion, as the applicant had not produced evidence of the value of her flat and how its value had been affected. In its judgment the court stated:[102]

> It is not enough to say this or that change of circumstances has occurred in the locality and leave it to the tribunal to translate it into an impact on property values.

It appears the High Court considered it was impossible for the tribunal to translate statistics in the report into an effect on house prices that would require a change in valuation band.

This has important implications, as it seems that the High Court now expects appellants to provide stricter proof of their grounds for an alteration in valuation, even though property valuation has always been considered more of an art than a science. In future cases, it may be that the best form of evidence will be a valuation report from an independent valuer demonstrating a link between the blighting and the price a dwelling would have fetched in a theoretical sale on 1 April 1991 (see Chapter 3). It leaves less scope for inference by a tribunal.

A further important decision is the Court of Appeal judgment in *Chilton Merryweather (LO) v Hunt and Others* in which the Court ruled that the word 'physical', in relation to physical changes in the environment, did not include changes in traffic and pollution and noise caused by greater car use on a motorway.[103]

You should expect to be asked questions by members of the tribunal and by the listing officer or local authority representative. For example, if you allege that your property value is affected by blighting or a nuisance of some kind, you may be asked what steps you have taken to remedy the problem. If you have taken no such steps, the conclusion might be drawn that the problem is not sufficiently serious as to make an impact on the property's value.

In appeals that do not relate to valuation matters, the local authority must give the other parties two weeks' notice if it wishes to produce evidence of information supplied in connection with a disability reduction or information in relation to liability. This information may be inspected and copies taken if at least 24 hours' notice is given to the local authority.[104] In a valuation appeal, the listing officer must give at least two weeks' notice of information s/he proposes to use at the hearing. Again, you and any other party to the appeal may, having given 24 hours' notice, inspect the documents and make a copy of all the documents or an extract if you wish.[105]

You have the right to inspect the relevant documents and to request information relating to a maximum of four comparable dwellings or, if the listing officer specifies more, the same number as is specified by the officer. The listing officer has a duty to produce both sets of documents at the hearing.[106]

Historic values

The government has indicated that it is prepared to allow the Valuation Office Agency greater freedom in the future to release information to taxpayers concerning property values obtained before 2000. This information could be of use, particularly with appeals in England where a taxpayer may be able to show a trend in rising house prices for properties with a particular banding and argue that her/his property is similar. Currently, such information is shared only once an appeal proceeds to a tribunal, but the government has proposed to make pre-2000 sales information available at an earlier stage.

Scotland

In Scotland, a valuation appeal committee may require a party to provide the other parties, by a set date, with:[107]

- a written statement outlining the evidence to be given at the hearing; *and*
- copies of all documents which are to be produced for the hearing.

If a committee has made such a requirement, no other material may be produced unless the committee allows it.[108]

If there is to be a hearing, the committee has the power to grant to any of the parties the same rights of access to documents as could be granted, or provided, by the Court of Session.[109] The committee may require:[110]

- someone's attendance at the hearing as a witness; *or*
- the production of any document relating to the appeal.

If someone fails to comply with such a written requirement, s/he is liable on summary conviction to a fine not exceeding level 1 on the standard scale.[111] No one need produce any material or answer any questions which s/he would not need to answer in a court of law (eg, professional confidences)[112] or questions that might incriminate a person to a criminal charge. Additionally, if someone is required to appear as a witness at the hearing and it takes place more than 10 miles from her/his home, s/he does not have to appear unless her/his necessary expenses are paid.[113]

Decisions

Following a hearing, the VTE/VTW or a valuation appeal committee in Scotland has the discretion to give an oral decision to the parties concerned.[114] Whether or not an oral decision is given, a written decision, together with a statement of reasons, must be supplied to the parties.

In **England and Wales**, this should be done as soon as is reasonably practicable after the decision has been made. If the tribunal does not give written reasons, you may request reasons in writing. Your request must be made within two weeks of the date on which the VTE panel sent or provided you with a final decision notice.[115] Sometimes a handwritten copy is given to the parties on the day, with a more formal typed copy supplied afterwards. In **Scotland**, it must be done within seven days of the decision. After the tribunal or committee has made a decision, it has the power to make orders to give effect to it.[117] An order may include a direction for the local authority to repay you any council tax owing or any bailiffs' fees or other charges, with interest at 6 per cent from the date(s) of payment.

Tribunals are expected to give reasons for their decisions. If a tribunal or committee fails to give adequate reasons, the decision is invalid.

The tribunal's decisions become public documents. In addition to being sent to the parties, they are placed on the website, except that, in the case where you are appealing about council tax liability decisions, your name and other identifying information is removed from the online version in the interests of privacy and family life.[118] You can request material to be omitted ('redacted') from the published decision, or ask that names and other identifying information to be omitted.[119]

The grounds on which the tribunal may decide not to publish certain information include:

- national security;
- public safety or public order;
- personal safety;
- privacy and family life;
- protection of children;
- protection of commercially sensitive information.

It is up to you to satisfy the tribunal that information should not be published.

Previous tribunal or committee decisions

When you begin an appeal, you may be told at some stage that a valuation tribunal or committee has already decided a particular matter and that your attempt to appeal on the same grounds will fail. You should not accept this as a reason for abandoning an appeal. Although local authorities and listing officers have tended to treat previous decisions involving points of law as binding, it should not be assumed that a tribunal or committee will automatically find against an appellant. Just because one appeal has been decided in a particular way does not necessarily mean that the same approach will be taken with a different appeal. Tribunals are not precedent-making bodies which are expected to follow decisions of earlier tribunals. In *West Midlands Baptist (Trust) Association (Incorporated) v Birmingham City Council*, Lord Salmon stated:[120]

> No doubt previous decisions of a tribunal on points of law should be treated by the tribunal with great respect and considered as persuasive *[sic]* local authority, even when made by a layman. But they should never be treated as binding.
>
> This is particularly so with valuation decisions, where there is room for legitimate disagreement or where better and more accurate evidence may be produced than at an earlier hearing regarding another property.

Similarly, in *Assessor for Highland and Western Isles Valuation Joint Board v Fraser*, it was held that a valuation appeal committee should not rely on an earlier ruling, but should consider any fresh evidence produced by the appellant on the subject of comparable dwellings.[121]

Records of decisions

In **Scotland**, each party has the right to make a recording of the hearing at her/his own expense. The committee should be informed of the intention to make a recording before the hearing begins.[122]

In **England and Wales**, the clerk has a duty to make arrangements for the tribunal's decisions to be recorded. The record may be kept in any form, whether documentary or otherwise. The record should contain the following information in appeals about proposals:[123]

- the appellant's name and address;
- the matter appealed against;
- the date of the hearing or determination;
- the names of the parties who appeared (if any);
- the decision of the tribunal and its date;
- the reasons for the decision;
- any order made in consequence of the decision;
- the date of any such order;
- any certificate setting aside the decision;
- any revocation.

Records of decisions are published at www.valuationtribunal.gov.uk.
For other appeals, the record must also contain:[124]

- the date of the appeal; *and*
- the name of the billing authority whose decision was appealed against.

A copy of the relevant entry in the record must, as soon as is reasonably practicable, be sent to each party to the appeal. Each record must be retained for six years.[125]

Anyone may inspect the records free of charge. If a person with custody of records intentionally obstructs someone from inspecting the records, without a reasonable excuse, s/he is liable on summary conviction to a fine not exceeding level 1 on the standard scale.[126]

The member who presided at the hearing or determination of an appeal may authorise that any clerical errors be corrected in the record. A copy of the corrected entry must be sent to the people to whom a copy of the original entry was sent.[127]

The production of a document certified by the clerk or the president is evidence of the decision and the facts it records in any proceedings in any court of law.[128]

5. Reviews of tribunal and committee decisions

There are limited circumstances in which a decision of the Valuation Tribunal for England (VTE), the Valuation Tribunal for Wales (VTW) or a valuation appeal committee decision in Scotland can be reviewed.

In **England and Wales**, except where a decision has been the subject of an appeal to the High Court, a tribunal may review its decision or set it aside.[129] This may only be done following a written application from any of the parties, provided it is in the interests of justice to do so, on the grounds that:

- a document relating to the proceedings was not sent to, or was not received at an appropriate time by, a party (or party's representative); *or*

- a document was not sent to the VTE/VTW; *or*
- a party did not appear and can show reasonable cause for this; *or*
- the decision is affected by a decision of, or on appeal from, the High Court or the Upper Tribunal; *or*
- there has been procedural irregularity; *or*
- in relation to a decision on a completion notice, new evidence has become available (unless it could have been established by reasonably diligent inquiry or foreseen previously).

An application for a review (or 'set-aside') must normally be made within 28 days of the day on which written notice of the decision was sent. In exceptional cases where there is a good reason, an application may be made outside 28 days.

The application must be considered by the tribunal president, who will decide whether one or more of the grounds are satisfied.[130] This is normally done without a hearing, but the president may call a hearing for the parties affected to make submissions.

All relevant parties are informed that a review is to take place and be invited to submit representations in writing within 14 days. A party may opt for a hearing to take place, which is then held within 28 days.

If a decision is to be set aside, the matter may be reheard or reconsidered by a differently constituted tribunal or, in England, treated as an appeal.[131] This can be done immediately if the parties consent.

As soon as is reasonably practicable after the outcome of the request for a review is known, the clerk to the tribunal must write to the applicant and every other party to the appeal informing her/him of the outcome. Additionally, if an appeal to the High Court remains undetermined, the clerk must also notify the High Court as soon as reasonably practicable after the decision has been made.[132]

Appeals to the High Court

If you are unsuccessful in the valuation tribunal, there is no further right of appeal except on a point of law – ie, where the law has been interpreted incorrectly. In **England and Wales**, this is made to the High Court; in **Scotland**, it is made to the Lands Valuation Appeal Court. The appellant, listing officer, assessor and local authority all have an equal right of appeal. In **England and Wales**, the High Court has made it clear that it will not normally interfere with findings of fact made by a tribunal, unless it can be shown that it has acted perversely – eg, the errors of fact are so severe that they amount to mistakes of law, and thus come within the jurisdiction of the High Court.[133]

It is not enough that you simply disagree with the tribunal's decision or that having heard the evidence the tribunal made a finding of fact which you dispute. It must be shown that the tribunal was irrational in that either there was no supporting evidence or that it left out relevant facts or considered irrelevant ones.[134]

Appeals may also be made if the tribunal fails to observe the rules of what is known as 'natural justice'. Examples of breaches of natural justice include the involvement of a person in the hearing who is barred from appearing (see p250), bias on the part of a panel or an appearance of tribunal and denial of cross-examination of witnesses or an opportunity to look at the evidence produced by the other side. A valuation tribunal which introduces legal points not made by parties of its own volition does not breach natural justice.[135]

You are strongly advised to seek legal advice before embarking on this course of action, as costs are likely to be in excess of £1,500 and could be much higher depending on the complexity of the case and whether the appeal is contested. The High Court has the discretion whether or not to award costs against an appellant, but the normal rule is that the loser pays the costs of the other side. However, the Court's decision depends on the facts and the conduct of the parties, whether they choose to appear and whether the matter could have been settled otherwise.

If the listing officer or the local authority brings the appeal, different rules apply. Costs cannot be awarded if the listing officer has brought the appeal or if the council taxpayer does not contest the appeal or attend the hearing. In cases where the local authority appeals to the High Court against a decision, the liability for costs will fall against the tribunal and not the council taxpayer.

In **England and Wales**, an appeal on a point of law to the High Court must be made within four weeks of:

- the date on which notice is given of the decision or order; *or*
- the date of a decision following review; *or*
- a determination by a tribunal that it will not review its decision where the application for review was made within four weeks of the original decision.

The High Court can hear appeals which are out of time (by judicial review) but this should not be relied on, as the right is purely discretionary.[136]

Details of how to appeal to the High Court are found in *The Supreme Court Practice*, known as *The White Book*.

If the VTE/VTW or valuation appeal committee has acted in breach of natural justice, an application for judicial review may also be made. Strict compliance with the time limits is expected.[137] You are required to complete and submit a form for a statutory appeal together with a skeleton argument. The High Court may place a stay on an application for a liability or any order until the appeal is determined.

The High Court may confirm, vary, set aside, revoke or remit the decision or order, and may make any order the tribunal could have made.

In **Scotland**, an appeal from a committee decision must be made within 14 days. The appeal is started by writing to the secretary of the committee to state a case for the Lands Valuation Appeal Court or to the Court of Session. Six copies of an appeal case must be lodged in the Court and six copies must be delivered to the solicitor for any other party to the appeal.

The Court of Session may intervene where a valuation appeal committee errs in the procedure it adopts and reaches conclusions that are illogical, erroneous in law and based on inadequate findings in fact.[138]

Matters excluded from High Court appeals

The High Court considers only matters which are relevant to the particular decision of the tribunal; it cannot consider complaints about the misconduct of individual listing officers or local authority staff involved.

The High Court cannot look at the validity of an Act of Parliament.[139] Claims that the Secretary of State should have created different bands or made other regulations, applying different valuation assumptions to those in force will not be successful, since the Secretary of State has made regulations in accordance with the wide powers granted under legislation. The High Court will not substitute different meanings or words to those used and will not consider challenges against the validity of regulations, unless it can be shown that the Secretary of State has made regulations which are *ultra vires* – ie, outside the scope of powers granted to her/him by Parliament under the main legislation.

Notes

1. **Valuation tribunals and valuation appeal committees**
   1 Regs 70A and 90A CTR(S) Regs
   2 *Future Oversight of Administrative Justice: the proposed abolition of the Administrative Justice and Tribunals Council*, Public Administration Select Committee, July 2013 para 27
   3 *Future Oversight of Administrative Justice: the proposed abolition of the Administrative Justice and Tribunals Council*, Public Administration Select Committee, July 2013
   4 Reg 90C CTR(S) Regs
   5 **E** Regs 3 and 4 Valuation Tribunal for England (Membership and Transitional Provisions) Regs 2009 No.2267 as amended

   W Regs 4-14 VTW Regs
   6 Sch 11 para A18A LGFA 1988 inserted by Sch 4 para 2 LGFA 2012

2. **Matters that can be appealed**
   7 **E** Reg 10(2) VTE(CTRA)(P) Regs
   8 **E** Reg 10(2) CT(ALA) Regs
   9 **E** Reg 10(3) CT(ALA) Regs
   10 **E** Reg 7(6) CT(ALA) Regs, as amended by reg 5 CT(VALA)(E) Regs
   W Reg 8(6) CT(ALA) Regs, as amended by reg CT(VALA)(E) Regs
   11 **E** Reg 7(7) CT(ALA)(E) Regs
   W Reg 8(7) CT(ALA) Regs, as amended
   12 **E** Reg 9(3) CT(ALA)(E) Regs
   W Reg 10(3) CT(ALA) Regs, as amended
   13 **E** Practice Statement: Points of Law and Principles of Valuation, VTE/PS/A10: 1 February 2013, para 1
   14 **EW** s16 LGFA 1992

S s81 LGFA 1992
15 **S** s81 LGFA 1992
16 **EW** s16 LGFA 1992
   E Reg 21 VTE(CTRA)(P) Regs
   W Reg 29 VTW Regs
17 **E** Reg 21(6) VTE(CTRA)(P) Regs
   W Reg 29(5) VTW Regs
18 **EW** Reg 37 VCCT(A) Regs
   E Reg 20A VTE (CTRA)(P)Regs as
   inserted by reg 2 VTE(CTRA)(P)(A) Regs
   W Reg 30(1) VTW Regs
19 **E** Reg 20A VTE(CTRA)(P) Regs inserted
   by reg 2(4) VTE(CTRA)(P)(A) Regs
   W Reg 30 VTW Regs as amended by reg
   2(4) VTW(W)(A) Regs 2013
20 Practice Statement: Council Tax
   Reduction Appeals, VTE/PS/A11: 22
   May 2013, para 5
21 Practice Statement: Council Tax
   Reduction Appeals, VTE/PS/A11: 22
   May 2013, Annex 4
22 Practice Statement: Council Tax
   Reduction Appeals, VTE/PS/A11: 22
   May 2013, Annex 4
23 **E** Reg 28(2) VTE(CTRA)(P) Regs
   W Reg 30(5) VTW Regs
24 **S** Reg 22 CT(ALA)(S) Regs
25 **S** Reg 22 CT(ALA)(S) Regs
26 **S** Reg 22 CT(ALA)(S) Regs
27 **S** Reg 7 CTR(S)A(No.2) Regs
28 **S** 90A(4)(c) CTR(S) Regs
29 **S** Reg 90B CTR(S) Regs
30 **S** Reg 90C(2) CTR(S) Regs
31 **S** Reg 90D(1) CTR(S) Regs
32 **E** Reg 21(5) VTE(CTRA)(P) Regs
   W Reg 29(4) VTW Regs
33 **E** Reg 21(6) VTE(CTRA)(P) Regs;
   reg 10 VTE(CTRA)(P) Regs
   W Reg 29(5) VTW Regs
34 **E** Reg 10(6) VTE(CTRA)(P) Regs
35 **E** Regs 25 and 28(2) VTE(CTRA)(P) Regs
   W Reg 40(5) VTW Regs
36 **S** Reg 24 CT(ALA)(S) Regs
37 **S** Reg 24 CT(ALA)(S) Regs
38 **S** Reg 24 CT(ALA)(S) Regs
39 **E** Reg 21(4) VTE(CTRA)(P) Regs
   W Reg 29(3) VTW Regs
40 **E** Reg 21(6) VTE(CTRA)(P) Regs
   W Reg 29(5) VTW Regs
41 **W** Reg 30 VTW Regs
42 **E** Reg 28 VTE(CTRA)(P) Regs
   W Reg 30(5) VTW Regs
43 **S** Reg 23 CT(ALA)(S) Regs
44 **S** Reg 23 CT(ALA)(S) Regs
45 **S** Reg 23 CT(ALA)(S) Regs
46 s13A(1)(c) LGFA 1992
47 *British Oxygen Ltd v Minister of
   Technology* [1971] AC 610

48 *Associated Provincial Picture Houses v The
   Wednesbury Corporation* [1948] 1 KB
   223
49 Practice Statement: Council Tax
   Reduction Appeals, VTE/PS/A11: 5
   November 2013, paras 25-30
50 Reg 19(8) VTE(CTRA)(P) Regs

3. **How appeals are dealt with**
51 **E** VTE(CTRA)(P) Regs
   W CT(ALA) Regs and VTW Regs
   S CT(ALA)(S) Regs
52 **EW** Reg 20 CT(ALA) Regs
   E Reg 29(1) VTE(CTRA)(P) Regs
   W Reg 33 VTW Regs
   S Reg 27 CT(ALA)(S) Regs
53 Reg 13 CT(ALA)(E) Regs
   E Reg 19(7) VTE(CTRA)(P) Regs as
   amended by reg 2 VTENDRCT(E)(A)
   Regs
54 **E** Reg 20 CT(ALA) Regs; reg 29(1)
   VTE(CTRA)(P) Regs
   W Reg 33(1) VTW Regs
   S Reg 27 CT(ALA)(S) Regs
55 **S** Reg 27 CT(ALA)(S) Regs
56 **S** Reg 27 CT(ALA)(S) Regs
57 **S** Reg 27 CT(ALA)(S) Regs
58 **E** Reg 6 VTE(CTRA)(P) Regs
   W Reg 21 CT(ALA) Regs

4. **Appeal hearings**
59 Reg 21 VTE(CTRA)(P) Regs; reg 10
   CT(ALA)(E) Regs
60 Practice Statement: extensions of time
   limits for making appeals, VTE/PS/AI, 15
   July 2010, para 7
61 Practice Statement: extensions of time
   limits for making appeals, VTE/PS/AI, 15
   July 2010, paras 8 and 9
62 **E** Reg 19 VTE(CTRA)(P) Regs
   W Reg 32(1) VTW Regs
63 **W** Reg 32(1) VTW Regs
64 **S** Reg 26 CT(ALA)(S) Regs
65 Reg 19(4) and (5) VTE(CTRA)(P) Regs as
   amended by reg 2 VTENDRCT(E)(A)
   Regs

4. **Appeal hearings**
66 **E** Reg 30 VTE(CTRA)(P) Regs
   W Reg 34(1) VTW Regs
67 **S** Reg 28 CT(ALA)(S) Regs
68 **W** Reg32(2) VTW Regs
69 **S** Reg 28 CT(ALA)(S) Regs
70 **W** Reg 33(3) Regs
   S Reg 28 CT(ALA)(S) Regs
71 **E** Reg 4 The Valuation Tribunal for
   England (Membership and Transitional
   Provisions) Regulations 2009 No.2267

W Reg 35 VTW Regs
72 **E** Reg 5(7) The Valuation Tribunal for England (Membership and Transitional Provisions) Regulations 2009 No.2267
73 **W** Reg 28 VTW Regs
74 **E** Practice Statement: Model Procedure, VTE/PS/B1, 22 May 2013
75 **E** Reg 13 VTE(CTRA)(P) Regs
   W Reg 36 VTW Regs
   S Reg 34 CT(ALA)(S) Regs
76 **E** Reg 13 VTE(CTRA)(P) Regs
   W Reg 36 VTW Regs
77 **S** Reg 13 The Valuation Appeal Committee (Procedure in Appeals under the Valuation Acts) (Scotland) Regulations 1995 No.572; reg 34 CT(ALA)(S) Regs
78 **E** Reg 13(1) VTE(CTRA)(P) Regs
   W Reg 36 VTW Regs
   S Reg 34 CT(ALA)(S) Regs
79 **EW** Reg 25 CT(ALA) Regs
   E Reg 32 VTE(CTRA)(P) Regs
   W Reg 37(2) VTW Regs
80 Practice Statement: Council Tax Reduction Appeals, VTE/PS/A11: 22 May 2013, para 34
81 **E** Reg 17(2) VTE(CTRA)(P) Regs
82 **W** VTW Best Practice Protocol, 1F Evidence, para 4
83 **E** Reg 6(1)(i) VTE(CTRA)(P) Regs
84 Practice Statement: Sending and Delivering Documents, VTS/PS/A8, 11 January 2011
85 **EW** Reg 25 CT(ALA) Regs
   E Reg 31 VTE(CTRA)(P) Regs
   W Reg 37 VTW Regs as amended by reg 2(6) VTW(A) Regs
86 **S** Reg 32 CT(ALA)(S) Regs
87 **EW** Reg 25 CT(ALA) Regs
   E Reg 10 VTE(CTRA)(P) as amended by reg 2 VTE(CTRA)(P)(A) Regs
   W Regs 32A(1)-(3) VTW Regs as amended by reg 2(5) VTW(W)(A) Regs
   S Reg 31 CT(ALA)(S) Regs
88 **E** Reg 40 VTE(CTRA)(P) Regs
   W Reg 42(5)(b) VTW Regs
89 **S** Reg 31 CT(ALA)(S) Regs
90 **EW** Reg 25(5) CT(ALA) Regs; reg 44(4) VCCT(A) Regs
   E Reg 32 VTE(CTRA)(P) Regs
91 Practice Statement: Model Procedure, VTE/PS/B1, 22 May 2013
92 Practice Statement: Model Procedure, VTE/PS/B1, 22 May 2013
93 Practice Statement: Appellant's Non-Attendance, VTE/PS/B3, April 2010
94 **E** Reg 17(1)(e) VTE (CTRA) Regs
   S Reg 33 CT(ALA)(S) Regs

95 Practice Statement: Appellant's Non-Attendance, VTE/PS/B3, April 2010, paragraph 25
96 Practice Statement: Appellant's Non-Attendance, VTE/PS/B3, April 2010, paras 26-30
97 **E** Regs 6 & 30 VTE(CTRA)(P) Regs; Practice Statement: Postponements and Adjournments, VTE/PS/A3, 1 December 2013
   W Reg 34(4) VTW Regs
98 Reg 18 VTE(CTRA)(P) Regs
99 **EW** *Garton v Hunter (Valuation Officer)* [1969] 2 QBD 37
   E Reg 17 VTE(CTRA)(P) Regs
   W Reg 37(9) VTW Regs
100 *Morgan v Dew* [1964] RA 294
101 *Tilly v Listing Officer of Tower Hamlets LBC* [2001] RVR 250
102 LJ Jowitt, *Tilly v Listing Officer of Tower Hamlets LBC* [2001] RVR 250
103 *Chilton-Merryweather v Hunt and Others* [2008] RA 357
104 **E** Reg 17 VTE(CTRA)(P) Regs
   W Reg 38 VTW Regs
105 **E** Reg 17 VTE(CTRA)(P) Regs
106 **E** Reg 17 VTE(CTRA)(P) Regs
107 **S** Reg 29 CT(ALA)(S) Regs
108 **S** Reg 29 CT(ALA)(S) Regs
109 **S** Reg 30 CT(ALA)(S) Regs
110 **S** Reg 30 CT(ALA)(S) Regs
111 **S** Reg 30 CT(ALA)(S) Regs
112 **S** Reg 30 CT(ALA)(S) Regs
113 **S** Reg 30 CT(ALA)(S) Regs
114 **E** Reg 36 VTE(CTRA)(P) Regs
   W Reg 40(2) VTW Regs
115 **E** Reg 37 VTE(CTRA)(P) Regs as amended by reg 2(6) VTE(CTRA)(P)(A) Regs
   W Reg 40(3) VTW Regs
116 **S** Reg 36 CT(ALA)(S) Regs
117 **E** Reg 38 VTE(CTRA)(P) Regs
   W Reg 41 VTW Regs
118 **E** Practice Statement: Publication of Decisions, VTE/PS/C3, 25 November 2013, para 2
119 **E** Practice Statement: Publication of Decisions, VTE/PS/C3, 25 November 2013, para 3
120 *West Midlands Baptist (Trust) Association (Incorporated) v Birmingham City Council* [1967] RVR 780 (CA)
121 *Assessor for Highland and Western Isles Valuation Joint Board v Fraser* [2001] SC 473
122 **S** Reg 35 CT(ALA)(S) Regs
123 **E** Reg 41 VTE(CTRA)(P) Regs
   W Reg 31 and Sch 4 CT(ALA) Regs

124 **E** Reg 41 VTE(CTRA)(P) Regs
125 **E** Reg 41 VTE(CTRA)(P) Regs
W Reg 43 VTW Regs
126 **E** Reg 41 VTE(CTRA)(P) Regs
W Reg 50 VTW Regs
127 **E** Reg 39 VTE(CTRA)(P) Regs
W Reg 43(7) VTW Reg
128 **E** Reg 41(6) VTE(CTRA)(P) Regs
W Reg 42(1) VTW Regs

5. Reviews of tribunal and committee decisions

129 **E** Reg 40 VTE(CTRA)(P) Regs
W Reg 42(1) VTW Regs
130 **E** Reg 40 VTE(CTRA)(P) Regs
W Reg 49 VTW Regs
131 **E** Reg 40(7) VTE(CTRA)(P) Regs
W Reg 44(2) VTW Regs
132 **E** Reg 41(10) VTE(CTRA)(P) Regs
W Reg 42(9) VTW Regs
133 *Bracegirdle v Oxley* [1947] 1 KB 349;
*Hayes v Humberside Valuation Tribunal
and Kingston Upon Hull City Council*
[1998] RA 37
134 *Vaughan v Valuation Tribunal* [2013]
EWHC 1885 (Admin)
135 *Macattram v London Borough of Camden*
[2012] RA 369
136 *R v London South Eastern Valuation
Tribunal and Neale (LO), ex parte Moore*
[2001] RVR 94
137 *R v London South West Valuation Tribunal
ex parte de Melo* [2000] RVR 73
138 *Dundee City Council v Dundee Valuation
Appeal Committee and another* [2011]
CSIH 73
139 *British Railways Board v Pickin* [1974]
EWCA 765

Chapter 13

Complaints to the Ombudsman

This chapter covers:
1. The work of the Ombudsman (below)
2. What is maladministration (p267)
3. Making a complaint (p270)
4. Action through the courts (p273)
5. Examples of complaints and settlements (p274)

1. The work of the Ombudsman

The remit of the Ombudsman is to examine and investigate complaints from members of the public who claim to have experienced injustice as a result of bureaucratic error or wrongdoing. Such mistakes and errors fall under the umbrella term of 'maladministration'. The Ombudsman has the power to look into many different types of error which do not generate a right to take court action, but nonetheless give grounds for complaint.

The Ombudsman may investigate maladministration by any district, borough, city or county council and, therefore, can deal with mistakes by billing authorities in administering council tax in their areas. The Ombudsman does not cover town or parish councils or improper behaviour by individual elected councillors, except if it involves wider wrongdoing in the administration of the council as a whole.

During 2005/06 in England, the Ombudsman received 18,626 complaints from the public about local government. Of these, 996 (5 per cent) related to local taxation matters. In 2009/10, the Ombudsman received 1,267 complaints and enquiries on local taxation. In 2010/11, the number increased to 1,623.[1]

2. **What is maladministration**

'**Maladministration**' is an open-ended term covering a wide range of bureaucratic mistakes and abuses. It is not defined in statute and when the term was first introduced into Parliament it was considered to include 'bias, neglect, delay, incompetence and inaptitude, arbitrariness and so on' on the part of public authorities.[2]

Maladministration can thus cover many forms of bureaucratic wrongdoing which may not be serious enough to justify court proceedings, but which nonetheless can cause injustice – eg, delays in answering letters or losing records. It can include many forms of improper behaviour by local government staff, whether through lack of care or deliberate wrongdoing. Other examples of maladministration include:[3]

- rudeness;
- bias;
- knowingly giving misleading advice;
- falsifying records and documents;
- unwillingness to recognise the rights of the taxpayer;
- failing to mitigate the effects of rigid adherence to the law where this results in inequitable treatment;
- not acting in a timely way;
- sending documents to the wrong address;
- allocating payments to the wrong account;
- generating numerous confusing and contradictory documents;
- wiping computer records or inserting inaccurate data;
- failing to notify a person of her/his loss of appeal rights;
- ignoring valid advice;
- taking disproportionate redress;
- operating faulty procedures;
- failing to follow Page 9 of the National Standards for Enforcement Agents regarding the use of bailiffs in collections from vulnerable persons (see Appendix 2).

Injustice

The Ombudsman intervenes in cases which have resulted in injustice, caused by a local authority but which it has failed to redress adequately or at all. As with maladministration, the concept of '**injustice**' is a wide one and open to different interpretations. Arguably, it should mean more than a trivial problem or minor inconvenience, although much will depend on the actual effect of the error on the individual taxpayer concerned. Maladministration causing nuisance, embarrassment, financial loss or serious inconvenience and distress to a taxpayer falls within the remit of injustice.

However, a complaint to the Ombudsman should not be used simply as a way of 'getting back' at a local authority or simply to get particular officials into trouble. Neither should a complaint be brought simply because you believe a decision to be wrong. Similarly, if a local authority has taken steps to correct an injustice and you are satisfied, the Ombudsman cannot be expected to take the matter any further.

Maladministration and council tax

In the *Digest of Cases* 2008/09, the Ombudsman stated:

> The Ombudsman receives many complaints about the way councils take recovery action over failure to pay council tax. Sometimes people receive summonses when they should not have done, and the consequences of that action can lead to councils granting liability orders that enable them to refer alleged debts to bailiffs. Where unjustified recovery action has been taken, the Ombudsman would expect an appropriate remedy to be provided.

Because of its complexity, the administration of council tax can frequently generate errors which, if uncorrected, may result in inconvenience, stress and embarrassment to taxpayers. Even when a mistake is discovered, the local authority may not act properly or quickly enough to remedy the problem.

For example, a local authority may fail to record an entitlement to a discount, repeatedly list the wrong person on a bill or fail to award payment to the correct account. This may result in sending reminder notices to, and summonses against, a person who has actually paid the tax or who is exempt. The authority may delay sending information or bills, causing 'prejudice' to the taxpayer (see p165). Problems may also be caused by sending demands in the names of people who have died after the local authority has been informed of the death, or failing to record that someone is severely mentally impaired.

Inadequate liaison between accounts and benefits sections in a local authority may generate problems. For example, although court action may be suspended, computerised enforcement systems may continue to issue warning letters even when the local authority has assured a person the mistake has been remedied. A local authority is not entitled to hide behind an excuse of 'computer error' to cover up inefficiency in such cases.

Another form of maladministration is an unreasonable delay in processing a council tax reduction (CTR) applications or refusing applications for discretionary relief without proper consideration, delays in referring an appeal to a tribunal, or failing to refer an appeal at all. Although you may ultimately receive CTR after a long delay, you may face considerable inconvenience, stress and financial difficulty and embarrassment in the meantime. Significantly, the Ombudsman does not consider automatically issuing a summons against a person who is waiting for her/his CTR to be calculated to be 'fair or reasonable' and that a local authority 'should take into account the circumstances of the individual before taking such action.'[4]

Other examples might include seeking a liability order against a person after an undertaking has been given not to obtain one, obtaining an order against a person who has offered to pay the sum in full, concealing the existence of a liability order or commencing enforcement action where an undertaking has been given by the local authority not to do so. Grounds may also exist for complaint if a local authority acts unreasonably by refusing to quash or cancel a liability order which has been obtained in error.

Matters that the Ombudsman cannot examine

There are a number of matters that the Ombudsman cannot investigate. These include:

- the amount of tax set by the local authority;
- decisions of courts or the Valuation Tribunal for England (VTE), Valuation Tribunal for Wales (VTW) and valuation appeal committees in Scotland;
- whether a person is liable for council tax;
- decisions about banding;
- the conduct of court proceedings.

These matters can only be challenged through the High Court or the VTE/VTW or valuation appeal committees in Scotland.

Refusal to accept evidence supplied by a taxpayer

In some cases maladministration occurs where the authority refuses to accept evidence submitted in an application for CTR or makes repeated requests for information that has already been supplied.

In such a case, you may serve a witness statement for establishing the truth of what you are saying, and also give notice of an intention to escalate the complaint to the civil courts or tribunal if the issue is not resolved in your favour.

A witness statement should set out the facts and calculations and deal with any matter the local authority has hitherto refused to be satisfied. It may also include copies of documents as exhibits and must carry a statement of truth.[5]

The witness statement should include the address of the local county court, as that is where an action may be founded against the authority and its staff, or alternatively the valuation tribunal where an appeal may be heard.

A sworn witness statement is evidence for all purposes in civil and criminal proceedings and is the strongest evidence that can be provided, save for sworn evidence given orally in proceedings. It is to be preferred to anything that a local authority may say or provide that is unsworn. Furthermore, it must be accepted by any court or tribunal as the truth unless contrary evidence is provided which undermines the truth of the statement or the witness is discredited by cross-examination.

Since a witness statement is the most conclusive evidence that you can provide, the local authority will err in law if it refuses to act upon the information contained in it. Refusal by the local authority to consider evidence placed before it can place the local authority in breach of its statutory duties, generating grounds for a complaint and potential legal action against the authority or officials concerned.

3. **Making a complaint**

The Ombudsman investigates complaints from:
- individuals;
- family members of individuals;
- advice agencies acting on behalf of individuals.

There is rarely public funding (formerly legal aid) available to bring a complaint to the Ombudsman. However, you could pursue a complaint via a solicitor who may be acting for you in a benefits case on a funded basis. However, after 2013 there is unlikely to be any legal aid provision at all.

No alternative remedy

In order to bring a complaint, there must be no other remedy available to you. In some cases, this may be because there is no right of appeal to a court or tribunal – eg, because the grounds of the complaint fall outside one of the issues which can be considered. Alternatively, the wrongful conduct may not provide a basis to start court action (eg, failing to reply to letters concerning council tax) but nonetheless can cause serious difficulties to an individual. In such cases, the Ombudsman can investigate.

Normally, if a legal remedy exists, you are expected to pursue it rather than make a complaint to the Ombudsman. Thus, in a dispute over benefit entitlement, you are expected to appeal to the First-tier Tribunal. However, there is also a limited provision which allows the Ombudsman to investigate if it would be unreasonable to expect you to pursue a legal remedy or appeal. A complaint to the Ombudsman would be appropriate, for example, if judicial review by the High Court is unavailable or impractical to pursue (eg, if you would find it difficult to obtain evidence), or if you are unlikely to have the means to pursue a legal remedy.[6]

How to make a complaint

The Ombudsman expects you to try to resolve your complaint with the local authority. In order to have a case taken up by the Ombudsman, you must normally have been through all the stages of your local council's internal complaints procedure. This usually involves a three-stage process, often ending with the chief executive, at least in name.

If you have experienced maladministration, you should therefore first make a complaint to the local authority concerned. Local authorities each have their own particular complaints procedure and should be prepared to provide details of it. Normally, details of the procedure can be obtained either by writing to the local authority or from its website.

The complaint should set out the specific details of what has taken place and the effect it has had on you. It is best that such complaints are written in clear and polite language and without using emotive or abusive language. (Extremes of language or unsubstantiated allegations are only likely to result in a complaint being viewed in a less favourable light on any impartial review.) **Note:** you should not threaten legal action generally against the local authority as an alternative to investigation by the Ombudsman, as the Ombudsman's jurisdiction only arises where there is no practical alternative or where it would be unreasonable to expect you to pursue legal action.

You will usually have to complete all stages of your local authority's complaints procedure before the Ombudsman will consider your complaint. Most have a three-stage procedure, with officers at increasing levels of seniority examining the case, usually ending at the office of the chief executive.

Information to support complaints can be obtained by way of requests under the Freedom of Information Act 2000. Use may be made of the Data Protection Act 1998 and subject access requests for personal data; subject access requests can be made by individuals and are often used by journalists.

Complaints and the monitoring officer

Although not necessarily sufficient in itself, a formal complaint to the council may be used in conjunction with other remedies; because time may be of the essence there are ways to short cut the process. Complaints are normally dealt with in a three-stage process and may take 12 weeks or more to clear all three stages, ending at the level of Chief Executive. Chief Executives vary in competence or understanding but seem to be highly media conscious. Where there is a complaint there is also scope for publicity, particularly with the local press.

To expedite or increase the effect of a complaint in a council tax matter, it can be worth copying the complaint direct to the Chief Executive. This may also be combined for a request to the local authority to exercise its discretionary powers to reduce or remit a sum in council tax.

Where an outsourced company is involved, a complaint should be taken to the senior officer in the authority responsible for contract compliance and liaison between the council and the contactor.

A further route to draw attention to a complaint where a local authority is acting in breach of any statutory duty or rule of law, a complaint may be made to the monitoring officer of the authority who is responsible for investigation and producing reports. The monitoring officer may also look into maladministration, though the duty only arises where the Ombudsman has investigated.[7]

Publicity can be an effective tactic against a local authority.

If you remain unhappy with the final outcome, or the council is taking too long to look into the matter (12 weeks is considered reasonable), you can complain to Ombudsman. Complaints should normally be brought within 12 months of the events.

The Ombudsman issues guidance on bringing a complaint. This is available at www.lgo.org.uk.

Complaint forms can normally be downloaded or completed online.

When bringing a complaint, it is usually a good idea to include a short chronology of events and correspondence, to provide a summary of key dates and the history of the matter, particularly if the case is complex. In the chronology, you should list the dates as accurately as possible and the event which occurred – eg, what the local authority did or did not do. Copies of all the relevant correspondence should also be submitted with the initial application, in order that the Ombudsman may begin analysis of the case with all the relevant information.

On receipt of a letter or application, the Ombudsman will normally assign a caseworker to deal with your complaint. The caseworker will contact you or your adviser as well as the local authority.

Action the Ombudsman can take

The remit of the Ombudsman is to obtain redress for the citizen. This may involve an investigation and publishing a report summarising the investigation and its findings (the complainant is normally given a pseudonym). The Ombudsman may issue directions to the local authority – eg, requiring it to make an apology or take appropriate action to remedy the maladministration and pay compensation to the person adversely affected. The Ombudsman also encourages local settlements.

There is no system to enforce an award of compensation but, in practice, local authorities usually accept the findings made by the Ombudsman and it is rare for a local authority to refuse to pay. Between 2005/06 to 2009/10, 99 per cent of Ombudsman recommendations were met by councils. Although the legal position is unclear, in such a case a victim of maladministration would potentially have grounds for taking civil action through the courts as actions or defaults giving rise to maladministration are likely to comprise actionable civil wrongs in themselves. Directions may also be issued to local authorities to change their procedures to prevent the problem reoccurring.

4. **Action through the courts**

The use of the civil courts is the ultimate recourse of the citizen who is a victim of bureaucratic wrong-doing.[8] The council tax enforcement regulations give a specific right to recover sums overpaid but more generally a local authority will fall within the general jurisdiction of the civil courts, including the arbitration procedure or 'small claims court'. Each billing authority is liable for acts and defaults by its employees or servants in civil law as with disputes between private parties. Local authorities may be sued for negligence, breach of statutory duty (eg, in refusing to process a council tax reduction application) or harassment in cases of wrongful debt recovery or for misfeasance in a public office. In addition to public authorities being liable in civil law, individual officials can be proceeded against on a personal basis where an individual officer has acted unlawfully, in bad faith or abused a position of trust.[9] Specific claims in tort may lie such as instigating malicious civil process or malicious instigation of bankruptcy proceedings. Most officers at senior level will be aware of this. The authority is liable in costs for the acts and defaults of its servants, as are individual officers if sued personally, or possibly even on a third part costs basis in exceptional circumstances.[10] Legal advice should be sought before commencing such civil claims.

In particular, the small claims jurisdiction of the County Court may be used for acts and omissions by local authority departments as it is relatively cheap to use and persons on low incomes or benefits may be entitled to obtain a fee waiver. The local authority faces the further problem that neither side in a claim for under £10,000 can claim for legal costs and, if the council does nothing in response to the issue of proceedings a default judgment may be entered against the authority, and any officer of the council named as a defendant.

In a small number of cases maladministration may also involve the deliberate commission of corrupt or criminal actions or defaults. Victims of maladministration have taken the matters to the police where maladministration has gone beyond negligence, into the realm of criminal liability for individual officers. There is a range of potential criminal offences that can arise from the production of false documents including the Forgery Act 1981, various offences involving theft or fraud, offences under the Criminal Attempts Act 1981 and the common law offence misconduct in a public office.[11]

The police are under a duty to investigate when a matter is reported to them, though officers may suggest that the matter is pursued as a civil matter. A private prosecution can also be commenced if the police fail to act.[12]

5. **Examples of complaints and settlements**

The following cases are examples of complaints of maladministration involving council tax which have been upheld. Cases often depend on their individual facts, but the settlement figures give an indication of the size of any award.

Suicide of taxpayer
Southwark Borough Council (00/A/19293 RVR [2002] 289)

The complaint was brought by relatives of a taxpayer who had committed suicide after receiving a summons for non-payment of council tax. The taxpayer was a single man with learning difficulties receiving benefits. In October 2000, his council tax benefit was cancelled and he was sent a fresh form to complete. Four days later he was sent a demand for £235.10 payable in instalments. The taxpayer visited the local authority's office and submitted a claim form, but the local authority continued recovery action. The taxpayer applied again for council tax benefit and provided information on his entitlement to jobseeker's allowance. Nonetheless, a summons was issued again for £235.10. The summons was accompanied by an additional sheet warning that bailiffs or imprisonment could follow the granting of liability order. The taxpayer hanged himself in his flat. Police called to the scene found the opened summons and a suicide note referring to his debt problems. Relatives of the deceased complained to the council but did not receive a satisfactory response.

On investigation, it was considered that the three-and-a-half-month delay in processing benefit amounted to maladministration. Further maladministration was found in sending out a summons while the relevant benefit claim had yet to be determined. The Ombudsman said that the summons had contributed to the distress and anxiety suffered by the deceased. The way in which the local authority had responded to relatives was also criticised.

Outcome: A settlement of £3,200 to the family of the deceased and £1,000 payment to a charity of their choice was approved.

Unnecessary recovery action
Hackney Borough Council (03/A/09613) 7 October 2004

The complainant, Ms Murray (pseudonym), set up a standing order to pay council tax in April 1998. In July 1998, Hackney Council realised that, because there was no council tax reference number on the standing order form, payments received were not being allocated to Ms Murray's account. Despite assurances from Hackney on several occasions that it would rectify the problem, this was not achieved until January 2004. Arrears for 1998/99 were wrongly carried forward each year and it began unnecessary recovery actions including summonses, liability orders and letters from bailiffs.

Outcome: The Ombudsman found maladministration and recommended that Hackney Council pay Ms Murray £1,800 compensation and undertake changes to its accounting systems.

Wrongful attribution of liability

Oxford City Council and Southwark Borough Council (02/B/09186 and 02/B/16542) 8 October 2003

A complaint was brought by Mr D Parry (pseudonym) that Oxford City Council was making deductions from his benefit for arrears of council tax. Mr Parry had been a student in Oxford over 30 years earlier but had not lived there since. The Ombudsman found that Oxford Council had believed that its debtor, another Mr D Parry, had moved from Oxford to London NW2, but when they could not find him there, they found the complainant living in SE15. This alone convinced it that it was the same debtor and it contacted Southwark Borough Council. Although Mr Parry had been a council tenant with Southwark for many years, Southwark Borough Council released information to enable deductions from the complainant's benefit and further compounded the error with delays in refunding his benefit. The Ombudsman found maladministration in the 'bizarre treatment' of the complainant and considered that depriving him of money while he was on a very low income must have resulted in difficulty.

Outcome: It was recommended that Oxford City Council pay £750 and Southwark pay £250 to the complainant.

Delay in housing and council tax benefit

Lambeth Borough Council (01/B/17580) 14 February 2003

The Ombudsman found maladministration in delays by Lambeth Council in assessing the council tax benefit and housing benefit claims of a married couple and in the delay in responding to a review of the decision. While considering the benefit claims, Lambeth Council began legal proceedings to take possession and obtained a liability order for non-payment of council tax. The delay in assessing benefits was 10-and-a-half months, and nine months to respond to the appeal. The decision to commence proceedings was also maladministration.

Outcome: Lambeth Council agreed to an apology and to ensure that benefits were being paid correctly and to make an *ex-gratia* payment of £1,000 to the complainants in recognition of their distress, inconvenience, time and trouble.

Delay in housing and council tax benefit

Allerdale District Council (03/C/07422) 12 January 2005

Allerdale District Council failed to assess and determine housing benefit and council tax benefit for the period September 2002 to March 2003. It also failed to respond to the complainants' letter of appeal regarding their claim and cancelled their benefit claim from 3 March 2003 without giving reasons. The circumstances of the complainants were complicated by the fact that they ran a small business at the time in question and they had failed to respond promptly to a request for information from the local authority.

Outcome: The Ombudsman found maladministration and recommended that Allerdale Council pay £500 for stress and court costs incurred and directed it to review its procedures.

Rating list errors and failures

Torbay Council (00/B/10806 1 August 2001 reported at [2001] RVR 194)

The Ombudsman held that Torbay Council should have taken reasonable steps to ensure that all the information about properties was accurate and that failure to do so was maladministration, the complainants having experienced considerable aggravation, uncertainty, time and trouble in pursuing the matter.

Outcome: The Ombudsman recommended an *ex-gratia* payment of £1,000 in compensation.

Delays in processing overpayment appeal

Liverpool City Council (01/C/07860) September 2002

An advice agency complained on behalf of a claimant about unreasonable delays in passing appeals against decisions to recover council tax benefit and housing benefit to the Appeals Service. The Ombudsman found a delay of nine months unreasonable.

Outcome: The Ombudsman considered an offer to pay £375 compensation a reasonable settlement to the complaint.

Delay in processing appeal

Liverpool City Council (01/C/15191) September 2002

An advice agency complained on behalf of a claimant that the council had delayed in passing an appeal against a decision to recover an overpayment of housing benefit and council tax benefit. The appeal had been brought in August 2001, but the papers were not passed to the Appeals Service until June 2002.

The Ombudsman found the delay of 10 months unreasonable and criticised the commencement of court proceedings after the appeal had been made.

Outcome: Liverpool Council agreed to pay £300, which included £50 to reflect the distress caused by the summons.

Unnecessary enforcement and attendance at court

Sandwell Metropolitan Council (No 03/B/12862) September 2004

Sandwell Council issued a summons when a council tax benefit claim was pending, the complainant having provided all the necessary information. It proceeded with court action even after the benefit claim had been assessed and the complainant did not owe the money that was being sought. As a result, the complainant overpaid his council tax by £400. A further incorrect bill was issued requiring the complainant to pay another £196. The taxpayer complained to Sandwell Council and the sums were later credited and repaid to him, but not for several months. The taxpayer was forced to attend an unnecessary court hearing and the local authority delayed in answering correspondence.

Outcome: Although the local authority had refunded money to the taxpayer, the Ombudsman found maladministration causing injustice. There had been inadequate liaison between the accounts and benefits sections of the revenues department and the taxpayer had experienced stress, inconvenience and an unnecessary attendance at court.

Sandwell Council had also delayed in replying to the taxpayer's complaints. The Ombudsman recommended £400 compensation be paid and that Sandwell Council review its procedures.

Delayed appeal and bailiff action

Waltham Forest Borough Council (03/A/01900) 28 October 2003

Mr Gower (pseudonym) complained that Waltham Forest Council had unreasonably delayed assessing claims for housing benefit and council tax benefit, did not provide reasons on appeal and unreasonably took recovery action before his appeal had been determined. The Ombudsman considered that a delay of three months in assessing his claim was unreasonable and amounted to maladministration. The Ombudsman found that Mr Gower was caused prolonged anxiety by the slow progress of his claims and the growth in his rent and council tax arrears. Recovery action caused further stress, which was compounded when, after being told that Waltham Forest Council would suspend bailiff action, he was nonetheless served with a bailiff notice threatening distress and removal of goods.

Outcome: The Ombudsman considered that an offer of £225 in settlement by Waltham Forest Council was too low and recommended £500, together with a review of the way in which it communicated with its bailiffs.

Housing benefit/discretionary housing payment delay

Lambeth Borough Council (04/B/1233) 22 November 2004

The claimant sought housing benefit and a discretionary housing payment. Lambeth Council delayed referring the matter to a rent officer until five months after a request by solicitors to do so and intervention by the Ombudsman. It then took a further five months from the rent officer's decision to decide her claim for a discretionary housing payment. During this period, the landlord of the property changed and payment was made to the previous landlord. High levels of rent arrears led to the claimant being evicted in May 2004.

Outcome: The Ombudsman found maladministration and directed Lambeth Council to pay £2,500 compensation and court costs incurred at the eviction hearing, apologise in writing for all errors, re-house the claimant permanently and undertake a review of procedures.

Delay in processing benefit and failure to respond to complaint

Waltham Forest Borough Council (04/A/10401) March 2005

Mr and Mrs Mohammed (pseudonyms) applied for council tax benefit and housing benefit after their circumstances changed. There was a delay in processing their claim and a reminder notice was issued for council tax arrears. Mr and Mrs Mohammed contacted Waltham Forest Borough Council and recovery action was stopped. However, proceedings recommenced and a summons was issued. A complaint was made by an advice service but not passed to the Council's complaints team. A second complaint was made, by which time a liability order had been obtained and a bailiff's letter issued.

Outcome: The Ombudsman found maladministration in the delay in assessing benefit, failure to halt recovery action and the failure to identify the advice service letter as a complaint. The Ombudsman approved a £500 compensation offer made by Waltham Forest Council, which also wrote off costs and paid the credit balance.

Mistake in determining discount leading to hardship
London Borough of Brent (05/A/17099) 26 February 2007

Brent Council wrongly awarded a 50 per cent empty property discount to the taxpayer in 2002. Having discovered the error in April 2004, it issued a retrospective bill for £4,649.96 and asked him to pay it back in the next 13 months. The taxpayer was a pensioner in poor health and unable to meet the bill in time. Brent Council failed to act in accordance with its anti-poverty strategy and to consider the means of the taxpayer. After the year expired, the local authority obtained a liability order.

Outcome: The Ombudsman identified several faults in the approach by Brent Council. He approved a reduction of £1,479.34 granted to the taxpayer as a suitable settlement. A report examining Brent Council's anti-poverty strategy and its approach to debt collection was published in the public interest.

Failure to communicate with taxpayer and inadequate record keeping
East Dunbartonshire Council (200600109) 19 December 2007

East Dunbartonshire Council failed to keep proper records and communicate about the account of Ms C, who disputed owing a sum of £242.

On investigation, the Ombudsman found the communication and advice from East Dunbartonshire Council was poor and its record-keeping in relation to council tax was inadequate.

Outcome: The Ombudsman recommended that East Dunbartonshire Council should ensure the accuracy of account details before taking recovery action on council tax accounts, and that an apology should be issued to Ms C, together with a payment equal to the disputed sum of £242.

Failure to respond properly to a liability appeal and complaint
City of Edinburgh Council (200603479) September 2007

The complainant (Mr C) raised a number of concerns about the way in which City of Edinburgh Council had dealt with his correspondence and subsequent appeal over council tax liability, and its complaints handling system. Edinburgh Council failed to respond to letters and to refer an appeal to the appeals committee or advise the complainant of his right to pursue the appeal.

The Ombudsman upheld Mr C's complaint that Edinburgh Council had unreasonably failed to treat a letter as an appeal and that the administration of his correspondence and the investigation of his complaint were inadequate.

Outcome: The Ombudsman recommended that the City of Edinburgh Council introduce a system to record all council tax appeals on receipt and set target dates for all appeals to be actioned within 10 days and, where cases are referred to the valuation appeal committee, within two months of receipt unless additional information has been requested. The Ombudsman also recommended a review of the complaints process.

Bankruptcy as a disproportionate method of enforcement
Wolverhampton City Council (06B16600) 31 March 2008
The local authority issued bankruptcy proceedings against a debtor owing council tax on a disputed debt of less than £2,000. This increased the debt to £38,000.
Outcome: The Ombudsman recommended that Westminster Council meet the costs of annulling the bankruptcy order. In his report, the Ombudsman said that a charging order should have been considered. The Ombudsman stated: 'The Council cannot, it seems to me, turn a blind eye to the consequences to the debtor of any recovery option it pursues. Some courses will no doubt be administratively more convenient and less costly than others. But in selecting those options, the impact on the debtor should be weighed in the balance. The dire and punitive consequences of bankruptcy, involving a multiplication of the original debt many times over and frequently incurring the loss of the debtor's home, must be a factor to be taken into account in deciding that the 'last resort' is indeed appropriate. I have seen no evidence that this relevant consideration was taken into account. And that too was maladministration.'

Maladministration causing injustice
London Borough of Camden (07A12661) July 2008
Camden Council's revenue team commenced bankruptcy proceedings for council tax arrears against a woman who, because of mental health difficulties, was unable to conduct her own affairs. Before doing so, it did not adequately record what checks it had made and did not check with the social care department, which would have shown that bankruptcy was not an appropriate recovery method.
Outcome: The Ombudsman found that one department of Camden Council knew of the woman's problems, but the revenue department did not find this out because it failed to make effective internal enquiries. Had it done so, Camden Council would most likely have taken different steps, with less serious consequences.
The Ombudsman ruled: 'I do not think it unreasonable for revenue officers to look beyond their own departmental information and consider a council's records as a whole.' This was in line with data protection guidance issued by the Information Commissioner.
The Ombudsman ruled that the failure to make checks led to unwarranted action and found maladministration causing injustice. Camden Council agreed to apply to court to annul the bankruptcy. On annulment, the Ombudsman recommended that Camden Council should contact credit rating agencies to advise them of the position and that it should change its procedures to make stringent checks for potential vulnerability before taking action leading to bankruptcy, a charging order or committal.

Wrongful pursuit of council tax debt after liability ceased
(Case reference confidential)

The taxpayer 'Mr J' was involved in a long-running dispute with the Council about liability for council tax on a property. He received a summons for two years' worth of arrears. Shortly before the hearing, the Council issued a letter accepting he did not have sole or main residence and that liability was with a 'Mrs K'. The Council requested details of when Mrs K vacated the property and a forwarding address. Nonetheless, the Council pursued a liability order against Mr J and he was threatened with bailiffs. Mr J made a complaint, but received no reply for three months. The Council still served four demand notices covering the previous three years.

Outcome: On investigation, the Ombudsman learned from the Council that it had continued to pursue Mr J because he failed to provide the information on Mrs K. The Ombudsman found that this approach was incorrect. While not criticising the Council for asking Mr J for that information, liability for the tax was not determined by the supply of information. The Council had no legal basis on which to pursue Mr J for arrears arising after the date from which it had decided he was no longer the liable person. The Council should not have proceeded with the court action.

The Council agreed to settle the complaint by apologising to Mr J for its errors and paying him £350 compensation.

Council tax recovery action against vulnerable woman with no income
Slough Borough Council (08 009 315) 4 April 2009

Slough Borough Council's council tax department failed to suspend bailiff action against a woman after being advised she was totally dependent on its own social services and had no means to pay.

'Mrs Carter' (psuedonym) who had entered the UK as a student in 2002 but was prevented from studying after developing cancer and was prohibited from working or claiming benefits. She was totally reliant on the council's social services department, who provided accommodation, a subsistence allowance, and had no income or belongings other than those they provided. She built up council tax arrears. In spite of being informed of these facts by Mrs Carter's social worker, the council instructed bailiffs to collect the council tax arrears, even though it had evidence that she was vulnerable, had no income, and was being supported by a different council department.

Outcome: The Ombudsman found the council at fault in failing to consider the information provided by the social worker and for failing to pass Mrs Carter's case to its welfare team. If the department had acted on the information provided then it is unlikely that bailiffs would have been involved and distress caused would have been avoided. The council was also criticised for the lack of effective liaison between different departments and for failing to have a written policy on dealing with vulnerable people.

The Ombudsman recommended that the council should:

– write off Mrs Carter's council tax arrears;

– pay her £250;

– implement a written policy on dealing with vulnerable people, and a policy on how to deal with people who are reliant on support from social services;
– establish a formal link between the council tax welfare team and social services.

Failure to administer council tax benefit and housing benefit and wrongful enforcement

Wandsworth Borough Council (09/008/990) 16 March 2010

The complainant Mr L had experienced repeated failures in the administration and payment of housing benefit and council tax over a seven-year period. Shortfalls in housing benefit resulted in rent arrears and eviction proceedings being commenced against Mr L and failures to pay council tax benefit resulted in three liability orders. Mr L attempted to settle the liability orders, whereupon bailiffs employed by Wandsworth Council imposed three sets of costs in respect of one levy. On receiving another summons, Mr L approached the authority before the hearing and was told that he would have to pay an additional £20 for seeking to make a repayment arrangement.

Mr L lodged a formal complaint which went through the three stages of Wandsworth Council's complaints procedure; he also complained separately to the bailiffs. The latter complaint resulted in bailiffs refunding the excessive charges, but the responses given by Wandsworth Council at each level to the wider issues of maladministration were inadequate and did not constitute a remedy.

Outcome: Following an investigation and review by the Ombudsman, Wandsworth Council offered a settlement of £630 to Mr L, which was accepted. Excessive bailiff fees of £50 were also repaid separately.

Charging of fees not permitted by law

Thurrock Council (09/006/694) 3 February 2010

Thurrock Council served a statutory demand for arrears of £1,367.57 and a further £400 for administrative costs for settling the debt. The complainant disputed the £400 fee. After a complaint failed to resolve the issue, an investigation took place by the Ombudsman who ruled that Thurrock Council had no power to charge a £400 fee since neither the Insolvency Rules, nor any other legislation, permitted recovery of fees for a statutory demand or an arrangement unless a bankruptcy order was made.

Outcome: The Ombudsman found there had been maladministration. Thurrock Council accepted it was not entitled to charge the fee and it ceased to do so in similar cases. It refunded the £400 to the complainant, restored the right to pay in instalments, waiving an additional £42.50 in bailiff fees incurred and making a £40 goodwill payment in compensation.

Bailiffs charging excessive fee for seizing a doormat

Slough Borough Council (10/007/469) 4 April 2011

A complaint was made against Slough Borough Council's bailiffs about a threat to remove a doormat and charge £230 in fees. The complaint was made by a man who had arrears of council tax and who was visited by bailiffs who could not gain entry. When he complained to the bailiff firm and then Slough Council, he was told the fees were legal.

Outcome: The Ombudsman considered that the levy on the doormat should not have been made. As the levy should not have been made, the fees should not have been charged. The bailiff was also at fault in charging an excessive amount for the levy. The Ombudsman found that the levying on such a low-value item as a doormat, the charging of the fees for this, and the lack of consideration of the reasonableness of this action amounted to maladministration. She noted the action Slough Council and the bailiffs had taken in acknowledging they were wrong and withdrawing the fees. Given this, and taking into account the complainant's failure to pay his council tax, she did not consider that any further remedy was needed in this case.

Ombudsman not satisfied by council's response after further report: 15 September 2011

Torbay Council (10 002 564) 12 May 2011

Torbay Council commenced bankruptcy proceedings against a man with mental health problems (given the pseudonym of 'Mr Castle') who owed a council tax debt of £2,248. He complained to the Local Government Ombudsman that Torbay Council had failed to have regard to his mental health issues.

Investigation by the Ombudsman established the council had difficulties engaging with the complainant. It was known that he did not open his post but left it to accumulate over a long period. None of the council's own officers visited Mr Castle at home. The council ignored the findings of a bailiff which indicated illness on the part of Mr Castle. The bailiff advised the council's solicitor that Mr Castle was suicidal.

While recognising that the council was short of enforcement options and that there was a duty to collect council tax, the Ombudsman found maladministration in its failures to keep proper records and the decision to commence bankruptcy proceedings.

Outcome: Maladministration was found. The Ombudsman did not consider that the council followed proper processes or kept accurate records. The council had not reviewed its decision to commence bankruptcy proceedings when information came to light that Mr Castle might be considered suicidal. The Ombudsman considered that, had such failings not occurred, then the council would not have continued bankruptcy proceedings and Mr Castle would not have incurred the costs of some £24,000. The Ombudsman recommended that Torbay Council paid Mr Castle £25,000 and issued a formal apology.

Note: In this case the bailiff appears to have acted in compliance with principles laid down by page 9 of the National Standards for Enforcement Agents (see Appendix 2). This requires an enforcement agent who discovers a vulnerable household to report it to the creditor for reconsideration. In this case the bailiff did, but the authority failed to act properly on receipt of the information.

Failure to control bailiff activity and fees

Blaby District Council (11 007 684) 18 July 2012

Mrs S owed arrears of council tax to Blaby Council. She complained that bailiffs employed by the council to collect her council tax arrears had not acted within the law and had overcharged her. She also complained that the council failed to properly respond to queries and complaints about these issues, including a serious allegation that four bailiffs tried to break into Mrs S's property and obtained money from her partner by clamping and taking occupation of a car that was not his.

Outcome: The Ombudsman's investigation found that the council failed to exercise proper control over the actions of its bailiffs and the fees it charged. The bailiffs had charged eight visit fees (because Mrs S had arrears for eight years – ie, there were eight accounts) on two occasions for one visit by one bailiff, and failed to carry out DVLA checks on the ownership of the vehicles. The council also failed to properly investigate Mrs S's complaints until she complained to the Ombudsman.

Once the Ombudsman became involved the council reduced the fees charged by £630.50, carried out DVLA checks on the vehicles, which showed they did not belong either to Mrs S or her partner, so removed the remaining levies and associated fees, and set out a new contract under which bailiffs could only charge one fee per levy.

Following a finding of maladministration the council agreed to pay £300 to Mrs S for the distress and inconvenience she was caused, which it offset against the outstanding council tax arrears. The Ombudsman also urged Mrs S to enter into a reliable regular payment arrangement with the council to avoid future action, such as an attachment of earnings either through her or her partner.

Notes

1. The work of the Ombudsman
1 Local Government Ombudsman *Annual Report* 2005/06 and 2010/11

2. What is maladministration
2 House of Commons debates; Parliamentary Commissioner Act 1967
3 UK Parliamentary Ombudsman Report 1993
4 Report by Commissioner Jerry White, Complaint 03/B/12862, 29 September 2004

3. Making a complaint
5 CPR rule 328 and Practice Direction 32
6 *R v Commissioner for Local Administration, ex parte Liverpool* CC [2001] All ER 462 (CA); Local Government Ombudsman Report into Manchester City Council (07B10432 FR), 29 March 2011
7 s5 Local Government and Housing Act 1989

8 *Ferguson v British Gas Trading Ltd* [2009] EWCA Civ 46

9 *Three Rivers DC v Bank of England (No 3)* [2003] 2 AC 1

10 See s51 Senior Courts Act 1981; *Dymocks Franchise Systems (NSW) Pty Ltd v Todd and others* [2004] UKPC 39; *R v Lambeth London Borough, ex parte Wilson* [1997] 3 FCR 437; *Flatman v Germany; Weddall v Barchester Healthcare Ltd* [2011] EWHC 2945 (QB)

11 For Crown Prosecution Guidance, see: www.cps.gov.uk/legal/l_to_o/misconduct_in_public_office/#a02; also Attorney General's Reference No.3 of 2003 [2004] EWCA 868

12 *R v Stewart* [1896] 1 QB 300

Appendix 1

Useful addresses

Valuation Office Agency

www.voa.gov.uk

England
Telephone: 03000 501 501

Wales
Telephone: 03000 505 505

Assessor for Central Scotland Valuation Joint Board

Hillside House
Laurelhill
Stirling FK7 9QJ
Phone: 01786 892200
Email: assessor@centralscotland-vjb.gov.uk
Website: www.saa.gov.uk/central

Valuation Tribunal for England

Doncaster office
Hepworth House
2 Trafford Court
Doncaster DN1 1PN
Telephone: 0300 123 2035
Email: vtdoncaster@vts.gsi.gov.uk

London office
Second Floor
Black Lion House
45 Whitechapel Road
London E1 1DU
Telephone: 0300 123 2035
Email: vtwhitechapel@vts.gsi.gov.uk

Council Tax Reduction Team
First Floor
Hepworth House
2 Trafford Court
Doncaster DN1 1PN
Telephone: 0300 123 1033
Email: appeals@vts.gsi.gov.uk

Valuation Tribunal for Wales

East Wales Region
22 Gold Tops
Newport NP20 4PG
Telephone: 01633 266 367
Email: VTWaleseast@vtw.gsi.gov.uk

North Wales Region
Government Buildings Block A(L1)
Sarn Mynach
Llandudno Junction LL31 9RZ
Telephone: 03000 625350
Email: VTWalesnorth@vtw.gsi.gov.uk

South Wales Region

22 Gold Tops
Newport NP20 4PG
Telephone: 01633 255 003
Email: VTWalessouth@vtw.gsi.gov.uk

West Wales Region

Llys y Ddraig
Penllergaer Business Park
Swansea SA4 9NX
Telephone: 0300 790 4530
Email: VTWaleswest@vtw.gsi.gov.uk

Council Tax Reduction Review Panel (Scotland only)

Europa Building
450 Argyle Street
Glasgow G2 8LH
Tel: 0141 242 0223
Email: ctrrpadmin@scotland.gsi.gov.uk
http://counciltaxreductionreview.scotland.gov.uk

Local Government Ombudsman

England

LGO Advice Team
PO Box 4771
Coventry CV4 0EH
Tel: 0300 061 0614 or 0845 602 1983
You can also text 'call back' to 0762 480 4299.
Email: enquiries@lgo.org.uk
www.lgo.org.uk

Public Services Ombudsman for Wales

1 Ffordd Yr Hen Gae
Pencoed CF35 5LJ
Tel: 0845 601 0987
Email: enquiries@ombudsman-wales.org.uk
www.ombudsman-wales.org.uk

Scottish Public Services Ombudsman

SPSO Freepost EH641
Edinburgh EH3 0BR
Tel: 0800 377 7330
www.spso.org.uk

Parliamentary and Health Service Ombudsman

Millbank Tower
Millbank
London SW1P 4QP
Tel: 0345 015 4033
Email: phso.enquiries@ombudsman.org.uk

The Adjudicator

The Adjudicator's Office
PO Box 10280
Nottingham
NG2 9PF
Te: 0300 057 1111
www.adjudicatorsoffice.gov.uk

Appendix 2

National Standards for Enforcement Agents (page 9)

Vulnerable situations

- Enforcement agents/agencies and creditors must recognise that they each have a role in ensuring that the vulnerable and socially excluded are protected, and that the recovery process includes procedures agreed between the agent/agency and creditor about how such situations should be dealt with. The appropriate use of discretion is essential in every case and no amount of guidance could cover every situation, therefore the agent has a duty to contact the creditor and report the circumstances in situations where there is potential cause for concern. If necessary, the enforcement agent will advise the creditor if further action is appropriate. The exercise of appropriate discretion is needed, not only to protect the debtor, but also the enforcement agent who should avoid taking action which could lead to accusations of inappropriate behaviour.
- Enforcement agents must withdraw from domestic premises if the only person present is, or appears to be, under the age of 18; they can ask when the debtor will be home – if appropriate.
- Enforcement agents must withdraw without making enquiries if the only persons present are children who appear to be under the age of 12.
- Wherever possible, enforcement agents should have arrangements in place for rapidly accessing translation services when these are needed, and provide on request information in large print or in Braille for debtors with impaired sight.
- Those who might be **potentially** vulnerable include:
  - the elderly;
  - people with a disability;
  - the seriously ill;
  - the recently bereaved;
  - single-parent families;
  - pregnant women;
  - unemployed people; *and*
  - those who have obvious difficulty in understanding, speaking or reading English.

Issued in January 2012 by the Ministry of Justice.

Appendix 3

Adjournment letter

TO: The Magistrates' Chief Executive
The [NAME] Magistrates' Court
[ADDRESS OF MAGISTRATES' COURT]

Dear Sir/Madam

RE: Summons number [INSERT REFERENCE NUMBER]
RE: Liability order application – Hearing date [STATE DATE]
RE: [NAME OF COUNCIL] v [NAME OF TAXPAYER]

I hereby apply to the court sitting at [GIVE NAME OF MAGISTRATES' COURT] for an adjournment of the above proceedings for the recovery of council tax to be heard on [STATE DATE CONTAINED ON SUMMONS].

The basis for seeking the adjournment is:
[GIVE DETAILS OF WHY ADJOURNMENT IS REQUESTED]
[IN A CASE WHERE AN APPEAL IS MADE TO A VALUATION TRIBUNAL ABOUT LIABILITY, EXEMPTION OR AN AMOUNT OF TAX, GIVE DETAILS OF THE APPEAL]

Accordingly, I have made an appeal to the valuation tribunal under section 16 of the Local Government Finance Act 1992 against this decision, and I would ask that the magistrates' court please consider adjourning this case until the tribunal has determined this matter.

Naturally, I hope that it will be possible to settle this matter without unnecessary proceedings and I await hearing from you with your decision.

Thanking you for your attention, I await hearing from you.

Yours faithfully

[NAME]

Note: a copy of the request should also be served on the local authority.

Appendix 4

Abbreviations used in the notes

AAC	Administrative Appeals Chamber	KB	King's Bench Reports
ACR	Appeal Case Reports	LJ	Lord Justice
ALR	Administration Law Reports	para(s)	paragraph(s)
All ER	All England Reports	PN	Practice Notes
Art(s)	Article(s)	QB	Queen's Bench Reports
CA	Court of Appeal	QBD	Queen's Bench Division
Ch	Chancery Division	r(r)	rule(s)
CO	Crown Office	RA	Rating Appeals
COD	Crown Office Digest	Reg(s)	Regulations(s)
CS	Court of Session	RVR	Rating and Valuation Reports
E	England	S	Scotland
EWCA	England and Wales Court of Appeal	s(s)	section(s)
		Sch(s)	Schedule(s)
EWHC	England and Wales High Court	UKUT	UK Upper Tribunal (Administrative Appeals Chamber)
GM	Housing Benefit and Council Tax Benefit Guidance Manual		
HC	High Court	VOA	Valuation Office Agency
HLR	Housing Law Reports	W	Wales
JP	Justice of the Peace Reports	WLR	Weekly Law Reports

Acts of Parliament

CSPSSA 2000	Child Support, Pensions and Social Security Act 2000
LA 2011	Localism Act 2011
LGA 1992	Local Government Act 1992
LGA 2003	Local Government Act 2003
LGFA 1988	Local Government Finance Act 1988
LGFA 1992	Local Government Finance Act 1992

* *

LGFA 2012	Local Government Finance Act 2012
SSAA 1992	Social Security Administration Act 1992
TCEA 2007	Tribunals, Courts and Enforcement Act 2007

Regulations and other statutory instruments

Each set of regulations has a statutory instrument (SI) number and date. You ask for them by giving their date and number.

CCCTNR(E)(MC) Regs	The Community Charges, Council Tax and Non-Domestic Rating (Enforcement) (Magistrates' Courts) England Regulations 2000 No.2026
CT(AE) Regs 1992	The Council Tax (Administration and Enforcement) Regulations 1992 No.613
CT(AE) Regs 2004	The Council Tax (Administration and Enforcement) Regulations 2004 No.927
CT(AE)(A)(E) Regs	The Council Tax (Administration and Enforcement) (Amendment) (England) Regulations 2004 No.297
CT(AE)(A)(No.2)(E) Regs	The Council Tax (Administration and Enforcement) (Amendment) (No.2) (England) Regulations 2012 No.3086
CT(AE)(A)(W) Regs	The Council Tax (Administration and Enforcement) (Amendment) (Wales) Regulations 2007 No.582
CT(AE)(AEO)(W) Regs	The Council Tax (Administration and Enforcement) (Attachment of Earnings Orders) (Wales) Regulations 1992 No.1741
CT(AE)(S) Regs	The Council Tax (Administration and Enforcement) (Scotland) Regulations 1992 No.1332
CT(ALA) Regs	The Council Tax (Alteration of Lists and Appeals) Regulations 1993 No.290
CT(ALA)(A)(W) Regs	The Council Tax (Alteration of Lists and Appeals) (Amendment) Wales Regulations 2010 No.77(W.10)
CT(ALA)(E) Regs	The Council Tax (Alteration of Lists and Appeals) (England) Regulations 2009 No.2270
CT(ALA)(S) Regs	The Council Tax (Alteration of Lists and Appeals) (Scotland) Regulations 1993 No.355
CT(APDD) Regs	The Council Tax (Additional Provisions for Discount Disregards) Regulations 1992 No.552
CT(APDD) Amdt Regs	The Council Tax (Additional Provisions for Discount Disregards) Amendment Regulations 1996 No.637
CT(CD)O	The Council Tax (Chargeable Dwellings) Order 1992 No.549

* * * *

CT(CVL) Regs	The Council Tax (Contents of Valuation Lists) Regulations 1992 No.553
CT(D)(S)(A) Regs	The Council Tax (Discounts) (Scotland) Amendment Regulations 1995 No.597
CT(D)(S)(A)O	The Council Tax (Discounts) (Scotland) (Amendment) Order 1993 No.343
CT(D)(S)A Regs	The Council Tax (Discounts) (Scotland) Amendment Regulations 1993 No.342
CT(D)(S)CAO	The Council Tax (Discounts) (Scotland) Consolidation and Amendment Order 2003 No.176
CT(D)(S)O	The Council Tax (Discounts) (Scotland) Order 1992 No.1408
CT(D)(S) Regs	The Council Tax (Discounts) (Scotland) Regulations 1992 No.1409
CT(DD)O	The Council Tax (Discount Disregards) Order 1992 No.548
CT(DD)(A)(E)O	The Council Tax (Discount Disregards) (Amendment) (England) Order 2006 No.3396
CT(DD)(A)(W)O	The Council Tax (Discount Disregards) (Amendment) (Wales) Order 2006 No.580
CT(DDED)(A)O	The Council Tax (Discount Disregards and Exempt Dwellings)(Amendment) Order 1995 No.619
CT(DIS) Regs	The Council Tax (Deductions from Income Support) Regulations 1993 No.494
CT(DN)(E) Regs	The Council Tax (Demand Notices) (England) Regulations 2010 No.2990
CT(DN)(E) Regs 2011	The Council Tax (Demand Notices) (England) Regulations 2011 No.3038
CT(DN)(E)(A) Regs	The Council Tax (Demand Notices) (England) (Amendment) Regulations 2012 No.3087
CT(DN)(W) Regs	The Council Tax (Demand Notices) (Wales) Regulations 1993 No.255
CT(DN)(W)(A) Regs	The Council Tax (Demand Notices) (Wales) (Amendment) Regulations 2013 No.63
CT(DPRS)(S) Regs	The Council Tax (Dwellings Part Residential Subjects) (Scotland) Regulations 1992 No.2955
CT(DUD)(S) Regs	The Council Tax (Discounts for Unoccupied Dwellings) (Scotland) Regulations 2005 No.51
CT(Dw)(E) Regs	The Council Tax (Prescribed Classes of Dwellings) (England) Regulations 2003 No.3011
CT(Dw)(S) Regs	The Council Tax (Dwellings) (Scotland) Regulations 1992 No.1334

CT(Dw)(S) Regs 2010	The Council Tax (Dwellings) (Scotland) Regulations 2010 No.35
CT(ED)O	The Council Tax (Exempt Dwellings) Order 1992 No.558
CT(ED)(A)(E)O	The Council Tax (Exempt Dwellings) (Amendment) (England) Order 2006 No.2318
CT(ED)(A)(E)O 2005	The Council Tax (Exempt Dwellings) (Amendment) (England) Order 2005 No.2865
CT(ED)(A)(E)O 2013	The Council Tax (Exempt Dwellings) (Amendment) (England) Order 2013 No.2965
CT(ED)(A)(W)O	The Council Tax (Exempt Dwellings) (Amendment)(Wales) Order 2000 No.1025
CT(ED)(S)O 1992	The Council Tax (Exempt Dwellings) (Scotland) Order 1992 No.1333
CT(ED)(S)O 1995	The Council Tax (Exempt Dwellings) (Scotland) (Amendment) Order 1995 No.598
CT(ED)(S)O 1997	The Council Tax (Exempt Dwellings) (Scotland) Order 1997 No.728
CT(ED)(S)O 2002	The Council Tax (Exempt Dwellings) (Scotland) Order 2002 No.101
CT(ED)(S)(A)O	The Council Tax (Exempt Dwellings) (Scotland) (Amendment) Order 2006 No.402
CT(ED)(S)(A)O 1995	The Council Tax (Exempt Dwellings) (Scotland) Amendment Order 1995 No.598
CT(ED)(S)(A)O 2012	The Council Tax (Exempt Dwellings) (Scotland) Amendment Order 2012 No.339
CT(EDDD)(A)O	The Council Tax (Exempt Dwellings and Discount Disregards) (Amendment) Order 1998 No.291
CT(LO) Regs	The Council Tax (Liability of Owners) Regulations 1992 No.551
CT(LO)(A)(E) Regs	The Council Tax (Liability of Owners) (Amendment) (England) Regulations 2003 No.3125
CT(LO)(A)(W) Regs	The Council Tax (Liability of Owners) (Amendment) (Wales) Regulations 2004 No.2920
CT(LO)(S) Regs	The Council Tax (Liability of Owners) (Scotland) Regulations 1992 No.1331
CT(PCD)(E) Regs	The Council Tax (Prescribed Classes of Dwellings) (England) Regulations 2003 No.3011
CT(PCD)(W) Regs	The Council Tax (Prescribed Classes of Dwellings) (Wales) Regulations 1992 No.3023
CT(RD) Regs	The Council Tax (Reductions for Disabilities) Regulations 1992 No.554

CT(RD)(S) Regs	The Council Tax (Reductions for Disabilities) (Scotland) Regulations 1992 No.1335
CT(RDTA)(W)(A) Regs	The Council Tax (Reductions for Disabilities and Transitional Arrangements) (Wales) (Amendment) Regulations 2005 No.702
CT(SVD) Regs	The Council Tax (Situation and Valuation of Dwellings) Regulations 1992 No.550
CT(SVD)(W)(A) Regs	The Council Tax (Situation and Valuation of Dwellings) (Wales) (Amendment) Regulations 2005 No.701
CT(TA)(W) Regs	The Council Tax (Transitional Arrangements) (Wales) Regulations 2004 No.3142
CT(VALA)(E) Regs	The Council Tax (Valuations and Alterations of Lists and Appeals) (England) Regulations 2008 No.315
CT(VD)(S) Regs	The Council Tax (Valuation of Dwellings) (Scotland) Regulations 1992 No.1329
CT(VD)(S)(A) Regs	The Council Tax (Valuation of Dwellings) (Scotland) (Amendment) Regulations 1993 No.354
CTNDR(DN)(E) Regs	The Council Tax and Non-Domestic Rating (Demand Notices) (England) Regulations 1993 No.191
CTR(S) Regs	The Council Tax Reduction (Scotland) Regulations 2012 No.303
CTR(S)A(No.2) Regs	The Council Tax Reduction (Scotland) Amendment (No. 2) Regulations 2013 No.218
CTR(SPC)(S) Regs	The Council Tax Reduction (State Pension Credit) (Scotland) Regulations 2012 No.319
CTRS(DFE)(E) Regs	The Council Tax Reduction Schemes (Detection of Fraud and Enforcement) (England) Regulations 2013 No.501
CTRS(DFE)(W) Regs	The Council Tax Reduction Schemes (Detection of Fraud and Enforcement) (Wales) Regulations 2013 No.588
CTRS(DS)(E) Regs	The Council Tax Reduction Schemes (Default Scheme) (England) Regulations 2012 No.2886
CTRS(DS)(W) Regs	The Council Tax Reduction Schemes (Default Scheme) (Wales) Regulations 2012 No.3145
CTRS(PR)(E) Regs	The Council Tax Reduction Schemes (Prescribed Requirements) (England) Regulations 2012 No.2885
CTRSPR(W) Regs	The Council Tax Reduction Schemes and Prescribed Requirements (Wales) Regulations 2012 No.3144
DFA Regs	The Discretionary Financial Assistance Regulations 2001 No.1167

HBCTB(DA) Regs	The Housing Benefit and Council Tax Benefit (Decisions and Appeals) Regulations 2001 No.1002
VCCT(Amdt) Regs	The Valuation and Community Charge Tribunals (Amendment) Regulations 1993 No.292
VT(A)(E) Regs	The Valuation Tribunals (Amendment) (England) Regulations 2000 No.409
VTE(CTRA)(P) Regs	The Valuation Tribunal for England (Council Tax and Rating Appeals) (Procedure) Regulations 2009 No.2269
VTE(CTRA)(P)(A) Regs	The Valuation Tribunal for England (Council Tax and Rating Appeals) (Procedure) (Amendment) Regulations 2013 No.465
VTENDRCT(E)(A) Regs	The Valuation Tribunal for England, Non-Domestic Rating and Council Tax (England) (Amendment) Regulations 2011 No.434
VTW Regs	The Valuation Tribunal for Wales Regulations 2010 No.713
VTW(W)(A) Regs	The Valuation Tribunal for Wales (Wales) (Amendment) Regulations 2013 No.547

Index